D1223622

Anti-Semitism and Its Metaphysical Origins

This book articulates a deeper understanding of the phenomenon of Jew hatred as a metaphysical aspect of the human soul. Proceeding from the Jewish thinking that the anti-Semites oppose, David Patterson argues that anti-Semitism arises from the most ancient of temptations, the temptation to be as God, and thus to flee from an absolute accountability to and for the other human being.

David Patterson holds the Hillel Feinberg Chair in Holocaust Studies at the Ackerman Center for Holocaust Studies at the University of Texas at Dallas. A winner of the National Jewish Book Award and the Koret Jewish Book Award, he has published more than thirty books and 150 articles and book chapters. His most recent books include *Genocide in Jewish Thought* (Cambridge, 2012), *A Genealogy of Evil: Anti-Semitism from Nazism to Islamic Jihad* (Cambridge, 2010), *Emil L. Fackenheim: A Jewish Philosopher's Response to the Holocaust* (2008), *Open Wounds: The Crisis of Jewish Thought in the Aftermath of Auschwitz* (2006), *Wrestling with the Angel* (2006), *Along the Edge of Annihilation* (1999), and *Sun Turned to Darkness* (1998). He is the editor and translator of *The Complete Black Book of Russian Jewry* (2002) and the coeditor (with Alan L. Berger) of the *Encyclopedia of Holocaust Literature* (2002).

BOOKS BY DAVID PATTERSON

Anti-Semitism and Its Metaphysical Origins

DAVID PATTERSON

University of Texas at Dallas

CAMBRIDGE
UNIVERSITY PRESS

CAMBRIDGE
UNIVERSITY PRESS

32 Avenue of the Americas, New York, NY 10013-2473, USA

Cambridge University Press is part of the University of Cambridge.

It furthers the University's mission by disseminating knowledge in the pursuit of education, learning, and research at the highest international levels of excellence.

www.cambridge.org
Information on this title: www.cambridge.org/9781107040748

© David Patterson 2015

This publication is in copyright. Subject to statutory exception and to the provisions of relevant collective licensing agreements, no reproduction of any part may take place without the written permission of Cambridge University Press.

First published 2015

Printed in the United States of America

A catalog record for this publication is available from the British Library.

Library of Congress Cataloging in Publication Data
Patterson, David, 1948–
Anti-semitism and its metaphysical origins / David Patterson.
pages cm
Includes bibliographical references and index.
ISBN 978-1-107-04074-8 (Hardback) – ISBN 978-1-107-64495-3
(Paperback) 1. Antisemitism. 2. Antisemitism–History. I. Title.
DS145.P368 2015   305.892′4–dc23
2014032225

ISBN 978-1-107-04074-8 Hardback
ISBN 978-1-107-64495-3 Paperback

Cambridge University Press has no responsibility for the persistence or accuracy of URLs for external or third-party Internet Web sites referred to in this publication and does not guarantee that any content on such Web sites is, or will remain, accurate or appropriate.

For Zsuzsanna and Pista Ozsváth

Contents

Preface

In the pages that follow I use the term *anti-Semitism* to refer to the phenomenon of Jew hatred throughout the centuries, even though the term did not come into popular usage until Wilhelm Marr founded the League of Anti-Semites in 1879. It should also be stressed that the usage of the words *anti-Semitism* or *anti-Semite* refers to a spectrum of phenomena and modes of thought. Rather than posing an either/or condition – either Jew hater or not a Jew hater – it is rather like asking whether a room is light or dark: there are degrees. I use the hyphenated form of the word as a matter of convention; it hardly need be said that anti-Semitism is about hatred of the Jews, and not about hatred of Semites in general. Hatred of Akkadians, Phoenicians, or Nabataeans is not a pressing issue. Hatred of the Jews, however, is not only pressing – it is deeply revealing. Exactly what it reveals is among the things to be examined in this book.

This book differs from other attempts to get at the essence and the origin of anti-Semitism. Although I draw on many of the existing studies on the history of anti-Semitism and make some use of a chronological organization, I have not written a history book. The centuries-old phenomenon of Jew hatred has been well documented by scholars such as Leon Poliakov, Joshua Trachtenberg, John Gager, Robert Wistrich, Walter Laqueur, Edward Flannery, George Mosse, Dan Cohn-Sherbok, Rosemary Radford Ruether, Robert Michael, Paul Grosser, and Edwin Halperin. Although the present volume draws on their valuable work, these authors do not address the metaphysical origins of anti-Semitism. Indeed, some of them reject the very notion of a metaphysical origin of anything; adopting the strict methods of historical studies and social sciences, their work is defined by strictly ontological parameters. One of the first to attempt to explain the cause of the phenomenon was Bernard Lazare, who was followed by Constantin Bruner, Peretz Bernstein, and Albert Lindemann; much more widely known attempts have been made by Jean-Paul Sartre, Hannah Arendt, Jacques Maritain, Bernard Lewis, Joel Carmichael, and Theodore Isaac Rubin. All of these efforts to get at the core of anti-Semitism are discussed in what follows. None of them, however, adopts the method that I have adopted in this work.

In contrast to almost all other studies of the origins of anti-Semitism, this book takes a conscientiously Jewish approach to understanding Jew hatred. Such an approach is rooted in the texts and the teachings of the Jewish tradition, including the Torah, Talmud, Midrash, the commentaries, writings of modern Jewish thinkers, and even some elements of Kabbalah. My reason for taking such an approach is calculated: the categories of thought and the teachings that guide this study are precisely what the anti-Semite is against. The overarching question to be answered in this volume, then, is this: How might the origins of Jew hatred be understood from the standpoint of the Judaism that the anti-Semites seek to eliminate? I shall show that anti-Semitism arises both from within and from beyond the human being, from a realm that transcends the contingencies of ethnic, religious, racial, or sociological differences. Having a metaphysical origin, anti-Semitism lurks in every soul, whether *in potentia* or *in actu*. It is not a question of We versus They; rather, it is a question of We – and, by extension, a question of *me*. To sound the depths of anti-Semitism, then, is to sound the depths of one's own soul.

David Patterson
Dallas, Texas

Acknowledgments

I would like first of all to express my deepest thanks to Cambridge University Press editor Lewis Bateman for his support, encouragement, and insightful suggestions in the preparation of this book. I am also indebted to the reviewers of the manuscript for their astute and helpful criticisms and suggestions for revision, and to Shaun Vigil for his good work at Cambridge University Press. Finally, I owe a debt of gratitude to the Ackerman Center for Holocaust Studies of the University of Texas at Dallas and to its provost, Dr. Hobson Wildenthal.

Introduction: Anti-Semitism as Deicide

> And the serpent said..., "You shall be as God..."
> Genesis 3:4–5

> If there were gods, how could I bear not being a god?
> Friedrich Nietzsche, *Thus Spoke Zarathustra*

Democritus of Thrace (ca. 460–370 BCE), known for his claim that all of matter is composed of atoms, was a rationalist and materialist philosopher who believed that everything happens according to the ineluctable laws of nature. He is also known for his *Maxims*, a volume of deft bits of wisdom for living a virtuous life.[1] And he is known as the first anti-Semite to invoke a blood libel, alleging that "every seven years the Jews captured a stranger, brought him to the temple in Jerusalem, and sacrificed him, cutting his flesh into bits."[2]

The noted Roman historian Tacitus (55–117) is a major source of information on the emperors Tiberius, Claudius, and Nero. He is also a source for some of the earliest diatribes against the Jews.[3] He attacked Jewish institutions as "sinister and shameful"[4] and complained that the

---

[1] Democritus, *Maxims*, trans. Jonathan Barnes, in Jonathan Barnes, ed., *Early Greek Philosophy* (New York: Penguin, 2002), 252–253.

[2] Joshua Trachtenberg, *The Devil and the Jews: The Medieval Conception of the Jew and Its Relation to Modern Antisemitism* (Philadelphia: Jewish Publication Society, 1983), 126.

[3] See, e.g., Tacitus, *The Histories*, in *The Annals and the Histories*, ed. Moses Hadas, trans. Alfred Church and William Brodribb (New York: Modern Library, 2003), 564–565.

[4] Dan Cohn-Sherbok, *Anti-Semitism* (Stroud, U.K.: The History Press, 2002), 17.

Jews "regard it as a crime to kill any newborn infant."[5] Yes, *complained*: he had an issue with the *absolute* prohibition against murder. There lay his anti-Semitism.

With the advent of Christianity as the official religion of Rome, Saint John Chrysostom of Antioch (347–407), famous for his eloquence and his moral teachings, declared that the Jews are the descendants not of Abraham but of the murderer Cain.[6] Indeed, in his *Homilies* the Church Father proclaimed that the Jews are "inveterate murderers, destroyers, men possessed by the devil" (1:4); hence for the Jews there is "no expiation possible, no indulgence, no pardon" (6:2).[7] Which means: if the Jews are *essentially* murderers, then the Jews are *necessarily* damned.

A millennium later an Augustinian monk broke away from the Church born of the doctrines of the Catholic Fathers. But he did not break away from the Jew hatred that many of them espoused. In his infamous diatribe *Von den Juden und ihren Lügen* (On the Jews and their lies, 1542) Martin Luther (1483–1546) declared that the Jews are "murderers of all Christendom..., often burned to death upon the accusation that they had poisoned water and wells, stolen children, and torn and hacked them apart."[8] The Nazis would be able to quote Luther without editing to serve their exterminationist ends.

With the eighteenth century came the Enlightenment, the age of reason and tolerance; among its leading exponents was the great German Idealist Immanuel Kant (1724–1804), the author of the Categorical Imperative, from which reason may deduce all morality: always act in such a way that, in accordance with your rational will, a universal maxim can be derived from your action.[9] He is also the author of the assertion that "the euthanasia of Judaism is the pure moral religion."[10] Why? Because the Jews, who derive their actions from

---

[5] Dennis Prager and Joseph Telushkin, *Why the Jews? The Reason for Antisemitism* (New York: Simon & Schuster, 2003), 71.

[6] See Rosemary Radford Reuther, *Faith and Fratricide: The Theological Roots of Anti-Semitism* (New York: Seabury Press, 1974), 134.

[7] Quoted in Edward H. Flannery, *The Anguish of the Jews: Twenty-three Centuries of Anti-Semitism* (New York: Macmillan, 1965), 48.

[8] Quoted in Raul Hilberg, *The Destruction of the European Jews* (Chicago: Quadrangle Books, 1961), 9.

[9] See Immanuel Kant, *Grounding for the Metaphysics of Morals*, trans. James W. Ellington (Indianapolis, Ind.: Hackett, 1981), 30–32.

[10] Immanuel Kant, *Conflict of the Faculties*, trans. Mary J. Gregor (New York: Abaris, 1979), 95.

divine commandment, and not logical deduction, pose a fundamental threat to the self-legislating autonomy of a free rational being.

Among the self-legislating, autonomous thinkers to emerge from the Enlightenment was Karl Marx (1818–1883), grandson of Rabbi Meir Halevi Marx of Trier and the inspiration for such mass murderers as Joseph Stalin and Mao Zedong. The primary author of *The Communist Manifesto* (1848), "throughout his life, Marx identified Jews and Judaism with all that he hated in capitalism."[11] Thus he asked and answered: "What is the profane basis of Judaism? *Practical need, self-interest.* What is the worldly cult of the Jew? *Huckstering.* What is his worldly god? *Money.*"[12] What, then, is to be done with the Jew?

One of capitalism's most successful devotees was Henry Ford (1863–1947), who at the age of twenty walked four miles every Sunday from his family's farm outside Detroit to attend their Episcopal church.[13] By the time he was fifty he was the chief executive and owner of the Ford Motor Company. When he reached the age of fifty-seven his book *The International Jew* came out, along with a series of articles in his newspaper *The Dearborn Independent* featuring selections from the infamous anti-Semitic forgery *The Protocols of the Elders of Zion*.

An avid believer in the lies of the *Protocols*, German-born Irma Grese (1923–1945) served the Third Reich in Ravensbrück, Auschwitz, and Bergen-Belsen. The Jews knew her as the Hyena of Auschwitz and the Beautiful Beast. The actions that earned her those titles led her to be among the accused at the Belsen war crimes trial. She was found guilty, and on 13 December 1945 she became the youngest of the female Nazis to be executed for crimes against humanity.

Among the Jihadist ideologues who were influenced by the Nazis is Sayyid Qutb (1906–1966), the Egyptian who was executed on 29 August 1966 under Gamal Abdel Nasser's regime. The author of *Our Struggle with the Jews* (1950), Qutb remains the most influential ideologue of the Muslim Brotherhood. He spread the Jihadist doctrine that "the Jews have confronted Islam with enmity from the moment that the Islamic state was established." Because the "Jews as Jews were by

---

[11] Prager and Telushkin, *Why the Jews?*, 125.
[12] Karl Marx, "On Bruno Bauer's *The Jewish Question*," in *Early Writings*, trans. and ed. T. B. Bottomore (New York: McGraw-Hill, 1964), 34.
[13] Harold Evans, *They Made America* (New York: Little, Brown, 2004), 237.

nature determined to fight Allah's Truth,"[14] they are "the eternal enemy of Islam."[15] The Jews, therefore, are the embodiment of evil and must be annihilated.

Contrary to Jihadists who deny that the Holocaust took place, Qutb extolled Adolf Hitler (1889–1945) as the instrument of Allah sent to exterminate the Jews.[16] Another ardent admirer of Hitler was Stokely Carmichael (1941–1998), who once declared that, although he had no love for white people, "the greatest of them, to my mind, was Hitler."[17] A former leader of the civil rights movement's Student Nonviolent Coordinating Committee, Carmichael worked with the Black Panthers, on whose behalf he "denounced 'kosher fascism' and 'white' Israel's oppression of the 'colored' Palestinians."[18]

And so we ask: What does Stokely Carmichael have in common with Democritus? Or Henry Ford with Karl Marx? Or Immanuel Kant with John Chrysostom? Or Irma Grese with Tacitus? Do they all need the Jews in order to have a scapegoat for society's misfortunes? Are they all xenophobes or racists? Do they all resent Jewish elitism? Are they all envious of the financial success of the Jews? The short answer is: No. Even if they have some of these things in common, why do they scapegoat the *Jews*? Of all "others," why are they afraid of the otherness of the *Jews*? Why do they resent the elitism or envy the success of the *Jews*? These anti-Semites have this in common: they all hate the *Jews*. They have one other thing in common: they each have a human soul.

In this book we shall see that the origins of anti-Semitism have little to do with racism, xenophobia, economic envy, Jewish elitism, scapegoating, psychological disorders, social structures, Manichean divisions of the world into We and They, and the like; such ontological contingencies simply provide the various occasions for an already dormant Jew hatred to surface. Nor does anti-Semitism arise from certain theological, philosophical, or ideological positions; rather, certain theological, philosophical, or ideological positions arise from anti-Semitism. Although he seeks

---

[14] Quoted in Ronald L. Nettler, *Past Trials and Present Tribulations: A Muslim Fundamentalist's View of the Jews* (Oxford: Pergamon, 1987), 35; emphasis added.
[15] Sayyid Qutb, "Our Struggle with the Jews," trans. Ronald L. Nettler, in Nettler, *Past Trials and Present Tribulations*, 81.
[16] Matthias Küntzel, *Jihad and Jew-Hatred: Islamism, Nazism and the Roots of 9/11*, trans. Colin Meade (New York: Telos Press, 2007), 84.
[17] Prager and Telushkin, *Why the Jews?*, 134.
[18] Robert Wistrich, *A Lethal Obsession: Anti-Semitism from Antiquity to the Global Jihad* (New York: Random House, 2010), 588.

the origins of anti-Semitism in an "ancient clash of civilizations," Robert Wistrich notes the difference between anti-Semitism and other forms of hatred of others by saying, "The sacral, quasi-metaphysical quality of anti-Semitism is singularly absent in other cases."[19] It is more than "quasi." Anti-Semitism has metaphysical origins that transcend its ontological manifestations. Because it arises from the depths of human subjectivity, beyond all ontological categories and contingencies, probing the depths of anti-Semitism entails probing the depths of the human soul – of one's own soul. That is why such disparate figures as Saint John Chrysostom and Karl Marx, Martin Luther and Sayyid Qutb, Henry Ford and Stokely Carmichael have Jew hatred in common: all of them are children of Adam with a human soul. There lies the metaphysical origin of anti-Semitism.

My thesis, of course, rests on a certain understanding – a Jewish understanding – of the soul as an emanation from the Holy One that transcends the coordinates of ontological, space-time reality. My method, then, is to turn to the object of the anti-Semite's hatred – Jews, Judaism, and Jewish teaching – in order to arrive at a deeper understanding of this primordial phenomenon.

THE SOUL OF THE CHILD OF ADAM

Elie Wiesel (b. 1928) has said that at Auschwitz not only was man murdered, but the very idea of man, of the human being, was obliterated.[20] Designed to exterminate the Jews, to be more precise, Auschwitz was designed to obliterate a Jewish idea of the human being. The term for "human being" in Hebrew is *ben adam*, which literally means "a child of Adam." Most fundamental to a Jewish understanding of the soul is the view that every human soul has a single origin in the Holy One and that, through its connection to the origin, every soul is tied to every other soul. Like a beam of light connected to the sun – and, through the sun, to every other beam of light – the soul is linked to its source and, through its source, to every other soul. In his commentary on Genesis 46:4 Chayim

---

[19] Ibid., 80. What Wistrich has in mind seems to be akin to Ernst Bloch's notion of "metaphysical anti-Semitism." Bloch uses the term in his analysis of Marcion, who wanted to eliminate the Hebrew Scriptures from the Christian canon, maintaining that the revealed truth of Christianity far transcends anything in Judaism: Christianity is the advent not only of a new covenant but new first principles. See Ernst Bloch, *The Spirit of Utopia*, trans. Anthony Nassar (Stanford, Calif.: Stanford University Press, 2000), 30.

[20] See Elie Wiesel, *Legends of Our Time* (New York: Avon, 1968), 230.

ben Attar (1696–1743), the Or HaChayim, affirms that souls are "parts of God's 'light' emanating from God's throne of glory." In addition to this primary metaphysical origin, every human soul has a physical origin in the first human being. Why did God begin with one, and not two? In the Tosefta, a collection of Jewish teachings from the third century, the sages explain: "So that in this world the righteous could not say, 'Our children are righteous, and yours are evil'" (*Tosefta Sanhedrin* 8:4). So that no one could say to another, "My side of the family is better than your side of the family." There is only one side of the family. The relationship to the Creator, therefore, is tied to the relationship to the other human being, and each needs the other in order to be what it is: the physical needs the metaphysical in order to have meaning, and the metaphysical needs the physical in order to be manifest.

According to this Jewish tradition, the wholeness of who we are lies in the oneness of our concrete, flesh-and-blood relation to other human beings and our transcendent, spiritual relation to the Creator. As the origin of the soul, the Creator is a persona and not a concept, a Who and not a What, one to whom we can say, "You." Likewise, the other human being is one to whom we can say, "You," so that who we are lies in both a vertical and a horizontal relation. That is why we find the phrase "I am the Lord" attached to the commandment "You shall love your neighbor as yourself" (*Veahavta lereakha k'mokha*, Leviticus 19:18): in that commanded relation to the other human being we encounter the One who commands. According to Chasidism's founder, the Baal Shem Tov (1700–1760), this commandment – this connection – is the basis of the entire Torah (see *Toledot Yaakov Yosef, Korach* 2).[21] If we examine the Hebrew word *k'mokha*, "as yourself," as well the *le-* in *lereakha*, "your neighbor," a better translation would be: "You shall show love *toward* your neighbor, for that loving relation *is* who you are": the life of the soul lies in the loving treatment of the neighbor, with hands ready to *give* to the neighbor. For the root of the verb to "love," *veahavta*, is *hav*, which means to "give." Whatever meaning a life might have lies in the divinely commanded love for the other human being manifest in the concrete act of giving; such love is the light that we are commanded to emanate into

---

[21] The *Toledot Yaakov Yosef* is a collection of teachings from the Baal Shem Tov gathered by his disciple Yaakov Yosef of Polnoe; the Baal Shem himself did not write anything. The reference to Korach is a reference to a weekly portion from the Torah (Numbers 16:1–18:32), as the *Toledot* is divided into sections in accordance with the weekly Torah portions.

the world. Indeed, says the sage Joseph Albo (ca. 1380–1444), with the divine summons of "Let there be light" (Genesis 1:3), the human soul and its meaning are born (*Sefer HaIkkarim* 4:30).

The metaphor of light is fundamental to a Jewish understanding of the soul. Two verses from the Book of Proverbs underscore this point: "The commandment is the candle and the Torah the light" (6:23), and "The soul of the human being is the candle of the Lord" (20:27). Schneur Zalman of Liadi (1745–1812), the first Lubavitcher Rebbe,[22] comments: "The soul is referred to as a *ner* [candle], and the commandment is called a *ner*. [In the metaphor] where the commandment is the candle, the soul is the wick and the commandment is the oil, producing two aspects of light, as it is written *Veahavta* ('and you shall love' [Deuteronomy 6:5]), which is twice the numerical value of *or* ('light')."[23] As the candle of God, the soul's task is to transform the darkness of the ego's isolation into the light that shines in the loving relation to another. The soul, in other words, derives its life from the divinely *commanded* loving relation to the other human being. To be sure, the root of the word *mitzvah*, or "command-ment" is *tzavta*, which means "connection," suggesting that in the com-mandment lies our connection to the soul's origin and to our fellow human being. Thus, according to the Midrash, the commandment is called a candle because when we perform a commandment, or *mitzvah*, it is as if we had kindled a light before God to "revive our soul" (*Shemot Rabbah* 36:3) by entering more profoundly into the relationship.[24] If knowing God means knowing what must be done, as Emmanuel

---

[22] In Chasidism, a rebbe is a wise and holy person whom God has supposedly sent to lead and to serve His flock. Each of the various Chasidic groups (with the exception of the Breslover Chasidim and now the Lubavitcher Chasidim) has its leader or its rebbe. The Lubavitcher Chasidim, also known as Chabad, formed around Schneur Zalman of Liadi, a town also known as Lubavitch. The term *Chabad* is an acronym for *chokhmah*, *binah*, and *daat* – "wisdom," "understanding," and "knowledge" – as the Lubavitcher Chasidim are known to place their emphasis on these qualities, rather than on the emotional aspect of religious life that other Chasidic groups underscore.

[23] Quoted in Adin Steinsaltz and Josy Eisenberg, *The Seven Lights: On the Major Jewish Festivals* (Northvale, N.J.: Jason Aronson, 2000), 355.

[24] *Shemot Rabbah* is the midrashic commentary on the Book of Exodus that is included in the ten-volume *Midrash Rabbah*, or *The Great Midrash*. The term *midrash* refers to a vast body of narrative and homiletic commentaries that stem from the Jewish oral tradition and that were gradually committed to writing after the destruction of the Second Temple in the year 70 CE; the *Midrash Rabbah* was compiled over about eight centuries. According to the religious tradition, its teachings go back to Mount Sinai; *Shemot Rabbah* was likely compiled in the tenth century. For a detailed discussion, see Barry W. Holtz, *Back to the Sources: Reading the Classic Jewish Texts* (New York: Simon & Schuster, 1984), 177–212.

Lévinas (1906–1995) has argued,[25] then knowing what must be done is the key to knowing who we are: the human being's *who* lies in the human being's commanded mission. And that mission is given to us in the first pronouncement of creation: "Let there be light" (Genesis 1:3).[26]

Just as the darkness of Egypt was such that no man could see the face of his neighbor (see Exodus 10:23), the light of the soul that illuminates the human relation reveals the face of the neighbor. To be sure, the darkness of Egypt is precisely the darkness of the ego that would eclipse the light of the divine commandment by making itself into its own god and its own ground. Blind to the face of the neighbor, the ego is the autonomous, self-legislating self, which is the opposite of the soul, the self that languishes in its narcissism, oblivious to the relation that is the source of its very life. The great sage of the Talmud,[27] Rabbi Akiva, maintained that the humanity and the dignity of the human being are revealed in the face: the face is a revelation of the soul and of its connection to every other soul.[28] According to Jewish tradition, then, the Hebrew word for "face," *panim*, is plural because each of us has two faces: the face of Adam, who came from the hand and mouth of God, and our own individual face. Just as each of us bears a trace of Adam's face, so each of us harbors a trace of Adam's soul. What distinguishes both the face and the soul is the word. Just as the light of the soul is a manifestation of divine speech, so is human speech an emanation of the light of the soul. The soul, as Saadia Gaon (882–942) states, "attains luminosity as a result of the light which it receives from God. . . . That is how it came to be endowed with the power of speech" (*Sefer Emunot Vedeot* 6:3). The light that the soul receives from God is precisely the word that God breathes into it.

The soul, therefore, is more an action than an object: it is a *speech act* of the Holy One. Our adherence to the commandments entails joining our

---

[25] Emmanuel Lévinas, *Difficult Freedom: Essays on Judaism*, trans. Sean Hand (Baltimore, Md.: Johns Hopkins University Press, 1990), 17.

[26] See Menachem M. Schneerson, *Torah Studies*, adapted by Jonathan Sacks, 2nd ed. (London: Lubavitch Foundation, 1986), 3–4.

[27] The Talmud was compiled in Babylon between the second and the sixth centuries of the Common Era. Its core text is the Mishnah, which is the recorded oral tradition of laws and commentaries. It also includes the Gemara, a text that explains and elaborates on the Mishnah; over the centuries remarks from later commentators were added. When scholars refer the "the Talmud," they have in mind the Babylonian Talmud or *Talmud Bavli*; there is also a Jerusalem Talmud compiled in Palestine, known as the *Talmud Yerushalmi*.

[28] See Louis Finkelstein, *Akiba: Scholar, Saint and Martyr* (New York: Atheneum, 1981), 103.

actions with the divine speech act, which is Torah. There lies our task in life, as Lévinas has suggested: "Being has meaning. The meaning of being, the meaning of creation, is to realize the Torah. The world is here so that the ethical order has the possibility of being fulfilled. The act by which the Israelites accept the Torah is the act which gives meaning to reality."[29] In this statement Lévinas echoes a teaching from the thirteenth-century mystic Abraham Abulafia: "God's intention in giving the Torah is that we reach this purpose, that our souls be alive in His Torah. For this is the reason for our existence and the intention for which we were created."[30] To be alive in His Torah is to burn with a devotion to our fellow human being; to be alive in His Torah is to be a soul on fire.

In the Jewish tradition fire, too, is a powerful metaphor for the soul; after all, the light that issues from a candle issues from its fire. "When man cleaves to God," says the Or HaChayim in his commentary on Genesis 23:2, "all his elements become transformed into the element fire, which forms the basis of the soul." Thus the great mystic Solomon ibn Gabirol (1022–1070) wrote a poem – or a prayer – on the soul, saying:

Thou hast imparted to it the spirit of wisdom
And called it the Soul.
And of flames of intellectual fire hast Thou wrought its form,
And like a burning fire hast Thou wafted it
And sent it to the body to serve and guard it,
And it is as fire in the midst thereof yet doth not consume it,
For it is from the fire of the soul that the body hath been created,
And goeth from Nothingness to Being,
"Because the Lord descended on him in fire." (Exodus 19:18)[31]

Just as the Torah is made of black fire on white fire (*Tanchuma Bereshit* 1; *Devarim Rabbah* 3:12; *Zohar* II, 226b),[32] so does the soul originate

---

[29] Emmanuel Lévinas, *Nine Talmudic Readings*, trans. Annette Aronowicz (Bloomington: Indiana University Press, 1990), 41.

[30] Quoted in Moshe Idel, *Language, Torah, and Hermeneutics in Abraham Abulafia* (Albany: SUNY Press, 1989), 37.

[31] Solomon ibn Gabirol, *Selected Religious Poems*, ed. Israel Davidson, trans. Israel Zangwill (Philadelphia: Jewish Publication Society, 1952), 104–105.

[32] The *Tanchuma Bereshit* is the commentary on the Book of Genesis from the *Midrash Tanchuma*, a commentary attributed to Rabbi Tanchuma bar Abba, a fourth-century sage who appears in the Talmud; it was likely compiled in the fifth century. *Devarim Rabbah* is the commentary on the Book of Deuteronomy from the *Midrash Rabbah*, probably compiled between the seventh and ninth centuries. The *Zohar* is the most prominent of the kabbalistic texts in Judaism; portions of the *Zohar*, in fact, can be found in the liturgy. Although it is attributed to Shimon bar Yochai of the

"in fire, being an emanation from the Divine Throne" (*Zohar* II, 211b). Therefore, it is written in the Midrash, when the angel tried to frighten Jacob as they wrestled at Peniel by making fire shoot up from the ground, Jacob cried, "Do you think you can frighten me with fire? Why, I am made of that stuff!" (*Bereshit Rabbah* 77:2).[33] If, as Elie Wiesel has said of the Holocaust, "fire was the dominant image of the Event,"[34] it is because the event was a radical assault on the soul. Indeed, the anti-Semitism that has its origin in the soul manifests itself as an assault on the soul, which always entails an assault on the flesh-and-blood body of the other human being. Judaism does not subscribe to the body–soul duality found in Greek philosophy (a theme that runs through Plato's *Phaedo*, for example). From a Jewish standpoint, the body does not have a soul; rather the soul has a body,[35] which is among the things that distinguish one soul from another. Such a distinction is essential to the relation, to the between space, from which the soul draws its breath.

In the Torah's account of the creation of the first human being, one finds a motif of distinction: light is separated from darkness, day from night, land from water, male from female – and human from God. This difference is essential to the fundamental relationship that is necessary for meaning in creation. For to take on meaning, to have significance, is to become a sign of the depth and the dearness of another; I can no more signify my own sanctity than I can lift myself up by my own hair. To become such a sign is to realize and act on an infinite responsibility to and for another, a responsibility that demands a radical vulnerability, which is why we often avoid it. Because this responsibility to and for another is essential to meaning and sanctity in life, God asserts that "it is not good for the human being to be alone" (Genesis 2:18). "Woman,"

second century, most scholars believe that it was compiled in the thirteenth century by the Spanish mystic Moshe de Leon.

[33] *Bereshit Rabbah* is the commentary on the Book of Genesis in the *Midrash Rabbah*; it was composed between the fifth and seventh centuries.

[34] See Elie Wiesel, *Evil and Exile*, trans. Jon Rothschild (Notre Dame, Ind.: University of Notre Dame Press, 1990), 39.

[35] The thirteenth-century mystic Shem Tov ibn Falaquera, for example, maintains that the soul assumes its concrete form at the level of *nefesh*; usually translated as "soul," it is the physical "form" of the soul in its union with the body, and its "appetites" are as much a part of the life of the soul as the ruminations of the mind (see *Sefer HaNefesh*, 3). Similarly, the great sage of the seventeenth century, Manasheh ben Yisrael, explains that, contrary to the Greek and Christian outlook, the soul permeates every part of the body, so that the body itself, precisely in its physical being, is holy (*Nishmat Chayim* 2:11). Thus "the soul and the body constitute a single agent," as Saadia Gaon has said (*Sefer Emunot Vedeot* 6:5).

Lévinas comments on this episode, "does not simply come to someone deprived of companionship to keep him company. She answers to a solitude inside this privation and – which is stranger – to a solitude that subsists in spite of the presence of God."[36] It is not good for the human being to be alone because it is not good for the human being to languish in a state of meaninglessness – that is the privation. Meaning is as essential to the soul as bread is to the body, and it is rooted in the primacy of a fundamental responsibility to and for *another*.

Inasmuch as creation transpires through a divine word, it is a movement into a relation of responsibility: the word is spoken by *someone* and implies someone to whom it is addressed, someone who is summoned to respond. The medieval sage Nachmanides (1194–1270) sees the Creator's movement of creation to be a movement into a *covenantal* relation, noting that the word *bara*, or "created," is a cognate of *brit*, which means "covenant."[37] The Zohar, moreover, reads *bereshit*, "in the beginning," as *brit esh*, "covenant of fire," to teach that all things were created through a covenant (*Zohar* I, 89a). Where there is covenant there is responsibility, which brings us back to the centrality of the You: prior to his appearance the first human being is *already* singled out for a relationship with another, to whom he may say, "You." Thus, looking further at the opening line of the Torah, we find another teaching from the Zohar. Instead of reading *Bereshit bara Elokim et ha-. . .* as "In the beginning God created the. . .," the Zohar reads it as "In the beginning God created the *alef*, *tav*, *hey* of *atah*: You." Says the Zohar, "The word *et* consists of the letters *alef* and *tav*, which include between them all the letters, as being the first and last of the alphabet. Afterwards *hey* was added, so that all the letters should be attached to *hey*, and this gave the name *atah* (You)" (*Zohar* I, 15b). What is most essential to the life of the soul is to answer, "*Hineni* – Here I am for *you!*" when summoned by another soul. According to the Chasidic master Levi Yitzchak of Berditchev (1740–1809), "All the hatred of the Jews" comes "from our constant defense of You,"[38] which is a defense of the eternal You as well as the You of flesh and blood, both of whom announce an infinite responsibility that can be neither fulfilled nor abrogated.

---

[36] Lévinas, *Difficult Freedom*, 33.

[37] See Nachmanides, *Commentary on the Torah*, vol. 1, trans. Charles B. Chavel (New York: Shilo, 1971), 112.

[38] Quoted in Victor Cohen, ed., *The Soul of the Torah: Insights of the Chasidic Masters on the Weekly Torah Portions* (Northvale, N.J.: Jason Aronson, 2000), 98.

Understanding that the substance of the soul lies in a relation of responsibility to and for the *other* human being, we understand more clearly Abraham Joshua Heschel's assertion that the ego or self is a self-deception.[39] The deception inheres in a preoccupation with *my* person, *my* space, *my* status, *my* material being, and even *my* spiritual being, as if anything that belongs to the essence of my soul could belong to *me*, *me*, and more *me*. Languishing in the egocentric illusion, the self lives in the dative case, forever trembling over the questions of what will happen "to me" and what is in it "for me." Understood in such terms, then, *the self is just the opposite of the soul*. As Yitzchak Ginsburgh states it, *bitul*, or the "obliteration of self," is the doorway to truth; "*bitul* produces a 'cavity' in the self, an opening and 'vessel' for truth to enter."[40] And truth enters when the soul enters into a responsive relation with another. To be sure, the soul, as Lévinas describes it, is "the other in me,"[41] which echoes the teaching from the Torah that refers to your "neighbor" as one *asher k'nafshekha*, one "who is like your soul" (Deuteronomy 13:7). The "other in me" is manifest in a certain disturbance arising in the encounter with the other, whether human or divine. It is the disturbance attendant on the emergence of the You, who shakes me from the sleep of my self-centered complacency, as I discover that I am not who I thought I was, that my self-styled self is a self-delusion, and that whoever I am lies in my responsibility to and for another, *despite* my counterfeit self. The counterfeit self is the ego that forever threatens to extinguish the light of the soul. It is the "strange god" that lurks within us.

If the Infinite One manifests Himself in the disturbance of His witness, as Lévinas claims,[42] it is the disturbance of an infinite claim on the witness. Precisely, this infinite assignation constitutes the infinite dearness of the soul. This claim on the soul is at the heart of the covenant with the soul, and it is precisely this claim, this covenant, that the ego would eradicate in its effort to hide from its responsibility. Thus Adam hid (Genesis 3:10) in a vain attempt to elude the One who alone, says Yechiel

---

[39] Abraham Joshua Heschel, *Man Is Not Alone* (New York: Farrar, Straus and Giroux, 1951), 47.

[40] Yitzchak Ginsburgh, *The Alef-Beit: Jewish Thought Revealed through the Hebrew Letters* (Northvale, N.J.: Jason Aronson, 1991), 72.

[41] Emmanuel Lévinas, *Otherwise Than Being or Beyond Essence*, trans. Alphonso Lingis (The Hague: Martinus Nijhoff, 1981), 69.

[42] Emmanuel Lévinas, *Ethics and Infinity*, trans. Richard A. Cohen (Pittsburgh, Pa.: Duquesne University Press, 1985), 109.

Mikhal of Zlotchov (d. ca. 1786), can utter the word *I*.[43] Thus it is He who asks, "Where are *you?*" (Genesis 3:9). This movement into hiding is a movement shared by every anti-Semite, and the temptation to hide is shared by every human being who bears a trace of the soul of Adam. In this original flight from this original question lies the metaphysical origin of anti-Semitism. With Adam, as with each of us, the flight from God comes in the wake of an even more fundamental temptation, the temptation to be like God, as when the serpent tempted Eve, saying, "On the day you eat of it [the fruit of the Tree of Knowledge], your eyes will be opened, and you will be like God, knowing good and evil" (Genesis 3:4). Stirring the longing to be like God, the serpent appeals to the longing of the ego to usurp God, which lurks in every soul. Thus in the *Pesikta de-Rab Kahana* it is written: "They put the question to the Holy One: A man who set up an idol in the Temple – can the repentance of such a man be accepted? The Holy One replied: If I do not receive him in his repentance, I shall be barring the door to all who would repent" (Piska 24:11).[44] For the one who would set up an idol of stone in the Temple is one who would set up the idol of the ego that eclipses God, and that can be anyone.

Those who turn against Jews and Judaism and toward the idol of their own making, David Mamet puts it, "award themselves the ability to *create* a God, in effect, in order to *become* God."[45] Of course, the God we would become is not the God of the Torah, who is loving and long-suffering (see Exodus 34:6–7), but the self-styled ego-god who is free of all limitations, in control, and self-justified, not only knowing but determining good and evil. Thus in the place of the God of the Torah and His uncompromising commandment, we fashion idols of reason and power (Democritus, Tacitus, and Kant), of credo and creed (Chrysostom, Luther, and Qutb), of ideology and race (Marx, Ford, Grese, and Carmichael). In a word, what the anti-Semites have in common is that they are all children of Adam, and they succumb to Adam's original temptation: deicide. For only in an act of deicide can one usurp the place of God.

---

[43] See Louis Newman, ed., *The Hasidic Anthology* (New York: Schocken Books, 1963), 423.

[44] The *Pesikta de-Rab Kahana*, or *The Verses of Rav Kahana*, is a midrashic text attributed to Rav Abba bar Kahana, who appears in the Talmud and lived in the late third century; the text dates from the fifth or sixth century.

[45] David Mamet, *The Wicked Son: Anti-Semitism, Self-Hatred, and the Jew* (New York: Schocken Books, 2006), 111.

DEICIDE: THE ORIGINAL SIN

According to the account in Genesis, God had just one commandment for Adam: do not eat from the fruit of the Tree of Knowledge of Good and Evil, where the word for "knowledge" is *daat*, which means to "join together." The deadly nature of the Tree, as the Chasidic master Yehudah Leib Alter (1847–1905) explains, is that it leads to a joining together of good and evil, a collapse of the distinction between the two, which always happens when the ego usurps the divine.[46] As Chayim Vital (1543–1620), chief disciple of the great mystic of Safed Isaac Luria (1534–1572), expressed it, the sin of succumbing to the temptation to be as God, "causes a mixing and confusion [of good and evil] throughout all the worlds,"[47] so that, for example, murder mutates into martyrdom. When good and evil become indistinguishable, murder ensues, and, because the soul suffers what it inflicts, death casts its shadow over the human being. That is why God tells Adam that on the day he succumbs to the tempta- tion to usurp the divine, he "will surely die" (Genesis 2:17). And yet he did not expire. How to understand this?

A look at the Hebrew will provide a clue. The phrase "surely die" is *mot tamut*, that is, "you will die the death." In other words, on the day you would become as God, death for you will not be the last but will be continually the last. Such a condition is the condition of despair, the "sickness unto death," as Søren Kierkegaard (1813–1855) understood it: "The torment of despair is precisely this, not to be able to die.... So to be sick *unto* death is, not to be able to die – yet not as though there were hope of life."[48] The sickness of despair is rooted in the "evil inclination," as the Chasidic master Nachman of Breslov has said,[49] and the evil inclination is an inclination to eliminate God. Therefore in despair, Kier- kegaard elaborates, the self longs to "tear itself away from the Power which constitutes it."[50] Indeed, the longing is not only to tear oneself away from God but to do away with God – that is what the tearing away amounts to. Here one realizes that the will to deicide, which is at the root

---

[46] Yehudah Leib Alter, *The Language of Truth: The Torah Commentary of the Sefat Emet*, trans. Arthur Green (Philadelphia: Jewish Publication Society, 1998), 10.

[47] Chayim Vital, *Kedushah* (Jerusalem: Eshkol, 2000), 19; my translation.

[48] Søren Kierkegaard, *The Sickness unto Death*, trans. Walter Lowrie (Princeton, N.J.: Princeton University Press, 1941), 15.

[49] Nachman of Breslov, *Restore My Soul (Meshivat Nefesh)*, trans. Avraham Greenbaum (Jerusalem: Chasidei Breslov, 1980), 23.

[50] Kierkegaard, *The Sickness unto Death*, 18.

of anti-Semitism, lies in despair, understood not as a mood, an emotion, or a psychological disorder but as a fragmentation of the soul that comes with the collapse of the relationship that constitutes the soul. If the Chasidim place such emphasis on joy, insisting that only prayers uttered with joy reach the ears of the Holy One,[51] it is not to urge us to be in a good mood; rather, it is to summon us to be who we are through an embrace of the "Power" that constitutes us.

Like the origin of the soul, then, original sin falls into a metaphysical category. It is not the first in a sequence of sins – it is the sin both primordial and perennial, the persistent compulsion, always already and always at hand. It is not the sin inherited from Adam, as if at some point in time he committed a transgression that now taints the generations that follow him. Such a view is alien to Jewish thought and at times has played into the hands of anti-Semitic thinking. Indeed, Adam himself had *already* inherited the potential for this sin that sleeps in the soul; hence the divine commandment concerning the Tree. Original sin belongs to an anarchic or immemorial past, an unrepresentable past, that pervades the present and hovers on the horizon of the future. Like the mission and the destiny of the soul itself, it lies outside the ontological coordinates of space-time. Or perhaps better: the coordinates of space-time are infused with the immemorial as part of what gives metaphysical meaning to the ontological landscape. Thus the immemorial chosenness of the human being – the assignation of the human being that is eternally *already* – lies not only in the summons to fulfill a mission but also in the commandment to refuse an original sin, the sin of usurping God in an effort to be as God. For the relation to the other, whether human or divine, requires the possibility of abrogating the relation through an appropriation of the other. To be sure, such an act of appropriation is the means by which we hide from the absolute assignation that defines our condition of being chosen, a condition announced in the question "Where are you?" The chosenness of the human being by a divine being, the summons to a higher relationship, is forever haunted by specter of original sin and the temptation to deicide.

God singles out the Jewish people – assigns the Jewish people – to announce to humanity that (1) every human being is chosen for a task that no other human being can perform and (2) every soul that enters creation is indispensable to all of creation. The longing to kill God is a

---

[51] See, e.g., Newman, *The Hasidic Anthology*, 203.

longing to undo this condition of singular chosenness, a condition couched in the individual's name: to be named is to be singled out. An emanation of the divine Name, the soul comes into being on the Creator's utterance of its name, as the Holy Shelah Isaiah Horowitz (1570–1626) has taught[52], and in its name lies both its destiny and identity. Thus, according to one tradition, when we die and lie in the grave the Angel of Death comes to us, so that he might bring us into the presence of the Holy One. But in order to draw nigh unto the divine presence, we must answer a question: "What is your name?"[53] In our surname is inscribed our past; in our given name abides our future. Knowing our name means knowing a tradition borne by those who have borne our names before us; it means knowing a teaching entrusted to our care and a destiny to which we are summoned by name; it means having the capacity to answer, "Here I am for you," when called to the task for which we are created.

According to this way of thinking, we are no more free to choose our destiny than we are to choose the Good; rather, we are free because we have been chosen for a destiny, chosen by the Good, before we have made any other choices. "The attachment to the Good," in the words of Lévinas, "precedes the choosing of this Good. How, indeed, to choose the Good? The Good is good precisely because it chooses you and grips you before you have had the time to raise your eyes to it."[54] That is what makes our choices *matter*: we are already responsible for the Good because we are already chosen by the Good, in whose image and likeness we are created. In this anarchic *already* lies the eternal. For Jewish thought, life eternal is precisely life conceived as responsibility and chosenness; life eternal is life *noad*, or "destined." Eternal life is not endless life; it is meaningful life. The Hebrew *yiud*, which is "mission" or "destiny," is the opposite of the Greek *moira* or "fate." A person's fate has no particular purpose. It is pointless, for example, to ask why Oedipus has to murder his father and marry his mother; he just *has* to, that's all – it is as necessary as it is arbitrary (can there be any horror greater than this merging of the necessary with the arbitrary?). Stealing away all genuine choice and thus undermining all genuine relation, fate is the hallmark of meaninglessness and the harbinger

---

[52] See Isaiah Horowitz, *The Generations of Adam*, trans. and ed. Miles Krassen (New York: Paulist Press, 1996), 99.

[53] See Nachman of Breslov, *Tikkun*, trans. Avraham Greenbaum (Jerusalem: Breslov Research Institute, 1984), 102; see also Rabbi Nathan of Nemirov, *Rabbi Nachman's Wisdom: Shevachay HaRan and Sichos HaRan*, trans. Aryeh Kaplan, ed. Aryeh Rosenfeld (New York: A. Kaplan, 1973), 148.

[54] Lévinas, *Nine Talmudic Readings*, 135.

of doom. Whereas fate strikes us dumb, however, destiny demands a response. How we respond determines whether we enter into a testimonial relation with another or whether we slip into the isolation of the ego that would eclipse God by transforming itself into a god. This self-apotheosis demands the murder of God.

Because this tension lies within the soul as it emanates from the Creator, and not in the ontological composition of creation, the view I propose cannot be construed as Manichean. I maintain that evil exists, not as a separate entity as in the God versus Satan scenario, but within each of us; I also maintain that, unlike an independent force at work in the world, evil can thrive only as we feed it. And we feed it by waging our own internal war against God. The Midrash illustrates this point with the teaching that when the Pharaoh decided to pursue the Israelites on their way to the sea, he declared, "It is not only against the Jews whom this war is directed. It is against their God Himself!" (*Midrash HaGadol* 14).[55] Taking himself for a god, Pharaoh was bent on eliminating the Creator. According to another midrashic teaching, when the nephew of Titus slashed his way through the Temple and emerged with his sword covered in blood, he boasted that he had slain the God of the Jews (*Midrash Tehillim* 5:121:3).[56] Teachings such as these may underlie why Maimonides (1135–1204) wrote in his letter to the Jews of Yemen, "Because of the Torah, all the kings of the earth stirred up hatred and jealousy against us. Their real intention is to make war against HaShem."[57] The real intention to make war against God is rooted in the ancient temptation to kill God. How? By killing the Jews, who proclaim that we are not God. Hence the exterminationist element of the more extreme forms of anti-Semitism: killing the God of Abraham requires killing the children of Abraham.

"We would, if we could, become deicides" – Richard Rubenstein makes a powerful observation. "Had we but the power, we would murder God, for we will never cease to be tempted by Ivan Karamazov's demonic

---

[55] See Moshe Weissman, ed., *The Midrash Says*, vol. 2 (Brooklyn, N.Y.: Bnay Yakov Publications, 1980), 121. Compiled in the late fourteenth century, the *Midrash HaGadol*, or The Great Midrash, is a collection of talmudic and midrashic teachings collected from earlier sources.

[56] The *Midrash Tehillim*, or Midrash on Psalms, is a midrashic commentary on the Book of Psalms dating from the eleventh century.

[57] Maimonides, *The Essential Maimonides*, trans. and ed. Avraham Yaakov Finkel (Northvale, N.J.: Jason Aronson, 1996), 8.

fantasy that if God were dead, all things would be permitted."[58] And: "*The wish to murder God makes sense only when all values derive from Him.* In such a system the deicidal act is an assertion of the will to total moral and religious license."[59] Rubenstein's observation, however, concerns a psychological condition, not a metaphysical origin. Although he sees the soul's impetus to deicide, he does not see the longing to kill God as a defining feature of anti-Semitism (he does, however, take it to be central to Christian anti-Semitism). We may not have the power to kill God the Creator and Lawgiver, but we have the power to destroy His children, beginning with His chosen, the Jews. In the Midrash we find a teaching that comes to bear in this connection: "Thy dwelling place is in heaven, and Thy dwelling place is also on earth. But because the enemies could not use their power against Thy dwelling place in heaven, they used it against Thy dwelling place on earth" (*Midrash on Psalms* 3:74:3), and, says the Zohar, His dwelling place on earth lies within the Knesset Yisrael, that is, among the Jewish people (*Zohar* II, 93a). The desire for unlimited power, free of every "thou shalt" and "thou shalt not," is a desire to get rid of the Jewish people. It is the essence of anti-Semitism.

The unlimited over against the limited is what distinguishes the false god of power from the true God of love – or rather, the God of the *commandment* to love. As Gershom Scholem has explained, according to kabbalistic teaching, in the act of creation God undergoes a "contraction" or "withdrawal," a self-limiting *tzimtzum*, so that the human being may have a relation to Him without being swallowed up by His infinity.[60] "When it arose in His simple will to create worlds," says the *Ets Chayyim* of Chayim Vital, "the Infinite contracted itself."[61] The God who is the Good is the God who is limited; He is what Lévinas calls the "otherwise than being," opposite the being that "is evil not because it is finite but because it is without limits."[62] The process of *tzimtzum* is rather like having the light and heat in the center of a star withdraw enough so that a candle could burn in its center without being obliterated by the star. Because human-to-divine and human-to-human relationships rest on the

[58] Richard L. Rubenstein, *After Auschwitz: History, Theology, and Contemporary Judaism*, 2nd ed. (Baltimore, Md.: Johns Hopkins University Press, 1992), 23.

[59] Ibid., 43; emphasis in the original.

[60] See Gershom Scholem, *Kabbalah* (New York: New American Library, 1974), 129–31.

[61] Chayim Vital, *The Tree of Life (Ets Chayyim)*, trans. D. W. Menzi and Z. Padeh (Northvale, N.J.: Aronson, 1999), 13.

[62] Emmanuel Lévinas, *Time and the Other*, trans. Richard A. Cohen (Pittsburgh, Pa.: Duquesne University Press, 1987), 51.

limitations outlined in the covenant of Torah – a covenant to which God binds Himself – the limiting principle is what characterizes the Good as a living presence that issues from the Holy One. The false god one would become through deicide, the god that the anti-Semite would become, is the god without limits, the totalitarian god, the god not of loving relation but of overwhelming domination, the evil god who will brook no alterity. Thus the original sin of deicide entails the elimination of all limits: killing the Infinite One requires an infinite transgression, an infinite breach of the limits of the permissible.

Why, it must be asked, are the *Jews specifically* accused of this original sin of deicide? It is not only because the Jews are the millennial witnesses to the uncompromising commandments of the God of Abraham, but also because, in a sense, the Jews are indeed the original deicides – *the deicides who slay the false gods of those who would be as God*. According to Jewish tradition, Abraham, the first to be called a Hebrew, was the original slayer of false gods. The Midrash relates a story about the young Abram, who was left alone one day to attend to his father Terach's idol shop. While his father was gone, Abram took a stick and smashed all the idols but one, the biggest one. When his father returned to the shop he was outraged and demanded to know what happened. Abram explained that the big idol smashed the other idols with the large stick. "Do you take me for a fool?" Terach demanded. "It is nothing but clay!" To which Abram answered, "Precisely" (*Bereshit Rabbah* 38:13).

Those who fall short of becoming a false god bow to a false god, always in expectation of some sort of payoff. Here too one sees that idolatrous adulation is the opposite of covenantal relation: we bow down in exchange for a favor, for power or pleasure, for possessions or prestige, and even for the remission of sin, as when Christians were told during the Crusades that killing a Jew would absolve them of all sin[63] or when Muslims are told that murdering Jews is a holy act pleasing to Allah.[64] The Jews, however, declare that there is no remission, that each is responsible not only for his or her own debts but for all debts, and that the accounts are never settled. The presence of the Jews, therefore, is unsettling. The Jews insist that those who would be as God – whether

---

[63] See Robert Michael, *Holy Hatred: Christianity, Anti-Semitism, and the Holocaust* (New York: Palgrave Macmillan, 2006), 67.
[64] Malise Ruthven, *A Fury for God: The Islamist Attack on America* (London: Granta, 2004), 206.

they would be all powerful on earth or the arbiters of salvation in heaven – are not as God. They insist that no matter how many times we have answered, "Here I am," to the question put to Adam, we must answer again and yet again.

FROM DEICIDE TO HOMICIDE: ANTI-SEMITISM AND THE ESSENCE OF EVIL

Rubenstein argues, correctly I think, that the centuries-old Christian accusation that the Jews are Christ killers and are therefore deicides is in fact an expression of the crime that the Christians long to commit.[65] One can find a comparable centuries-old accusation in Islam, where in the Hadith it is claimed that the Jews poisoned Muhammad (*Sahih Bukhari*, Vol. 3, Book 47, #786): as the purported murderers of prophets, the Jews are the murderers of the quintessential prophet of Islam, whose word has the status of the divine Word. The blood libel, which, as Wistrich has pointed out, the Muslims have picked up from the Christians,[66] bears similar implications. "When the anti-Semite accuses the Jew of ritual murder," says Rubenstein, "he accuses him of the very crime that he himself intends to commit."[67] As sacralized murder, ritual murder transforms the transgression of the divine prohibition against murder into something holy; it is therefore a fundamental expression of the elimination of the divine. From the first recorded case of the Christian blood libel in 1144 Norwich to contemporary dramatizations of the blood libel on Arab Muslim television,[68] the accusation leveled at the Jews is an expression of the original desire that, as Rubenstein maintains, lurks in each of us: the desire to kill God. The Jews reveal to all this desire rooted in the soul, and they are hated for it.

"'The jews,'" as Jean-François Lyotard (1924–1998) puts it, are for this reason "the irremissible in the West's movement of remission and pardon. They are what cannot be domesticated in the obsession to

---

[65] Rubenstein, *After Auschwitz*, 43.

[66] Robert S. Wistrich, "Islamic Judeophobia: An Existential Threat," in David Bukay, ed., *Muhammad's Monsters: A Comprehensive Guide to Radical Islam for Western Audiences* (Green Forest, Ark.: Balfour Books, 2004), 202.

[67] Rubenstein, *After Auschwitz*, 42.

[68] In 2003 a private Syrian film company produced a series titled "Ash-Shatat" (The Diaspora), which was based in part on the infamous *Protocols of the Elders of Zion* and portrayed dramatic re-enactments of the blood libel; the series was aired on the Hezbollah satellite television station Al-Manar.

dominate."[69] And if they cannot be domesticated, they must be annihilated. Thus, Lyotard outlines the history of anti-Semitism: "One converts the Jews in the Middle Ages, they resist by mental restriction. One expels them during the classical age, they return. One integrates them in the modern era, they persist in their difference. One exterminates them in the twentieth century"[70] – which is the final, postmodern solution to the Jewish Question. It is *post*modern because the modern thinking of the Age of Reason at least tried to find an absolute ground for the prohibition against murder, whereas the postmodern period has done away with all absolutes. What is said of the Jews, moreover, can be said of God: He cannot be domesticated. One makes God into a Christian or a Muslim; He resists by mental restriction. He is expelled and replaced by the "I think" in the classical age; He returns. He is integrated into a cultural phenomenon in the modern era; He persists in His otherness. One exterminates Him in the postmodern age by exterminating His people.

Because the Jews have been singled out for the thankless task of unmasking the false gods and attesting to an absolute limiting principle, the desire to kill God is a desire to kill the Jews, which is the deepest desire of the anti-Semitic aspect of the soul. The dynamic of Jew hatred, moreover, works in two directions, with each fueling the other: in order to eliminate God, one must eliminate the divine prohibition against murder, and in order to eliminate the divine prohibition, one must eliminate God. The crimes of the Nazis, therefore, were not unimaginable but everything imaginable, for their actions were limited only by their imagination and their will. There was no measure too extreme: it was impossible to go too far, to be too brutal, or to murder too many Jews. Just the opposite: the principle that guided them in their actions was "Thou shalt murder *every* Jew." For this reason, as Emil Fackenheim (1916–2003) has maintained, murder was not a by-product of National Socialism – it was its very essence.[71] Why? Because anti-Semitism was its very essence: deicide demands the murder of every Jew, the silencing of every Hebrew prayer, and the burning of every Torah scroll.

---

[69] Jean-François Lyotard, *Heidegger and "the Jews,"* trans. Andreas Michel and Mark S. Roberts (Minneapolis, Minn.: University of Minneapolis Press, 1990), 22.

[70] Ibid., 23.

[71] See Emil L. Fackenheim, *The Jewish Return into History* (New York: Schocken Books, 1978), 246.

Jean Améry (1912–1978) has a related insight: "Torture was not an accidental quality of this Third Reich, but its essence."[72] Indeed, torture is central to the movement from deicide to homicide and is the incarnation of evil. The soul is in the blood (Genesis 9:4), and in his appropriation of the soul the torturer invades, curdles, and drains the blood of his victim. In torture, the god-like torturer is the purveyor of the soul, the master of word and silence, the arbiter of immortality. Like the murderer, the torturer holds in his hands what belongs only to God: death. Hence the horror of torture is that the victim *cannot die*. During the Spanish Inquisition doctors, including "the most brilliant university professors," were present at all torture sessions to be sure that the victim would not find relief from his or her agony in death.[73] Murder is of the essence where there is an *assault* on God; torture is of the essence where there is an *appropriation* of God. Both entail an assault on and an appropriation of the other human being, beginning with the Jew; both are essential expressions of anti-Semitism. The torturer waxes infinite in his ascent to becoming a god, expands "into the body of his fellow man," as Améry puts it, and extinguishes "what was his spirit."[74] It is no accident that totalitarian regimes that routinely engage in torture and mass murder are also anti-Semitic.

Both murder and torture entail an assault on the soul of the other in an effort to hide from the first question put to the first human being: "Where are you?" Hiding, like Adam, from the responsibility that constitutes my subjectivity, I renounce the first utterance from Mount Sinai, "I am God" (Exodus 20:2), which amounts to an abrogation of the commandment "Thou shalt not murder" (Exodus 20:13). For it is written that we are to read the commandments not from top to bottom but from right to left (in Hebrew): "I am God" means "Thou shalt not murder" (see, e.g., *Mekilta Bachodesh* 8; *Pesikta Rabbati* 21:19; *Zohar* I, 90a),[75] so that in "whoever sheds human blood renounces the Likeness," as it is written

---

[72] Jean Améry, *At the Mind's Limits: Contemplations by a Survivor on Auschwitz and Its Realities*, trans. Sidney Rosenfeld and Stella P. Rosenfeld (New York: Schocken Books, 1986), 24.

[73] Joseph Pérez, *The Spanish Inquisition: A History*, trans. Janet Lloyd (New Haven, Conn.: Yale University Press, 2005), 118.

[74] Améry, *At the Mind's Limits*, 35.

[75] The *Mekilta*, also known as the *Mekilta de-Rabbi Ishmael*, is a midrashic commentary on the Book of Exodus attributed to the talmudic sage Rabbi Ishmael, who lived in the second century. The *Pesikta Rabbati* is a midrashic commentary composed by an anonymous author around 845 CE.

in the Tosefta (*Tosefta Yevamot* 8:4), the "Likeness" is not only within one's own soul but also within the soul of the other. For the anti-Semite, as for every child of Adam, the soul suffers what it inflicts: killing Abel, Cain killed Cain in a mad attempt to kill God.

"Cain killed to become God. To kill God," writes Elie Wiesel.[76] And: "Every murder is a suicide: Cain killed Cain in Abel."[77] In Cain's action we see the move from deicide to homicide, as well as from homicide to suicide. "Whoever kills Jews," says Wiesel, "will end up killing himself and his own God."[78] The movement from deicide to homicide begins with "the anti-Semitic remark," which, writes Lévinas, "is like no other. Is it therefore an insult like other insults? It is an exterminating word, through which the Good that glorifies Being sees itself brought to unreality and shrivels up in the deepest recesses of a subjectivity,"[79] a subjectivity that would be as God. The evil of anti-Semitism lies in the egocentric will to deicide, which shows itself concretely as a will to homicide: killing God requires killing human beings, from Abel onward. Already at work in the murder of Abel, the anti-Semite proceeds from Abel to the extermination of the Jewish people. Very often the movement is from killing Jews to killing other human beings; what happens to humanity happens to the Jews first. Inasmuch as the evil inclination, which is the soul's anti-Semitic inclination, is an inclination to get rid of God, it is an inclination to commit murder. Perhaps that is why the Chasidic master Rabbi Simcha Bunim of Pshyshka (1765–1827) taught that "the evil inclination should be imagined as if it were a murderer,"[80] a murderer of God and humanity.

Understanding the essence of anti-Semitism as a move to eliminate God through the elimination of the prohibition against murder, we come to a startling realization: the essence of anti-Semitism is the essence of evil, so that to understand anti-Semitism is to understand evil. Which means: the problem of Jew hatred is the problem of evil. Evil, it must be carefully

---

[76] Elie Wiesel, *Messengers of God*, trans. Marion Wiesel (New York: Simon & Schuster, 2005), 58. Recall the remark made by the character Cain in Wiesel's novel *Twilight*: "When I killed my brother, it was really Him I wanted to kill. And He knows it. Any fool knows that he who kills, kills God"; see Elie Wiesel, *Twilight*, trans. Marion Wiesel (New York: Summit Books, 1998), 58.

[77] Wiesel, *Messengers of God*, 61.

[78] Elie Wiesel, *Against Silence: The Voice and Vision of Elie Wiesel*, vol. 1, ed. Irving Abrahamson (New York: Holocaust Library, 1985), 137.

[79] Lévinas, *Difficult Freedom*, 262.

[80] Quoted in Milton Aron, *Ideas and Ideals of the Hassidim* (Secaucus, N.J.: Citadel, 1969), 243.

noted, lies not in the *violation* of the commandment, but rather in its *elimination* through the elimination of the One who commands. Lévinas argues that "evil claims to be the contemporary, the equal, the twin, of the Good. This is an irrefutable lie, a Luciferian lie. It is the very egoism of the ego that posits itself as its own origin, an uncreated sovereign principle, a prince."[81] Such is the ego of the anti-Semite, who is "completely enclosed within" himself, "to the point of not revealing" himself even to himself, which is another way in which Lévinas defines evil.[82] And, he adds, evil refuses "any synthesis in which the wholly otherness of God would become visible."[83] All of these definitions and descriptions of evil point to one thing: evil lies in the radical undermining of both the human-to-divine and the human-to-human relation, which are of a piece. The undermining of those relations manifests itself most radically in deicide and homicide, which, again, are of a piece. Underlying both is the metaphysical origin of anti-Semitism.

In the light of what has been said, it turns out that, strictly speaking, anti-Semitism is not reducible to Jew hatred, although that is where it finds its most immediate and most venomous expression. Anti-Semitism is God hatred and human hatred. Lévinas claims that anti-Semitism is present in every form of racism[84] and that it is "in its essence hatred for a man who is other than oneself – that is to say, hatred for the other man."[85] Anti-Semitism is present in every form of racism precisely because it is not a form of racism; if it is hatred of the other person, it is hatred of the holy image and likeness in which the other person is created. Steven Katz states that "what is definitive in antisemitism is ontology, not psychology,"[86] but it does not have an ontological origin. Tied to the essence of evil, anti-Semitism has a metaphysical origin: it is not of this world, any more than the human soul is of this world. With its origins lying outside the ontological coordinates of space-time, anti-Semitism reveals itself in the mad struggle to return being to the chaos and void that God overcomes in the act of creation, something that Lévinas senses when he notes that a certain nihilism is part of anti-Semitism.[87] It is an

---

[81] Emmanuel Lévinas, *Collected Philosophical Papers*, trans. Alphonso Lingis (Dordrecht: Martinus Nijhoff, 1987), 138.

[82] Lévinas, *Nine Talmudic Readings*, 108.

[83] Lévinas, *Collected Philosophical Papers*, 183.   [84] Lévinas, *Difficult Freedom*, 261.

[85] Ibid., 281.

[86] Steven T. Katz, *The Holocaust in Historical Context*, vol. 1: *The Holocaust and Mass Death before the Modern Age* (New York: Oxford University Press, 1994), 396.

[87] Lévinas, *Difficult Freedom*, 261.

attempt to expel the Divine Presence from creation, an attempt to reduce all there is to all there is. Anti-Semitism, in other words, is the ontological project *par excellence*, the totalitarian project to appropriate the other, both human and divine. It lurks in the despairing, fragmented soul of every human being, and that is why we find it in such disparate figures as Democritus and Stokely Carmichael.

I

Preliminary Explanations

To the superficial mind, Antisemitism is simply another form of race prejudice, and only those are guilty who willfully indulge in it.

Franklin Littell, *The Crucifixion of the Jews*

Commenting on the task of fathoming the origin of anti-Semitism, Jean Améry once declared, "I would play into their unclean hands if I began investigating what share religious, economic, or other factors have in the persecution of the Jews. If I were to engage in such investigations I would only be falling for the intellectual dupery of so-called historical objectivity, according to which the murdered are as guilty as the murderers, if not even more guilty. A wound was inflicted on me. I must disinfect and bind it, not contemplate why the ruffian raised his club, and, through the inferred 'That's Why,' in the end partly absolve him."[1] Although Améry and I have little in common with regard to the ground of our thinking, we share much the same view on the shortcomings of most of the attempts to explain anti-Semitism. If I am trying get at the Why, it is a Why that lies outside "the intellectual dupery of historical objectivity." My concern is not with the history of anti-Semitism but with what drives that history. The "religious, economic, or other factors" that Améry refers to are central to most of the investigations into the phenomenon of Jew hatred. Most explanations, in other words, are rooted in ontological contingencies and contexts – whether social or political, cultural or economic – that in the end may indeed place the blame on the murdered by rendering the

[1] Jean Améry, *At the Mind's Limits*, trans. Sidney Rosenfeld and Stella P. Rosenfeld (Bloomington: Indiana University Press, 1980), 92.

actions of the murderers "understandable," if not absolvable. To the extent that any explanation of anti-Semitism falls into this trap, it plays into the hands of the anti-Semites, and any explanation rooted in onto-logical contingencies runs such a risk. Améry speaks from the depths of a wound, as he says. The wound is a wound in the soul. And it is in the depths of the soul that an explanation – if, indeed, that is the right word – must be sought.

Proceeding from the contextual framework of the ontological land-scape, the prevailing analyses of the phenomenon fall into five categor-ies: the theological, sociological, ideological, psychological, and composite. All of them are relatively recent, given the fact that, having been with us ever since the Amalekites attacked the Israelites coming out of Egypt (see Exodus 17:8–15), Jew hatred is indeed the longest hatred, as Robert Wistrich has aptly described it.[2] The first person to offer a systematic explanation of anti-Semitism was Bernard Lazare (1865–1903), who published his *Antisemitism: Its History and Causes* in 1894, within months of the arrest of Alfred Dreyfus (1859–1935), the Jewish French officer wrongly accused of treason and espionage. Although his historical facts are sometimes inaccurate, Lazare traces a detailed history of anti-Semitism and anti-Semites, from Apollonius Molon (first century BCE) and Pliny the Elder (23–79) to Saint Jerome (ca. 347–420) and Isidore of Seville (ca. 560–636), from Theophanes the Confessor (ca. 760–818) and Pope Innocent IV (1195–1254) to King Edward I of England (1239–1307) and King Ferdinand II of Spain (1452–1516). In addition to the history of pagan and Christian anti-Semitism, Lazare briefly examines the notorious "intellectual" anti-Semitic work *Entdecktes Judenthum* (Judaism Unveiled, 1700) by Johann Andreas Eisenmenger (1654–1704), as well as the work of some of the early French proponents of the myth of Jewish world domination, such as Roger Gougenot des Mousseaux (1805–1876) and Jacques Crétineau-Joly (1803–1875). He also identifies anti-Semitic race theor-ists such as Heinrich von Treitschke (1934–1896), Wilhelm Marr (1819–1904), and Arthur de Gobineau (1816–1882), even though it seems that Gobineau was actually philo-Semitic, arguing as he did in his *Inequality of Human Races* that the Jews "became a people that succeeded in everything it undertook, a free, strong, and intelligent

---

[2] See Robert Wistrich, *Antisemitism: The Longest Hatred* (New York: Schocken Books, 1994).

people."[3] The fundamental cause of the Jew hatred, says Lazare, is xenophobia,[4] which in his day largely expressed itself as "national protectionism."[5] What is the understandable reason for the xenophobia and national protectionism that lead to Jew hatred? According to Lazare, it is the Jews, who insist on being "different."

A Jew who desperately longed to assimilate into an enlightened social-ist world, Lazare was at once a pro-Zionist and a potential anti-Semite, inasmuch as he had a profound hatred of the Jewish religious tradition, which is the source of Jewish identity. He was a social activist who maintained that "the general causes of antisemitism have always resided in Israel itself.... Everywhere up to our own days the Jew was an unsoci-able being. Why was he unsociable? Because he was exclusive, and his exclusiveness was both political and religious, or rather he held fast to his political and religious cult, to his law,"[6] that is, to his Torah. The Jews, according to Lazare, were to blame for their persecution because "they instinctively had a taste for domination, as they believed themselves to be superior to all others by their origin, their religion, their title of a 'chosen race.'"[7] Above all, the origin of anti-Semitism lay in the Jews' embrace of the Talmud.[8] Although the gentile world opened its doors to the Jews in the eighteenth century, says Lazare, "they could not help giving themselves up to their usual commerce, their vices, their passion for gold. Dominated by the Talmudists, they succeeded in producing nothing beyond commentaries of the Talmud."[9] Not just the Talmud, he argues, but also the Bible is the justifiable reason for Jew hatred, and the Jews should abandon it,[10] a view typical of an "emancipated" Jew who would trade the Talmud for any Kantian tractate. Lazare's solution to the Jewish Question is total assimilation: once the Jews have totally assimilated, with nothing Jewish about them remaining, anti-Semitism will come to an end.[11]

It is not surprising that this first attempt to explain anti-Semitism, drawing as it does on what Améry describes as "the intellectual dupery of so-called historical objectivity," should prove to be anti-Semitic. Indeed, in his introduction to Lazare's work Wistrich notes that "most French Jews were hostile to Lazare's history of antisemitism or

---

[3] Arthur de Gobineau, *The Inequality of Human Races*, trans. Adrain Collins (New York: G. P. Putnam's Sons, 1915), 59.

[4] Bernard Lazare, *Antisemitism: Its History and Causes* (Lincoln: University of Nebraska Press, 1995), 176.

[5] Ibid., 103.   [6] Ibid., 9.   [7] Ibid., 62.   [8] Ibid., 65.   [9] Ibid., 80.

[10] Ibid., 120.   [11] Ibid., 179–180.

embarrassed by its often harsh criticisms of Jewry. Antisemites, on the other hand, frequently praised it.... [Edouard] Drumont [1844–1917] considered it a highly informative work," and "the founder of the Action Française, Charles Maurras [1868–1952], was another anti-Semite who admired Lazare's work."[12] Lazare's tendency to blame the Jews for being an object of hatred sets a precedent for some, although not all, of the subsequent attempts to explain the phenomenon of anti-Semitism, even when the explanation is rooted in an ostensibly genuine concern for the Jews. All too often the Jew hater is somehow exonerated, since his hatred issues from cultural, psychological, or sociological forces outside his control. Indeed, Jew hatred becomes not only understandable but "natural."

Although Lazare avoided any religious explanation of anti-Semitism, the religious aspect of Jewish identity cannot be avoided, as Lazare himself realized. Like many other modern thinkers, he viewed religion not as the unfolding of a divine revelation but as a cultural curiosity. Hence, the Jews could be blamed for insisting on remaining a curiosity and refusing to assimilate into the host culture. Even those who viewed religion as a manifestation of the divine were often inclined to blame the Jews for Jew hatred, not because they refused cultural assimilation but because they refused spiritual salvation. And so we begin with the attempts made by theologians and theological thinkers to explain the phenomenon.

THEOLOGICAL EXPLANATIONS

Among the first of the Christian theologians to attempt to explain the phenomenon of Jew hatred was James Parkes (1896–1981). In *The Conflict of the Church and the Synagogue* (1934), Parkes systematically outlines the development of a tradition of contempt for the Jews in early Church history and called Christians to a reevaluation of their relationship to Jews and Judaism.[13] His book, however, is much more about the early history of an insidious teaching than about the origins of Jew hatred; or rather, he argues that the history is itself the origin, as if there were no specific hatred of the Jews until the Church Fathers made it a part of their theology. In 1939, when the Nazis' war against the Jews was much

---

[12] Robert Wistrich, introduction to Lazare, *Antisemitism*, xv.

[13] See James William Parkes, *The Conflict of the Church and the Synagogue: A Study in the Origins of Antisemitism* (New York: ACLS Humanities E-Book, 2008).

further along, a more prominent Christian thinker sought to explain Christian anti-Semitism on a deeper level. Responding to the Nazi Jew hatred that had appeared in the heart of Christendom, the French Catholic philosopher Jacques Maritain (1882–1973) published his slim volume *Antisemitism*.

One of Maritain's deepest insights lies in his realization that with anti-Semitism "everything proceeds as though a profound hatred of the Scriptures, wherein God testifies to Himself, rebounds on Israel itself as a mystical body, and Israel, as a mystical body, is never afflicted without Israel, as a people, feeling the same blow."[14] The physical and the metaphysical are always interconnected. By their very presence in the world, Maritain maintains, the Jewish people represent the presence of the Infinite One, who disturbs our sleep from beyond the world, from the inside, by proclaiming our infinite responsibility to and for the other human being: "Israel, which is not of the world, is to be found at the very heart of the world's structure, stimulating it, exasperating it, moving it. . . . It gives the world no peace, it bars slumber, it teaches the world to be discontented and restless as long as the world has not God; it stimulates the movement of history. It seems to me that these considerations explain something of the spiritual essence of antisemitism. . . . If the world hates the Jews. . ., it is because the world detests their passion for the absolute and the unbearable stimulus which it inflicts."[15] What Maritain refers to as an "unbearable stimulus" is the unsettling presence of the Jews in a world that longs to have matters settled, particularly matters of salvation and redemption. The "spiritual essence" of anti-Semitism, as Maritain calls it, lies in the anti-Semite's refusal of a transcendent ethical authority at work in the world. If the Jews will always be "outsiders" in a spiritual sense, it is because through them a spiritual Presence will always call us into the open and demand of us a reckoning.

Maritain believes that the perilous task for which the Jews are chosen – the task of waking up a slumbering humanity – also falls to the Christians, insisting as he does that *"spiritually we are Semites."*[16] And yet this move, which might at first glance seem to side with the Jews, actually displaces them by collapsing the difference between Christian and Jew and thus rendering superfluous anything that might set the Jews apart. "According to Paul," Maritain justifies his position, "we gentile Christians have been grafted on to the predestined olive tree of Israel *in place of the branches*

[14] Jacques Maritain, *Antisemitism* (London: Centenary Press, 1939), 31.
[15] Ibid., 20.   [16] Ibid., 27; emphasis in original.

which did not recognize the Messiah foretold by the prophets.... Christianity, then, is the overflowing expansion and the supernatural fulfillment of Judaism."[17] Judaism thus fulfilled is Judaism justly superseded – superseded because of a failing of the Jews to recognize the Messiah. For all of its depth and insight, Maritain's explanation of anti-Semitism fails to avoid this basic anti-Semitic element in traditional Christian teaching.

A more liberal Christian theologian who has attempted to get at the theological roots of anti-Semitism is Rosemary Radford Ruether (b. 1936), the author of *Faith and Fratricide* (1974). Similar to Parkes, she maintains that anti-Semitism has its origins in the Christian teaching of contempt and not, strictly speaking, in the pre-Christian Greco-Roman world.[18] Such a teaching, says Ruether, "is the proof of the election of the gentile Church and its inheritance of the election of the rejected Jews.... Essentially, there is one covenant, *promised* to Abraham, *foretold* by the prophets, and *fulfilled* in the gentile Church."[19] This anti-Semitic seed, according to Ruether, was planted in the soil of Christian Scripture and nourished by the dualism of Hellenistic thinking, where the body is viewed as the enemy of the soul. Thus, a Hellenized Christianity came to view Judaism as the old, carnal body, with Christianity portrayed as the new, liberated soul, which overcomes not only death but also the body.[20] Here lies one of Ruether's more profound insights; it is an insight into what characterizes anti-Semitic thinking, rather than the origin of anti-Semitism itself. The concrete ethical demand as taught in Judaism devolves on the body; the ethical obligation is to attend to the body, not to the soul, of the other human being. To be sure, Jewish thought opposes the Hellenistic dualism, maintaining as it does that the body is part of the soul,[21] and most traditions that promote such dualism also promote anti-Semitism. To divorce the body from the soul is to eliminate the ethical demand that allows us no sleep. The Hellenistic roots of Christian anti-Semitism, then, may run deeper than Ruether thinks.

---

[17] Ibid., 16; emphasis added.
[18] Rosemary Radford Ruether, *Faith and Fratricide: The Theological Roots of Anti-Semitism* (New York: Seabury Press, 1974), 28
[19] Ibid., 137. It must be noted that, while the Church indeed thinks of itself as elect, the Jews do not: to be chosen is not to be among the "elect," if *elect* means being assured of some sort of salvation. To be chosen is to be chosen for a deeper responsibility, a notion that appears to be absent from the Church's notion of the election of the gentiles.
[20] Ibid., 95.
[21] See, e.g., Abraham Joshua Heschel, *The Prophets*, vol. 2 (New York: Harper & Row, 1975), 37.

In any case, she believes that, thanks to the teaching of contempt for the Jews, "anti-Judaism is too deeply embedded in the foundations of Christianity to be rooted out entirely without destroying the whole structure."[22] This entrenchment in tradition threatens the whole structure not only because of how history has formed Christianity but, according to Ruether, due to the nature of the Christian psyche: "The assertion that the Jews are reprobate because they did not accept Christ as having already come is really a projection upon Judaism of that unredeemed side of itself that Christianity must constantly deny in order to assert that Christ has already come and founded 'the Church.' The Jews represent that which Christianity must repress in itself, namely the recognition of history and Christian existence as unredeemed. In this sense, the Jews do indeed 'kill Christ' for the Christian."[23] To be sure, the temptation to see oneself as God, which lies at the core of anti-Semitism, is a temptation to see oneself as redeemed, washed as clean as the unblemished Lamb, who is Himself God. To kill Christ is to kill this illusion that the Christian is Christ-like. Once again, the Jews are hated because, insisting on attending to the body, they allow the soul no sleep.

In contrast to Ruether, John Gager argues that the anti-Semitism systematized in Christian theology has its origins in antiquity, particularly in the Roman world. Roman officials, he points out, "saw Judaism as a persistent 'threat' among their own people. Not unlike later Christians – Ignatius, John Chrysostom, and others – whose negative reactions to Judaism can be plotted as a function of Judaizing tendencies among their own faithful, Roman political and intellectual leaders responded to pagan Judaizers for essentially the same reasons."[24] In fact, several of the emperors of the pre-Christian and early Christian period had their anti-Semitic advisors: Tiberius (42 BCE–37 CE) had Sejanus, Caligula (12–41) had Helicon, Nero (37–68) had Seneca (ca. 4–65), and Domitian (51–96) had Quintilian.[25] The Roman world, on Gager's view, provides the context for Paul's de-Judaizing of the Christian message,[26] as well as his inversion of the gentiles into "a light unto Israel."[27] According to Gager, the origin of the teaching of contempt for the Jews lies not in Christianity but in the Roman thinking of Paul. If anti-Semitism is rooted in Pauline

---

[22] Ruether, *Faith and Fratricide*, 228.   [23] Ibid., 245.

[24] John G. Gager, *The Origins of Anti-Semitism: Attitudes toward Judaism in Pagan and Christian Antiquity* (Oxford: Oxford University Press, 1983), 59; see also E. Mary Smallwood, *The Jews under Roman Rule: From Pompey to Diocletian: A Study in Political Relations* (Leiden: Brill, 1976), 205–210.

[25] Ibid., 62.   [26] Ibid., 242.   [27] Ibid., 262.

Christian theology, that theology itself has a distinctly Roman element. It is no accident, then, that in 380 CE under the emperor Theodosius I (347–395) Christianity became the official religion of *Rome* and that the first anti-Semitic legal codes, such as the Codex Theodosianus (438) and the Justinian Code (529), were *Roman*.

In *The Satanizing of the Jews* (1992), Joel Carmichael argues that the Christian thinkers added a mystical dimension to Roman Jew hatred. After the Bar Kochba Revolt (132–136), the Jews were scattered throughout the empire and had lost virtually all cultural, political, and religious significance in the Roman world, a world that was becoming increasingly Christian. Among the major Church Fathers of that early Christian period were Ignatius of Antioch (ca. 50–110), Justin Martyr (103–165), Tertullian (c. 160–c. 225), and Origen of Alexandria (ca. 185–254), all of whom wrote diatribes against the Jews.[28] For these early theologians, Carmichael explains, the Jews "were to embody a strange, eerie power, despite all appearances, through their being integrated into a new world view that assigned them their peculiar status – enemies of Jesus Christ, and hence of God, through their rejection of the Incarnation."[29] What Carmichael calls "mystical anti-Semitism" has its origins in this invisible ubiquity of the Jews, which lends itself to Satanizing the Jews: "they were all-powerful *secretly*."[30] According to Carmichael's account, anti-Semitism has a theological origin in the morphing of the Jew into this metaphysical category that explains every evil. Note well: the Jew is not the transgressor – he or she is the origin and essence of transgression as such.

The Jews' rejection of the Incarnation, moreover, is crucial: "What would otherwise have been mere exoticism, a cluster of normal dissimilarities between different groups, was escalated by the Jewish role as a Counter-Incarnation to a level of lofty horror that, in the very process of 'sparing' the Jews, heightened their demonically powerful character."[31]

---

[28] See Ignatius of Antioch, "To the Philadelphians," in Andrew Louth, ed., *Early Christian Writings: The Apostolic Fathers*, trans. Maxwell Staniforth (London: Penguin Books, 1987), 91–98; Justin Martyr, *Dialogue with Trypho*, trans. Thomas B. Falls (Washington, D.C.: Catholic University of America Press, 2003); Tertullian, "Against the Jews," in Geoffrey D. Dunn, *Tertullian (The Early Church Fathers)* (London: Routledge, 2004), 43–73; and Origen, *An Exhortation to Martyrdom, Prayer, and Selected Works*, trans. Rowan A. Greer (Mahwah, N.J.: Paulist Press, 1988), 171ff.

[29] Joel Carmichael, *The Satanizing of the Jews: Origin and Development of Mystical Anti-Semitism* (New York: Fromm International Publishing Corporation, 1992), 32.

[30] Ibid., 36; emphasis in original.   [31] Ibid., 52.

The rejection of the Incarnation is much more than a rejection of salvation or a matter of disbelief – it is the refusal of a category, a renunciation of the very notion of the merging of God and man in the Christ. Since the Incarnation represents the attainment of the greatest good, the rejection of the Incarnation is the greatest evil. The God of the Torah, who refuses the Incarnation as a category, is Himself transformed into a devil, so that the only way the Hebrew Scriptures can be legitimized is to be systematically Christianized, as Ruether had noted.[32] This Christian abstraction of the Jew into a metaphysical category, according to Carmichael, is tied to the abstract thinking that characterized the Enlightenment,[33] as well as the subsequent centuries. That is why someone as devoutly antireligious as the socialist anarchist Pierre-Joseph Proudhon (1809–1865) could assert, "It is not for nothing that the Christians call them deicides. The Jew is the enemy of the human race,"[34] not for what he does – since killing God is an ontological absurdity – but for what he *is*.

Carmichael's insight leads us to the realization that the theological move to make man into God has its modern counterpart in the philosophical move to make the thinking ego into the ground of all being and all value (much more will be said about this in subsequent chapters). Once the thinking ego becomes such a ground, God becomes superfluous, and mystical anti-Semitism becomes exterminationist anti-Semitism: "When theology became obsolete through the cooling of faith and atheistic indifference, the Jews became *pure* Evil. There was then no rationale for their existence – no reason they should *not* be exterminated. They no longer had to be sustained as Witnesses to the Truth of the Cross. They no longer *meant* anything: in the imaginations of all those released from the sustaining harmonizing force of theology, the Jews were simply monsters, and nothing else."[35] If one should wonder how a notion of evil can remain after the elimination of God, the answer is that modern thought has not gotten rid of God – it has usurped Him. Throughout his argument Carmichael situates the origin of anti-Semitism in the Christian theological mystification of the Jew, and not in the human soul, as if to say that were it not for Christian theology, there would be no anti-Semitism. However, where Carmichael saw a mystification of the Jew even in a modern, post-religious world, others set out to demystify the modern hatred of the Jew.

---

[32] Ruether, *Faith and Fratricide*, 161.   [33] Carmichael, *The Satanizing of the Jews*, 102.
[34] Pierre-Joseph Proudhon, *Carnets de P.-J. Proudhon*, ed. Pierre Haubtmann (Paris: Marcel Rivière, 1960–1961), 337–338.
[35] Carmichael, *The Satanizing of the Jews*, 133.

SOCIOLOGICAL EXPLANATIONS

In 1926, the same year that the second volume of *Mein Kampf* appeared, the German-born Zionist Perez Bernstein (1890–1971) published *Jew-Hate as a Sociological Problem*. He explains the phenomenon by arguing that because the minority group "is always a readily available and defenseless target for every need to discharge hatred, the excessive supply of suffering resulting from disasters can transform itself immediately into hostile acts against the minority group."[36] Unlike Carmichael, who maintains that anti-Semitism persists as a metaphysical category, Bernstein assumes that because the Enlightenment invalidated all religious forms of hatred, "metaphysical convictions were leveled down to the same value – or lack of value."[37] Nor does he take economic envy to be at the root of the problem. "The Jewish proletariat," says Bernstein, "is exposed to no lesser enmity than the well-to-do Jews."[38] Therefore, the origins of anti-Semitism must lie in racial animosity based on "the *outward appearance* of the Jew."[39] Because the Jew cannot undo his racial look, the attempt to assimilate not only must fail but "ratifies [the Jew's] own inferiority and contemptibility."[40] Zionism, then, is the only solution: "A Jewish nation which lives in close settlement within its own country will probably be exposed to the hostility of the surrounding nations..., but the enmity between the Jews and their neighbours will then be no more than a normal enmity between one nation and another, and not the onesided and accursed hatred which has haunted the fragments of a tortured people."[41] Sadly, Bernstein underestimated the exterminationist fanaticism of the Islamic Jihadists who currently surround the Jewish state.

Not everyone in Bernstein's time, however, understood race in terms of appearances. His contemporary, Alfred Rosenberg (1893–1946), for example, conflates outward appearance with inner essence, and in the inner essence lies the profound religious belief of the Jew: "One has only to visualize a face with hooked nose, drooping lips, piercing black eyes and wool hair to understand the plastic impossibility of embodying the European God in a Jewish face (to say nothing of the Jewish body). This insight also suffices to show why even the *inner* God-idea of

---

[36] Perez Bernstein, *Jew-Hate as a Sociological Problem*, trans. David Saraph (New York: Philosophical Library, 1951), 225.

[37] Ibid., 237. [38] Ibid., 244. [39] Ibid., 277–278. [40] Ibid., 229.

[41] Ibid., 291–292.

Judaism – which, together with the Jewish external form constitutes *one* essence – has to be completely rejected."[42] The European God is the self-styled idol of the ego constituted by will and power; the God-idea of Judaism is an idea of weakness and submission to arbitrary whim, which belongs to the ineluctable essence of the Jew. The God of Abraham, therefore, is not only ridiculous – He is dangerous and must be eliminated. Since the God of Abraham – or rather, the *idea* of the God of Abraham – is part of the Jewish essence, the only ultimate solution to the Jewish problem as a God-of-Abraham problem is the extermination of the Jews, which must be as fanatic and total as the totalitarian state.

A thinker who understood totalitarian fanaticism very well and who took up a social-political examination of anti-Semitism is German-born Hannah Arendt (1906–1975). Brought up in a family of secular Jews, Arendt studied under Martin Heidegger (1889–1976) and Karl Jaspers (1883–1969). In 1933, she fled from Germany to Paris, and in 1941 she immigrated to the United States, where she pursued a career as a scholar and a social philosopher. Her assessment of the origins of anti-Semitism can be found in her study *Antisemitism*, which is part one of *The Origins of Totalitarianism* (1951). Although Arendt places much of the blame for anti-Semitism on the Jews for taking Judaism to be "superior to other religions,"[43] she maintains that the phenomenon stems from "a secular nineteenth-century ideology" quite distinct from religious Jew hatred.[44] A shift in the social standing of the Jews brought anti-Semitism to "its climax," says Arendt, "when Jews had similarly lost their public functions and their influence, and were left with nothing but their wealth."[45] The social-historical process leading to this climax, she explains, proceeded in four stages:

1. In the seventeenth and eighteenth centuries Jews enjoyed a privileged status as court Jews who financed state affairs.
2. After the French Revolution, Jews used their international connections to set up a large banking industry and acquired privileges that only court Jews had known.
3. With the rise of nation-states, Jews lost their privileged status.

---

[42] Alfred Rosenberg, *Race and Race History and Other Essays*, ed. Robert Pois (New York: Harper & Row, 1974), 131.
[43] Hannah Arendt, *Antisemitism: Part One of the Origins of Totalitarianism* (New York: Harcourt Brace Jovanovich, 1968), viii–ix.
[44] Ibid., vii. [45] Ibid., 4.

4. Jews became "an object of universal hatred because of [their now] useless wealth, and of contempt because of [their] lack of power."[46]

Arendt thus situates the origin of anti-Semitism in the dynamics of social-economic history and not in religious tradition, historical testimony, or any mode of thought that the Jews might represent. She makes no distinction between who the Jews are and the social situation into which they are thrown.

For Arendt, then, anti-Semitism has nothing to do with any Jewish view of God and humanity, good and evil, or meaning and meaninglessness that the anti-Semites might perceive as a threat. She even attributes the Nazis' exterminationist anti-Semitism to social and political elements, maintaining that "the Nazi brand of antisemitism had its roots in these social conditions as well as in political circumstances,"[47] as if the Nazis would never have wanted to murder the Jews if circumstances had been different. Her approach cannot account for Rosenberg's insistence that the German spirit or mind – the German *Geist* – had been poisoned not just by Jewish blood but by Judaism.[48] She is correct in her understanding that the loosening of "old bonds of religious and spiritual tradition" in "Western culture for the first time threatened the very existence of the Jewish people."[49] She also notes a shortcoming in the ontological tradition that "cannot conceive of" the "radical evil [that] has emerged in connection with a system in which all men have become equally superfluous."[50] What she fails to see, however, is that the process of thinking God out of the picture that characterizes the Western ontological tradition led to the collapse of any limiting principle or absolute that might curb the excesses of the will to power. Such deadly, often anti-Semitic thinking can be found among those who attempt an ideological explanation of anti-Semitism.

IDEOLOGICAL EXPLANATIONS

Here we begin with the well-known work *Anti-Semite and Jew* (1946) by the existentialist Marxist Jean-Paul Sartre (1905–1980), who is specifically interested in modern French anti-Semitism. As an existentialist, he claims that anti-Semitism originates within the anti-Semite, who is in a

---

[46] Ibid., 14–15. [47] Ibid., 87. [48] Rosenberg, *Race and Race History*, 131–132.
[49] Arendt, *Antisemitism*, 27.
[50] Hannah Arendt, *The Origins of Totalitarianism* (New York: Harcourt Brace & Company, 1979), 459.

state of flight from his existential situation; "the Jew," says Sartre, "only serves him as a pretext; elsewhere his counterpart will make use of the Negro or the man of yellow skin. . . . Anti-Semitism, in short, is a fear of the human condition."[51] Hence, "if the Jew did not exist, the anti-Semite would invent him."[52] As a Marxist, Sartre insists that "anti-Semitism would have no existence in a society without classes and founded on collective ownership of the instruments of labor,"[53] claiming with incredible naiveté that "we find scarcely any anti-Semitism among workers."[54] Thus, Sartre makes a move much like the one made by the anti-Semite. Whereas the anti-Semite would purify society of the Jewish presence, he would purify society of the capitalist presence that generates anti-Semitism, so that the Jew may disappear into the proletarian body politic.

Sartre explains the difference between the anti-Semite and the capitalist democrat by saying, "The anti-Semite reproaches the Jew with *being* Jewish; the democrat reproaches him with willfully *considering himself* a Jew."[55] And, yet, Sartre's solution to the Jewish question plays into the hands of both of these existentially inauthentic figures, as Jonathan Judaken points out: "The antisemite wants to destroy the man and leave nothing but 'the Jew,' the democrat wants to destroy 'the Jew' and leave nothing but the man. . . . Sartre's solution to this impossible existential situation is for 'the Jew' to support the socialist revolution, which will end all antinomies in its explosion of the antithetical constructs 'the Jew' and the antisemite."[56] Because Jew hatred is what binds Jews together as Jews, says Sartre, there will be no Jew hatred in the Marxist utopia because there will be no Jews.[57] The authentic Jew will no longer have to be the one who "wills himself into history as a historic and damned creature" and who "ceases to run away from himself and to be ashamed of his own kind."[58] Once the Jews have thus been freed of the interminable and intractable struggle for authenticity, there will be no context to define the inauthentic Jews, who "are men whom other men take for Jews and who have decided to run away from this insupportable situation."[59] In short, there will be no Jews, inauthentic or otherwise: no Jew, no problem.

Sartre's solution to the Jewish Question smacks of the refined anti-Semitism that characterizes much of the thinking of left-wing

---

[51] Jean-Paul Sartre, *Anti-Semite and Jew: An Exploration of the Etiology of Hate*, trans. George L. Becker (New York: Schocken Books, 1976), 54.

[52] Ibid., 13.   [53] Ibid., 150.   [54] Ibid., 35.   [55] Ibid., 58.

[56] Jonathan Judaken, *Jean-Paul Sartre and the Jewish Question: Antisemitism and the Politics of the French Intellectual* (Lincoln: University of Nebraska Press, 2006), 139.

[57] Sartre, *Anti-Semite and Jew*, 91.   [58] Ibid., 136.   [59] Ibid., 93.

intellectuals. "If it is true," he writes, "that a community is historical to the degree that it remembers its history, then the Jewish community is the least historical of all, for it keeps memory of nothing but a long martyrdom, that is, of a long passivity."[60] As the least historical people, on Sartre's view, the Jewish people have little claim or capability to be part of history; although he recognized the need for a haven for the Jews in a world that detests them, he no doubt had high hopes for the emergence of a socialist state created by socialist Jews in Palestine. Rejecting any metaphysical view of anti-Semitism, Sartre refuses to allow for any connection between Judaism and Jew hatred. It is a social-political problem with a social-political solution that robs the Jews of all identity as Jews. For these reasons Emmanuel Lévinas's critique of Sartre rings true: Sartre's primary concern was "to generate disengagement in the midst of engagement."[61] In his assessment of anti-Semitism Sartre falls prey to the *mauvais foi* that the existentialist railed against.

Historian Albert S. Lindemann, author of *Esau's Tears: Modern Anti-Semitism and the Rise of the Jews* (1997), situates the cause of modern anti-Semitism in modern ideological movements that have reacted to the increasing influence of the Jews. His basic thesis is that "the rise of the Jews in modern times" is "the most fundamental cause of racial and political anti-Semitism"[62] and that the reason for this Jew hatred lies as much with the Jews as with the anti-Semites themselves. "As human beings," he says, "Jews have been as capable as any other group of provoking hostility in the everyday secular world."[63] In Russia, for example, the land of the pogroms, says Lindemann, anti-Semitism had "understandable cause" and was "related to real factors."[64] Why? Because while "modern secular Jews would be credited with bringing progress, new industrial techniques, [and] scientific discoveries..., they could also be credited with exploitation, corruption, crime, prostitution, alcoholism, social disintegration, and cultural nihilism."[65] Lindemann's anti-Semitic point is not that the Jews are necessarily prostitutes, alcoholics, and nihilists; rather, they are *the source* of these evils.

Elsewhere in his analysis Lindemann is less even-handed. Noting that European anti-Semites claimed that the Jews were behind the Boer War

---

[60] Ibid., 66–67.
[61] Emmanuel Lévinas, *Difficult Freedom: Essays on Judaism*, trans. Sean Hand (Baltimore, Md.: Johns Hopkins University Press, 1990), 212.
[62] Albert S. Lindemann, *Esau's Tears: Modern Anti-Semitism and the Rise of the Jews* (Cambridge, U.K.: Cambridge University Press, 1997), 532.
[63] Ibid., xvii.   [64] Ibid., 280.   [65] Ibid., 200.

(1899–1902) and the Russo-Japanese War (1904–1905), he embraces the anti-Semitic "world Jewish conspiracy" canard to maintain that there was in fact "clandestine Jewish involvement" in these events.[66] And, he asserts, the Romanian nationalist charge that international Jewry was trying to gain control of Romania "was hardly without foundation."[67] Anti-Semitism, then, has little to do with Jewish teaching, testimony, or tradition; even the categories of race and ethnicity, says Lindemann, are invoked simply to justify a deeper ideological and political hatred of the Jews.[68] He insists that the Jews brought this virulent hatred on themselves through their rise to power, but he does not explain why others who have risen to power have not become the target of a similar hatred. Indeed, the Jews have become the victims of mass murder precisely in places where they were powerless.

The anti-Semitic nature of Lindemann's analysis goes even further. Taking anti-Semitism to have a justified ideological origin, he mitigates the anti-Semite's hatred of the Jews by casting the Jews in the role of ideological competitors. To make such an argument, he minimizes the depth of the Jew hatred found in some of the nineteenth century's most notorious anti-Semites, such as Heinrich von Treitschke and Adolf Stoecker (1935–1909).[69] He notes that when Theodor Herzl (1860–1904) published *Die Judenstaat* (The Jewish State) in 1896, Édouard Drumont gave it a good review,[70] ignoring Drumont's claim that a world Jewish conspiracy was bent on the destruction of France.[71] He avers that Viennese mayor Karl Lueger (1844–1910) – who in a 1902 interview with Hermann Bielohlawek declared, "Yes, we want to annihilate the Jews!"[72] – was more an opportunist than an anti-Semite and certainly not a precursor to Adolf Hitler,[73] even though in *Mein*

---

[66] Ibid., 275.   [67] Ibid., 314.   [68] Ibid., 78.

[69] See ibid., 139ff. Heinrich von Treitschke was the author of what became the Nazi propaganda slogan *Die Juden sind unser Unglück!* (The Jews are our misfortune!); see Heinrich von Treitschke, "A Word about Our Jews," trans. Richard S. Levy, in Richard S. Levy, ed., *Antisemitism in the Modern World: An Anthology of Texts* (Lexington, Mass.: D. C. Heath and Company, 1991), 72. Adolf Stoecker identified the Jews as "the single greatest threat to German national life"; see Adolf Stoecker, "Our Demands on Modern Jewry," trans. Richard S. Levy, in Levy, *Antisemitism in the Modern World*, 60.

[70] Lindemann, *Esau's Tears*, 329.

[71] Édouard Drumont, *Les Juifs contre la France* (Paris: Librairie Antisémite, 1899), 25.

[72] Hermann Bielohlawek, "Yes, We Want to Annihilate the Jews!" trans. Richard S. Levy, in Levy, 117.

[73] Lindemann, *Esau's Tears*, 344.

Kampf Hitler repeatedly expressed his admiration for Lueger.[74] He implies that Houston Stewart Chamberlain (1855–1927), another man whom Hitler admired, was not so bad, since Albert Schweitzer, Winston Churchill, George Bernard Shaw, and D. H. Lawrence could be counted among his fans[75] – as if such a following obviates Chamberlain's proclamation that "we cannot understand Judaism and its power, as well as its ineradicable tenacity, we cannot form a just and proper estimate of the Jew among ourselves, his character and way of thinking, until we have recognised his demonical genius."[76]

Finally, Lindemann touts private remarks attributed to Hitler that were inconsistent with anti-Semitism,[77] as if such remarks trumped the Führer's frequent diatribes against the Jews, not to mention his project to annihilate them. As for the other Nazis, Lindemann does everything he can to let them off the hook of exterminationist Jew hatred, insisting that under the Third Reich it was not so much the Nazis' anti-Semitic ideology "as the chaotic dynamics of that regime itself ... that best explains the complicated set of initiatives and often competing agendas that finally led toward mass murder."[78] Really? The bankruptcy of Lindemann's assessment of the origins of modern anti-Semitism is so blatant as to require no further comment.

PSYCHOLOGICAL EXPLANATIONS

Whereas sociological and ideological explanations of anti-Semitism are oriented toward the world around us, psychological explanations turn inward to the dark recesses of the psyche. This orientation inward distinguishes the psychological argument from my own argument, which situates the metaphysical origin of anti-Semitism in the soul and not in the psyche; the psyche is not an emanation from God but part of the inherent makeup of the human being. It lies only within, and not in any transcendent beyond. Therefore, the psyche is an ontological category, rather than a metaphysical reality. The difference is that, whereas the psychological explanation looks inside, my account looks to the higher and human relationships through which the soul lives. Distinct from the categories of "inside" and

---

[74] Adolf Hitler, *Mein Kampf*, trans. Ralph Mannheim (Boston: Houghton Mifflin, 1971), 99–101,121.

[75] Lindemann, 351.

[76] See Houston Stewart Chamberlain, *The Foundations of the Nineteenth Century*, vol. 1, trans. John Lees (London: John Lane, 1911), 488.

[77] See Lindemann, *Esau's Tears*, 492–494.   [78] Ibid., 536.

"outside," the operative pre-position from my perspective is *between*. Nonetheless, let us consider the psychoanalytical movement inward.

Israeli psychoanalyst Avner Falk holds a view that generally characterizes psychological explanations of the origins of anti-Semitism. "Judeophobia, Jew-hatred, and anti-Judaism, known by the 'scientific' euphemism of 'anti-Semitism,'" he maintains, "are highly complex psychological phenomena on both the individual and collective levels. In addition to the economic, political, social, historical, religious, and conscious-psychological causes of anti-Semitism, there are also unconscious defensive psychological processes, such as the individual's splitting, projection, and externalization, and the majority group's collective needs for identity, boundaries, and enemies.... It is only by considering both the conscious and unconscious, individual and collective psychological processes active in anti-Semitism that this most pernicious and dangerous phenomenon can be understood."[79] There is nothing of the metaphysical here, nothing pertaining to the transcendent vertical dimension of the soul.

Of course, Sigmund Freud (1856–1939) was the first to contemplate the psychological origins of anti-Semitism. Identifying the root of anti-Semitism as a fear of castration on the part of uncircumcised non-Jews in *Moses and Monotheism* (1938),[80] he goes on to argue that among Christians the hatred of the Jew is a manifestation of an unconscious hatred of the Jew Jesus.[81] Jesus (the superego) demands that the Christian take up the cross in an imitation of his own love for humanity: Christ calls the Christian to be Christ-like, not through supreme faith but through supreme sacrifice. Terrified of this intransigent summons to Golgotha, the Christian abhors his Lord; thus his lower nature (the id) surfaces in a desire to kill Jesus. Because Judaism was the father religion and Christianity the son religion, moreover, Christianity had to kill the father, but the Christians have confessed their crime and have received absolution.[82] The implication is that anti-Semitism is not an evil but a disease of the mind that falls outside any ethical categories and that, with the help of some highly trained psychoanalysts, can be treated, if not cured. Here too we see a distinction between a psychoanalytical approach to

---

[79] Avner Falk, *Anti-Semitism: A History and Psychoanalysis of Contemporary Hatred* (Westport, Conn.: Praeger, 2008), 202.

[80] Sigmund Freud, *Moses and Monotheism*, trans. Katherine Jones (New York: Vintage Books, 1955), 116; see also Falk, *Anti-Semitism*, 67.

[81] Freud, *Moses and Monotheism*, 117.   [82] Ibid., 116; see also Falk, *Anti-Semitism*, 68.

anti-Semitism and the metaphysical approach taken in this volume: there is no "treating" the metaphysical.

One of the most thorough of the psychological explanations of anti-Semitism is *Anti-Semitism: A Disease of the Mind* (1990) by Theodore Isaac Rubin (b. 1923). Elaborating on Freud's main points, Rubin posits the notion of the "S gap" or "symbol sickness" as the key to understanding the disorder. He identifies five elements at work in the dynamics of symbol sickness:

1. First the symbol – that is, the Jew – is removed from any attachment to an object, so that it becomes an abstraction, with no concrete reference.
2. Once removed from its object, the symbol slips out of the conscious control of the individual, and logic no longer applies.
3. The symbol becomes polarizing and is used as an object of projection and displacement.
4. The distorted symbol becomes the stereotype of the object of hatred.
5. Envy plays a major role in the hatred of the symbol, that is, the abstract Jew.[83]

Rubin's first point is a good one: the object of Jew hatred is never a flesh-and-blood individual or anything else that meets the eye. Like the world Jewish conspiracy, the hated Jew is hidden. The invisibility of the Jew does indeed have a polarizing effect, inasmuch as he or she is now aligned with an invisible, projected "evil," something satanic that lurks in the shadows. And yet all the while, the devil in the darkness is the anti-Semite himself. If the anti-Semite would be as God, the God he or she would be like is the Devil-God that Rubin describes, saying, "Killing Jews makes way for the Devil-God, the dehumanized God, the noncompassionate self-glorifying narcissistic God, the nationalized God, the hierarchical (*Deutschland Über Alles*) Aryan God, the Wagnerian primeval German-God – Hitler himself."[84] Such a dark presence is envied not for its righteousness but for its power. Even though Rubin would not say so, I would argue that the perversion of the Jew into Satan lies in the secret knowledge that the Jew signifies the presence of a covenantal God – not

[83] See Theodore Isaac Rubin, *Anti-Semitism: A Disease of the Mind* (New York: Continuum, 1990), 27–38.
[84] Ibid., 108.

the superego within, but the God of Abraham above, who continually puts to us the question put to the first man: Where are you?

To the extent that the anti-Semite's hatred of the Jew is tied to the righteousness of the Jew, Rubin says that three points should be kept in mind whenever envy is a defining feature of anti-Semitism:

1. The envious one has exaggerated feelings of inadequacy, deprivation, impoverishment, and powerlessness.
2. The envious one feels abused and entitled.
3. Projection or displacement is almost always present in envious people.[85]

The more egocentric we are, the more these three points apply. In this case, the Jew is envied not because he or she has what I do not have, but because he or she represents what I am not, what I am summoned to become, and what I fear to become, namely, a person who takes on all the responsibilities of one who is created in the image and likeness of the Holy One, "provoked," in the words of Lévinas, "as irreplaceable, as devoted to the others, without being able to resign, and thus as incarnated in order to offer itself, to suffer and to give."[86] For the Christian, that person, unique and irreplaceable, is embodied in the Incarnation of the Holy One, so that for the Christian the suppressed object of hatred is the Christ.

The fact that Jesus was a Jew, Rubin asserts, is "the single and most significant factor in the explosion of the disease [of anti-Semitism]."[87] As a psychoanalyst, Rubin transforms what I would regard as metaphysical categories into psychological ones. Where I maintain that hatred of the Jews is a hatred of the commanding covenantal God, he argues that Christians hate Jews as "god producers and Jesus is the foremost of the gods," displacing their "unconscious hatred of God to Jews, who produced Him."[88] Thus, the deicide charge is nothing but a projection of a desire deeply rooted in the Christian unconscious: "The Jews are hated for contributing Christ to the world (as moral restriction – conscience) rather than for the fiction that they are Christ killers. In fact, I believe that rabid anti-Semites who have convinced themselves of the historical delusion that Jews killed Christ unconsciously really admire and envy them for doing so. . . . The louder the cry of 'Christ killer,' the greater the

---

[85] Ibid., 39–40.
[86] Emmanuel Lévinas, *Otherwise Than Being or Beyond Essence*, trans. Alphonso Lingis (The Hague: Martinus Nijhoff, 1981), 105.
[87] Rubin, *Anti-Semitism*, 54.   [88] Ibid.

effort at burying the unthinkable – hatred of Him."[89] In other words, where I would argue that the anti-Semite sets out to get rid of God, Rubin maintains that he or she wants to get rid of conscience, or the superego. Thus, "the Jew is hated for being a conscience giver rather than a Christ killer,"[90] not for announcing to the nations that the Creator of heaven and earth has chosen each of us for a mission and a meaning that cannot be abrogated. If, as superego, "Jesus is hated for insisting on compassion, love, forgiveness, and consideration of others," it is because he gets in the way of the "primitive and self-satisfying urges" of the id, which, when dominant in the personality, are "characteristic of people suffering from symbol sickness and stunted emotional and social development."[91] Did the anti-Semites mentioned in the first chapter, from Democritus to Chrysostom, from Martin Luther to Sayyid Qutb, suffer from stunted emotional and social development? Is *that* what they all have in common?

Another question for Rubin arises in this connection: how does his insightful analysis of Christian Jew hatred apply to Jew hatred on the part of non-Christians? Perhaps he can argue from the same basic terms with regard to Hellenistic Jew hatred, but without invoking Jesus: the Jew is somehow representative of a conscience or superego that the Greek cannot abide. The dynamic might be similar for the Muslim anti-Semite, from Mohammad onward. Still, like Freud, Ruben relies so heavily on Christian categories in his analysis that it is doubtful whether it applies to Democritus or Qutb, not to mention left-wing intellectuals. To be sure, as something that emerged in the midst of Christendom, psychoanalysis itself may be an attempt to disarm the absolute demands of a commanding God by providing a scientific explanation of conscience and thus avoid anything about the Jews themselves – their teachings, traditions, and testimonies – that might become an object of fear, resentment, and contempt even for the psychoanalyst.

COMPOSITE EXPLANATIONS

It is no accident that in the explanations of anti-Semitism considered thus far we find an overlap of the disciplines of theology, history, psychology, sociology, and philosophy. Some thinkers who have attempted to offer an account of the phenomenon conscientiously draw on a variety of

---

[89] Ibid., 59.   [90] Ibid., 58.   [91] Ibid., 57.

disciplines in their analysis. Among the first to draw on theology, sociology, philosophy, and psychology to get at the root cause of anti-Semitism was the German Jewish thinker Constantin Brunner (1862–1937). In his writings, which were quite popular at the time, he consistently draws a distinction between spirituality and religiosity, between understanding and superstition, between mysticism and moralism. He regards Judaism not as a religious doctrine but as a "spiritual path," and he views Jesus as a great Jewish mystic whose teachings Christianity has perverted. Brunner goes so far as to maintain that Jews must "take Christ unto themselves," since they cannot understand Judaism if they fail to see that Christianity is Jewish.[92] He is *not* suggesting that Jews should convert to Christianity, nor does he mean for Christians to convert to Judaism when he affirms that "Christianity at its noblest is Judaism."[93] Affiliating with no particular religious tradition, Brunner envisioned a human community centered on the life of the mind or spirit (*Geist*), through which humanity would realize its true freedom. That vision, however, dissolved into the reality of the rise of the Nazis in 1933, when he fled Germany and settled in The Hague.

In *The Tyranny of Hate/The Roots of Antisemitism* (1919), Brunner declares that "hatred of Jews is more than moral hatred: it is hellish hatred."[94] Well before the advent of the Third Reich, he understood that the calumnies of the anti-Semites "are already murderous. They tend towards murder. ... From civil liquidation there is a strong impetus towards physical liquidation and *total annihilation*."[95] Some of Brunner's insights appear to be in keeping with the position that I am arguing in this volume. He asserts, for example, that "fundamentally, all are anti-Semites,"[96] suggesting, as I have, that the evil inclination to hate the Jews lurks in the recesses of the human soul – or rather, in the self that would eclipse the soul. "Jews," says Brunner, "belong in a significant way to the life of humanity; the Jewish race is evidently something that penetrates the whole of humanity, in time, in space, and inwardly."[97] While this statement may have some metaphysical overtones, its invocation of "the Jewish race" places it in an ontological category. By "race" Brunner seems to have in mind something like an "essence" that "penetrates the

---

[92] Constantin Brunner, *The Tyranny of Hate/The Roots of Antisemitism*, trans. Graham Harrison, ed. Aron M. Rappaport (Lewiston, Idaho: Edwin Mellen Press, 1992), 174–175.
[93] Ibid., 39.   [94] Ibid., 146.   [95] Ibid., 88; emphasis added.   [96] Ibid., 126.
[97] Ibid., 167.

whole of humanity," so that the Jew signifies something as inescapable as conscience. Therefore, unlike Lazare, Lindemann, and others, Brunner holds that "it is impossible that the Jews should really be the cause of the anti-Semites' judgment against them."[98] His argument that the Judaic "religion of love" has led to Jew hatred also has some resonance with my claim that Jewish teaching implicates us in our responsibility to and for our fellow human being.[99] The commandment to love can never be altogether fulfilled, so that we are forever in arrears, a condition that we do not want to be reminded of.

Because the very presence of the Jew proclaims a responsibility to and for our fellow human being, Brunner understands that hatred of the Jews is basically hatred for the other person: "By keeping Jew hatred alive, they keep hatred of human beings alive too,"[100] a statement that anticipates Lévinas's assertion that anti-Semitism is "hatred for the other man."[101] The crucial point here is that hatred of the other man stems from hatred of the Jew, and not the other way around: anti-Semitism, in other words, is not a subcategory of racism – it is a transcendent, metaphysical category that must be determined in order to arrive at a racist position. Brunner, however, does not take the origin of anti-Semitism to be metaphysical. He argues, rather, that "antisemitism comes chiefly from the interest of pride."[102] And: "Everyone who belongs to this society stinks of pride against the Jews."[103] He does not, however, take this line of reasoning any further; although he realizes that Jew hatred is tied to hatred of the other person, Brunner does not argue that Jew hatred is a manifestation of the hatred of God that haunts the self who would be as God. Instead, he sees the Jew as a scapegoat,[104] who is defined by his being an object of hatred, as much as his being the bearer of a testimony: "Without anti-Semitism and unmerited suffering, therefore, there would soon be no Jews at all,"[105] a position reminiscent of Sartre but coming from quite a different perspective.

Two later scholars who systematically sorted out the causes of anti-Semitism are Paul E. Grosser and Edwin G. Halperin, authors of *Anti-Semitism: The Cause and Effects of a Prejudice* (1979). Their historically based research led them to identify ten specific "comprehensible causes" of anti-Semitism, some of which may overlap in certain situations:

---

[98] Ibid., 40.   [99] Ibid., 145.   [100] Ibid., 139.
[101] Lévinas, *Difficult Freedom*, 281.   [102] Brunner, *The Tyranny of Hate*, 41.
[103] Ibid., 84.   [104] Ibid., 44.   [105] Ibid., 108.

1. Jews, explain Grosser and Halperin, "found themselves in Western countries as a foreign, cohesive, powerless, landless, unique, despised 'nation,'" despised, that is, *because* they were foreign.[106] Why the Jews, among all the foreign elements, should be specifically despised they do not explain.

2. Religious conflict and attitudes "during the early Christian centuries and the consequent de-Judaizing of Christianity created antagonisms between the two faiths," whereby the Jews "were trapped in the theological role of God-killer, God-blasphemer, and devil."[107]

3. Religious conflict led to "psycho-Christian demands," which led Christianity to discredit its parent religion: "The Christian, guilt-ridden through theological dictate, sought to alleviate this guilt by nurturing Christianity's anti-Semitism and justifying its past, present and future by finding fault with the Jews. He was thus able to accuse them of his own condemned emotions and to resist any realization that his anti-Semitism was unjustified."[108] This approach is similar to Rubin's psychological explanation.

4. Despite living in proximity to each other for centuries, Jews remained "perpetual strangers in conflict."[109] Because the Jew refuses to disappear from history, he or she is an eternal alien. *Why* the Jew – and *the Jew specifically* – is so recalcitrant Grosser and Halperin do not say.

5. "Man has a psychological need to rationalize his fears, shut out inconvenient truths, release, act out and justify his repressed hostilities and dreams. Prejudice against Jews helped fill this need."[110] Once again, however, there is no explanation of why the Jews in particular should fill this need.

6. Due to their social and economic status, Jews were forced into occupations such as merchants, middlemen, and financiers, which fueled a vicious resentment of them.[111] This is basically the resentment and envy argument. But, as Dennis Prager and Joseph Telushkin point out, "*Jews were not hated because they lent money; they lent money because they were hated.*"[112]

---

[106] Paul E. Grosser and Edwin G. Halperin, *Anti-Semitism: The Cause and Effects of a Prejudice* (Secaucus, N.J.: Citadel Press, 1979), 290.

[107] Ibid., 291.   [108] Ibid., 293.   [109] Ibid., 295.   [110] Ibid., 296.   [111] Ibid., 298.

[112] Dennis Prager and Joseph Telushkin, *Why the Jews? The Reason for Antisemitism* (New York: Simon & Schuster, 2003), 59–60; emphasis in original.

7. Anticipating the question of *why the Jews in particular*, Grosser and Halperin answer that, given their dress and residence restrictions they were particularly conspicuous and vulnerable.[113] The questionable implication is that assimilation would eliminate this particular cause of anti-Semitism; it certainly does not explain the case of the German Jews, who were all but indistinguishable from their non-Jewish German neighbors.

8. With the development of the modern world, "anti-Semitic expressions in art, literature, language, education, history, sermons, religious writings (especially lectures and textbooks), traditional conversations and folk myth became ubiquitous, insidious, and profound."[114] To view this dissemination of anti-Semitic material as the cause of anti-Semitism, however, leads to the circular argument that anti-Semitism is caused by anti-Semitic cultural material, and anti-Semitic cultural material comes from anti-Semitism.

9. Grosser and Halperin's ninth cause, "resistance to solution," explains the persistence of anti-Semitism, rather than its origin. Simply stated, anti-Semitism exists because we do not know how to get rid of it.

10. Finally, anti-Semitism persists simply because it has a life of its own: "Western history created and nurtured a symbiotic, interacting prejudice against the Jews – deep-rooted, obsessive, cumulative, self-perpetuating, the old sustaining the new, and effect often becoming new cause."[115] Here we have a hint of the metaphysical origin of anti-Semitism, but not in the sense that Grosser and Halperin intend. Contrary to their analysis, my contention is that it has a life of its own because it is part of the life of the soul – or rather, it is part of what the soul must overcome if it is to have a life.

Grosser and Halperin's work deserves our attention for outlining these causes of anti-Semitism in such an organized manner. One can see in their explanation elements of previous explanations, covering theological, sociological, ideological, and psychological aspects of Jew hatred. However, it all remains ontological and often circular, as already suggested: religious conflict leads to social restriction, and social restriction leads to alienation. Or is it the other way around? In the end, despite the

---

[113] Grosser and Halperin, *Anti-Semitism*, 299.   [114] Ibid., 300.   [115] Ibid., 307.

thoroughness of their research, Grosser and Halperin have to throw up their arms: the Jews refuse to go away, and the problem refuses solution.

Also proceeding from historical research but combining it with a study of religion, Stanford medievalist Gavin I. Langmuir argues in his *History, Religion, and Antisemitism* (1990) that anti-Semitism, "both in its origins and in its recent most horrible manifestation, is the hostility aroused by irrational thinking about 'Jews,'... an irrational reaction to repressed rational doubts."[116] Drawing largely on a psychological explanation of the phenomenon, Langmuir explains that "the deicide accusation camouflaged Christian awareness that the continued existence of Jewish disbelief challenged Christian belief. The accusation enabled Christians to repress doubts about Jesus' resurrection by imagining that no one who was not blind could have encountered Jesus without perceiving he was God."[117] This is a bit different from Rubin's claim that Christians hate Jews because of an absolute moral demand that the Jew Jesus places on them; with Rubin's explanation, the problem is precisely that Christians do *not* doubt the truth of the demand placed on them and truly believe that they *ought* not doubt it. With Langmuir, Christians are so ridden with the guilt of repressed doubt that they see something satanic about the Jews, because only a satanic creature would willfully and conscientiously refuse salvation through faith in Christ Jesus. The phenomenon of anti-Semitism as such, Langmuir maintains, did not appear until the twelfth century, with the spread of such "chimerical beliefs or fantasies about 'Jews.'"[118] Thus he distinguishes between the anti-Judaism of the early Christian era and the irrational hatred of the Jews of subsequent centuries.

This irrational hatred of the Jews, says Langmuir, led to scapegoating, as it happened, for example, during the Black Death (1347–1350).[119] If one supposed that the coming of the Enlightenment and the Age of Reason would mitigate such irrational hatred, Langmuir points out that xenophobia was aggravated by Romanticism, which "reinvigorated trust in nonrational thought, reinforced traditional forms of religious expression, spawned new ones, and revived interest in what seemed the most religious period of European history, the Middle Ages."[120] Stemming from xenophobic Romantic nationalism, Volkish mythology combined with race theory to provide "irrational" Jew hatred with a scientific basis. Such beliefs, explains Langmuir, "emphasized the centrality of nonrational

---

[116] Gavin I. Langmuir, *History, Religion, and Antisemitism* (Berkeley: University of California Press, 1990), 275–76.
[117] Ibid., 288.   [118] Ibid., 297.   [119] Ibid., 301.   [120] Ibid., 320.

thinking which was so prominent a feature of Volkish mythology, and they also claimed to be the product of rational empirical thinking, which most Germans valued highly. They were not incompatible with the attitudes of many Protestants, some of whom tried to argue for a Nordic Jesus, and they were also or even more compatible with atheistic disbelief."[121] Tracing the origins of anti-Semitism to a lack of confidence in one's beliefs – which led to scapegoating, xenophobia, and racism – Langmuir suggests that irrational thinking is the real cause of anti-Semitism, with the corollary implication that rational thought might cure it. And, yet, the autonomous rational thought that Langmuir would champion allows no room for the heteronomous thinking that characterizes Jewish thought.

Langmuir's explanation of the origins of anti-Semitism is rooted in a speculative mode of thought that allows no room for thinking from the categories of creation and revelation, of covenant and commandment – categories that define Jewish thought. Indeed, Langmuir's claim is that anti-Semitism arises when one departs from an ontological mode of thought grounded in reason. The difficulty with this view is that the rational thinking that would eliminate Jew hatred would also eliminate the Jews, since it cannot abide the categories of thought that shape Judaism. Hence, the Jew hatred expressed by such champions of reason as Johann Gottlieb Fichte (1762–1814)[122] and G. W. F. Hegel (1770–1831).[123] To fathom the origins of Jew hatred in such a way that would allow room for the discrete existence of the Jews, one must shift into a different mode of thought, a Jewish mode of thought. That is where Dennis Prager and Joseph Telushkin come in.

A JEWISH EXPLANATION

In the introduction to their book *Why the Jews? The Reason for Antisemitism* (2003), Prager and Telushkin point out that "you are likely

---

[121] Ibid., 339–340.

[122] "The only way to give them [the Jews] citizenship," said Fichte in his *Beitrag zur Berichtung der Urteils des Publikums über die französischen Revolution* (1793), "would be to cut off their heads in the same night in order to replace them with those containing no Jewish ideas"; quoted in Berel Lang, *Act and Idea in the Nazi Genocide* (Syracuse, N.Y.: Syracuse University Press, 2003), 169.

[123] Jews live an "animal existence," according to Hegel; they are in a "state of total passivity," of total ugliness" and are to blame for refusing to "die as Jews"; see G. W. F. Hegel, "The Spirit of Christianity and Its Fate," in *Early Theological Writings*, trans. T. M. Knox (Chicago, Ill.: University of Chicago Press, 1948), 201–205.

to be given every reason for antisemitism except, amazingly, that it is a response to anything distinctively Jewish."[124] Explanations from sociology, culture, ideology, psychology, and other speculative modes of thought confirm the truth of this statement. Such approaches to the issue may address why specific people hate Jews under specific circumstances, but they do not address the matter of how Jews themselves might understand the hatred directed toward them. In many cases, explaining anti-Semitism in distinctively Jewish terms would undermine the premise and the method behind the explanation. Explanations of the origins of anti-Semitism, as Prager and Telushkin observe, "include, most commonly, economic factors, the need for scapegoats, ethnic hatred, xenophobia, resentment of Jewish affluence and professional success, and religious bigotry. But ultimately these answers do not explain anti-Semitism."[125] Indeed, such explanations often play into the hands of the anti-Semites by de-Judaizing the phenomenon. They do not explain anti-Semitism because they answer every question except one: Why the Jews? And responding to that question entails thinking from a Jewish point of view, as these two authors do.

Turning to Jewish categories of thought to offer their own analysis of the origins of anti-Semitism, Prager and Telushkin cite four reasons for Jew hatred, from ancient to modern times:

1. Jews affirm the one law-giving God of all humanity, and they live "by their own all-encompassing set of laws."
2. Jews were chosen by God to bring the nations of the world to God.
3. Jews insist on "changing the world for the better," which entails elevating the world through a realization of ethical responsibility.
4. "As a result of the Jews' commitment to Judaism, they have led higher-quality lives than their non-Jewish neighbors."[126]

The one God whom the Jews affirm is the one God before whom all humanity must answer for its actions. He who would be as God must obviate this higher accountability, so that a basic element of anti-Semitism is a rebellion "against the 'thou shalts' and 'thou shalt nots' introduced by the Jews in the name of a supreme moral authority."[127] Chosen to bring the nations of the world to God, the Jews are chosen to say to the world, "Each of us is summoned to an absolute responsibility to God for how we treat our neighbor." Hence, "the Jews' chosenness confers neither

[124] Prager and Telushkin, *Why the Jews?*, xi.
[125] Ibid., 6.   [126] Ibid., 8–9.   [127] Ibid., 14.

privilege nor superiority, only obligation and frequent suffering,"[128] a suffering that extends to anyone who takes on him- or herself a loving care for his or her neighbor. Changing the world for the better is much more than a matter of picking up litter or promoting tolerance; beyond that, it entails the sanctification of this realm by answering ever more profoundly, "Here I am for you!" to the human outcry all around us. Because answering the cry of our neighbor places us in a position of profound vulnerability, "from earliest times the Jews have suffered for representing, even when not embodying, obedience to God."[129] If Jews live lives of higher quality than their neighbors, that quality lies not in the enjoyment of material goods but in the insistence on moral standards and responsibilities.

Many of the solutions to the problem of anti-Semitism, such as the ones proposed by Lazare and Sartre, amount to one thing: Jews should cease being Jews. Prager and Telushkin, by contrast, insist that "a solution to antisemitism must by definition include the survival of Jewry, just as a solution to an illness must by definition include the survival of the patient. We seek solutions to antisemitism that enable Jews to live as Jews,"[130] that is, as the millennial witnesses of Torah. Thus, these two Jewish thinkers seek a solution to the problem in the very "Jewishness" that the anti-Semites oppose: "The Jewish role is to bring humankind not to Judaism but to universal, God-based morality. *It is the exquisite irony of Jewish history that this task, which has been the ultimate cause of antisemitism, must be fulfilled to end antisemitism.*"[131] Thus approaching the issue from a Jewish standpoint, Prager and Telushkin see anti-Semitism not as a mental disorder or a social malady, not as flawed theology or insidious ideology, but as an ethical issue. In a word, anti-Semitism is *evil*, if not the embodiment of evil itself. Prager and Telushkin's analysis has at least one important ramification: theological, psychological, ideological, and social scientific explanations of anti-Semitism make it much safer for us to engage the problem, precisely because such explanations render irrelevant the ethical categories of good and evil. Since I am not an Augustinian monk or a Nazi, since I suffer from no mental disorder or economic envy, since I am tolerant of others and some of my best friends are Jews – I cannot be an anti-Semite. No, not me: *they* are the anti-Semites. To confront the issue in ethical terms, however, is for each of

---

[128] Ibid., 28.   [129] Ibid., 15.   [130] Ibid., 181.   [131] Ibid., 190; emphasis in original.

us to be implicated by how we understand the origin of anti-Semitism: if it is an ethical matter, then it is about *me*, not them.

Although Prager and Telushkin turn to what the Jews represent in order to understand anti-Semitism, they do not quite sound the depths of its metaphysical origins. That is, like their predecessors, they are thinking in ontological terms of cause and effect, without considering the metaphysical ramifications of covenant, creation, chosenness, and so on, all of which are categories that lie outside the ontological confines of cause and effect. Of course, explanations characteristically seek causes; they differ only in where they situate the cause.

What is needed is not a better explanation of the *cause* of anti-Semitism but a mode of thought that understands anti-Semitism to lie outside the coordinates of cause and effect, a mode of thinking that situates it in what Lévinas refers to as the "immemorial," which is prior to all beginnings. He describes "the Good" that lays claim to us from "beyond being" and thus determines an absolute responsibility beyond context as "the trace of a past which declines the present and representation, the trace of an immemorial past."[132] Similarly, what would draw us away from the anarchic Good is an anarchic temptation to be as God, prior to every beginning, and there lies the origin of anti-Semitism, outside the contexts and coordinates of being. Just as "the pre-original responsibility for the other" escapes "the measurements of being,"[133] so does the seed of the longing to hide from that responsibility escape speculative thought. If many of the explanations of the cause of anti-Semitism are themselves, to varying degrees, anti-Semitic, it is because they seek an ontological cause, and not a metaphysical origin. Which is to say: they adopt a mode of thought that is antithetical to the categories that shape Torah-based Jewish thought, the very thinking – the very teaching and testimony – that the anti-Semite would eliminate, first through conversion, then through assimilation, and finally through extermination.

Examining the theological, philosophical, and National Socialist manifestations of anti-Semitism, the next three chapters parallel this sequence of conversion, assimilation, and extermination. As we shall see, in each of these manifestations the soul of the anti-Semite – or the anti-Semite in the soul – seeks its own means of the usurpation and appropriation of the divine that lies at the origin of anti-Semitism.

---

[132] Emmanuel Lévinas, *Collected Philosophical Papers*, trans. Alfonso Lingis (The Hague: Martinus Nijhoff, 1987), 136.
[133] Ibid., 138.

2

The Arrogation of God: Christian Theological Anti-Semitism

He who believes in the Son has everlasting life; and he who does not believe in the Son shall not see life, but the wrath of God abides on him.

(John 3:36)

According to Martin Buber, Christian "theologians argue that God rejected this people, who no longer have any heritage because that heritage has now passed over to Christianity. But the Jewish people continued to exist, book in hand; and even though they were burned at the stake, the words of the book were still on their lips. That is the perennial source of anti-Semitism."[1] The words of the book still on their lips were the words of the *Shema*: "Hear, O Israel, the Lord our God the Lord is One!" (Deuteronomy 6:4). Briefly stated, on Buber's view the aim of anti-Semitic Christian theology was to silence the *Shema*. True enough. But the perennial source of Christian anti-Semitism was not the Jews' intractable recalcitrance. It lay, rather, in the human longing to be Christ-like, God-like, washed clean of all sin. More than rejecting Christianity, the Jews rejected the temptation to be Christ-like, insisting that no one can take upon himself the accountability for another person's sins. That is what they affirmed with the words of the *Shema*, even as they were engulfed in the flames of the auto-da-fé.

In this chapter I examine the roots of anti-Semitism manifest in certain forms of dogmatic Christian theology, as it arose with the merging

---

[1] Martin Buber, *On Judaism*, trans. Eva Jospe, ed. Nahum N. Glatzer (New York: Schocken Books, 1967), 186.

of Hellenistic philosophy and the new Christian religion.[2] As Clement of Alexandria (ca. 150–ca. 215) stated it, Greek philosophy was "a preparation, paving the way for him who is perfected in Christ."[3] My argument is that in this case anti-Semitism stems not from the theology as such but from the theological longing to conceptually possess God, to presume to know the judgment of God, and thus to be as God. In its effort to determine the judgment of God from the content of doctrine, dogmatic theology conceptualizes, thematizes, and thus appropriates God; as Emmanuel Lévinas states it, "in thematizing God, theology has brought him into the course of being, while the God of the Bible signifies ... the beyond of being."[4] In a word, the God of the theologians is not the God of Abraham, Isaac, and Jacob. Among history's most prominent Christian theologians, almost without exception, the aim has been to accommodate the God of Abraham to the God of the philosophers, and not the other way around. The point of such a theological endeavor is not only to define the attributes of God but also to determine the content of belief necessary for salvation. Thus thematizing God, theology twists Him into an object not only of belief but also of thought; in this way the theologian *comprehends* God and thus becomes the arbiter of redemption itself. Grasping God, the religious authority assumes an authority over the soul by insisting on a *belief* in the God of the theologians as the pathway to paradise.

Strictly speaking, there is no Jewish theology, inasmuch as theology means thematizing God and then insisting on a specific content of belief. If one should refer to the thirteen attributes of God's mercy affirmed in the Jewish liturgy,[5] those attributes are not to be believed in but acted on: they *command* us concerning how we must behave toward others, not what we are to believe within ourselves. In Jewish tradition the closest

---

[2] The renowned classicist Werner Jaeger demonstrates that Christianity is a hybrid of Hellenism and Hebraism, with Hellenism dominating, quite convincingly in his classic work *Early Christianity and Greek Paideia* (Cambridge, Mass.: Harvard University Press, 1961).

[3] Clement of Alexandria, *The Miscellanies or Stromata*, trans. William Wilson, in Alexander Roberts and James Donaldson, eds., *Clement of Alexandria: Ante Nicene Christian Library Translations of the Writings of the Fathers to AD 325, Part Four* (Whitefish, Mont.: Kessinger, 2007), 366.

[4] Emmanuel Lévinas, *Of God Who Comes to Mind*, trans. Bettina Bergo (Stanford, Calif.: Stanford University Press, 1998), 56

[5] (1) The Lord! (2) The Lord! (3) God, (4) Compassionate and (5) Gracious, (6) Slow to anger and Abundant in (7) Kindness and (8) Truth, (9) Preserver of kindness for thousands of generations, Forgiver of (10) iniquity, (11) willful sin, and (12) error, and (13) Who cleanses (Exodus 34:6–7).

thing to a statement of a creed is to be found in the thirteen principles of Maimonides as articulated in his commentary on the Mishnah (*Sanhedrin* 10).[6] What is to be kept in mind, however, is that Maimonides made his list of what Jews believe in, as Christians and Muslims were forcing Jews to adopt a different belief; he was briefly stating for those Jews just what Jews believe, so that they might be able to answer their tormentors when asked what they believe. There was no implication that nonbelievers are damned, and he was not interested in rooting out heresy.

Once comprehended and turned over to a concept, the God of theology is no longer a persona, no longer a *Who* with whom we enter into a relation and from whom we receive a commanding revelation; rather, the conceptualized God is a *What*, an object to be seized and an authority to be invoked when attempting to justify what is otherwise unjustifiable. To clarify the contrast with Jewish teaching, it is worth noting that the first name for God that appears in the Torah is *Elohim*. The Zohar explains the origin of this name:

When the most Mysterious wished to reveal Himself, He first produced a single point which was transmuted into a thought, and in this He executed innumerable designs, and engraved innumerable engravings. He further engraved with the sacred and mystic lamp a mystic and most holy design, which was a wondrous edifice issuing from the midst of thought. This is called *Mi*, or "Who," and was the beginning of the edifice, existent and non-existent, deep buried, unknowable by name. It was only called *Mi*. It desired to become manifest and to be called by name. It therefore clothed itself in a refulgent and precious garment and created *Eleh*, or "These," and *Eleh* acquired a name. The letters of the two words intermingled, forming the complete name *E-l-o-h-i-m*. (*Zohar* I, 2a)

My purpose here is not to delve into the mystical depths of this passage, but I do want to point out that underlying the names of the Holy One is the mystery of the *Who*, and not the principle of a *what*, as systematic theology often would have it. A *Who* can neither be grasped nor thematized, neither known nor appropriated.

---

[6] Briefly stated, the Thirteen Principles are: (1) God exists, (2) God is one and unique, (3) God is incorporeal, (4) God is eternal, (5) prayer is to be directed to God alone and to no other, (6) the words of the prophets are true, (7) Moses' prophecies are true and Moses was the greatest of the prophets, (8) the Written Torah (first five books of the Bible) and Oral Torah (teachings now contained in the Talmud and other writings) were given to Moses, (9) there will be no other Torah, (10) God knows the thoughts and deeds of men, (11) God will reward the good and punish the wicked, (12) the Messiah will come, and (13) the dead will be resurrected. The *Mishnah* is the oral tradition put into writing in the form of commentary on the Torah, Jewish law, and tales; it forms the core text of the Talmud.

Once the persona is eclipsed by the concept, the living word is subsumed under the authoritarian doctrine. Central to the theological appropriation of God, then, is the appropriation of the Word. In the case of Christianity this begins with Jerome's translation of the sacred texts from Hebrew into Latin between 390 and 405, a move that coincided with the establishment of Christianity as the official religion of the Roman authority in 380: the language of power and the language of Scripture became one and the same. Although Jerome himself viewed the Hebrew texts as the ultimate source of truth, over the centuries that followed relatively few Christian theologians actually studied the Scriptures in Hebrew but rather relied on the Vulgate, so that in the Roman Church Latin superseded Hebrew as the new holy tongue.[7] In Christian theology, the Word was further appropriated by reading it through the lens of Christology, particularly in the early centuries of the religion, so that the Scripture could be made to conform to the formalized creed, and not the other way around.[8] As Augustine (354–430) expresses the Christological approach to the "Old Testament," "What does the term 'old covenant' imply but the concealing of the new? And what does the term 'new covenant' imply but the revealing of the old?"[9] Thus the Suffering Servant of Isaiah 53 is identified as Jesus, and the maiden (*almah*) of Isaiah 7:14 is identified as the Virgin Mary; just as the Binding of Isaac prefigures the crucifixion, so does Jacob's election over Esau prefigure Christianity's supersession of Judaism. Thus, the content of belief reigns supreme, reigns over the revealed Word itself.

CREED-BASED THINKING AND THE USURPATION OF GOD

After legalizing Christianity in 313 under the Edict of Milan, in 325 the Roman Emperor Constantine (272–337) called for the first ecumenical council at Nicaea, so that Christianity might have an officially sanctioned statement of doctrine. Beginning with the Council of Nicaea, there arose a series of official creeds that succinctly stated the basic tenets of the Christian doctrine. This is the Nicene Creed:

---

[7] See Andrew Cain and Josef Lössl, eds., *Jerome of Stridon: His Life, Writings and Legacy* (Surrey, U.K.: Ashgate Publishing, 2009), 124–125.

[8] For a general treatment of this topic, see Donald Juel, *Messianic Exegesis: Christological Interpretation of the Old Testament* (Minneapolis, Minn.: Fortress Press, 1992).

[9] Augustine, *The City of God*, trans. Marcus Dods (New York: Random House, 2000), 496.

We believe in one God, the Father, the Almighty, maker of heaven and earth, of all that is, seen and unseen. We believe in one Lord, Jesus Christ, the only son of God, eternally begotten of the Father, God from God, Light from Light, true God from true God, begotten, not made, of one Being with the Father. Through him all things were made. For us and for our salvation he came down from heaven: by the power of the Holy Spirit he became incarnate from the Virgin Mary, and was made man. For our sake he was crucified under Pontius Pilate; he suffered death and was buried. On the third day he rose again in accordance with the Scriptures; he ascended into heaven and is seated at the right hand of the Father. He will come again in glory to judge the living and the dead, and his kingdom will have no end. We believe in the Holy Spirit, the Lord, giver of life, who proceeds from the Father and the Son. With the Father and the Son he is worshiped and glorified. He has spoken through the Prophets. We believe in the holy Catholic Church and Apostolic Church. We acknowledge one baptism for the forgiveness of sins. We look for the resurrection of the dead, and the life of the world to come.

The Apostles' Creed, elements of which are older than the Nicene Creed, is basically the same:

I believe in God, the Father, almighty, creator of heaven and earth. I believe in Jesus Christ, His only son, our Lord. He was conceived by the power of the Holy Spirit and born to the Virgin Mary. He suffered under Pontius Pilate, was crucified, died, and was buried. He descended to the dead. On the third day he rose again. He ascended into heaven and is seated at the right hand of the Father. He will come again to judge the living and the dead. I believe in the Holy Spirit, the holy Catholic Church, the communion of saints, the forgiveness of sins, the resurrection of the body, and the life everlasting.

The Athanasian Creed (formulated between 381 and 428) sets forth the doctrine of the Trinity and the Incarnation and states that anyone who does not believe in that doctrine is condemned to eternal damnation. The Chalcedonian Creed was adopted at the Fourth Ecumenical Council, held at Chalcedon, in what is now Turkey, in 451, as a response to certain heretical views on what one must believe with regard to the nature of Christ. It established the view that Christ has two natures (human and divine) that are unified in one person.[10] Thus wielding the keys to the kingdom articulated in the doctrine, the Church came to wield more and more power. To be sure, wielding power is often an underlying interest in the institutional formulation of doctrine. When the Emperor Theodosius (347–395) declared the Nicene Christianity of the Catholic Church to be the only legitimate Imperial religion in 380, the deification of the doctrine was all but accomplished.

[10] For a thorough treatment of the early Christian creeds, see J. N. D. Kelly, *Early Christian Creeds*, 3rd ed. (London: Continuum, 1972).

In the time of the formulation of Christian doctrine, the Jews had difficulty not only with the content of the doctrine but also with the very notion of doctrine. Even under the Hasmoneans, when the Jews enjoyed a measure of political autonomy in Judea from 140 to 37 BCE, they had no officially sanctioned creed. When the Christians were articulating their doctrine and defining the heresies, the Jews were gathering their oral tradition into what would become the Talmud, an endeavor that unfolded between the years 200 and 600, with later additions and redactions. Emphasizing how to live rather than what to believe, the Talmud contains no doctrine, no statement of a creed. Whereas, the Christian emphasis on a certain belief necessitated the formulation of a doctrine for Christians to believe in, the Jewish insistence on a certain behavior necessitated the transmission of a teaching that Jews could live by, regardless of whether they had any political power. The Christians asked, "What do we believe?" The Jews asked, "What do we do?"

In Christian dogmatic theology culling out the damned from the saved on the basis of espoused belief is central to usurpation of the seat of divine judgment. Here the lesson of history is: beware of those who would save your soul. When a human authority presumes to separate the damned from the saved, the torture and murder of the damned often ensue. For Christian theologians of this ilk, laying claim to the seat of judgment begins with separating the Jews and everything Jewish from the dogma. From the early centuries of Christianity onward Christian thinkers set out to theologically delegitimize Jewish teaching and therefore Jewish existence by invoking the "Judaizing heresy." Ignatius of Antioch is a good example, insisting as he did in his "Letter to the Magnesians" that "it is absurd to have Jesus Christ on the lips and at the same time to practice Judaism. Christianity did not base its faith on Judaism, but Judaism on Christianity" (10:3).[11] Less than a century after Ignatius, Marcion of Sinope (ca. 95–160) went so far as to maintain that the God of the Abrahamic Covenant had no connection to the God incarnate in Jesus.[12] Although his teachings were deemed heretical by figures such as Justin Martyr and Irenaeus (130–202), his heresy lay in his renouncement of the "Old Testament," not in his effort to de-Judaize Christianity;

[11] See Ignatius of Antioch, "Letter to the Magnesians," in William A. Jurgens, ed., *The Faith of the Early Fathers*, vol. 1 (Collegeville, Minn.: The Order of St. Benedict, 1970), 19–20.
[12] See Todd D. Still, "Shadow and Light: Marcion's (Mis)Construal of the Apostle Paul," in Michael F. Bird and Joseph R. Dodson, eds., *Paul and the Second Century* (London: T&T Clark, 2011), 91–107.

Christian commentators, in fact, would soon de-Judaize the Hebrew Scriptures. In the fourth century, John Chrysostom described Judaizing as a "disease,"[13] and his contemporary Jerome "wrote to Augustine that if converted Jews were allowed to practice even one fragment of their former religion, 'they will not become Christians, but they will make us Jews.... The ceremonies of the Jews are pernicious and deadly; and whoever observes them, whether Jew or Gentile, has fallen into the pit of the devil.'"[14] Indeed, Augustine maintained that Christians who observed even the slightest of Jewish rituals were heretics (one wonders whether this included Jesus and his disciples).[15] The Council of Antioch (341), moreover, prohibited Christians from celebrating Passover, and the Council of Laodicea (434–481) forbade Christians to observe the Jewish Sabbath.[16] Centuries later Judaizing would become the primary heresy targeted by the Spanish Inquisition (1478–1834); according to Henry Kamen, of the more than two thousand people put to the auto-da-fé between 1480 and 1530, approximately 99% were so-called crypto-Jews.[17]

As we have seen, the theological ascent to the seat of divine judgment rests on the premise that belief is the key to one's personal salvation and that the Church has determined what must be believed. From the standpoint of Christian dogmatic theology, whoever *believes* in Jesus as their Lord and Savior is promised everlasting life (John 3:16); "I am the Way, the Truth, and the Life," says Jesus. "No man comes unto the Father except through me" (John 14:16). What, then, becomes of the nonbeliever? And how is he or she to be treated? It is well known that, in keeping with his Judaism, Jesus teaches us to love the stranger: "I was a stranger, and you took me in" (Matthew 25:35). Similar affirmations of the godliness of treating the stranger with loving kindness are found in 1 Timothy 5:10 and 3 John 1:5, as well as in Hebrews 13:2, where it is written, "Be not forgetful to entertain strangers: for thereby some have entertained angels unawares." But Jesus also teaches that the flock will not follow a stranger, that is, one who has not "entered through the door," for

---

[13] John Chrysostom, *Discourses against Judaizing Christians*, trans. Paul W. Harkins (Washington, D.C.: Catholic University Press of America, 1979), 15.

[14] Robert Michael, *Holy Hatred: Christianity, Anti-Semitism, and the Holocaust* (New York: Palgrave Macmillan, 2006), 21.

[15] Quoted in ibid., 29.

[16] See Dan Cohn-Sherbok, *Anti-Semitism* (Stroud, U.K.: The History Press, 2002), 48.

[17] Henry Kamen, *The Spanish Inquisition: A Historical Revision* (New Haven, Conn.: Yale University Press, 1998), 60.

"they know not the voice of strangers," adding, "I am the door of the sheep" (John 10:5–8). To be "without Christ," Paul declares to the Gentiles, is to be "strangers in the covenants of promise, without hope" (Ephesians 2:12), and those who believe are "no more strangers and foreigners" (Ephesians 2:19). To be a nonbeliever, then, is to belong to an alien category, trapped in an error most grave – not because of any act committed but because of a failure to affirm the creed.

These Pauline teachings are in sharp contrast to the commandments of the Torah concerning the treatment of strangers. In Exodus 22:20, for example, we read, "You shall not wrong a stranger, nor shall you oppress him; for you were strangers in Egypt." Whereas in the eyes of some psychologists, having been abused has become an excuse for becoming an abuser, in Judaism the fact that Jews were oppressed as strangers means precisely that they will *not* oppress non-Jews. Why? Because "you know the soul of a stranger, as you were strangers in Egypt" (Exodus 23:9). The phrase "for you know the soul of the stranger" is *yedaatem et-nefesh hager*, where the word for "know," *daat*, also means to "be joined together with." This suggests that because every soul is an emanation from the Holy One, each is bound to the other, Jewish and non-Jewish. The stranger who dwells among you shall be as one of your own, not because of a doctrine you share but because you and the stranger are *essentially* and *physically* tied to one another as *benei Adam*, children of Adam. Hence "the stranger who dwells among you shall be as one of your own, and you shall love him as yourself. For you were strangers in the land of Egypt: I am the Lord" (Leviticus 19:34). That is, you shall love him *k'mokha*, "as yourself," an echo of the commandment to love your neighbor, your fellow Jew, *k'mokha* (Leviticus 19:18). What does it mean? Rendered as "that is what you are like," it means the stranger is no stranger: "You shall love the stranger, because your love for the stranger *is* your self." Indeed, the Baal Shem Tov taught that the love for the stranger is the foundation of the Torah (see *Toledot Yaakov Yosef, Korach* 2).

Related to the view that the nonbeliever lies outside the circle of salvation is another key creedal component of the Christian appropriation of the seat of divine judgment: the doctrine of inherited sin. Ever since the fall of Adam, "all have sinned and fall short of the glory of God," as Paul states it (Romans 3:23) – *all*, from infants to elders, by the mere fact of existing. Two things are required for the remediation of this inherited sin: (1) the blood sacrifice of the Christ, followed by the resurrection that conquers death, and (2) belief in the blood sacrifice of the Christ. Without that belief, even Mother Teresa's loving embrace of widows, orphans, and strangers, as commanded by the Torah (Deuteronomy 10:18), is not enough to attain salvation, because "man is justified by faith alone, without the deeds of the law" (Romans 3:28). Hence Christians guided by dogmatic theology have no concept of the age-old Jewish teaching on the Righteous among the Nations, because anyone who does not believe cannot be righteous. Although the Gospel teaches that people who do good works shall have life (John 5:29), the epistles teach that damnation comes to anyone who no longer believes (e.g., 1 Timothy 5:12). If, as Paul says, God takes vengeance on "those who do not obey the Gospel of our Lord Jesus Christ" (2 Thessalonians 1:8–9), "obey" in this instance means "believe in." While it is true that the Christian Scriptures teach that "if it has no works faith is dead" (James 2:17), these words have been construed to mean that deeds derive from faith, not faith from deeds. Such thinking is in sharp contrast to what we find in the Torah: when Moses read aloud from the Torah, the Israelites cried out, "*Naaseh venishma* – We will do and we will hear!" (Exodus 24:7). That is to say, we will cultivate the deeds, and then our understanding and our devotion – our faith – will follow.

The determination of who is damned and who is redeemed has often been invoked as a justification for wielding absolute power, as during the time of the Crusades (1096–1291) and the conquest of the New World. The latter sparked the famous Valladolid Debate (1550–1551) held in Spain's Colegio de San Gregorio over the question of whether the indigenous peoples of the Americas were in fact human beings with souls. Opposing each other were Juan Ginés de Sepúlveda (1494–1573), who maintained that the Indians were soulless savages who lay outside the usual protections accorded to humanity, and Bartolomé de las Casas (1484–1566), who argued against the killing and cruelty inflicted on the Native Americans and maintained that their souls must be saved.[18] Thus, added to the matter of who is damned and who is redeemed is the matter of who is human and who is not, as determined by ecclesiastic authority. In my view, it is no coincidence that the Valladolid Debate arose in the aftermath of the expulsion of the Jews from Spain, when the Spanish Inquisition was engaged in the task of the removal of the Jews from the stage of history. Otherwise Christianity itself, which measures the dating

---

[18] See Lewis Hanke and Jane M. Rausch, eds., *People and Issues in Latin American History: The Colonial Experience* (Princeton, N.J.: Markus Wiener Publishers, 2006), 160–184.

of history from its own advent, would have its own place in history forever threatened by the very presence of Jews in the world.

The drive to establish such a dogmatic theology is rooted in the anti-Semitic longing to be as the God of history, not only knowing good and evil but holding the keys to the kingdom that awaits humanity when the Christ returns at history's end. Once again we find that in this theological manifestation of the anti-Semitic longing, the one who would be Christ-like is the one who would be God-like, inasmuch as Christology has determined that Christ and God are one and the same. And the Christian who is God-like has no more need for the law than God does (or does He?). Indeed, the law must be eliminated, and the elimination of the law requires the theological elimination of its signifier: the Jew. The vilification of the Jew and the vilification of the law, then, go hand in hand. If "Christ redeemed us from the curse of the law" (Galatians 3:12), then the curse that falls on the Jews who reject Christ is precisely the curse of the law, the curse of Torah, under which the Jews labor in vain for a salvation that can never come. Subsequently, the Church Fathers saw circumcision not as the sign of the Covenant of Torah but as the sign of the curse.[19]

Here it is important to underscore what was noted above, namely that the one who ascends to the throne of divine judgment condemns the Jews not for any crime committed, not for the violation of any law, but for embracing the law and rejecting the creed – that is, *for rejecting the very appropriation of God that Christian dogmatic theology has itself undertaken.* If the path to God lies in the observance of the commandments of the Torah, then the ecclesiastical authority is rendered powerless; wherever it lies in the affirmation of the creed, however, the ecclesiastical authority is all powerful. Once such a power becomes the arbiter of salvation, the usurpation of God brings with it an eclipse of the love that the Christian Scripture identifies with God Himself (1 John 4:8) – especially and most importantly a love for the stranger. To lose the law is to lose the thirty-six times that the Torah commands us to love and care for the stranger. Only a divine law steeped in divine love – and not in demagogic judgment – can command a loving relation to the stranger. Therefore, when Christians lose the law, they lose love: the supersession of Judaism is a supersession of love. It is true that the Christian Scripture invokes the importance of faith, hope, and love, declaring that "the

---

[19] See Rosemary Radford Ruether, *Faith and Fratricide: The Theological Roots of Anti-Semitism* (New York: Seabury Press, 1974), 147–148.

greatest of these is love" (1 Corinthians 13:13). But when Christian theology goes dogmatic, the formula is faith, hope, and dogma, and the greatest of these is dogma, where dogma determines the creed that unlocks the gates of paradise.[20] In its dogmatic aspect, Christian theology has necessarily been grounded in a contempt for the Jews.

THEOLOGICAL FALLOUT: SUPERSESSION, DEICIDE, BLOOD LIBEL

Central to the de-Judaizing project is the supersession of the Covenant with the Jews, the Covenant of Abraham and Moses. Although in his *Against Heresies*, Irenaeus argues that the two dispensations "differ according to accident, not substance (4.9.2)," he maintains that "the Old Covenant is suited to a spirit of bondage, the New to the spirit of freedom (4.9.2); the old is appropriate for 'one nation only,' the new for the whole world (4.9.2); the old is passing, earthly, and figurative, the new eternal, heavenly, and unsurpassable (4.19.1). When the new comes, therefore, the old is done away with."[21] In *The City of God* Augustine invokes the old covenant as "the other city" that "ran its course, not in light, but in shadow ... from the time of Abraham."[22] There has been some debate on whether or not Thomas Aquinas (1225–1274) was a supersessionist, but Rabbi Eugene Korn and Catholic thinker John Pawlikowski conclude that "when one sees all the evidence, it appears that there is no continuing validity of the old covenant in Thomas's perspective."[23] As for Martin Luther, to take an example of a Protestant theologian, one only need quote from *On the Jews and Their Lies*:

[It is] going on fifteen hundred years since Vespasian and Titus destroyed Jerusalem and expelled the Jews from the city.... Such ruthless wrath of God is sufficient evidence that they assuredly have erred and gone astray.... For one dare not regard God as so cruel that he would punish his own people so long, so terribly, so unmercifully, and in addition keep silent, comforting them neither with words nor with deeds, and fixing no time limit and no end to it.... Therefore

[20] For a very good essay on this matter, see Harry James Cargas, *Reflections of a Post-Auschwitz Christian* (Detroit, Mich.: Wayne State University Press, 1989), 61–65.

[21] R. Kendall Soulen, *The God of Israel and Christian Theology* (Minneapolis, Minn.: Augsburg Fortress, 1996), 46–47.

[22] Augustine, *The City of God*, 609.

[23] Eugene B. Korn and John Pawlikowski, *Two Faiths, One Covenant? Jewish and Christian Identity in the Presence of the Other* (Lanham, Md.: Rowman & Littlefield, 2005), 53.

this work of wrath is proof that the Jews, surely rejected by God, are no longer his people, and neither is he any longer their God.[24]

With the supersession of the Covenant comes the usurpation of the Giver of the Covenant, and once the displacement of the God of the Covenant of Abraham is accomplished, so is the displacement of the prohibition against striving to be as God. With the elimination of the prohibition, the appropriation of God attendant on the new dispensation becomes an appropriation of divine judgment. The one who holds the key to salvation also deals out damnation, and the one who deals out damnation inevitably deals out death, beginning with the Jews.

Hence "the superseding or displacement myth," post-Holocaust Christian theologian Franklin Littell states it, "already rings with the genocidal note."[25] Darrell Fasching adds, "If no interpretation other than the myth of supersession can be derived from the New Testament and embraced in practice by Christians, then Christianity is immoral and obscene."[26] The Christian Scriptures are perhaps a bit ambiguous on the supersessionist teaching. Paul, for example, insists that God has not cast away His people, the Jews (Romans 11:1), yet in a New Testament comment on Jeremiah 31:31 we read, "In speaking of a new covenant [the prophet] treats the first as obsolete. And what is becoming obsolete and growing old is ready to vanish away" (Hebrews 8:13).[27] Therefore the Jews should vanish away, presumably by becoming Christian, for the sake of their own souls. In this way Christian theology paints itself into an inescapable corner: if the only path to salvation lies in the New Covenant of the blood of Jesus, as it is written (e.g., Acts 4:10–12), then anyone who consciously and conscientiously says "No" to that path is damned, beginning with the Jews. As for peoples of distant lands who have not received the Good News, Catholic theologians such as Karl Rahner allow them some latitude, arguing that, in their own way, they follow Jesus, even if they are not cognizant of the fact.[28] Not so the Jews:

---

[24] Martin Luther, *On the Jews and Their Lies, 1543*, trans. Martin H. Bertram, available at http://www.jrbooksonline.com/PDF_Books/JewsAndTheirLies.pdf, 2001, 2.

[25] Franklin H. Littell, *The Crucifixion of the Jews: The Failure of Christians to Understand the Jewish Experience* (Macon, Ga.: Mercer University Press, 1986), 2.

[26] Darrell J. Fasching, *Narrative Theology after Auschwitz: From Alienation to Ethics* (Minneapolis, Minn.: Fortress Press, 1992), 43.

[27] In Jeremiah 31:31 it is written, "Behold the days are coming, says the Lord, when I shall make a new covenant with the House of Israel and with the House of Judah."

[28] See Karl Rahner, *Foundations of Christian Faith: An Introduction to the Idea of Christianity*, trans. William V. Dych (New York: Crossroad, 1994), 311–321.

they have no mitigating circumstances, as Aquinas points out. The Jews, he says, "could not claim the excuse of ignorance," because they "have heard enough about the Christian religion to be guilty of rejecting it."[29] And their contempt for the self-evident truth makes them contemptible.

If one should wonder how someone could be offered salvation through the grace of God and knowingly reject it, the supersessionist theologian answers: there must be something demonic about the Jews, something satanic in their rebellion against God. They must be "emissaries of Satan" who "serve demons," as John Chrysostom stated it in his "Homilies against the Jews."[30] Once the Jews become such a theological category, they become "a *mythic* creature," Steven Katz observes. "Jews, a Jew, can be God incarnate; they can be the Devil incarnate (or his lieutenants); but they can never again be *merely* human beings."[31] No one, therefore, is more deserving of disdain than the Jews. Significantly, the teaching of contempt for the Jews as creatures who are somehow demonic is inextricably tied to the deicide charge, a charge that masks the secret desire of the anti-Semite to kill God. There is a link, therefore, between dogmatic theology and the dogma of deicide. That the Crucifixion came about in keeping with divine will and nothing could have been done to change it is irrelevant. What is essential to the Christian theological appropriation of God is that the Jews killed God. To be sure, as the story of the Crucifixion is related in the Christian Scriptures, prior to any systematic Christian theology, the blame for the murder of the Son of God clearly falls on the Jews. Pilate poses the rhetorical question, "What evil has this man done?" (Matthew 25:23), and when the Jews insist that Jesus be crucified, Pilate washes his hands of all liability in the matter, declaring, "I am innocent of the blood of this righteous person" (Matthew 27:24); the Blood of the Lamb is on the heads of the Jews and their children (Matthew 27:25). And there can be no crime worse than murdering God (whatever that might mean). Not only are the Jews the murderers of God, but they are the *unrepentant* murderers of God: even when offered forgiveness and salvation in Jesus – even when confronted with irrefutable evidence that he is the Redeemer – they still refuse that redemption.

---

[29] Quoted in Korn and Pawlikowski, *Two Faiths, One Covenant?*, 53.

[30] Quoted in Arthur Lukyn Williams, *Adversus Judaeos: A Bird's-Eye View of Christian Apologiae until the Renaissance* (Cambridge, U.K.: Cambridge University Press, 1935), 98.

[31] Steven Katz, *The Holocaust in Historical Context*, vol. 1 (New York: Oxford University Press, 1994), 256.

Examples of how the deicide charge found its way into the Christian theological tradition abound in the earliest stages of that tradition's development. One of the first to vent his hatred on the murderers of God was second-century theologian Justin Martyr, who declared that the Jews should "rightly suffer," for they have "slain the Just One."[32] Hippolytus (ca. 170–236) maintained that the Jews will forever receive God's just punishment for having murdered Jesus, and Origen of Alexandria agreed.[33] If the Covenant of Abraham has been superseded, as Cyprian (200–258) insisted,[34] it is because the children of Abraham "would fasten Christ to the cross."[35] Augustine of Hippo, the most influential of the early Christian theologians, wrote, "The Jews held him; the Jews insulted him, the Jews bound him, they crowned him with thorns, dishonored him by spitting upon him, they scourged him, they heaped abuses upon him, they hung him upon a tree, they pierced him with a lance."[36] Well into the time of the Crusades, Pope Innocent III (ca. 1161–1216) proclaimed that "the blood of Jesus Christ calls out" against the Jews and condemns them, like Cain, to forever wander the face of the earth.[37] Thomas Aquinas held a similar view: "It would be licit ... to hold Jews, because of their crime [of deicide], in perpetual servitude."[38] Whatever reforms the Protestant Reformation may have brought, the deicide charge endured, as Luther declared that "they would

---

[32] See Justin Martyr, *Dialogue with Trypho*, trans. Thomas B. Falls (Washington, D.C.: Catholic University of America Press, 2003), 27–29.

[33] See Ruether, *Faith and Fratricide*, 37.

[34] See Cyprian, "Three Books of Testimonies against the Jews," in Alexander Roberts and James Donaldson, eds., *The Writings of Cyprian Bishop of Carthage II: Ante Nicene Christian Library Translations of the Fathers down to AD 325, Part Thirteen* (Whitefish, Mont.: Kessinger, 2004), 80.

[35] Ibid., 98.

[36] Quoted in Edward H. Flannery, *The Anguish of the Jews* (New York: Paulist Press, 1965), 50. Rosemary Radford Ruether notes other texts from early Christianity that laid the groundwork for the teaching of contempt: *Adversos Judaeos* by Tertullian, *Demonstrations against the Jews* by the Syrian Aphrahat (ca. 270–345), and *Contra Judaeos* by the Arian bishop Maximinus (fifth century). The most famous sermons against Jews are those of Chrysostom in Antioch in 386–388; other sermons are from the Syrian Fathers Ephrem (ca. 306–373), Isaac of Antioch (fifth century), and Syrian Jacob of Serug (ca. 451–521). Anti-Jewish dialogues include *Dialogue of Timothy and Aquila* (fifth century), *Dialogue of Athanasius and Zacchaeus* (fourth century), *Discussion between Simon the Jew and Theophilus, a Christian* by Evagrius (344–399), *Dialogue of Papiscus and Philo* (fourth century), the *Discussion of St. Sylvester with the Jews at Rome* (fourth century), and the *Dialogue on the Blessed Trinity* by Saint Jerome; see Ruether, *Faith and Fratricide*, 119.

[37] Quoted in Flannery, *The Anguish of the Jews*, 102.   [38] Ibid., 95.

crucify ten more Messiahs and kill God himself if this were possible,"[39] and John Calvin (1509–1564) "believed that Jews were collectively guilty of deicide."[40]

If the Crucifixion was a necessary part of the divine plan, it was also necessary to the predetermined fate of a demonic, irredeemable Jewry: deicide was to become the sin not only projected on the Jews but ascribed to their demonic *essence*. Indeed, the Jews refuse salvation in Christ not because they fail to recognize that Jesus of Nazareth is the Messiah, the Son of God, but precisely because they *do* recognize him as such. And that is why they would murder him. Hence Gregory of Nyssa (ca. 335–ca. 395), who was a vocal proponent of the deicide charge,[41] also taught that the Jews are "confederates of the devil, offspring of vipers,... utterly vile,... enemies of *all that is good*."[42] Jerome asserted that the Jews "come from the synagogue of Satan,"[43] saying, "If you call it [the synagogue] a brothel, a den of vice, the Devil's refuge, Satan's fortress, a place to deprave the soul, an abyss of every conceivable disaster or whatever you will, you are still saying less than it deserves."[44] These examples run counter to Joshua Trachtenberg's claim that the "unique demonological character" of anti-Semitism is "of medieval origin."[45] Following the Middle Ages, in *Von Schem Hemphoras* (1543) Martin Luther wrote that "the God of the Jews is the devil."[46] As the ones whose father is the devil, the Jews are the antithesis of the ones whose father is God; as the embodiment of the Antichrist, they must necessarily reject the Christ. Their contempt for the self-evident truth makes them not only contemptible but the quintessential enemies of Truth, the children of the Father of Lies.

---

[39] Luther, *On the Jews and Their Lies*, 40.

[40] Michael, *Holy Hatred*, 106.

[41] See Gregory of Nyssa, *Against Eunomius*, in Philip Schaff and Henry Wace, eds., *A Select Library of Nicene and Post-Nicene Fathers of the Christian Church: Select Writings and Letters of Gregory, Bishop of Nyssa*, trans. William Moore and Henry Austin Wilson (New York: The Christian Literature Company, 1893), 189.

[42] Quoted in Mark R. Cohen, *Under Crescent and Cross* (Princeton, N.J.: Princeton University Press, 1995), 171; emphasis added; see also Gregory of Nyssa, *Against Eunomius*, 101.

[43] Jerome, *Commentary on Galatians*, trans. Andrew Cain (Washington, D.C.: Catholic University of America Press, 2010), 266.

[44] Quoted in Robert Wistrich, *Anti-Semitism: The Longest Hatred* (New York: Pantheon Books, 1991), 19.

[45] Joshua Trachtenberg, *The Devil and the Jews: The Medieval Conception of the Jew and Its Relation to Modern Anti-Semitism* (Philadelphia: Jewish Publication Society, 1983), 6.

[46] Quoted in Michael, *Holy Hatred*, 111.

Here the hatred of the Jews is no longer the unfortunate outcome of the new dispensation or even the result of social or economic circumstance; now it is a religious duty incumbent on pious Christians, something holy and pleasing to God. Thus, Ephraim of Syria (ca. 306–373) added Jew hatred to the Christian liturgy,[47] Eusebius of Alexandria (d. 444) systematically incited hatred of the Jews,[48] and Athanasius of Constantinople (1230–1310) asserted, "It is the duty of Christians to hate the deicidal Jews."[49] During the First and Second Crusades, in fact, the belief that anyone who kills a Jew will have his sins forgiven was widespread,[50] resulting in the massacres of 1096 in Speyer, Worms, Mainz, and Cologne, as well as in Metz, Trier, Rouen, and Monieux. Thus, in a perverted twisting of the sacrificial rite of atonement, the Jews take the place of Jesus: their blood, not his, washes away all sin. Placed in such a position, the Jews are placed outside the circle of salvation: the one whose blood brings you redemption is not subject to redemption. Situating the Jews outside the circle of salvation constitutes a new but inevitable move in their demonization.

The only appropriation of the divine that might exceed the murder of God would be the consumption of God, becoming God by making God part of oneself. There lies the real meaning of the blood libel, the claim that Jews murder children – unblemished lambs – and consume their blood, appropriating the Christ by absorbing the one who is Christ-like into themselves; thus the accusation often included the claim that the child was not just slaughtered but crucified.[51] To consume the blood is to consume the soul, for the soul is in the blood, as it is written (see Genesis 9:4); it means arrogating the essence of what is consumed. In the blood libel we see a grim perversion of the Sacrament of the Eucharist, whereby the believer consumes the blood and the body of Christ – in an act not of appropriation but of absorption. This is not to say that the ritual of communion is expressive of the desire to lay claim to God by consuming Him, but when the anti-Semite projects it on the Jew in the form of the blood libel, it is indeed expressive of his or her own desire to be as God by killing and consuming Him. This Eucharistic association underscores the ritualized nature of this murder; indeed, it is

---

[47] Flannery, *The Anguish of the Jews*, 46.   [48] Michael, *Holy Hatred*, 39.
[49] Ibid., 40.
[50] Ibid., 67; see also Ruether, *Faith and Fratricide*, 206. It should be noted that during the Second Crusade Bernard of Clairvaux (1090–1153) spoke against killing Jews.
[51] See ibid., 85.

cast not precisely as murder but as a kind of satanic blood sacrifice, sanctioned not by the Holy One but by the Evil One.

By the fourteenth century the ritual was associated with the observance of Passover, which, of course, is the season of the Crucifixion. Here the charge of host desecration – taking the sacred bread of communion and defiling it, even driving nails into it – is associated with the blood libel as a reenactment of the murder and consumption of God. In 1298, for example, it was rumored in Rottingen that Jews had desecrated the host, whereupon, led by a German nobleman and Franconian knight named Rindfleisch, the *Judenschächter*, or "Jew slaughterers," murdered 100,000 Jews in Germany and destroyed 140 communities.[52] In the murderous ritual, it was alleged, Jews did not merely kill Christian children but crucified them and consumed their blood. Although several popes declared that the Jews were innocent of such a crime (e.g., Innocent IV in 1247, Gregory X in 1272, Martin V in 1422, Nicholas V in 1447, and Paul III in 1540), the accusation persists in the modern period. In 1881, the Vatican journal *Civilita Cattolica* attempted to demonstrate that ritual murder was an integral part of Judaism; much of the claim was based on the work of German Catholic theologian August Rohling (1839–1931),[53] who ascribes to the Jews the teaching that "whoever spills the blood of a godless one [i.e., a non-Jew] thereby brings a sacrificial offering to God."[54] To be sure, according to Robert Michael there were as many cases of blood libel accusations between 1880 and 1945 as there were during the entire Middle Ages.[55]

So why is the Jew the designated target for the deicide charge and demonization, for the blood libel and degradation? From the standpoint of dogmatic Christian theology, the very presence of the Jew unseats anyone who presumes to sit in judgment; thus the Jew unsettles the one who would have matters settled, particularly the matter of sorting out the damned from the redeemed. The only way to settle matters is to unseat God, and the very presence of the Jew stands in the way of such a project. Franz Rosenzweig (1886–1929), in fact, sees this unsettling presence of the Jew as the source of Christian anti-Semitism: "The existence of the Jew constantly subjects Christianity to the idea that it is not attaining the

---

[52] Flannery, *The Anguish of the Jews*, 106–107.
[53] See Bernard Lewis, *Semites and Anti-Semites: An Inquiry into Conflict and Prejudice* (New York: W. W. Norton, 1999), 106–107.
[54] August Rohling, *Der Talmudjude*, 4th ed. (Münster: Adolph Russell's Verlag, 1872), 41; my translation.
[55] Michael, *Holy Hatred*, 170.

goal, the truth, that it ever remains – on the way. That is the profoundest reason for the Christian hatred of the Jew."[56] Remaining "on the way" means affirming, with the Jews, that the Messiah is still on the way and that the matter of redemption remains unsettled, a position that is anathema to Christian dogma. If the Jews did not kill Christ historically, they kill him theologically, simply by insisting that he is not the Anointed One who brings redemption to all humanity.

Judaism tends to place as much or more importance on working for the coming of the Messiah than on his arrival. Indeed, the Messiah is precisely the one who is forever *yet* to arrive, thus underscoring the infinite task of hastening the coming of the Messiah. Said the talmudic sage Rabbi Samuel ben Nachman, in the name of Rabbi Yonatan, "Cursed be the bones of those who calculate the end. For they would say, since the predetermined time has come, and yet the Messiah has not come, he will never come. Nevertheless, await him" (*Sanhedrin* 97b). Nevertheless prepare the way for him. In that *nevertheless* lies the infinite aspect of my responsibility. Each may be responsible for all, but *I* am more responsible than the others, so that *I* am the one who must bring the Messiah. Instead of personal salvation, I am left with personal responsibility, and no one – not even the Messiah – can assume that responsibility for me. From a Jewish standpoint, then, Jesus cannot do it for me. *I* am the one who must mount the Cross: *for me there is no remission of sin but only a reckoning* – a rather unsettling realization. Because the issue is my responsibility, and not my redemption, the matter of a heavenly reward for *me* is irrelevant. And so it is written in the *Sifre* on Deuteronomy 3:23, "Says the Torah: whether You redeem us or not, whether You heal us or not, we shall seek to know You."[57] Our task is not to know God but to *seek* to know God, to know God in the mode of "not knowing," particularly not knowing who is damned and who is redeemed. Contrary to dogmatic Christian theology, therefore, Judaism does not divide the world into the damned and redeemed on the basis of belief.

This point is profoundly illustrated in the story of Jonah. For a Christian, to bring the people of Nineveh to God would mean converting them to Christianity; for the Jew Jonah, it does not mean enjoining them to convert to Judaism – it means leading them to realize that their

---

[56] Franz Rosenzweig, *The Star of Redemption*, trans. William W. Hallo (Boston: Beacon Press, 1972), 413.

[57] The *Sifre* on Deuteronomy is a rabbinic commentary on the Book of Deuteronomy dating from around the year 300 CE.

treatment of one another is an expression of their relation to God. The anti-Semitic essence of Christian dogmatic theology manifests itself when the fixed formulas and ready answers of the creed are challenged by the prospect that the creed is not enough. Longing to finalize the matter of redemption, dogmatic theology would have the final word, settle the accounts, and slip into a sleep that would draw everyone else into the circle of its slumber. Here we realize, with Lévinas, that "anti-Semitism is the archetype of internment."[58] But the Jews continually and stubbornly break free of the internment. Thus, the anti-Semites begin by assimilating and end by annihilating the Jews in order to resolve the Jewish Question. What is the Jewish Question? It is the eternal irritant that began with the questions put to Adam and his firstborn: Where are you? Where is your brother? And what have you done? Inasmuch as I would be the Judge who asks, I grow deaf to the one who cries out.

DOES CHRISTIAN THEOLOGY HAVE TO BE ANTI-SEMITIC?

By now one might wonder whether there can be a Christian theology that is not anti-Semitic. If it is indeed possible, then it would have to be a theology that is free of supersessionism – there lies the key. If the Jews appear to be so stiff-necked in their refusal to embrace the "new covenant," it is not because they are somehow demonic. It is because of a teaching essential to Judaism, namely that the Covenant of Torah is set and eternal *as it stands*; hence there can be no new covenant, as it is written: "You shall not add to the word which I command you, nor take from it; that you may keep the commandments of the Lord your God which I command you" (Deuteronomy 4:2). Also essential to the covenantal teaching of Torah is the principle that the commandments of Torah revealed at Mount Sinai are humanity's *only* link to God. In its traditional supersessionist mode, Christianity rejects theses teachings from the Torah. For example, when we read, "For by grace you have been saved through faith, and that not of yourselves; it is a gift of God, not of works" (Ephesians 2:8–9), it might suggest that *only* faith in Jesus Christ brings salvation to the human being. The word *faith* or *belief*, in fact, appears about one hundred times more frequently in the New Testament than in the so-called Old Testament. Inasmuch as the Christian new covenant insists on the shibboleth of *sola fide*, "by faith [in Christ] alone," as the

[58] Emmanuel Lévinas, *Difficult Freedom: Essays on Judaism*, trans. Sean Hand (Baltimore, Md.: Johns Hopkins University Press, 1990), 153.

guarantor of salvation, then Christianity *has* to oppose itself to any way of thinking that insists on the commanded acts of loving kindness as the true path to God.

The real issue, however, is not faith or deeds. The real issue lies in whether I shall turn away from the usurpation of God that lies at the core of anti-Semitism, or whether I shall presume to be as God. If Christian theology is to avoid the anti-Semitic usurpation of God, then it must be guided by the realization that I am not God, that I therefore have no idea of who is damned and who is redeemed, and that God alone determines such things, my sincere affirmation of the creed notwithstanding. But theology, by its very nature, tends to get in the way of such a move. When Christian theology indulges in Christology, for example, in order to determine what must be *believed* about the Christ, difficulties can arise. If one were to ask what the Jews believe about the Messiah, there are a few basic tenets, namely that he comes from the House of David, that he will bring an end to the exile of the Jews, and that he will somehow lead all of humanity to realize the oneness of the human-to-human and the human-to-divine relationships. Beyond that, the teachings are rather confused and often conflicting.[59] In any case, the Messiah whom the Jews await bears little resemblance to the Messiah who, according to the Christians, has come. What is essential to Christian teaching about the Messiah is unintelligible to a Jewish understanding of the Anointed One, namely that he was born of a virgin, was the incarnation of God, was offered up as the son of God in sacrifice for our redemption, and is forever part of a divine trinity – in other words, the defining tenets of the Christian creeds. All of these teachings hinge on the doctrine of inherited sin, according to which, since the fall of Adam all of humanity – indeed, the very essence of humanity – has been tainted with sin, for which only the unblemished Lamb of God can atone. Judaism, by contrast, has no such doctrine.

The Christological doctrine, moreover, is central to the de-Judaizing of Christianity, for once the doctrine determines the Messiah to be divine, he cannot be a Jew or reducible to any other ethnic origin. Of course, the mystery or paradox of the Christ is that he is both divine and human, both God and Jew. Which is to say: both unsurpassable and superseded. Related to this paradox is another conundrum: because Christian theology needs the Hebrew Scriptures, it continually confronts the Jewish Covenant that is both indispensable and undermining to Christianity;

[59] For a good anthology of Jewish texts and teachings on the Messiah, see Raphael Patai, *The Messiah Texts* (New York: Avon, 1979).

without the Covenant of Torah there can be no Christianity, yet the Covenant of Torah declares that there can be no "new" covenant. Without the divinely chosen status of the Jews, there can be no Christianity; if the divinely chosen status of the Jews is undone or superseded, then Christianity itself is undone.

Precisely such paradoxes, however, may open up a theological opportunity for Christian theology to find within its own teaching a way to free itself from what might otherwise appear to be its anti-Semitic essence. Some Christian theologians, at least, seem to think so. Franklin Littell, for example, maintains that anti-Semitism is not merely one among the many sins of racism, bigotry, prejudice, and the like; nor does it lie in a xenophobic "fear of the other," in some psychological need for a scapegoat, and even less in a perverse envy of the Jewish people (who, indeed, would envy the lot of the Jews?). No, says Littell, anti-Semitism is *blasphemy*, the "sin against the Holy Spirit,"[60] which, according to the Gospel, *cannot be forgiven* (Matthew 12:31). But *blasphemy* is a very strong word, and Littell does not use it lightly. If anti-Semitism is blasphemy, then much of Christian theology is blasphemy. If it is blasphemy, it is because, like anti-Semitism, this dogmatic theology has its metaphysical origin in the primal longing to be as God and thus to get rid of Him. But is *that* the sin against the Holy Spirit?

The sin against the Holy Spirit is generally identified as blasphemy, but that remains a bit vague. Augustine understood the sin against the Holy Spirit to be the persevering "hardness of an impenitent heart."[61] In a similar vein, Thomas Aquinas argued that the blasphemy that constitutes the sin against the Holy Spirit assumes various forms, such as obstinacy, impenitence, envy, resistance to truth of Christ's divinity, and the presumption that salvation can come without repentance – all of which, he says, can assume the form of thought, word, and deed.[62] As for the Protestants, Martin Luther used to end his sermons with a warning about the sins against the Holy Spirit,[63] which he viewed as "first, presumption; second, despair; third, opposition to and condemnation of the known

[60] Littell, *The Crucifixion of the Jews*, 65.
[61] Augustine, *Nicene and Post-Nicene Fathers: First Series Volume VI: Sermon on the Mount, Harmony of the Gospels, and Homilies on the Gospels*, ed. Philip Schaff (New York: Cosimo, 2007), 326.
[62] Thomas Aquinas, *Summa Theologica: Volume III – Part II, Second Section*, Dominican trans. (New York: Cosimo, 2007), 1228–1230.
[63] Bernhard Lohse, *Martin Luther's Theology: Its Historical and Systematic Development* (Minneapolis, Minn.: Augsburg Fortress, 1999), 235.

truth; fourth, not to wish well, but to grudge one's brother or neighbor the grace of God; fifth, to be hardened; sixth, to be impenitent."[64] And according to John Calvin, "he sins against the Holy Spirit who, while so constrained by the power of divine truth that he cannot plead ignorance, yet deliberately resists, and that merely for the sake of resisting."[65] In other words, he sins against the Holy Spirit who persists in his impenitence. Thus, the thread that runs through these theologians' understanding of the sin that cannot be forgiven is the sin, the blasphemy, of obstinate impenitence, which was generally associated with the Jews. If Littell is right, however, then the true sin against the Holy Spirit lies in leveling this very accusation against the Jews. Therefore, it is not the Jews but the anti-Semites who are guilty of the sin against the Holy Spirit: as they project on the Jews their own desire to kill God and ascend to the divine throne of judgment, so they project on the Jews their own blasphemy.

As a move to unseat God as the sole judge of who is redeemed and who is not, the sin against the Holy Spirit amounts to an effort to drive the Divine Presence, the Holy Spirit, from the world. From a Jewish standpoint, the presence of the Jewish people in the world signifies the presence of the Holy One – of the *Shekhinah*, or Indwelling Presence of God (see *Zohar* II, 98a). The longing to rid the world of the Jews, then, is a longing to rid the world of the Holy Spirit. Further, if the Holy Spirit enters the world where it is allowed to enter – through Scripture, prayer, and acts of loving kindness – then anti-Semitism is a sin against the Holy Spirit, for anti-Semitic acts of cruelty against the Chosen of God are based on a denial of the Scripture that views the Jews as God's Chosen (see, e.g., Numbers 18:19). Each time the Christians consigned to the flames the folios of Talmud or the scrolls of Torah, each time there was a call for restrictions on Hebrew prayers and Hebrew tomes, each time accusations of the blood libel or the desecration of the host were leveled at the Jews, the effort to rid their world of the Jews amounted to an effort to rid their world of God. That is why anti-Semitism is blasphemy. From both Jewish and Christian standpoints, blasphemy entails such a denial of God and His Torah, and any hatred of the Jews or desire to eliminate the Jews, whether by extermination or by conversion, amounts to a denial of God and His Torah. For, according to the Jewish teaching of the Koretzer

---

[64] Martin Luther, *The Table Talk*, trans. and ed. Thomas S. Kepler (New York: Dover, 2005), 85.

[65] John Calvin, *Institutes of the Christian Religion*, trans. Henry Beveridge (Peabody, Mass.: Hendrickson, 2003), 400.

Rebbe (1726–1791), a disciple of the Baal Shem Tov, "God and Torah are one. God, Israel, and Torah are one."[66] As many of the sages have said, to launch an assault on the Jewish people is to launch an assault on the Holy One. The renowned medieval commentator Rashi (1040–1105), for example, wrote, "Whoever attacks Israel is as though he attacks the Holy One, blessed be He" (commentary on Numbers 31:3).

If Christian theology is to rid itself of its anti-Semitic elements, it must find a way to subscribe to a similar view, without abandoning the core teachings of Christianity. Christianity itself is at stake here: if Christian theology is necessarily anti-Semitic, then Christian theology is necessarily blasphemy and a sin against the Holy Spirit, a sin that cannot be forgiven. Rosemary Radford Ruether has suggested that "anti-Judaism is too deeply embedded in the foundations of Christianity to be rooted out entirely without destroying the whole structure."[67] I believe, however, that Christian theology can free itself from its anti-Semitic aspect, as well as from its anti-Judaism, and remain essentially Christian. In fact, one way to do that is to reverse the matter of Judaizing from its heretical status to something that adds to the depth and substance of Christianity itself.

Christian theologians could begin, for example, with Paul's declaration that God has not cast away His people, the Jews (see Romans 11:1). Then there are Christian Scriptures that forbid dispensing judgment, such as "Judge not lest you be judged. With the judgment you pronounce you will be judged, and the measure you mete will be the measure meted unto you" (Matthew 7:1–2). Of course, this teaching from the Jew Jesus stems from the Jewish oral tradition, where it is taught, "He who judges his neighbor in a scale of merit is himself judged favorably" (*Talmud Bavli, Shabbat* 129b), and "In the measure with which a man measures, it is meted unto him" (*Mishnah Sotah* 1:7). This emphasis on Christian teachings rooted in Judaism would have to be accompanied by a new and different understanding of fundamental precepts such as "none comes unto the Father except by me" (John 14:6) and "other foundation can no man lay than that is laid, which is Jesus Christ" (1 Corinthians 2:11). Christian theologians can avoid the blasphemy of anti-Semitism only by committing what until now would have been viewed as another blasphemy, namely by adopting the view that for the Jews, Jesus is *superfluous to salvation*. If such a shift comes with staggering

---

[66] Louis Newman, ed., *The Hasidic Anthology* (New York: Schocken Books, 1963), 147.
[67] Ruether, *Faith and Fratricide*, 228.

ramifications with regard to Christian identity and the essence of Christianity, it is because anti-Semitism has a metaphysical aspect that transcends theological categories; if anything, it shapes the categories of theologies that deal with the Jews. Indeed, to maintain that anti-Semitism is blasphemy is to imply that it has a much deeper origin than many have imagined, that it has the kind of metaphysical origin that I have described. For blasphemy lies precisely in the usurpation of God, the appropriation of absolute divine truth, and the distribution of divine judgment.

More than a few Christian thinkers – among them pastors, scholars, and theologians such as Edward Flannery, Harry James Cargas, Alice Eckardt and A. Roy Eckardt, John K. Roth, Didier Pollefeyt, Henry Knight, Juergen Manemann, and Martin Rumscheidt – have found the courage to try to purge traditional Christian theology of its anti-Semitic elements. I know from personal conversations with several of these thinkers that they reject the view that the salvation of the Jews rests on the embrace of Jesus Christ as their Lord and Savior; they maintain, rather, that the Torah is sufficient for the redemption of the Jews and that such judgment is in God's hands alone.

Others, however, such as Palestinian Anglican priest Naim Ateek, founder of the Sabeel Ecumenical Liberation Theology Center, have persisted in the blasphemy of anti-Semitism. In fact, Ateek's hatred of the Jews extends to a hatred of Christians who support the Jewish people, as he declares Christian Zionism to be heresy.[68] Echoing elements of the deicide charge, he compares the Israeli oppression of the Palestinians to the crucifixion of Jesus, crying out, "Palestine has become one huge Golgotha."[69] He drums up the blood libel that Jews kidnap Christian children and slaughter them by claiming that Israelis seek out babies in order to kill them.[70] And he continues the tradition of demonizing the Jews by insisting that the Zionists are the incarnation of the very "spiritual hosts of wickedness against which Christians are called to struggle (Ephesians 6:12–13)."[71] Not surprisingly he sympathizes with Jihadist Muslims in their struggle to eliminate the Jewish State: "As Muslims have ultimately prevailed against the nineteenth- and twentieth-century colonialists, most of them believe that in the long run they will prevail against the State of Israel, this foreign Western body in the heart of the Arab East. Such a view is not alien to the basic concept of *jihad* that

---

[68] Stephen Spector, *Evangelicals and Israel: The Story of American Christian* Zionism (New York: Oxford University Press, 2009), 131.
[69] Quoted in ibid., 132.   [70] Ibid.   [71] Ibid., 134.

Muslims espouse. The word means not only 'holy war' but 'striving' as well. There is a *jihad* of preaching and persuasion, as well as a *jihad* of perseverance and endurance."[72] Among the Jihadists, who benefit from Ateek's demonization of the Jews and the Jewish State, the jihad of preaching and persuasion is always a preaching and persuasion to murder within the framework of determining who will have a place in paradise and who will not. Among the Jihadists who would thus usurp the throne of judgment, anti-Semitism assumes a religious fanatic form.

---

[72] Naim Stifan Ateek, *Justice and Only Justice: A Palestinian Theology of Liberation* (Maryknoll, N.Y.: Orbis Books, 1989), 160.

3

Islamic Jihadism: Religious Fanatic Anti-Semitism

Surely Allah has cursed the unbelievers and has prepared for them a burning fire. (Quran 33:64)

If the Jews left Palestine to us, would we start loving them? Of course not. . . . They would have been enemies even if they did not occupy a thing. . . . Our fighting with the Jews is eternal, and it will not end . . . until not a single Jew remains on the face of the Earth. . . . As for you Jews, the Curse of Allah upon you, you pigs of the earth!

Sheikh Muhammad Hussein Yaqoub, Al-Rahma TV, 17 January 2009

In this chapter, I examine the roots of anti-Semitism manifest in the foundational Jew hatred of Islamic Jihadism. In its current form Jihadist anti-Semitism is the issue of a synthesis of modern totalitarian ideology and modern purist movements in Islam, with some motifs borrowed from centuries of European Christian Jew hatred. Highly influential among the modern Jihadist ideologues is Abdul Al'a Maududi (1903–1979), who on 26 August 1941 in Lahore, India, founded the Jihadist group Jamaat-e-Islami. On that day he declared, "The Message of Islam is meant for the whole of mankind and whatever relates to human life necessarily concerns Islam as well. Hence the Islamic movement is universal in nature." He followed this statement with a call for worldwide jihad.[1] Islam, says Maududi, is "a revolutionary ideology and program which seeks to alter the social order of the whole world and rebuild it in conformity with its own tenets and ideals. . . . The

---

[1] Abdul Al'a Maududi, *Selected Speeches and Writings*, vol. 1, trans. S. Zakir Aijaz (Karachi: International Islamic Publishers, 1981), 5.

80

purpose of Islam is to set up a State on the basis of its own ideology and programme, regardless of which nation assumes the role of the standard bearer of Islam."[2] Among the Jihadists, then, the aim is to pervert the God of Abraham into the God of a totalitarian ideology and thus to determine the belief and the behavior necessary for salvation: the belief according to the Shahadah – "There is no God but Allah, and Muhammad is the messenger of Allah" – and the behavior according to the law of Sharia.

As in the case of Christianity, in order to appropriate the judgment of God, the Jihadists must appropriate the word of God. One important theological difference, however, between Christianity and Islam vis-à-vis the Hebrew Scriptures and the Covenant of Abraham is that, unlike Christianity, Islam does not understand itself to supersede Judaism and the Covenant of Torah, because, according to the Quran, the Jews had no covenant to be superseded; rather, the Jews falsified the Scriptures to suit their own evil ends (see Quran 2:59; 3:78). Indeed, Abraham was not a Jew but a Muslim (3:67), and the heir in the way of Allah was Ishmael, not Isaac (2:127). As for the Jews, the Quran declares that, far from being the people of the true Covenant, Allah has cursed them because of their refusal to believe (2:88; 4:46) and that they are damned both in this world and in the next (5:41). If the Quran claims that Muslims are closer in their beliefs to Christians than to the Jews (5:82), the likeness lies more in a hatred of the Jews than in any theological claims. In fact, Islamic Jihadists play on the supposed likeness to Christianity by invoking the age-old Christian charge of deicide in order to incite hatred of the Jews, despite the Quran's denial that the crucifixion took place (4:157). On a television program titled *Religion and Life*, aired in February 2005, for example, Muslim Brotherhood leader Youssef al-Qaradawi (b. 1926) declared, "There is no doubt that the Jews had a far-reaching [role] in crucifying Jesus.... We believe Jesus was not crucified, but the crime was committed.... And we believe that the Jews, I mean, they committed this crime."[3] As ever, hatred trumps reason.

Although most Muslims are not Islamic Jihadists, as I am using the term, it is not an accident that Islamic Jihadism has emerged, in part, from certain traditions in Islam. They are traditions that provide a sacred ground both for Jihadism and for Jew hatred.

---

[2] Abdul Al'a Maududi, *Jihad in Islam* (Lahore: Islamic Publications, 2001), 8–10.
[3] Quoted in Robert Wistrich, *A Lethal Obsession: Anti-Semitism from Antiquity to the Global Jihad* (New York: Random House, 2010), 809–810.

ISLAMIC ROOTS OF JIHADIST FANATICISM

Often used with the phrase *fi sabil Allah* or "in the path of Allah,"[4] *jihad fi sabil Allah* means "to strive in the path of Allah."[5] Closely associated with jihad is the term *qital*, which means "fighting" or "killing."[6] On the most fundamental level, it "consists of military action with the object of the expansion of Islam."[7] Islamic studies scholar Majid Khadduri elaborates: "The term *jihad* is derived from the verb *jahada* (abstract noun, *juhd*) which means 'exerted'; its juridical-theological meaning is exertion of one's power in Allah's path, that is, the spread of the belief in Allah and in making His word supreme over this world. The individual's recompense would be the achievement of salvation, since *jihad is Allah's direct way to paradise*. This definition is based on a Quranic injunction which runs as follows: 'Believe in Allah and His Apostle and carry on warfare (jihad) in the path of Allah with your possessions and your persons'" (61:11).[8] Because the Quran contains numerous imperatives of this kind,[9] an understanding of jihad as (1) violent and (2) a sacred religious duty has been part of Islamic thinking since the advent of Islam itself. As so it must be if the religious movement is to appropriate God to become the arbiter of ultimate truth in this world.

From the time of the spread of Islam under the sword in the seventh century, writes Rudolph Peters, "expansionist jihad is a collective duty (*fard 'ala al-kifaya*) ..., considered to be a fulfillment of a religious duty."[10] Early on jihad came to hold a prominent place in the four main schools of Islamic thought: the Hanafi, founded by Abu Hanafi

---

[4] Michael Bonner, *Jihad in Islamic History: Doctrine and Practices* (Princeton, N.J.: Princeton University Press, 2006), 2.

[5] Andrew G. Bostom, "Jihad Conquests and the Imposition of Dhimmitude – A Survey," in Andrew G. Bostom, ed., *The Legacy of Jihad: Islamic Holy War and the Fate of Non-Muslims* (Amherst, N.Y.: Prometheus Books, 2005), 26–27.

[6] Reuven Firestone, *Jihad: The Origin of Holy War in Islam* (Oxford: Oxford University Press, 1999), 18.

[7] David Cook, *Understanding Jihad* (Berkeley: University of California Press, 2005), 2.

[8] Majid Khadduri, "The Law of War: The Jihad," in Andrew G. Bostom, ed., *The Legacy of Jihad: Islamic Holy War and the Fate of Non-Muslims* (Amherst, NY: Prometheus Books, 2005), 307; emphasis added.

[9] Other verses in the Quran urging the believers to jihad include 2:191, 2:216, 2:217, 2:218, 4:74, 4:76, 4:95, 8:15–16, 8:39, 8:41, 8:65, 9:5, 9:29, 9:73, 9:111, 9:123, and 47:20. The Sura of Combat (47) and the Sura of Victory (48) also have extensive verses on fighting in the path of Allah. See Firestone, *Jihad*, 60–65, 84–91.

[10] Rudolph Peters, *Jihad in Classical and Modern Islam: A Reader* (Princeton, N.J.: Markus Wiener, 1995), 3.

(699–765); the Maliki, founded by Imam Malik ibn Anas (714–796); the Shafi'i, founded by Muhammad ibn Idris ash-Shafi'i (767–820); and the Hanbali, founded by Ahmad ibn Hanbal (780–855). Among the leading scholars in these schools are Maliki jurist Ibn Abi Zayd al-Qayrawani (922–996), Shafi'i jurist al-Mawardi (d. 1058), Hanafi jurist Burhanuddin Ali (d. 1196), and Hanbali jurist Taqi ad-Din Ahmad ibn Taymiyyah (1263–1328), all of whom extolled jihad as holy war. Especially influential among today's Jihadist movements is Ibn Taymiyyah, who is quoted, for example, in the Al-Qaeda Manual.[11] Jihad, he maintained, "is the finest thing in this world and the next, and to neglect it is to lose this world and the next. . . . This means: either victory and triumph or martyrdom and paradise."[12] Following Ibn Taymiyyah, Muslim sage Ibn Khaldun (1332–1406) stated Islam's consensus view of jihad by saying, "In the Muslim community, the holy war is a religious duty, because of the universalism of the [Muslim] mission and [the obligation to] convert everybody to Islam either by persuasion or by force. . . . Islam is under obligation to gain power over other nations."[13] From the standpoint of traditional Islam, it seems, to speak out against jihad is tantamount to heresy, which may explain why so few Muslim clerics decry the Jihadist movements.

Just as important as the law is the hadith, those texts containing the oral traditions on the teachings of the Prophet. The six main collections that comprise the hadith are Sahih al-Bukhari, compiled by Muhammad ibn Ismail al-Bukhari (810–870); Sahih Muslim, collected by Muslim ibn al-Hajjaj (821–875); Sunan Abu Daud, gathered by Abu Daud al-Sijistani (817–888); Sunan al-Tirmidi, put together by Eesa Muhammad ibn Eesa al-Tirmidi (824–892); Sunan Ibn Majah, collected by Muhammad ibn Yazid ibn Majah (824–887); and Sunan al-Nasai, compiled by Ahmad ibn al-Nasai (829–915). Michael Bonner observes that "in the hadith, [there] is a central theme of the jihad, namely *the propagation of the Faith*

---

[11] Al-Qaeda Manual, in Walter Laqueur, ed., *Voices of Terror* (New York: Reed Press, 2004), 405.

[12] Quoted in David Aaron, *In Their Own Words: Voices of Jihad* (Santa Monica, Calif.: Rand Corporation, 2008), 46.

[13] Ibn Khaldun, *The Muqudimmah: An Introduction to History*, trans. Franz Rosenthal (New York: Pantheon, 1958), 473. Hasan al-Banna invoked this support for Jihadism on the part of all four of the major schools of Islam when he made his case for the Muslim Brotherhood's pursuit of their murderous program; see Hasan al-Banna, *Five Tracts of Hasan al-Banna: A Selection from the Majmuat Rasail al-Imam al-Shahid Hasan al-Banna*, trans. Charles Wendell (Berkeley: University of California Press, 1978), 146–151.

through combat."[14] In the hadith of al-Bukhari, for example, it is written, "No slave [of God] who dies and has goodness with God wants to return to the world, ... except the martyr (*illa al-shahid*), for when he sees the greatness of martyrdom (*fadl al-shahada*), he will want to return to the world and be killed again"[15] – killed again, that is, in the act of killing for Allah. For "he who dies without fighting or believing in fighting," says the al-Bukhari, "dies as a kind of dissenter."[16] These texts are second only to the Quran as authoritative sources on what to believe and how to live.

Muslim scholar Khaleel Mohammed notes further that the hadith is the primary source of the most anti-Semitic Islamic teachings.[17] In the hadith, for example, we find the teaching that "the last hour would not come unless the Muslims will fight against the Jews and the Muslims would kill them until the Jews would hide themselves behind a stone or a tree and a stone or a tree would say: Muslim, or the servant of Allah, there is a Jew behind me; come and kill him" (Sahih Muslim 41:6985; Sahih Bukhari 4:56:791).[18] Not only are "Jews as Jews ... *by nature* determined to fight Allah's Truth and sow corruption and confusion," as Muslim Brotherhood ideologue Sayyid Qutb says,[19] but in the days of the world's final purification nature itself will vomit up the Jewish evil as something truly *unnatural* and that therefore has no place in existence. It is no accident that this hadith is quoted in Article Seven of the Hamas "Charter of Allah," with the implication that the Hamas is Allah.

Why in the days of the final purification of creation must all the Jews be killed and not, say, all the Zoroastrians? Because the Jews are the falsifiers of God's truth and therefore the source of all that defiles creation. Here, too, Islam shares a certain similarity, as well as an important difference, with Christianity. Both traditions insist on being purified of sin either by belief and blood, as the Christians maintain, or by belief and obedience, as the Muslims preach. And as the one whose voice declares that no human being can assail the seat of God by any means, the Jew is the primary source of contamination. Therefore anyone who would presume to sort out the defiled from the pure must silence the Jew. And

---

[14] Michael Bonner, *Jihad in Islamic History: Doctrine and Practices* (Princeton, N.J.: Princeton University Press, 2006), 49; emphasis in the original.

[15] Quoted in Firestone, 100.   [16] Quoted in ibid., 101.

[17] Khaleel Mohammed, "Antisemitism in Islamic Texts and Traditions," lecture given at the University of Memphis, 14 March 2007.

[18] Quoted in Aaron, *In Their Own Words*, 43–44.

[19] Quoted in Ronald L. Nettler, *Past Trials and Present Tribulations: A Muslim Fundamentalist's View of the Jews* (Oxford: Pergamon, 1987), 35; emphasis added.

one must be pure in body and belief in order to carry out that holy mission. Not surprisingly, in the modern period, with the advent of a mode of thought that renders God meaningless, Islam witnessed the rise of purist movements, such as Wahhabism and Salafism, as precursors to Islamic Jihadism. The predominant form of Islam in Saudi Arabia today, Wahhabism is based on the *Kitab at-tawhid* (Book of Unity), written by Muhammad ibn 'Abd al-Wahhab al-Tamini (1703–1792), who founded the Wahhabi movement in 1744.[20] In accordance with its doctrine of unity, or *tawhid*, Wahhabism seeks to purify the planet of everything that does not belong to Islam. Al-Wahhab believed that the unbeliever (*kafir*) should be put to death and that political power was therefore necessary to carrying out the aims of Islam.[21] Because sending the unbelievers to the damnation they deserve is a holy act pleasing to Allah, paradise is guaranteed to any Muslim who dies in that effort.

The movement that has had a more direct influence on modern Jihadism, however, is Salafism; the seminal Salafist thinker Rashid Rida (1865–1935), in fact, was the teacher of Hitler's Grossmufti Haj Amin al-Husseini (1897–1974) and had a decisive influence on Hasan al-Banna (1906–1949), the founder of Islamic Jihadism's most pervasive group, the Muslim Brotherhood. Deriving its name from the word *salaf*, which means "pious ancestor," Salafism emerged in the middle of the nineteenth century as a purist movement based on the untainted teachings of the first three generations of Islamic sages. Like the Wahhabis, Salafists embrace the dogma of *tawhid*; also like the Wahhabis, they understand the oneness of God to be rooted in the oneness of humanity's worldview.[22] In this insistence on a strict, worldwide conformity with Islamic dogma lies the Jihadist appropriation and usurpation of God. The Jihadist dogma of *tawhid* leads to a dogmatic justification of murder, the prohibition of which is what defines the authority of the Holy One. Thus, true to the Salafist outlook, Sayyid Qutb holds that it is incumbent on Islam to "establish its universal aims" through war.[23] The chief enemy to be engaged in that war is the Jew, for the Jew is "the eternal enemy of

[20] See Christina Phelps Harris, *Nationalism and Revolution in Egypt: The Role of the Muslim Brotherhood* (The Hague: Mouton & Co., 1964), 112–113.

[21] See Robert A. Burns, *Christianity, Islam, and the West* (Lanham, Md.: University Press of America, 2011), 60.

[22] See Roel Meijer, ed., *Global Salafism: Islam's New Religious Movement* (New York: Columbia University Press, 2009), 4–5.

[23] Sayyid Qutb, *Social Justice in Islam*, trans. John B. Hardie (New York: Octagon Books, 1963), 167–168.

Islam."[24] As the primary means of purification, jihad is Islam's highest duty, and, as the primary source of contamination, the Jews are the first target of jihad. Therefore a Jihadist must, by definition, *fight and kill Jews in order to be righteous.*

ANTI-SEMITISM AS THE CORNERSTONE OF ISLAMIC JIHADISM

If true jihad lies in an inward struggle, then turning it outward, into a violence directed toward one's fellow human beings, is a perversion of the concept from a struggle to serve God into a struggle to kill God: in the end, killing for the sake of Allah is an act of killing Allah. As we have seen, this is the metaphysical origin of anti-Semitism, which was manifest in Islam from the beginning. "Islam's political theology," Ronald Nettler explains, "emerged in the crucible of [Muhammad's] war against the Meccans and the Jews. On the Jewish question, Islam emerged from all this with shattered expectations and an indelibly fixed notion of the Jews as a great enemy of Muslims and their god, Allah."[25] If God and His Truth are one and the same and if the Jews are falsifiers of God's truth, then the Jews are, in effect, deemed the murderers of God; thus the deicide charge made explicit in Christian theology is implicit to Islamic theology.[26] To be sure, according to the Sahih al-Bukhari (3:47:786), a Jewish woman named Zaynab bint al-Harith poisoned Muhammad; when asked whether she should be executed, the Prophet said, "No,"[27] much like Jesus who from the cross cried out, "Father forgive them, for they know not what they do" (Luke 23:34). Like many Christians, however, many Muslims did not forgive.

According to the Muslim chronicler Baladhuri (d. 892 CE), during the conquest of Palestine in the 630s, all 40,000 Jews living in Caesarea disappeared without a trace.[28] Between 789 and 791, Idris I, founder of the Idrisid dynasty, engineered the massacre of Jewish communities throughout Morocco. Under the Abbasid caliphates of Harun al-Rashid (786–809) and al-Mutawakkil (847–861), Jews and Christians were

---

[24] Nettler, *Past Trials and Present Tribulations*, 81.   [25] Ibid., 5.

[26] If one should wonder whether in Islam Muhammad enjoys a status similar to that of Jesus in Christianity, compare the Muslim reaction to the cartoons of Muhammad in Denmark's *Jyllands-Posten* with the Christian reaction to Andres Serrano's *Piss Christ*.

[27] See Robert Spencer, *The Myth of Islamic Tolerance: How Islamic Law Treats Non-Muslims* (Amherst, N.Y.: Prometheus Books, 2005), 140–141.

[28] See Bat Ye'or, *The Decline of Eastern Christianity under Islam: From Jihad to Dhimmi-tude* (Madison, N.J.: Fairleigh Dickinson University Press, 1996), 47.

required to wear yellow patches attached to their garments. In 850, consistent with Quranic verses associating the Jews with Satan and hell (e.g., 16:63), al-Mutawakkil decreed that they must attach woolen images of devils to the doors of their homes.[29] As the Muslim invasion extended across North Africa and into Spain, so did the Muslim violence against the Jews, with pogroms taking place in Fez in 1032 and 1033.[30] According to the Spanish sage Abraham ibn Daud (ca. 1110–ca. 1180), the Muslim Ibn Tumart (ca. 1080–ca. 1130), founder of the Almohad movement, waged a campaign of extermination against the North African Jews and "wiped out every last 'name and remnant' of them from all his empire."[31] Then came the decrees ordering the destruction of synagogues in Egypt and Syria (1014, 1293, and 1301), Iraq (854–859 and 1344), and Yemen (1676). Jews were often forced to convert to Islam or face death, for example, in Yemen (1165 and 1678), Morocco (1275, 1465, and 1790–1792), and Baghdad (1333 and 1344).[32] There was also the killing of five thousand Jews in Granada in 1066, as well as the Almohads' slaughter of Jewish and Christian populations in Spain and North Africa from 1130 to 1232.

The fifteenth century brought more Muslim violence against the Jews: in 1465 Arab mobs in Fez killed thousands of Jews, and thousands more suffered under the Ottoman conquests. In 1535, for example, there were mass killings and expulsions of Jews in Tunisia, and the Jews of Jerusalem endured numerous attacks between 1625 and 1627.[33] Then came Ali Burzi Pasha's massacre of hundreds of Libyan Jews in 1785, followed by the slaughter of Jews in Algeria (1805), Safed (1834, 1838), and Morocco (1859).[34] There were pogroms against the Jews in Aleppo (1853), Damascus (1848 and 1890), Cairo (1844 and 1901–1902), Alexandria (1870 and 1881), and Fez (1912). Between 1864 and 1880 more than 500 Jews were murdered in Morocco.

With the coming of modernity, drawing on certain Christian manifestations of Jew hatred came naturally to much of the Muslim world. In the previous chapter we saw the relation between the deicide charge and the blood libel, between the blood libel and the demonization of the Jews.

---

[29] Bostom, "Jihad Conquests and the Imposition of *Dhimmitude* – A Survey," 47–48.

[30] See Paul E. Grosser and Edwin G. Halpern, *Anti-Semitism: The Cause and Effects of a Prejudice* (Secaucus, N.J.: Citadel Press, 1979), 380.

[31] Abraham ibn Daud, *Sefer Ha-Qabbalah: The Book of Tradition*, trans. Gerson D. Cohen (Philadelphia: Jewish Publication Society, 1967), 88.

[32] Bat Ye'or, *The Dhimmi* (Teaneck, N.J.: Fairleigh Dickinson University Press, 1985), 61.

[33] See Grosser and Halpern, *Anti-Semitism*, 381.   [34] See ibid., 382.

The Damascus Affair of 1840, when eight of the city's Jews were accused of ritual murder on the disappearance of the Capuchin monk Father Thomas,[35] is perhaps the most infamous of the blood libels in Arab lands, but it was not the first. There had already been cases in Hama (1829), Beirut (1824), and Antioch (1826); in 1872 there was a pogrom against the Jews of Smyrna in the wake of yet another blood libel.[36] Among the supporters of Islamic Jihadism, the blood libel continues to this day. In 1962, the Egyptian Ministry of Education reissued *The Talmudic Human Sacrifices* by Habib Faris (1890), with the stated aim of demonstrating the talmudic basis for ritual murder.[37] On 24 April 1970, Fatah radio reported that the Zionists were kidnapping children from the streets to take their blood. In 1983, Syria's former Defense Minister Mustafa Tlas (b. 1932) published a book titled *The Matzo of Zion*, in which he maintained that Jews murder children to obtain blood for Passover matzo.[38] A year later, at a United Nations Human Rights Commission Conference on Religious Tolerance, Saudi representative and World Muslim Congress President Dr. Maruf al-Dawalibi (1909–2004) averred, "If a Jew does not drink every year the blood of a non-Jewish man, then he will be damned for all eternity."[39] In 2002, Dr. Umayma Ahmad al-Jalahma of King Faisal University published an article in the Saudi news-paper *Al-Riyadh* accusing the Jews of the blood libel.[40] During Ramadan 2003, Hezbollah produced a television dramatization of the blood libel, which was first aired through their Al-Manar television station.

The blood libel that the Jihadists lay on the Jews is a projection of their own deicidal thirst for blood. On 28 November 1971, Jordan's Prime Minister Wasfi al-Tal was assassinated by the Palestinian group Black September in front of Cairo's Sheraton Hotel, whereupon one of the assassins went over, bent down, and licked his victim's blood.[41] Even

---

[35] See Jonathan Frankel, *The Damascus Affair: "Ritual Murder," Politics, and the Jews in 1840* (Cambridge, U.K.: Cambridge University Press, 1997).

[36] See Wistrich, *A Lethal Obsession*, 787.

[37] See Dennis Prager and Joseph Telushkin, *Why the Jews? The Reason for Antisemitism* (New York: Simon & Schuster, 2003), 107.

[38] See Barry Rubin, *Revolution until Victory?: The Politics and History of the PLO* (Cambridge, Mass.: Harvard University Press, 1994), 125.

[39] See Bernard Lewis, *Semites and Anti-Semites: An Inquiry into Conflict and Prejudice* (New York: W. W. Norton, 1999), 194.

[40] See Kenneth R. Timmerman, *Preachers of Hate: Islam and the War on America* (New York: Three Rivers Press, 2004), 74–76.

[41] See Rubin, *Revolution until Victory?*, 37–38. Black September was formed in 1970 to avenge the Jordanian killing of several thousand Palestinians in September 1970.

more telling is the video that Hamas produced in February 2006. It was a homicide bomber's final testimony to the world, in which he declared, "My message to the loathed Jews is that there is no god but Allah [and] we will chase you everywhere! We are a nation that drinks blood, and we know that there is no blood better than the blood of Jews. We will not leave you alone until we have quenched our thirst with your blood, and our children's thirst with your blood."[42] Then there are the photographs of kindergarten children, hands raised and painted blood red, imitating the gesture of the blood-covered murderers who butchered Yossi Avrahami and Vadim Norjitz in Ramallah on 13 October 2000. Episodes such as these bring to mind a rabbinic interpretation of the meaning of *Amalek*, the tribe who attacked the children and the elders among the Israelites as they came out of Egypt. *Amalek*, it is said, means *Am Lak*, "people" who "lick" blood.[43] Whether they lick blood or dip their hands into it, the Jihadists thrive on the blood of Jews.

Although modern Islamic Jihadists include Christians or "Crusaders" among their enemies in the holy war they wage, according to Qutb, the Christians were corrupted by the Jews.[44] Whereas, the Christians are historical enemies of Islam, the Jews are metaphysical enemies, as they must be for those whose "holy war" against the Jews is against the Holy One Himself: unlike the Christians, who have been corrupted, the Jews are Satan incarnate, a theme that pervades the diatribes of modern Jihadist ideologues. Maududi, for example, refers to world Jewry as "the devil" that threatens all humanity,[45] and for Qutb the Jews are "the blackest devil and source of the worst anti-Islamic machinations."[46] Parallel to the opposition between *dar al-Islam* and the *dar al-harb*, the "realm of Islam" and the "realm of war," says Qutb, is the distinction between *hizb Allah*, or "Party of Allah," and the *hizb al-shaytan*, or "Party of Satan."[47] The universal threat to the house of Islam and the

[42] Itamar Marcus and Barbara Cook, "Hamas Video: 'We will drink the blood of the Jews,'" *Palestine Media Watch*, 14 February 2006, available at http://www.pmw.org.il/latest%20bulletins%20new.htm#b140206.

[43] See Moshe Weissman, ed., *The Midrash Says*, vol. 2 (Brooklyn: Bnay Yakov Publications, 1980), 158.

[44] Sayyid Qutb, *Basic Principles of the Islamic Worldview*, trans. Rami David (North Haledon, N.J.: Islamic Publications International, 2006), 27.

[45] Abdul Al'a Maududi, *Selected Speeches and Writings*, vol. 2, trans. S. Zakir Aijaz (Karachi: International Islamic Publishers, 1981), 62–63.

[46] Quoted in Nettler, *Past Trials and Present Tribulations*, 28.

[47] Quoted in Ahmad S. Moussalli, *Radical Islamic Fundamentalism: The Ideological and Political Discourse of Sayyid Qutb* (Beirut: American University of Beirut, 1992), 168.

Party of Allah is the satanic evil of the Jews and Judaism. Nettler comments on the significance of Qutb's assertion, saying that from Qutb's

> judicious use of ancient sources applied imaginatively to contemporary crises, there arose familiar ideas: the Jews as inherently decadent and anti-religious; the Jews as being driven by an obsessive urge to destroy the only true religion, Islam; the Jews as the organizers and agents of the Western political threat to Islam; the Jews as the main purveyors of the cultural Westernization which has so damaged Islam; the Jews as the modern "Hypocrites" continuing the work of their ancient predecessors; and the Jews as the power behind the Westernizing "Muslim" politicians. The monstrous evil exemplifying these specific Jewish evils was the Jewish Satan of Zionism and Israel.[48]

The notion of the "Jewish Satan of Zionism" is examined in detail in Chapter 7. For now, it should be noted that the Jihadist politico-theologians, who from Maududi to Qutb demonized the Jews, have their successors.

In 1974, for example, Abd al-Halim Mahmoud (1910–1978), the Grand Imam of Al-Azhar University from 1973 to 1978, published *Holy War and Victory*, in which he portrayed the struggle against the Jews as a struggle against Satan. It was he who stated, "Allah commands Muslims to fight the friends of Satan wherever they may be found. And among Satan's friends – indeed, his best friends in our age – are the Jews."[49] Then we have Hassan Nasrallah (b. 1960), the leader of Hezbollah, who insists that Muslims are obligated "to use *any means at their disposal*" to kill Jews.[50] They are "behind all evil," he would later reiterate.[51] Which means: the Jews are a mortal threat not only to the body *but also to the soul* of humanity – hence the metaphysical nature of the Jewish contagion and hence the politico-theological manifestation of the metaphysical origin of anti-Semitism.

In the Introduction it was noted that, according to Jewish tradition, the assertion "I am God" means "Thou shalt not murder," to which the actions of the Jihadist seem to retort, "No, *I* am God. And I command the faithful to murder." In reply to the God who chose the Jewish people to be a light unto the nations and commanded them to thus "choose life" (Deuteronomy 30:19) – a light that forbids murder – the Jihadists choose

---

[48] Nettler, *Past Trials and Present Tribulations*, 69.   [49] Quoted in ibid., 18–19.
[50] Hassan Nasrallah, *Voice of Hezbollah: The Statements of Sayyed Hassan Nasrallah*, ed. Nicholas Noe, trans. Ellen Khouri (London: Verso, 2007), 231; emphasis added.
[51] Ibid., 295.

the Jewish people for extermination, thus extinguishing such a light for the sake of their own dark aim of dominating humanity and usurping divinity. The most profound way to effect such a transformation is to ritualize murder, and the morphing of murder into martyrdom is the highest expression of ritualized murder, the very thing of which the usurpers of God accuse the Jews. In most sacred traditions martyrdom is not a commodity for which martyrs expect due compensation – it is a summons from on high to which they respond, often against their will. The true martyrs of many traditions choose martyrdom not by committing murder but *instead of* committing murder. Whereas in Jewish tradition, as in other traditions, martyrdom means dying in a refusal to commit murder and thus to sanctify life and the Creator of life (see *Talmud Bavli, Sanhedrin* 74a), in Jihadist teaching it means dying precisely in order to commit murder for the glorification of God. But Jihadist "martyrs" neither glorify God nor sanctify life. No, they glorify an ego made into Allah and thereby sanctify murder by perverting it into martyrdom; in the process they pass both the children of the Jews and their own children through fire – there lies the evil of Islamic Jihadism. The morass that has spawned most of today's Jihadist movements is the Muslim Brotherhood.

THE MUSLIM BROTHERHOOD

In his memoirs, Hasan al-Banna recalls the founding of the Muslim Brotherhood in March 1928 by saying, "We determined in solemn oath that we shall live as brethren, work for the glory of Islam and launch *Jihad* for it."[52] A major source of his inspiration was not only the purist movement of Salafism but also National Socialism. Proof of the Nazi influence on al-Banna can be found in a report issued by the British Political Intelligence Centre Middle East, which found that al-Banna had "made a careful study of the Nazi and Fascist organizations. Using them as a model, he has formed organizations of specially trained and trusted men who correspond respectively to the Brown Shirts and Black Shirts."[53] J. E. Jacobs from the American Embassy in Cairo also had

---

[52] Hasan al-Banna, *Memoirs of Hasan al Banna Shahid*, trans. M. N. Shaikh (Karachi: International Islamic Publishers, 1981), 142.
[53] Jeffrey Herf, *Nazi Propaganda for the Arab World* (New Haven, Conn.: Yale University Press, 2009), 225.

similar findings about the Brotherhood.[54] Al-Banna professed his admiration for Hitler[55] as well as for the Nazis' method of inciting hatred of the
Jews through the use of propaganda.[56] One understands why the Brotherhood distributed Arabic translations of *Mein Kampf* and the *Protocols
of the Elders of Zion* at the Parliamentary Conference for Arab and
Muslim Countries held in Cairo in October 1938.[57] Pressing for a return
to Muslim religious law, or Sharia, as the law governing all humanity,
al-Banna sought a theocratic totalitarianism that was essentially anti-
Judaic, as any such attempt to be godlike must be. He understood the
purification of Islam led by the Brotherhood to be a return to the rule of
the Caliphate,[58] and he admired the Caliphate because it "warred against
guileful Judaism" and "struggled against Christianity," the two main
sources of the defilement of Islam and the world.[59] Judaism was, of
course, the worse of the two, because it is the source of Christianity's
contamination.

Jihad, he maintained, was the only means of purifying the world of the
contagion of Judaism. Therefore "God," he declares, usurping the seat of
divine judgment, "has imposed *jihad* as a religious duty on every Muslim,
categorically and rigorously, from which there is neither evasion nor
escape. . . .. He regards abstention and evasion of *jihad* as one of the major
sins, and one of the seven mortal sins that guarantee annihilation."[60]
Either you take up arms in service to the hatred that drives Jihadism,
beginning with Jew hatred, or you are destined for the Fire. The more
mercilessly you kill, the more mercy you earn and the greater your
reward: in the Quran, al-Banna points out, "Forgiveness" and "Mercy"
are "associated with slaying and death."[61] Thus "a good man," he
affirms, "takes delight in launching *Jihad*,"[62] that is, takes delight in
indiscriminate murder for the sake of Allah and Islam, beginning,
again, with the murder of Jews. Yes: a *good* man, one who embraces
the "Word of the Truth."[63] What sanctifies the "Word of the Truth"

---

[54] Ibid., 226.   [55] See, e.g., al-Banna, *Five Tracts of Hasan al-Banna*, 97.
[56] Ibid., 45–46.
[57] Matthias Küntzel, *Jihad and Jew-Hatred: Islamism, Nazism and the Roots of 9/11*, trans.
Colin Meade (New York: Telos Press, 2007), 25.
[58] Charles Wendell, Introduction to Hasan al-Banna, *Five Tracts of Hasan al-Banna:
A Selection from the Majmuat Rasail al-Imam al-Shahid Hasan al-Banna*, trans. Charles
Wendell (Berkeley: University of California Press, 1978), 3.
[59] Al-Banna, *Five Tracts of Hasan al-Banna*, 17.   [60] Ibid., 133.
[61] Ibid., 134.   [62] Al-Banna, *Memoirs of Hasan al Banna Shahid*, 117
[63] See al-Banna, *Five Tracts of Hasan al-Banna*, 93.

is not the wisdom of the sages but the "blood of martyrs,"[64] so that the more blood is spilled, the more truth is justified.

Within a few years of the assassination of al-Banna, on 12 February 1949, Sayyid Qutb emerged as the Muslim Brotherhood's most influential ideologue. A turning point in his outlook came in 1948, when he traveled to the United States to earn a master's degree from Wilson Teacher's College (now the University of the District of Columbia). When he returned to Egypt in 1951 he officially joined the Brotherhood, and by 1953 he was appointed editor-in-chief of the weekly newspaper *The Muslim Brotherhood*. He was arrested, however, after Gamal Abdul Nasser (1918–1970) banned the Brotherhood in January 1954. He spent ten of the next twelve years in prison, until his execution on 29 August 1966. Like al-Banna, Qutb equated the authority of Islam with the divine authority, which wields power over "every aspect of life"[65] and "extends into all aspects of life; it discusses all minor or major affairs of mankind; it orders man's life – not only in this world but *also in the world to come*."[66] During his time in prison he wrote one of his most influential books, *Maalim fi al-Tariq* (Milestones), a work in which he declares, "Wherever an Islamic community exists which is a concrete example of the Divinely-ordained system of life, it has a God-given right to step forward and take control of the political authority so that it may establish the Divine system on earth."[67] He advocates jihad against all non-Muslim countries, since what they pass off as freedom grounded in responsibility is nothing but slavery to sensuality and self-interest, both of which are born of corruption from the Jews.[68] The uppermost aim of jihad, declares Qutb, is "to abolish all the Satanic forces and Satanic systems of life,"[69] which is to say, all forces and systems of life that are not Islamic, beginning with the Jews and Judaism. Why? Because by their very presence in the world, the Jews and their traditions undermine the equation of the human project with divine authority.

Qutb's "main principle," Nettler explains, "was that of the Jews as First Cause – First Cause of resistance to Islam's Truth in its early quest for fulfillment."[70] Here the Jewish Question is far more than a Zionist Question – it goes to the question of human sanctity and divine authority:

---

[64] Ibid., 115. [65] Qutb, *Social Justice in Islam*, 98.
[66] Sayyid Qutb, *Ma'alim fi al-tariq (Milestones)*, 13th legal ed. (Cairo: Dar al-Da'wa, 1989), 32; emphasis added. [67] Ibid., 76.
[68] Ibid., 7; see also Qutb, *Social Justice in Islam*, 235. [69] Ibid., 70.
[70] Nettler, *Past Trials and Present Tribulations*, 28.

it is a metaphysical question that opens up the metaphysical origins of anti-Semitism. As corruptors of the law and the teachings of Allah, "the Children of Israel, both before and after Moses, tarnished and perverted his message."[71] The Jews, then, are the *essential* evil that plagues humanity, and the solution to the eradication of this evil is Islam: "The war that the Jews have launched against Islam," Qutb writes, "has been much longer lasting and wider in spectrum than that launched against it by pagans and unbelievers both in old and modern times.... Theirs is a wicked nature which is full of hatred for Islam, its Prophet and its followers.... Our modern world will not be saved from this wicked nature except by Islam."[72] And there can be no rehabilitation of a "wicked nature": it must be eradicated. By 1950, Qutb had already written a brief but vitriolic diatribe against the Jews that would ultimately enjoy massive circulation; it was titled *Ma'rakatuna Ma'a al-Yahud* (Our Struggle with the Jews). Jeffrey Herf compares this work to *Mein Kampf*, noting, "Whereas the Nazis depicted Jewry as obsessed with plans to destroy Germany, Qutb ... presented the Jews as preoccupied with an effort to destroy Islam. Whereas Nazism attacked the Jews for undermining the values of the nation, ... Qutb saw Jews as agents of confusion and doubt about religious belief. Where Nazis appealed to the authority of ... Hitler, ... Qutb evoked the even more unshakable authority of the Koran and Allah himself."[73] These parallels between Qutb's manifesto and Hitler's hardly seem coincidental.

The three themes that run throughout "Our Struggle with the Jews" are (1) the Jewish goal of Islam's destruction, (2) the evil essence of the Jews, and (3) the balance of power in this situation. In the last two one can see a repetition of some of the themes of *Mein Kampf*. Turning to history, as Hitler often does in his manifesto, Qutb invokes the Muslims' enmity with the Jewish tribe Banu Qurayzah, pointing out that "the Jews have confronted Islam with enmity from the moment that the Islamic state was established in Medina"; therefore the Jews are "the eternal enemy of Islam."[74] Like Hitler and many others, Qutb promulgated the "world Jewish conspiracy" calumny, citing the Jews' passion to control others as a "driving force in their national character."[75] Like Hitler, he argued

---

[71] Sayyid Qutb, *Basic Principles of the Islamic Worldview*, trans. Rami David, preface by Hamid Algar (North Haledon, N.J.: Islamic Publications International, 2006), 207.
[72] Qutb, *In the Shade of the Quran*, 220–221.
[73] Herf, *Nazi Propaganda for the Arab World*, 256.
[74] Quoted in Nettler, *Past Trials and Present Tribulations*, 81.   [75] Ibid., 37–38.

that Zionism was not about the creation of a Jewish haven or homeland but rather was the first move toward the Jews' conquest of the world.[76] Like Hitler, he viewed Zionism and Marxism as part of the same conspiracy.[77] Thus, like Hitler, Qutb played on the fear of an invisible, insidious, and ubiquitous evil that preys on the body and soul of all humanity. And, like Hitler, he provides the key to the salvation and liberation of humankind: the exterminationist program of jihad and the universal rule of Islam.

Today "the Muslim Brotherhood is the largest of the Islamic groups, both in numbers and in influence," writes Islamist scholar Ziad Abu-Amr. "These groups make no distinction between religion and state and consider the Koran and the *sunna* as the basis for all aspects of life."[78] The collapse of distinctions between religion and state reflects the collapse of distinctions between God and man in the Jihadists' appropriation of God. As always, the appropriation of God demands the elimination of the chosen of God, that is, of those first chosen to bring to the world God's message that every human being is chosen for an absolute responsibility to and for the other. The key to the Muslim Brotherhood's assault on the Holy One, then, is their assault on the Jews, so that "the history of the Muslim Brothers," as Matthias Küntzel has demonstrated, "shows that revolutionary antisemitism is no mere supplementary feature of modern jihadism; it is its core."[79] The truth of this statement, as well as the metaphysical origin of the anti-Semitism that defines Islamic Jihadism, can be seen in the ideologues and the movements spawned by the Brotherhood.

THE PROLIFERATION OF ISLAMIC JIHADIST JEW HATRED

When Haj Amin al-Husseini turned up in Egypt on 20 June 1946 after having been on the run as a Nazi war criminal, Hasan al-Banna and Sayyid Qutb greeted him with open arms, thus sealing his association with the Muslim Brotherhood.[80] Known as "Hitler's Grossmufti" ever since their meeting in Berlin on 28 November 1941, he had the Führer's

---

[76] Ibid., 49. Qutb's Saudi editor underscores this point with reference to the *Protocols of the Elders of Zion*.

[77] Qutb, "Our Struggle with the Jews," 84.

[78] Ziad Abu-Amr, *Islamic Fundamentalism in the West Bank and Gaza: Muslim Brotherhood and Islamic Jihad* (Bloomington: Indiana University Press, 1994), xiv.

[79] Küntzel, *Jihad and Jew-Hatred*, 59.

[80] See Herf, *Nazi Propaganda for the Arab World*, 242–244.

assurance that the Nazis and the Arabs were engaged in the same struggle, namely, the struggle to exterminate the Jews.[81] Indeed, at a war crimes trial on 26 July 1946 Adolf Eichmann's deputy Dieter Wisliceny testified that "the Mufti was one of the initiators of the systematic extermination of European Jewry and had been a collaborator and advisor of Eichmann and Himmler in the execution of this plan."[82] Al-Husseini had at his disposal six radio stations, from which he issued regular Arabic-language broadcasts inciting Muslims with cries of "Kill the Jews wherever you find them. This pleases God, history and religion. This saves your honor. God is with you."[83] He recruited Muslims to serve in SS killing units, the most infamous of which was the Handschar Division of 21,065 men.[84] Other Muslim SS killing units included the Skanderbeg Division in Albania and the Arabisches Freiheitskorps in Macedonia. All of them played a major role in rendering the Balkans *Judenrein* in the winter of 1943–1944.

Soon after getting situated in Egypt, al-Husseini brought his distant relative Yasser Arafat (1929–2004) to Egypt for training in the Brother-hood; Arafat would go on to become the founder of the Jihadist organiza-tion Fatah in 1959 and the leader of the Palestine Liberation Organization in 1969. The PLO gained renown worldwide in 1972, when their Black September terrorists murdered eleven Israeli athletes at the Olympic Games in Munich, whereupon Arafat declared that every Jew everywhere – *every Jew* – is a target.[85] From the time of the founding of Fatah, Arafat continually proclaimed, "The end of Israel is the goal of our struggle.... Peace for us means the destruction of Israel and nothing else."[86] Following the U.N.'s welcoming the PLO as the representative of the Palestinians in 1974 (Resolution 3236), PLO chief Salah Khalaf asserted, "An independ-ent state on the West Bank and Gaza is the beginning of the final solution,"[87] obviously imitating the Nazi discourse that informed the PLO's Jihadist outlook. Like the Nazis and echoing Qutb, Arafat deemed the Jews "dogs. Filth and dirt," adding that "treachery flows in their

---

[81] Joseph B. Schechtman, *The Mufti and the Fuehrer: The Rise and Fall of Haj Amin el-Husseini* (New York: Thomas Yoseloff, 1965), 306.

[82] Ibid., 160.

[83] Quoted in Chuck Morse, *The Nazi Connection to Islamic Terrorism* (New York: iUni-verse, 2003), 62.

[84] David G. Dalin and John F. Rothman, *Icon of Evil: Hitler's Mufti and the Rise of Radical Islam* (New York: Random House, 2008), 55.

[85] Quoted Laurent Murawiec, *The Mind of Jihad* (Cambridge: Cambridge University Press, 2008), 34.

[86] Ibid., 41.   [87] Quoted in Rubin, *Revolution until Victory?*, 47.

blood, as the Quran testifies."[88] In 1994, then, it was no surprise that he appointed Ikrima Sabri Mufti of Jerusalem, a man who denounced the Jews as "descendants of pigs and apes," accusing of them of involvement in the "world Zionist conspiracy" and blaming them for every ill that has befallen humanity.[89] When his health began to fail Arafat appointed Holocaust denier and avowed anti-Semite Mahmoud Abbas the new Palestinian prime minister on 13 March 2003.

One of the key outside figures to establish connections with the Muslim Brotherhood early on was Muhammad Navab-Safavi (1924–1955), an Iranian Jihadist in exile who lived in Cairo during the 1930s. In 1937, both he and Ruhullah Khomeini (1902–1989), already an avid reader of al-Banna's writings, met the Brotherhood's leader.[90] Two years later Navab-Safavi became Khomeini's tutor.[91] Khomeini went on to translate several volumes of Sayyid Qutb's eight-volume work *Fi Zilal al-Quran* (In the Shade of the Quran, 1952) into Persian.[92] For good reason the Qutbists are often referred to as "Egyptian Khomeinists."[93] Between 21 January and 8 February 1970, Khomeini gave a series of lectures that would comprise his notorious work *Islamic Government*. One theme that runs through his volume is that the Jews are the source of the corruption that has pervaded Islam.[94] In that work Khomeini declares, "Islam contains everything. Islam includes everything. Islam is everything."[95] In a word, Islam is godlike. Islamic government, Khomeini maintains, must be rooted in the hadith,[96] and *"there is no place for doubting"* the hadith.[97] He further argues that in Islamic government the power of legislation is confined to God and that no one may rule who has not been given that power by God.[98] Who determines which of the leaders has been given such divine authority? At the time it was Khomeini himself, who just happened to be God's chosen Supreme Guide.

Modeled after the Jihadist anti-Semitism of the Muslim Brotherhood, the Islamic Revolution in Iran was a Jihadist revolution that resulted in the establishment of the first Jihadist state in February 1979, with the

---

[88] Ibid., 180.   [89] Ibid., 103–104.   [90] Murawiec, *The Mind of Jihad*, 40.
[91] Ibid., 41.
[92] Ahmad S. Moussalli, *Radical Islamic Fundamentalism: The Ideological and Political Discourse of Sayyid Qutb* (Beirut: American University of Beirut, 1992), 48.
[93] Amir Taheri, *Holy Terror: Inside the World of Islamic Terrorism* (Bethesda, Md.: Adler & Adler, 1987), 187–188.
[94] Baqer Moin, *Khomeini: Life of the Ayatollah* (New York: St. Martin's Press, 1999), 154.
[95] Ruhullah Khomeini, *Islamic Government* (New York: Manor Books, 1979), 2.
[96] Ibid., 28.   [97] Ibid., 47, emphasis added.   [98] Ibid., 31.

Ayatollah Khomeini as its supreme leader. In a speech he gave in Bihisht-i Zahra on 2 February 1979 he declared, "The government I intend to appoint is a government based on divine ordinance, and to oppose it is to deny God."[99] This ascendancy to the seat of the Judge of the World demands the elimination of the Jews from the world, as Khomeini well understood. To be sure, in *Islamic Government* he justifies the extermination of the Jews by invoking Muhammad himself, pointing out that the Prophet "annihilated the Banu Qurayzah Jews to the last man because of the harm he realized they were causing the Moslem society, his government and all the people."[100] Repeating the diatribes of Sayyid Qutb, elsewhere he writes, "From the very beginning, the historical movement of Islam has had to contend with the Jews, for it was they who first established anti-Islamic propaganda."[101] Indeed, the Jew is "the enemy not only of Islam but of all humanity,"[102] an absolute evil that must be annihilated as a matter of *religious duty.*[103] Therefore the imperative to murder the Jews is prior to context and circumstance; it is rooted in a metaphysical principle and not in an ontological contingency, such as racism, ethnocentrism, or politics.

Because the Jew must be eliminated, if Islam is to embody the will of God on earth, Khomeini's confidant Ayatollah Sadeq Khalkhali (1927–2003) once declared, "Those who are against killing have no place in Islam."[104] Indeed, Khomeini's teacher Navab-Safavi once asserted, "Killing is tantamount to saying a prayer."[105] If, according to the Jihadists, having a place in Islam requires killing, then having a place in paradise requires killing. In this precept, which undermines the prohibition against murder, we see a fundamental expression of the Jihadist evil. To be sure, among Khomeini's most infamous statements is this: "Islam says: Whatever good there is exists thanks to the sword and in the shadow of the sword!... The sword is the key to paradise, which can be opened only for holy warriors!"[106] And the primary target on the other end of the sword is the Jew: kill a Jew and go to heaven. When the priests of Europe made such a proclamation during the Second Crusade, Bernard of Clairvaux (1090–1153) voiced his objection; among the

---

[99] Ruhullah Khomeini, *Islam and Revolution: Writings and Declarations of Imam Khomeini (1941–1980)*, trans. Hamid Algar (Berkeley, Calif.: Mizan Press, 1981), 259.
[100] Khomeini, *Islamic Government*, 66.   [101] Khomeini, *Islam and Revolution*, 27.
[102] Ibid., 195   [103] Ibid., 276.   [104] Quoted in Taheri, *Holy Terror*, 44.
[105] Quoted in Lawrence Wright, *The Looming Tower: Al-Qaeda and the Road to 9/11* (New York: Alfred A. Knopf, 2006), 32.
[106] Ibid., 47.

Jihadists, by contrast, there is no such voice.[107] For "the very fact of being born Jewish," Khomeini taught, "makes one an 'enemy of Islam,'"[108] thus placing the Jew in a metaphysical category and thereby eliminating all possibility of redemption for the Jew.

An insidious offshoot of the Islamic Revolution is Hezbollah, the Party of Allah. According to Naim Qassem, Deputy Secretary General of Hezbollah, the Party of Allah emerged from the activities of three Iranian clerics: Imam Mussa al-Sadr (1929–1978), Ayatollah Muhammad Mahdi Shamseddine (1936–2001), and Ayatollah al-Sayyed Muhammad Hussein Fadlallah (b. 1935).[109] Al-Sadr is the author of the infamous Hezbollah slogan "Israel is an utter evil."[110] Indicative of the Jihadist appropriation of God is Hezbollah's "theoretical booklet" *Rah e Ma* (Our Party), published in Tehran in 1982, which declares that the Party of God "is a way of life, an 'army of civilians,' a semi-secret fraternity, and, last but not least, a 'clearinghouse for mankind,' where those who will be admitted into paradise are separated from those destined for hell."[111] Whereas, Allah had once been the one to decide who will be redeemed and who will be damned, that prerogative now falls to the Party of Allah, to Hezbollah, thus rendering Allah superfluous: Allah and Hezbollah are one and the same.

On 16 February 1985, "Sheik Ibrahim al-Amin publicly declared the group's manifesto, which included three goals: the eradication of Western imperialism in Lebanon, the transformation of Lebanon's multi-confessional state into an Islamic state, and the complete destruction of the state of Israel."[112] To be sure, Qassem identifies the annihilation of the Jews as one of the three pillars of the Party of God.[113] Thus "our struggle will end," it is written in "The Hezbollah Program," "only when this entity [the Jewish State] is obliterated. We recognize no treaty with it, no cease fire, and no peace agreements, whether separate or consolidated. We vigorously condemn all plans for negotiation with

[107] Dan Cohn-Sherbok, *Anti-Semitism* (Stroud, U.K.: The History Press, 2002), 65.
[108] Wright, *The Looming Tower*, 150–151.
[109] See Naim Qassem, *Hizbollah: The Story from Within*, trans. Dalia Khalil (London: SAQI, 200), 14–16.
[110] Ibid., 15.   [111] Ibid., 87.
[112] Dimitry Kapustyan and Matt Nelson, *The Soul of Terror: The Worldwide Conflict between Islamic Terrorism and the Modern World* (Washington, D.C.: International Affairs Press, 2007), 89.
[113] Qassem, *Hizbollah*, 19; the other two pillars are Islam and the principle of one-man rule of the Party.

Israel, and regard all negotiators as enemies."[114] More than viewing jihad as a war against the infidels, Hezbollah views jihad chiefly as a war against the Jews.

The current head of Hezbollah, Hassan Nasrallah, has been Secretary General since 1992. In a speech delivered on 13 September 1997 he made it clear that the Jihadist enemy is not the state of Israel but the Jew: "If we search the entire globe for a more cowardly, lowly, weak, and frail individual in his spirit, mind, ideology, and religion, we will never find anyone like the Jew – and I am not saying the Israeli."[115] Choosing the Jew as the designated target, Hezbollah makes no distinction between military and civilian targets, both in Israel and elsewhere. According to Qassem, in fact, targeting civilians is a "prime directive" for Hezbollah.[116] More than a political directive, the battle against "the Jewish cancer" is commanded from on high: "Anyone who reads [the Quran] cannot think of co-existence with them [the Jews], of peace with them, or about accepting their presence."[117] Far more than a source of deadly contagion, the Jews are "satanic," Nasrallah insisted in an interview on 21 June 1999.[118] They are "behind all evil," he would later reiterate.[119] Which means: the Jews are a mortal threat not only to the body *but also to the soul* of humanity. Hence the metaphysical nature of the Jewish evil – and the metaphysical origin of the Jihadist Jew hatred: the hatred of what is deemed a threat to the soul stems from the soul.

A Jihadist organization that explicitly identifies itself as part of the Muslim Brotherhood is the Islamic Resistance Movement (Harakat al-Muqawama al-Islamiya), more widely known by its acronym Hamas; it was founded on 9 December 1987 by Sheikh Ahmed Yassin (1937–2004) and his comrades.[120] After his assassination on 22 March 2004 Yassin was followed by Abdel Aziz al-Rantisi, who met the same fate on 18 April 2004; Rantisi was succeeded by Khalid Mashal, the current head of Hamas. Hamas embraces the Brotherhood's position that the Jews are "the dirtiest and meanest of all races" and makes

---

[114] "The Hizballah Program," *The Jerusalem Quarterly*, No. 48 (Fall 1988), available at http://peacebuffs.com/index.php?page=hezbollah-charter.

[115] Nasrallah, *Voice of Hezbollah*, 171.   [116] Qassem, *Hizbollah*, 74.

[117] Quoted in Andrew G. Bostom, ed., *The Legacy of Islamic Antisemitism: From Sacred Texts to Solemn History* (Amherst, N.Y.: Prometheus Books, 2008), 682.

[118] Ibid., 196.   [119] Ibid., 295.

[120] See Zaki Chehab, *Inside Hamas: The Untold Story of the Militant Islamic Movement* (New York: Nation Books, 2007), 25.

"no distinctions between Jews, Zionists, and Israelis."[121] As always, where the Jew is the enemy, Judaism is the enemy. Beverley Milton-Edwards further notes the modern nature of Hamas's animosity toward Jews and Judaism: "While Hamas, like other modern-day Islamic Jihadists, has developed its argument on the Jewish question by relying on Qur'anic and other Islamic sources, it also ... [borrows] from such classical Western anti-Semitic sources as *The Protocols of the Elders of Zion*."[122] Distinctively modern, and not a throwback to a medieval mindset, Hamas represents an *exterminationist* manifestation of anti-Semitism, which informs the very core of their worldview. Therefore, for Islamic Jihadists, Jew hatred is a *metaphysical* category, a first principle, that defines the essence of their thinking. And this metaphysical nature of their anti-Semitism stems from anti-Semitism's metaphysical origin.

Nowhere is the Jihadist usurpation of God more evident than in the charter of Hamas, which is called "The Charter of Allah": Hamas *is* Allah.[123] The charter's preamble opens with a quote from Hasan al-Banna: "Israel will exist and will continue to exist until Islam will obliterate it," where Israel is a reference to the Jewish people, not to the Jewish state. The al-Bukhari hadith, no. 3,593, cited in Article Seven of the charter, affirms the eschatological and therefore the metaphysical essence of this guiding principle: "The Prophet, Allah bless him and grant him salvation, has said: 'The Day of Judgment will not come about until Moslems fight the Jews (killing the Jews), when the Jew will hide behind stones and trees. The stones and trees will say, 'O Moslems, O Abdulla, there is a Jew behind me, come and kill him.'" Nature itself rebels against the existence of the Jews: natural law, therefore, requires the eradication of the Jews. This ultimate aim brings Hamas into harmony with "the laws of the universe" and defines its place "in the stream of destiny" (Article Thirty-three), and, in accordance with the will of Allah, which shapes human destiny and natural law, the Jews must be exterminated. To ask a Muslim to negotiate peace with the Jews is to ask him to renounce Islam, so that "there is no solution for the Palestinian question except through

---

[121] Abu-Amr, *Islamic Fundamentalism in the West Bank and Gaza*, 26.
[122] Beverley Milton-Edwards, *Islamic Politics in Palestine* (London: I. B. Tauris, 1999), 188.
[123] For the complete text of the charter, see "The Covenant of the Islamic Resistance Movement (HAMAS)," *Jewish Virtual Library*, available at http://www.jewishvirtuallibrary.org/jsource/Terrorism/Hamas_covenant_complete.html; see also Kapustyan and Nelson, *The Soul of Terror*, 122–151; Yonah Alexander, *Palestinian Religious Terrorism: Hamas and Islamic Jihad* (Ardsley, N.Y.: Transnational Publishers, 2002), 47–69.

Jihad" (Article Thirteen). Thus Article Fifteen ends with the refrain: "I will assault and kill, assault and kill, assault and kill." Article Eighteen affirms that Muslim children must be indoctrinated for this task of "martyrdom," which means murdering Jews in suicide attacks. Once again we see that, like the ancient idolaters against whom God warned the Israelites (see, e.g., Deuteronomy 18:10), those who would exterminate the Jews pass their children through fire and worse: making their children into sacrificial offerings consumed by the flames of their bombs, they transform them into murderers.

Like all anti-Semites, Hamas invokes the metaphysical nature of the evil embodied by the Jew only to expose the metaphysical aspect of its own evil. Article Twenty-two of the charter states:

With their money, they [the Jews] took control of the world media, news agencies, the press, publishing houses, broadcasting stations, and others. With their money they stirred revolutions in various parts of the world.... They were behind the French Revolution, the Communist revolution and most of the revolutions.... With their money they were able to control imperialistic countries and instigate them to colonize many countries in order to enable them to exploit their resources and spread corruption.... They were behind World War I.... They obtained the Balfour Declaration, formed the League of Nations through which they could rule the world. They were behind World War II.... It was they who instigated the replacement of the League of Nations with the United Nations and the Security Council to enable them to rule the world through them. There is no war going on anywhere, without having their finger in it.

In a word, the Jews are the hidden source of every evil, and Hamas is the salvation of humanity. Therefore, declares Article Twenty-eight, "The Zionist invasion [of the world] is a vicious invasion. It does not refrain from resorting to all methods, using *all evil* and contemptible ways to achieve its end.... They aim at undermining societies, *destroying values*, corrupting consciences, *deteriorating character* and annihilating Islam. It is behind the drug trade and alcoholism in all its kinds so as to facilitate its control and expansion.... *Israel, Judaism and Jews* challenge Islam and the Moslem people" (emphasis added). Here too we see the metaphysical dimensions of the Jihadists' anti-Semitic assault on Jews and Judaism, both of which they associate with evil *as such*: hence, in a departure from traditional Islam but in keeping with Qutb,[124] the Jews *cannot be rehabilitated*; they fall outside the circle of redemption. Another

---

[124] See quotes of Qutb in Nettler, *Past Trials and Present Tribulations*, 35–44.

important departure from traditional Islam can be found in Article Thirty-two, where Hamas invokes not the Quran or the hadith but the *Protocols of the Elders of Zion* as proof that the aim of the Jews is to dominate the entire world: they are the Jihadists' chief competitors in the aspiration to unseat God and ascend to the throne of creation.

Hamas is not the only outgrowth of the Muslim Brotherhood, however, whose hatred of the Jews is tied to an aspiration to world domination. Rohan Gunaratna describes al-Qaeda as "the natural offshoot of the Muslim Brotherhood."[125] More a network than a group, al-Qaeda was founded on 20 August 1988 under the leadership of Muslim Brotherhood members Abdullah Azzam, Ayman al-Zawahiri, and Osama bin Laden.[126] Their stated goals are "(1) establishing the rule of God on earth, (2) attaining martyrdom in the cause of God, and (3) purification of the ranks of Islam from the elements of depravity," where the Jews are the primary source of depravity.[127] "The enmity between us and the Jews," bin Laden stated in 1998, "goes back far in time and is deeply rooted. . . . The Hour of Resurrection shall not come before the Muslims fight the Jews."[128] More than bin Laden, however, Azzam laid the ideological foundations for al-Qaeda as a jihadist network. "The word Jihad," he insists, "only means combat with weapons."[129] Therefore "every Muslim who passes away without a gun in his hand faces Allah with the sin of abandoning fighting."[130] For Azzam, as for all Islamic Jihadists, Islam is more about shedding blood than bleeding, more about appropriating God than serving God. In his most famous work, *Al-Defaa aan Ardh al-Muslimeen aham furood al-ayaan* (Defense of the Muslim Lands, 1987), Azzam asserts, "If only the Muslims would apply their Lord's command [to jihad] and implement the laws of their *Shariah* concerning the General March for just one week in Palestine, Palestine would be completely purified of Jews."[131] The language of purification is clearly in line with the modern exterminationist anti-Semitism that portrays the Jews as a contagion.

---

[125] Rohan Gunaratna, *Inside Al Qaeda: Global Network of Terror* (New York: Columbia University Press, 2002), 96.

[126] Wright, *The Looming Tower*, 133. [127] Ibid., 302.

[128] Küntzel, *Jihad and Jew Hatred*, xxi.

[129] Quoted in Aaron, *In Their Own Words*, 68.

[130] Quoted in Cook, *Understanding Jihad*, 130.

[131] Abdullah Azzam, *Defense of the Muslim Lands: First Obligation after Iman*, trans. Brothers in Ribat, available at http://www.ayyaz.com.pk/Books/Shaykh.Abdullah .Azzam/Defence.of.the.Muslim.Lands.-.the.First.Obligation.After.Iman.pdf, 36.

Since the assassination of Azzam on 24 November 1989, Ayman al-Zawahiri has been widely considered al-Qaeda's principal ideo-logue.[132] When Sayyid Qutb was executed in 1966, al-Zawahiri vowed to put his vision into action.[133] He points out, for example, that Qutb "greatly helped the Islamic movement to know and define its enemies,"[134] as, for example, in "Our Struggle with the Jews." After serving three years in prison for his role in the murder of Anwar Sadat in 1981, al-Zawahiri traveled first to Jedda and then to Peshawar, where he met Abdullah Azzam and Osama bin Laden.[135] By that time he had thoroughly studied the works of Ruhullah Khomeini and the strategies of the Islamic Revo-lution in Iran. In 1990 he returned to Egypt, where he led the Egyptian Islamic Jihad in a series of terrorist actions. He rejoined bin Laden in 1998, at which time he merged the Egyptian Islamic Jihad with al-Qaeda.[136] On 23 February of that year he and bin Laden put their names to a fatwa that in all likelihood al-Zawahiri himself had written; it was called "World Islamic Front against Jews and Crusaders." In keeping with his Jihadist anti-Semitism, al-Zawahiri asserts that the hatred of Israel "in the hearts of Islamists is genuine and indivisible."[137] Not only does "the global Jewish government" control the United States,[138] the Jews manipulate the "propaganda tools" throughout the West.[139] Thus they corrupt the West, so that "the West ... does not know the language of ethics, morality, and legitimate rights."[140] The Jews, in short, are a cosmological, metaphysical enemy.

As for Osama bin Laden, his induction into the worldview of the Brotherhood dates back to his studies at King Abdul University in Jeddah in the late 1970s; there he attended lectures by Sayyid Qutb's brother Muhammad Qutb and studied under Abdullah Azzam.[141] Reflecting this training, bin Laden once declared his conviction that "the Muslim nation was created to stand at the center of hegemony and rule," for it is "the divine rule that the entire earth must be subject to the religion of Allah."[142] The determination that the rule of Islam is "divine rule"

---

[132] Aaron, *In Their Own Words*, 70.   [133] Wright, *The Looming Tower*, 37.

[134] Ayman al-Zawahiri, *His Own Words: Translation and Analysis of the Writings of Dr. Ayman al-Zawahiri*, trans. and analysis by Laura Mansfield (Lulu.com, 2006), 47.

[135] See Gunaratna, *Inside Al Qaeda*, 25–26.   [136] Aaron, *In Their Own Words*, 70.

[137] Al-Zawahiri, *His Own Words*, 72.   [138] Ibid., 125.   [139] Ibid., 77.

[140] Ibid., 199.   [141] Wright, *The Looming Tower*, 79.

[142] Matthias Küntzel, "National Socialism and Anti-Semitism in the Arab World," *Jewish Political Studies Review* (17, Spring 2005), available at http://www.jcpa.org/phas/phas-kuntzel-s05.htm.

characterizes the Jihadist appropriation of God. Just as the Jews are the chief stumbling block to the project of unseating God, so are they the chief obstacle to the Jihadists' aim of ruling the world. "The Jews," bin Laden says, projecting his own evil, "believe as part of their religion that people are their slaves, and whoever denies their religion deserves to be killed."[143] *Any* peace with "the Jews," he insists, "is a disaster for Muslims."[144] He affirms that Jew hatred, as a hatred of evil, is "part of our belief and our religion."[145] He pleads with the Americans to awaken to the fact that "the Jews have taken control of your economy, through which they have then taken control of your media, and they now control all aspects of your life" through "immoral acts of fornication, homosexuality, intoxicants, gambling, and trading with interest."[146] Bin Laden thus casts the Jew in the mold of the eternal enemy of all humanity. Justifying his fanaticism, he quotes the Quran, saying, "The most implacable men in their enmity to the believers are the Jews" (5:82). Bin Laden further perverts the Quran (8:60) in a Jihadist appropriation of Allah by averring that "whoever refuses the principle of terror against the enemy also refuses the commandment of Allah,"[147] which, of course, is the commandment of al-Qaeda: as ever, al-Qaeda *is* Allah.

A CLOSING REFLECTION ON RAMIFICATIONS

Very few Islamic theologians and thinkers have cried out against the vicious Jew hatred that lies at the core of Islamic Jihadist politico-theology; among those who have taken genuine risks to even broach the topic are Bassam Tibi, Riffat Hassan, Bülent Şenat, and Khaleel Mohammed. They are aware of a truth that becomes increasingly evident with every Jihadist terrorist action: the exterminationist anti-Semitism of Islamic Jihadism poses an extreme danger not only to the Jews but to all of humanity, including the Muslims themselves. To be sure, Azzam insisted that fellow Muslims can be killed in terrorist actions, if it promotes the killing of the "unbelievers."[148]

Although the Christians would like for all of humanity to seek salvation in Jesus, their attitude toward the nonbeliever is quite different from

---

[143] Osama bin Laden, *Messages to the World: The Statements of Osama bin Laden*, ed. Bruce Lawrence, trans. James Howarth (London: Verso, 2005), 190.

[144] Ibid., 9.   [145] Ibid., 87.

[146] Küntzel, "National Socialism and Anti-Semitism in the Arab World"; bin Laden's letter was published in *The Observer* on 24 November 2002. Al-Zawahiri wrote a similar letter dated 10 January 2006; see al-Zawahiri, 297.

[147] Ibid., 54.   [148] Azzam, *Defense of the Muslim Lands*, 20.

the Jihadists' stance. The Jews may pose a theological and metaphysical threat to both Christians and Muslims, but, in a much more fanatic fashion, the Jihadists cast that threat in ontological, existential terms. In some ways similar to the dogmatic Christians, however, Islamic Jihadists hate the Jews because the very presence of the Jews robs them of their authority over the matter of salvation. Indeed, the presence of the Jews robs them of their own salvation. It robs them of their salvation because it signifies the infinite responsibility that makes the wait for salvation infinite and that makes us infinitely responsible for the life and well-being of other human beings. In a word, it robs them of their salvation because it disturbs the sleep that would settle the matter of redemption through belief in a creed. Jihadist versions of Jew hatred are manifest in the claim to the last line in the syllogism, to a truth that is purified, resolved, and guaranteed. Absolute security is attained through absolute control over all humanity, "in this world and the next,"[149] as al-Banna says. But the Jews announce that those who would wield absolute control over the truth are not in control. For the truth is in control of us – not the other way around, despite our theological and ideological machinations.

Perhaps the most important difference between Christian anti-Semitism and Islamic Jihadist anti-Semitism lies in how the two have responded to modernity, particularly in its post-Holocaust contexts. In some quarters, though not all, the scandal of the systematic extermination of the Jews has led the Christians to reexamine their traditions and to seek a deeper, more dialogical relationship with the Jews. Among the Jihadists, however, it has led to a more venomous hatred of the Jews, with an accompanying exploitation of anti-Semitic canards that have come both from the centuries-old Christian hatred of the Jews and from the modern expressions of Jew hatred, such as the blood libel and world Jewish conspiracy accusations. Although modernity has witnessed the rise of a certain contempt for revealed religion and its "superstitions," the secular philosophical and cultural outlook of modernity is no less anti-Semitic than the "backward" views of revealed religion. There, too, we discover the longing to be as God.

---

[149] Al-Banna, *Five Tracts of Hasan al-Banna*, 46–47.

4

The Elimination of God: Philosophical Anti-Semitism in Modern Thought

> To think is to be God. The act of thought, as such, is the freedom of the immortal gods from all external limitations.
>
> Ludwig Feuerbach, *The Essence of Christianity*

A story is told of the first philosopher, Thales of Miletus (ca. 636–ca. 546 BCE), who was walking along one night gazing up at the stars, when he fell into a well.[1] He climbed out of the pit and immediately vowed to never again take a step without being certain of the firm ground beneath his feet. And so he clambered to consume the fruits of the tree of knowledge, that his eyes may be opened. Here we have the birth of the speculative tradition of ontological thought. Philosophy seeks security; to be as God is to be secure, and knowledge provides security – at least that is the illusion. The philosopher "retreats from the flow of reality to the protected circle," Franz Rosenzweig states it. "Slowly he submerges to the depths, to the region of the essences. Nothing can disturb him there. He is safe."[2] Like God.

In his analysis of anti-Semitism from 1700 to 1933 Jacob Katz claims that "it was the image of the Jew that was inherited from Christianity that determined the secular perception of the Jew."[3] Modern philosophical anti-Semitism, however, runs much deeper and is to be distinguished from

---

[1] See Plato, *Theaetetus*, trans. Benjamin Jowett (Rockville, Md.: Serenity Publishers, 2009), 131.

[2] Franz Rosenzweig, *Understanding the Sick and the Healthy: A View of World, God, and Man*, trans. Nahum Glatzer (Cambridge, Mass.: Harvard University Press, 1999), 42.

[3] Jacob Katz, *From Prejudice to Destruction: Anti-Semitism, 1700–1933* (Cambridge, Mass.: Harvard University Press, 1980), 320.

Christian Jew hatred. Theology appropriates God in the name of God, making man into the godman, or what might be called "the infinite without finitude." Philosophy eliminates God in the name of man, making man into the mangod, or what Emmanuel Lévinas calls "finitude without the infinite."[4] Both are manifestations of how we succumb to the temptation of the serpent: eat and you will know, your eyes will be opened, and you will be as God, safe and secure, redeemed and pure. In the modern period philosophy supersedes theology as a manifestation of anti-Semitism; once the ego is as God, both theology and God are superfluous. And so are the Jews: in the Western unfolding of the manifestations of the metaphysical origins of anti-Semitism, first theology and then philosophy labor to get rid of the Jew, whose very presence cries out, "Don't listen to the serpent!" Within two or three generations, what begins with a philosopher's head scratching ends up as a cultural outlook. In the thinking ego's elimination of God the manifestations of modern anti-Semitism go from the philosophical to the cultural to the political. Michael Mack outlines this sequence: "German Idealists attempted to pave the way for such redemption through the workings of 'freedom' and 'reason' (Kant's autonomy, Hegel's dialectics). According to Schopenhauer, an aesthetic transcendence of the world enacts Kantian rationality. In a further move Feuerbach attempted to translate Christianity's rationality into the anthropological. Finally, Wagner syncretized, in his total work of art (*Gesamtkunstwerk*), 'reason,' 'politics,' and 'Christianity's anthropological essence.'"[5] In this chapter, I examine in some detail, the philosophical manifestation of anti-Semitism in modern thought and then briefly consider its impact on cultural and political manifestations, particularly in Germanic Volkism and in European political movements such as socialism and communism. But the philosophy is seminal. And it stems from Athens.

"In order to understand ourselves," writes Leo Strauss (1899–1973), "we must understand Jerusalem and Athens."[6] Among the matters Strauss understood best was the tension between Athens and Jerusalem. Whereas the former, he explains, signifies "free inquiry," the latter

---

[4] Emmanuel Lévinas, *God, Death, and Time*, trans. Bettina Bergo (Stanford, Calif.: Stanford University Press, 2000), 36.

[5] Michael Mack, *German Idealism and the Jew: The Inner Anti-Semitism of Philosophy and German Jewish Responses* (Chicago, Ill.: University of Chicago Press, 2003), 7.

[6] Leo Strauss, *Studies in Platonic Political Philosophy* (Chicago, Ill.: University of Chicago Press, 1985), 147.

signifies "obedient love."[7] Insisting that the path to truth lies in the "free inquiry" of autonomous reason, philosophy would first deduce the right path and then take a step. In contrast to this paralyzing hesitation we have the Israelites' response when Moses presented them with the Torah: "All that the Lord has said, we shall do and we shall hear" (Exodus 24:7). Philosophy, in other words, would first hear – first understand – and then do. "By saying that we wish to hear first and then to act," Strauss notes, "we have already decided in favor of Athens against Jerusalem."[8] To decide in favor of Athens is to decide in favor of the *What* of a conceived principle over the *Who* of a commanding voice, in favor of the reflective isolation of the I over a responsive relation to the other, in favor of deduction over revelation. Ridding ourselves of the divine *Who*, we reduce ourselves and others to an *It*. Reduced to an It, we are of neutral value and a matter of indifference: to think God out of the picture is to think the other human being out of the picture. We may complain about the absence of God, but, as Abraham Joshua Heschel has noted, "God did not depart of His own volition; He was expelled."[9] Concerned only for itself, the thinking ego has elbowed Him out of the way. The more the world is thus "pervaded by a sense of 'I,'" says Adin Steinsaltz, "the more it is subject to the obscuring of the divine essence."[10] If the difference between Athens and Jerusalem lies in free inquiry over against obedient love, it lies in autonomous self-legislation over against divine commandment. And if that is the case, then one may trace a path leading from Athens to Auschwitz, where no one was ever more autonomous, more self-legislating than the Nazis. What began with thinking God out of the picture ended with shoving the Jews into the gas chambers.

Although almost without exception the philosophers of the modern speculative tradition were known for their anti-Semitic statements, their anti-Semitism is rooted in the categories of ontological thought itself. A mode of thought shaped by autonomous reason, rather than revealed commandment, *has* to oppose Jewish thought, Judaism, and the Jewish people. Ever since the Enlightenment, as Emil Fackenheim has pointed

---

[7] Leo Strauss, *The Rebirth of Classical Political Rationalism: An Introduction to the Thought of Leo Strauss*, selected by Thomas L. Pangle (Chicago, Ill.: University of Chicago Press, 1989), 72.

[8] Strauss, *Studies in Platonic Political Philosophy*, 150.

[9] Abraham Joshua Heschel, *Man Is Not Alone* (New York: Farrar, Strauss and Giroux, 1951), 153.

[10] Adin Steinsaltz, *The Thirteen Petalled Rose: A Discourse on the Essence of Jewish Existence and Belief*, trans. Yehuda Hanegbi (New York: Basic Books, 1980), 20.

out, "the denial of the living God was an essential aspect of man's scientific and moral self-emancipation. If man was to be fully free in his world, God had to be expelled from it. . . . The living God had to become a mere 'Deity,' a 'Cosmic Principle' – remote, indifferent, and mute"[11] – again, a *What*, and not a *Who*. As noted in the Introduction, he adds: "The moment the living God became questionable, Jewish existence became questionable."[12] Why? Because the essence of Jewish existence, like the essence of Jewish thought, lies in the living presence of the divine revealed in the Torah, Covenant, Hebrew prayers, Sabbath observance, and so on. Once the living God is rendered superfluous, such things are empty, and if such things are empty, Jewish life is not only meaningless but threatening.

Further, just as we saw an appropriation of the Word in the creed-based religions of Christianity and Islam, so we witness an assault on the Word with the advent of philosophical anti-Semitism, as manifest in so-called biblical criticism or the historical study of the Bible and above all in the *Wissenschaft des Judentums*, or the "scientific study of Judaism," which reduces the Torah to a mere text and the prohibition against murder to the whim of a tribal chieftain. Proceeding from the premise that nothing is revealed but everything is deduced, such an engagement with the Word proceeds from a premise that is antithetical to the basis of the Word itself. Here the Scripture that the Jews deem "the primary foundation of meaning,"[13] as Lévinas laments, is deemed just one text among many and thus rendered meaningless. No longer is the Torah the Word of God revealed to humanity through the Israelites; instead, it is just another quaint and curious volume of forgotten lore. As Jonathan Sacks has understood, "the assault on the Word could not but be an assault on the Jewish God. Nor can we escape reflection on the fact that within a century, the culture which had reduced the book of the Covenant to fragments had reduced a third of the people of the Covenant to ashes."[14] This unfolding of the philosophical assault on the Word illustrates perfectly the teaching from the Koretzer Rebbe:

[11] Emil L. Fackenheim, "Jewish Existence and the Living God: The Religious Duty of Survival," in Arthur A. Cohen, ed., *Arguments and Doctrines: A Reader of Jewish Thinking in the Aftermath of the Holocaust* (New York: Harper & Row, 1970), 260.

[12] Ibid., 261.

[13] Emmanuel Lévinas, *New Talmudic Readings*, trans. Richard A. Cohen (Pittsburgh, Pa.: Duquesne University Press, 1999), 69–70.

[14] Jonathan Sacks, *Crisis and Covenant: Jewish Thought after the Holocaust* (Manchester, U.K.: Manchester University Press, 1992), 242.

"God and Torah are one. God, Israel, and Torah are one."[15] As each one comes under assault, so do the other two.

What is targeted for elimination in the assault on Torah is not just the content of the text but the categories of the thinking. Because the Word is a *revealed* Word, chief among the categories of thought most dangerous to modern philosophy is revelation. "If revelation is impossible," Fackenheim has said, "then there is no significance to the human situation in general, even though God is accepted. . . . But this [acceptance of God as a concept] makes individual men and historic moments universally interchangeable,"[16] and therefore universally expendable. "If the belief in the creation of the world, the reality of biblical miracles, the valid law based on revelation at Sinai, is the foundation of Judaism," Fackenheim asserts further, "then one must say that modern Enlightenment has undermined its foundations"[17] – precisely by undermining revelation as a reality. Ultimately, from the standpoint of such thinking, the Jew is not the "other" – the Jew is the unenlightened and is therefore dangerous. For the Jew represents the most fundamental threat to autonomous freedom; the hegemony of race, class, culture, and gender; and the dialectics of materialism, insisting as he does that freedom lies neither in autonomous reason and resolve nor in the accidents of nature but in the heteronomous adherence to Torah. The implication? Either the Jew is evil or modern thought is evil. And those who have the will and the power to act on the implication have done so.

THE MODERN PHILOSOPHICAL MANIFESTATION
OF ANTI-SEMITISM

"*Cogito, ergo sum*," declared René Descartes (1596–1650), "I think, therefore I am."[18] Thus equating thought with being, the Father of Modern Philosophy ushered in a new understanding of the human being, one that equates the being of the human being with thought: I *think*, therefore I *am*. Equally significant is the *I* in the "*I* think": *my* thought is

---

[15] See Louis Newman, ed., *The Hasidic Anthology* (New York: Schocken Books, 1963), 147.

[16] Emil L. Fackenheim, *Quest for Past and Future: Essays in Jewish Theology* (Bloomington: Indiana University Press, 1968), 107.

[17] Emil L. Fackenheim, *Jewish Philosophers and Jewish Philosophy*, ed. Michael L. Morgan (Bloomington: Indiana University Press, 1996), 48.

[18] René Descartes, *Meditations on First Philosophy*, 3rd ed., trans. Donald A. Cress (Indianapolis, Ind.: Hackett, 1993), 19–20.

the ground of my being. Here the being of the human being issues not from a Creator in whose image and likeness humans are created, as taught in the Torah, but from the *res cogitans*, the "thinking thing,"[19] which is the autonomous ego. In the Cartesian equation of thought with being, God is usurped by a counterfeit I, an illusory and delusional I, the I who would be as God – in short: the I of the anti-Semite. In the ego's usurpation of God, evil itself is unmasked, as Lévinas points out, saying, "Evil ... is the very egoism of the ego that posits itself as its own origin, an uncreated sovereign principle, a prince."[20] Anti-Semitism has its metaphysical origin in this "very egoism of the ego" that eclipses the light of the Holy One. With the waxing of the Cartesian *lumen natural*, or "natural light,"[21] there is a waning of the divine light, so that modern thought slips into the darkness, into the evil, of egocentric anti-Semitism. For nothing is more threatening to the natural light of autonomous reason than the heteronomous Judaism embodied in the Jewish people.

What comes to mind in this connection is the talmudic assertion that the heart cannot contain both the ego and the *Shekhinah*, God's Indwelling Presence, at the same time (*Pesachim* 66b). Thus the talmudic contempt for philosophy: "Cursed be the man who would teach his son Grecian Wisdom" (*Bava Kama* 82b). And: "When Ben Damah, the son of Rabbi Ishmael's sister, asked when he may study the wisdom of the Greeks, the Rabbi answered, 'Go find a time that is neither day nor night and then learn the Greek wisdom'" (*Menachot* 99b). Opposite philosophy's *cogito* is Judaism's *bitul hayesh*, the "annulment of the self" or the ego that eclipses the soul. Recall the teaching, as articulated by the Chasidic master Yechiel Mikhal (d. ca. 1786), that only God can say I,[22] *Anokhi*, which is the first word in the first utterance at Mount Sinai. The premise is that God is not the projection of my ego or my I; rather, I am a projection of the divine I. God says *Anokhi*, therefore I am. Which is to say: God commands me, therefore I am. The God whose existence Descartes sets out to prove is a philosophically, egocentrically determined "supreme being" and not the Creator of all being, who is otherwise than being. If I derive God from my reasoning, then I am higher than God, which is to say: I am God. From a Jewish perspective, it is the other way

---

[19] Ibid., 5.
[20] Emmanuel Lévinas, *Collected Philosophical Papers*, trans. Alphonso Lingis (Dordrecht: Martinus Nijhoff, 1987), 138.
[21] See, e.g., Descartes, *Meditations on First Philosophy*, 26.
[22] See Newman, *The Hasidic Anthology*, 423.

around: God derives me, as it were, from His thinking, His will, and His Word. There lies the danger that the presence of the Jew poses for modern philosophy. And the philosophers know it.

There are several anti-Semites among the notable *philosophes* of the Enlightenment.[23] For example, Jean-Baptiste Mirabaud (1675–1760), the permanent secretary of the Académie Française, believed that the Jews merited the hatred aimed at them, saying that all the nations who hated the Jews "believed they were as justified in hating as in despising them. They were hated because they were known to hate other men."[24] Along similar lines the German-born encyclopedist Paul Henri Dietrich d'Holbach (1723–1789) wrote that the Jews had their revenge on the Romans because "from the ruins of their country, a fanatic sect emerged which gradually polluted the whole of Empire," a sect deemed fanatic because of its adherence to the Torah.[25] Then there was Voltaire (1694–1778), author of the *Philosophical Dictionary*, where he described the Jews as a "totally ignorant nation who, for many years, have combined contemptible miserliness and the most revolting superstition with a violent hatred of all those nations that have tolerated them."[26] As Sacks has pointed out,

It is no accident that almost all the great continental philosophers of the eighteenth and nineteenth centuries ... delivered sharp attacks on Judaism as an anachronism. Voltaire described it as a "detestable superstition." Kant called for its euthanasia. Hegel took Judaism as his model of a slave morality. Nietzsche fulminated against it as the "falsification" of all natural values. In the twentieth century, Sartre could see no content to Jewish existence other than the defiance of anti-Semitism. Martin Heidegger, the greatest German philosopher of his time, became an active Nazi. Modern Western philosophy, promising a new era of tolerance, manifestly failed to extend that tolerance to Judaism and the Jews. Against this background, the transition from Enlightenment to Holocaust is less paradoxical than it might otherwise seem.[27]

Berel Lang adds this insight: "There are few figures of the Enlightenment in fact who in their common defense of toleration do not qualify that principle where the Jews are concerned. This ... attitude toward the Jews

[23] See, e.g., Joel Carmichael, *The Satanizing of the Jews: Origin and Development of Mystical Anti-Semitism* (New York: Fromm International Publishing Corporation, 1992), 130.

[24] Quoted in Dennis Prager and Joseph Telushkin, *Why the Jews? The Reason for Anti-semitism* (New York: Simon & Schuster, 2003), 119

[25] Quoted in ibid.

[26] Quoted in ibid., 115; see also Voltaire, *Philosophical Dictionary*, trans. Theodore Besterman (New York: Penguin, 1984), 144, 306–307.

[27] Sacks, *Crisis and Covenant*, 268–269.

was not accidental or simply the recrudescence of earlier prejudices, but was engendered by the doctrines of the Enlightenment itself."[28] I have just one correction to Lang's insight: the anti-Semitic stance toward the Jews was not engendered by the doctrines of the Enlightenment. Rather, the doctrines of the Enlightenment were engendered by a mode of thought that was inherently anti-Semitic: if it was to be true to itself, the philosophy of the Enlightenment *had* to be anti-Semitic.

The lie of the "enlightened" thinking that promised tolerance to all was declared long before Sacks and Lang arrived at their insights. With the same clarity of vision that led him to declare that those who burn books will end by burning people,[29] in 1834 Heinrich Heine (1797–1856), himself a child of the Enlightenment, wrote:

The German revolution will not be milder and gentler because it was preceded by Kant's *Critique*, by Fichte's transcendental idealism, and even by the philosophy of nature. These doctrines have developed revolutionary forces that wait only for the day when they can erupt and fill the world with terror and admiration. There will be Kantians forthcoming who will hear nothing of piety in the visible world, and with sword and axe will mercilessly churn the soil of our European life, to exterminate the very last roots of the past. Armed Fichteans will enter the lists, whose fanaticism of will can be curbed neither by fear nor by self-interest.[30]

Armed Fichteans? Yes. In fact, Hans Sluga calls Johann Gottlieb Fichte (1762–1814) "the first National Socialist philosopher."[31] One reason he says this is Fichte's infamous comment on whether or not Jews should be given citizenship: "The only way to give them citizenship would be to cut off their heads in the same night in order to replace them with those containing no Jewish ideas."[32] The Fichteans to whom Heine refers are armed with Fichte's notion that "the real destiny of the human race . . . is

---

[28] Berel Lang, *Act and Idea in the Nazi Genocide* (Syracuse, N.Y.: Syracuse University Press, 2003), 185.

[29] In his tragedy *Almansor* (1831) Heine's character Hassan declares, *Das war ein Vorspiel nur, dort wo man Bücher/Verbrennt, verbrennt man auch am Ende Menschen*: "That was just a prelude; wherever books are burned, in the end people will also be burned." See Heinrich Heine, *The Complete Poems of Heinrich Heine: A Modern English Version*, trans. Hal Draper (Boston: Suhrkamp/Insel, 1982), 187.

[30] Heinrich Heine, "The German Revolution," in *Words of Prose*, trans. E. B. Ashton (New York: L. B. Fischer, 1943), 51–53.

[31] Hans Sluga, *Heidegger's Crisis: Philosophy and Politics in Nazi Germany* (Cambridge, Mass.: Harvard University Press, 1993), 29.

[32] From "Beitrag zur Berichtung der Urteils des Publikums über die französischen Revolution" (1793); cited in Lang, *Act and Idea in the Nazi Genocide*, 169.

in freedom to make itself what it really is originally."[33] Instead of the
creation of the human being in the divine image, we have the free resolve
of the human being to forge his or her own essence. To make such a move,
not just Jewish "ideas" but a Jewish mode of thought rooted in creation
and revelation must be eliminated.

Of course, Fichte stood on the shoulders of Immanuel Kant, who
understood freedom in terms of a self-legislating autonomy, declaring,
"Freedom and self-legislation of the will are both autonomy and hence
are reciprocal concepts."[34] Paul Guyer has said that "at the philosophical
level of the transformation of the Western concept of a human being from
a mere spectator of the natural world and a mere subject in the moral
world to an *active agent in the creation of both*, no one played a larger
role than Immanuel Kant."[35] The elimination of the testimony of a
heteronomous, earthbound, and therefore tainted Judaism is essential to
becoming an active agent in the creation of the natural and moral worlds.
Philosophy, therefore, must be de-Judaized and purged of such influences.
"Kant," Mack points out, "saw in the Jews the opposite of reason's
purity: they embodied the impurity of empirical reality, of 'matter.'"[36]
In a word, Kant's *reine Vernunft* or "pure reason" is conscientiously
Judenrein.

Living according to divine commandment, and not according to their
own autonomous self-legislation, the Jews represented for Kant the height
of heteronomy and self-enslavement. As a free, autonomous, self-
legislating anti-Semite, Kant derived the Good from the natural light of
reason, and from the Good he derived God – or rather the *concept* of
God – in a usurpation of God.[37] Once God is reduced to a human
concept, He is rendered superfluous, as Kant himself understood: "All
that does depend upon the direct will of God," he writes in his *Universal
Natural History*, "is the creation of matter."[38] In everything else, instead

[33] Johann Gottlieb Fichte, *Addresses to the German Nation*, ed. George Armstrong Kelly
(New York: Harper & Row, 1968), 40; emphasis added.
[34] See Immanuel Kant, *Grounding for the Metaphysics of Morals*, trans. James W. Ellington,
3rd ed. (Indianapolis, Ind.: Hackett, 1993), 52.
[35] Paul Guyer, Introduction to Paul Guyer, ed., *The Cambridge Companion to Kant*
(Cambridge, U.K.: Cambridge University Press, 1992), 3; emphasis added.
[36] Mack, *German Idealism and the Jew*, 3.
[37] See, e.g., Immanuel Kant, *Critique of Pure Reason*, trans. and ed. Marcus Weigelt (New
York: Penguin Classics, 2008), 43–44.
[38] Quoted in Frederick C. Beiser, "Kant's Intellectual Development: 1746–1781," in Paul
Guyer, ed., *The Cambridge Companion to Kant* (Cambridge, U.K.: Cambridge University
Press, 1992), 39.

of the will of God we have the will of the thinker. Because God is thus rendered all but superfluous, the human being, says Kant, is "determinable only by laws which he *gives to himself* through reason"[39] and not by anything like commandments revealed from on high. Thus we eliminate God, revelation, and the dimension of height, a move necessary for establishing the autonomy of the self. Making such a move, Kant transforms Jew hatred from a religious obligation into a moral duty, as his contemporary Saul Ascher (1767–1822) understood, saying, "A totally new adversary is developing before our eyes, armed with more awful weapons than his predecessors."[40] The use of the weapons of religion is contingent on belief; the use of the weapons of moral principle is a logical necessity.

Insisting that religion and God derive from morality, and not the other way around,[41] Kant embraced a rationalism that is opposed to revelation, beginning with the revelation from Mount Sinai that emanates into the world through the nation of Israel. The revelation of the *Anokhi*, the I, of the Holy One is followed by the revelation of the Name, the *yud-hey-vav-hey* (Y-H-V-H), of the Holy One. And so we see the transition from Descartes to Kant. Descartes eliminated the *Anokhi* uttered at Mount Sinai; situating the ground of moral law in the autonomous, self-legislating ego that declares, "I"; Kant eliminated the Y-H-V-H, the Name of the Holy One, for, according to Jewish teaching, the revealed *mitzvah* or commandment issues from the revealed Name. Kalonymos Kalmish Shapira (1889–1943), Rebbe of the Warsaw Ghetto, explains this point by noting that the word *mitzvah* (spelled *mem-tzadee-vav-hey*) contains the four-letter Holy Name (spelled *yud-hey-vav-hey*), so that God, the *Infinite* One, is revealed *in* the *mitzvah*. While the last two letters, *vav-hey*, are the same in both words, first two letters of the Name are hidden in the first two letters, *mem-tzadee*, of *mitzvah*; for when transformed according to the *At-Bash* hermeneutic, the *mem* and *tzadee* of *mitzvah* become the *yud* and *hey* of the divine Name.[42] The mitzvah, therefore, is

---

[39] Immanuel Kant, *The Critique of Practical Reason*, trans. Lewis White Beck (New York: Macmillan, 1985), 101; emphasis added.

[40] Quoted in Katz, *From Prejudice to Destruction*, 68.

[41] See, e.g., Immanuel Kant, *Religion within the Limits of Reason Alone*, trans. Theodore M. Greene and Hoyt H. Hudson (New York: Harper & Brothers, 1960, 95ff. For a good discussion of Kant's views in this regard, see Allen W. Wood, "Rational Theology, Moral Faith, and Religion," in Guyer, *The Cambridge Companion to Kant*, 394–416.

[42] Kalonymos Kalmish Shapira, *Sacred Fire: Torah from the Years of Fury 1939–1942*, trans. J. Hershy Worch, ed. Deborah Miller (Northvale, N.J.: Jason Aronson, 2000), 61.

a portal through which the Holy One enters the world. With the Kantian erasure of the revealed commandment, then, comes the erasure of the Name. Indeed, once God is reduced to a concept, He – or It – neither bears a personal name nor enters into a personal relation.

Recall at this juncture the etymological root of *mitzvah* mentioned in the Introduction: it is *tzavta*, which means "connection." Without the mitzvah, God has no connection, no relation to the world; when God has no connection to the world, evil flourishes; and when evil flourishes, we have no relation to one another. Eliminating the higher commandment, philosophy opts for the isolation of the ego over the relation to the other human being. And so it must be for the philosophical genius of the Enlightenment, as Michael Mack realizes: for Kant, he says, autonomy "denotes the refusal of the self to engage with the other,"[43] whether human or divine. The refusal of any such engagement is essential to the enthronement of the self who would be as God. The implication? Rosenzweig understood it perhaps better than anyone: far from glorifying the human being, this elimination of any relation to the other is radically dehumanizing. "Corresponding to the Copernican turn of Copernicus which made man a speck of dust in the whole," says Rosenzweig, "is the Copernican turn of Kant, which, by way of compensation, placed him upon the throne of the world, much more precisely than Kant thought. To that monstrous degradation of man, costing him his human-ity, this correction without measure was, likewise, at the cost of his humanity."[44] Insisting on the creation of himself after his own image, the human being loses his human image. In the end he dehumanizes and murders the *other* human being. At stake in anti-Semitism is not the status of the Jew – it is the sanctity of the other human being.

The Kantian Idealism that deprecates the concrete material world parallels the Christian thinking that is likewise characterized by a *contemptus mundi*. Like the Christian who rejects the things of this world for the world to come, Kant understood the autonomous freedom of the individual to lie in a "liberation from one's inclination to depend on objects in the empirical world."[45] There lies a key to Kantian Idealism:

The *At-Bash* transformation is a means of interpretation, whereby the first letter of the alphabet is interchanged with the last letter, the second letter with the penultimate letter, and so on.

[43] Mack, *German Idealism and the Jew*, 16.
[44] Franz Rosenzweig, *Franz Rosenzweig's "The New Thinking,"* trans. and ed. Alan Udoff and Barbara Galli (Syracuse, N.Y.: Syracuse University Press, 1999), 96.
[45] Mack, *German Idealism and the Jew*, 24.

the "real" world lies in the idea or the concept and not in the flesh-and-blood reality; those who are fixated on a material, concrete reality are the deluded slaves to the empirical. Because the Jews and Judaism are concretely oriented toward the things of this world, Kant viewed Judaism as a superstition rooted in "reason's subjection to external facts,"[46] which is the Kantian definition of enslavement.

In keeping with the premise of Idealism, G. W. F. Hegel (1770–1831) maintained that revealed religion is superseded by the absolute knowledge of reason,[47] which means that "the self has to guard itself against being swayed by the arbitrariness of otherness. In short, it has to protect its posited sameness against the external world of 'matter,' of heteronomy,"[48] that is, the world of the Jew. With the Hegelian "posited sameness" of the self, the other, both human and divine, is absorbed into the autonomous thinking ego. Such, for Hegel, is the meaning of the incarnation of God in the Christ: God and man merge *in essence* through the autonomous, egocentric spiritualization of the self.[49] With this synthesis the individual attains his true identity as a "spiritual individuality,"[50] which ultimately disappears into the universality of spirit. With this disappearance of the self into universal abstraction, God is swallowed up into the self. In Hegel, Fackenheim explains, "divinity comes to dwell, as it were, in the same inner space as the human self."[51] Which in the end means: the ego is divine. Here we see more clearly that theological and philosophical manifestations of anti-Semitism have a common metaphysical origin in the ego's longing for apotheosis. For Hegel, philosophy does not abandon the theological project but rather consummates it: the collapse of the divinity into the self is the ultimate synthesis to be attained in the Hegelian dialectic. Resisting this dialectic, Jews live an "animal existence," in Hegel's words; they are in a "state of total passivity, of total ugliness" and are to blame for refusing to "die as Jews."[52] To be sure, the

---

[46] Ibid., 40.

[47] See, e.g., G. W. F. Hegel, *Phenomenology of Spirit (The Phenomenology of Mind)*, trans. J. B. Baillie (Digireads.com Publishing, 2009), 39. For a good discussion of this point, see Edith Wyschogrod, *Spirit in Ashes: Hegel, Heidegger, and Man-Made Death* (New Haven, Conn.: Yale University Press, 1985), 69–72.

[48] Mack, *German Idealism and the Jew*, 18–19.

[49] See Hegel, *Phenomenology of Spirit*, 354–355.   [50] See ibid., 147.

[51] Emil L. Fackenheim, *Encounters between Judaism and Modern Philosophy* (New York: Basic Books, 1993), 190–191.

[52] See G. W. F. Hegel, "The Spirit of Christianity and Its Fate," in *Early Theological Writings*, trans. T. M. Knox (Chicago: University of Chicago Press, 1948), 201–205.

Jews *must* die as Jews if the Hegelian dialectic – the project of modern philosophy and the culture it engenders – is to be realized.

The Hegelian spiritualization of material reality is essential to the formation of the perfect body politic, which is realized in the transformation of the state into a spiritualized political entity. "The state," says Hegel, "is the will which manifests itself, ... raised to the plane of the universal.... This substantive unity is its own motive and absolute end."[53] And so the state becomes absolute and totalitarian. The Jews threaten this totalitarian apotheosis of the state, inasmuch as they "symbolize the worldly, which resists an immanent and imminent transformation into the otherworldly."[54] It is no accident that totalitarian regimes are characteristically anti-Semitic. The worldview embodied in Judaism is not just an alternative worldview – for Hegel, it is precisely the worldview that threatens both the totalitarian absolute and, more importantly, philosophy itself. Therefore Judaism must be eliminated. Hegel argued that "Kantian moral freedom can only become a politically (*Sittliche*) binding one by means of an intrusion of spirit into matter. Spirit needs to encounter matter not to spiritualize but to destroy it,"[55] and this project of destruction is best undertaken by the state. If, in the end, the destruction of matter meant the destruction of Judaism, then it meant the destruction of the Jews. Such a project would become the project of the state, as realized with the ascent of the Nazis.

In the Hegelian destruction of the empirical by the spiritual, the flesh-and-blood individual is consumed by the state. This Hegelian meaninglessness of the single individual opposes itself to the Jewish understanding of the infinite dearness of every human being. According to the Hegelian view, every individual is expendable; according to the Jewish view, every individual is indispensable. This view is reflected in the Torah's emphasis on our care for the widow, the orphan, and the stranger (e.g., Deuteronomy 10:8), as well as the Talmud's repeated insistence on the dignity of every person (e.g., *Shabbat* 81b; *Eruvin* 41b). In the Mishnah it is written that he who saves a single life saves the world entire (*Sanhedrin* 4:5). Elsewhere in the Mishnah we have the teaching that says if the gentiles declare, "'Give us one of you that we may make her unclean, but if not, lo, we will make all of you unclean' – let them make all unclean, but they should not hand over a single Israelite" (*Terumot* 8:12). Which means: if

[53] G. W. F. Hegel, *The Philosophy of Right*, trans. S. W. Dyde (New York: Cosimo, 2008), 132–133.
[54] Mack, *German Idealism and the Jew*, 4–5.   [55] Hegel, *Phenomenology of Spirit*, 47.

an enemy should demand that a community turn over to them even a single innocent person, the community must refuse, even if the entire community is threatened with death. Here we have a stark illustration of a *limiting principle* imposed by Torah, a principle that would affirm the absolute, infinite sanctity of every human life. When the ground of such a principle is situated within the will of the state, the state absorbs the individual into itself in the name of the collective, so that every limiting principle is erased and the eclipse of God is accomplished.

There is an important difference, then, between the Christian theological manifestations of anti-Semitism and its modern philosophical manifestations. When the Christian Crusaders slaughtered the Jews, a Christian could object to the slaughter and remain a Christian, as Bernard of Clairvaux did, invoking his own Christian texts and teachings to declare, "We are going too far." Once divinity occupies the same space as the self, however, the limiting principle vanishes; once thought has eliminated God, the first limit to vanish is the prohibition against murder. Undertaking an assault on the commanding Voice of the Infinite One who spoke from Mount Sinai, the evil of philosophical anti-Semitism approached the limitless: it waxed as infinite as the imagination. In the neo-Hegelians we discover a quintessential manifestation of this philosophical anti-Semitism. For the neo-Hegelians, as Fackenheim has noted, "divinity vanishes in the process of internalization, to be replaced by a humanity *potentially infinite* in its modern 'freedom,'"[56] which is nothing more than modern license unchecked by anything resembling a divine commandment.

From a philosophical standpoint, however, Christians do not pose the same threat that the Jews do, because Christians espouse the confluence of God and humanity in the Incarnation in such a way as to free humanity from the commandments of Torah (see, e.g., Galatians 3:13); after Kant and Hegel had accomplished the philosophical de-Judaizing of Christianity, philosophy was able, at least for a time, to come to some accommodation with Christianity, albeit in a way that ultimately required the elimination of God. Neo-Hegelians, Fackenheim observes, are "post-Protestant atheists. Hegel's 'identity of the divine nature and the human' becomes actual not in a generally religious but rather in a specifically Christian-Protestant world. As the left-wing Hegelians 'transform' Hegel's identity into an appropriation of the divine nature

---

[56] Fackenheim, *Encounters between Judaism and Modern Philosophy*, 191; emphasis added.

by the human, it must under no circumstances be overlooked that they affirm and produce, not a generally postreligious, but rather a specifically post-Christian-Protestant world. Hegel's all-comprehensive philosophy requires not 'religion' but Protestant Christianity."[57] Christians could, in fact, accommodate the modern freedom that issues from modern thought, which is an absolute freedom determined by an absolutely autonomous self.

Ludwig Feuerbach (1804–1872) is a good example of a neo-Hegelian who merged Christian theological Jew hatred with modern philosophical anti-Semitism. With Feuerbach, God is reduced to nothing more than a projection of one's own psyche onto the cosmos.[58] Therefore, "consciousness of God is self-consciousness, knowledge of God is self-knowledge. By his God thou knowest the man, and by the man his God; the two are identical. Whatever is God to a man, that is his heart and soul; and conversely, God is the manifest inward nature, the expressed self of a man."[59] And: "God is the highest subjectivity of man *abstracted* from himself."[60] And: "To think is to be God. The act of thought, as such, is the freedom of the immortal gods from all external limitations."[61] Like Hegel, Feuerbach understood the essence of Christianity in terms of a fundamental opposition to the essence of Judaism. "Feuerbach took over, from Hegel, the idea that history is the realization of theology's ethical and political content.... He did not set out to negate religion as such but only 'the inhuman' (*das Unmenschliche*) aspects of it. He located such inhumanity in the God of the Jews, who caused a rift between immanence and transcendence."[62] Thus Feuerbach contrasted Judaism's "desire for *earthly happiness*" with Christianity's "longing for *heavenly bliss*,"[63] locating the human not in this realm of flesh and blood but in the ethereal imperium of philosophical abstraction. From here it would be just a few generational steps to launching the ashes of flesh-and-blood humanity into the heavens.

Understanding the inherently anti-Semitic nature of this thinking, Joseph Soloveitchik (1903–1993) observes that the path of development from Hegel to Feuerbach is one in which the philosopher sees God as no more than "an infinite ideal to which he aspires. His philosophical

[57] Ibid., 137.
[58] See Ludwig Feuerbach, *The Essence of Christianity*, trans. George Eliot (New York: Harper & Row, 1957), 12–13.
[59] Ibid., 12–13.   [60] Ibid., 31; emphasis added.   [61] Ibid., 41.
[62] Mack, *German Idealism and the Jew*, 7.
[63] Feuerbach, *The Essence of Christianity*, 121.

religiosity is anthropocentric and anthropocratic. The point of departure is not God but the universal experience (of Him), which is considered creative, redeeming, and inspiring – the maximum bonum of mental life. He is absorbed in his own self rather than in a transcendent God"[64] and, more dangerously, rather than in a relation to the other human being. Transcending God and humanity, the transcendent self transcends all limitations and is divorced from all human relations. Here the other human being does not summon who I am in my infinite responsibility for another, but rather threatens who I am in my infinite being-for-myself. The I-Thou relation that Feuerbach famously espoused is not a flesh-and-blood relation, a being-for-the-other; rather, the Thou is tied to the I as an object of thought,[65] a shared "essence,"[66] which the I appropriates through thought, absorbing the other into the same. As one who disturbs the sleep of my philosophical reflection, the other, flesh-and-blood human being is a threat to my freedom, conceived as my self-legislating autonomy, which is now limited only by the will, as Friedrich Nietzsche (1844–1900) understood.

Acting as philosophy's self-appointed coroner, the man whom Alfred Rosenberg described as *"the greatest figure of the German and European intellectual world of his day"*[67] pronounced God D.O.A.[68] Although Nietzsche rejected the primacy of rational thought found in German Idealism, his thinking is the logical outcome of that tradition, inasmuch as the implementation of the Kantian categorical imperative rests on the egocentric *will*: "Act as if the maxim of your action were to become through your will a universal law of nature"[69] – *through your will*, and not through divine commandment, as the Jews would have it. Understanding that there is no reason for the will to go in one direction over another – or rather, understanding that if the will is guided in a preconceived ethical direction, then it is already undermined – Nietzsche denounced Kant's "inferior" knowledge of human nature, as well as

---

[64] Joseph Soloveitchik, *The Halakhic Mind: An Essay on Jewish Tradition and Modern Thought* (New York: Free Press, 1986), 78.

[65] Feuerbach, *The Essence of Christianity*, 2.   [66] Ibid., 158.

[67] Alfred Rosenberg, *Race and Race History and Other Essays*, ed. Robert Pois (New York: Harper & Row, 1974), 145.

[68] Nietzsche's pronouncement on the death of God appears in Section 125 of *The Gay Science*; see Friedrich Nietzsche, *The Gay Science*, trans. Walter Kaufmann (New York: Vintage Books, 1974); see also Friedrich Nietzsche, *Also sprach Zarathustra*, in *Werke*, vol. 1 (Munich: Carl Hanser Verlag, 1967), 549.

[69] Kant, *Grounding for the Metaphysics of Morals*, 30.

Kant's "moral fanaticism."[70] Nevertheless, he needs something akin to Kant's view of freedom as autonomous self-legislation; with Nietzsche, the road to freedom lies in a will to power, through which the individual attains a god-like ascendancy over the herd. As for the connection to Hegel, Edith Wyschogrod offers a penetrating insight: "The intellectual implications of Hegel's radical vision [of the internalized God] are first realized in Nietzsche's depiction of the madman who not only declares the death of God, but makes the equally important and unthinkable claim that man is the killer."[71] Nietzsche understood that with the elimination of God, the ego becomes God. "The 'ego,'" he writes, "subdues and kills: it operates like an organic cell: it is a robber and violent. ... It wants to give birth to its god and see all mankind at his feet."[72] Killing God, man becomes the mass murderer of men, beginning with the Jews.

Thus yawns the abyss of freedom infinite in its potentiality, beyond any law, resolute, and decisive. "*Measure*," Nietzsche states, "is alien to us; let us own it, our thrill is the thrill of the infinite, the unmeasured."[73] Unmeasured is the will and the imagination of the ego that would be as God, unmeasured and reeling in the swoon of the thrill that only God can know, drunk in a bacchanalia of blood. In that thrill, however, we collide with the abyss of our own nothingness, where we equate our being – and our thinking – with the will to power and imagination, free of all the limitations that lie at the core of Judaism and are affirmed by the Jewish presence in the world. And so the motif of the philosophical surrender to the serpent continues to play itself out, as we succumb to the most ancient temptation: not only would the philosopher be like god, knowing good and evil, but he would be a self-legislating god, creator, and destroyer of his own good and evil. "*Genuine philosophers*," Nietzsche asserts, are "*commanders and legislators*: they say, '*Thus* it *shall* be!'... Their 'knowing' is *creating*, their creating is a legislation, their will to truth is – *will to power*,"[74] so that *truth* "is a word for the 'will to power,'"[75] its meaning determined precisely by the will. Thus the outcome of the collapse and the eclipse of reality that came with German Idealism: with Nietzsche's proclamation that "life itself is *will to power*,"[76] more became real than

---

[70] Friedrich Nietzsche, *The Will to Power*, trans. Walter Kaufmann and R. J. Hollingdale, ed. Walter Kaufmann (New York: Random House, 1968), 64.

[71] Wyschogrod, *Spirit in Ashes*, 146.   [72] Nietzsche, *The Will to Power*, 403.

[73] Friedrich Nietzsche, *Beyond Good and Evil*, trans. Walter Kaufmann (New York: Vintage Books, 1966), 153.

[74] Ibid., 136.   [75] Nietzsche, *The Will to Power*, 298.

[76] Nietzsche, *Beyond Good and Evil*, 21.

was possible. Just as Kant had reduced reality to the perceiving self, so Nietzsche reduced reality to the willing self: "As long as you still experience the stars as something 'above you,'" he wrote, "you lack the eye of knowledge."[77] Indeed, like truth, knowledge itself is nothing more than the will to power: I know what I *will* to know.[78]

With Nietzsche, what is sought is a salvation not from sin or death but from others, from the herd. To rise above the herd and thus attain the state of the higher man, or the *Übermensch*, the self must bring to bear its inner will to power, and that entails either the elimination or the enslavement of others. "My ideas," says Nietzsche, "do not revolve around the degree of freedom that is granted to the one or to the other or to all, but around the degree of *power* that the one or the other should exercise over others or over all."[79] With Nietzsche, then, God is what one aspires to become in a self-apotheosis into the *Übermensch*, and other human beings are mere *Untermenschen*. With this philosophical heritage, the Jews would be logically counted as chief among the *Untermenschen*, inasmuch as they pose the greatest, most fundamental threat to the birth of the new Messiah, the mangod, from the womb of modern philosophy.

Nietzsche understood that the Hegelian project of the merging of the human and the divine is realized not through the dialectic of reason but through the will to power – not through the godman but through the mangod: "in man," Nietzsche announced, "*creature* and *creator* are united."[80] Thus we have the Nietzschean reversal of Christology: "Jesus said this to the Jews: 'The law was for servants – love God as I love him, as his son! What are morals to us sons of God!'"[81] Because one cannot create a God of truth through conjecture, says Nietzsche, we must become such a God, through our will to power.[82] In the will lies the "salvation"[83] that the ego longs for; it is precisely the longing to be as God, for only God is "saved." *That* is the longing that forever fuels anti-Semitism in all its manifestations.

MANIFESTATIONS OF ANTI-SEMITISM SPRUNG FROM THE SOIL OF MODERN PHILOSOPHY

Here I briefly consider the social-political and cultural-national manifestations of anti-Semitism in the nineteenth century. As with modern

---

[77] Ibid., 80.   [78] See, e.g., Nietzsche, *The Will to Power*, 266.   [79] Ibid., 458.
[80] Nietzsche, *Beyond Good and Evil*, 154.   [81] Ibid., 91.
[82] See Nietzsche, *Also sprach Zarathustra*, 600–601.   [83] Ibid., 682.

philosophy, these instances of anti-Semitism were, and continue to be, tacit expressions of a totalitarian longing to eliminate the God of Abraham as transmitted through the centuries-old and ongoing testimony of the Jews as a people. No matter how much the "emancipated" Jews of Europe attempted to assimilate into an anti-Judaic world, that world understood very well what the children of Abraham signified. It was a world in which the socialist and nationalist elements of Jew hatred would come together in the twentieth century's most rabid, most definitive form of Jew hatred: National Socialism. The interest here, however, is not so much in the expressions of hatred, which are rampant and well documented, but in the metaphysical origins of the hatred. The hatred, in other words, is symptomatic of a deeper issue within the soul, tied as much to an ontological outlook as to an emotional state. Where the theologian wished to speak for God and the philosopher to silence Him, the political ideologue now wished to speak for the collective, as the voice of the state that would take the place of God. Indeed, philosophically speaking, Hegel had already made such a move.

We have seen the displacement of theology on the part of modern philosophy, as the anti-Semitic impetus shifted from the apotheosis of man into godman to the apotheosis of man into mangod. This had its social-political, cultural-national manifestation, which drew on a philosophy of ideas and essence to affix essence to ethnicity and race, to nationality and culture. Because the existence of the Jews could no longer be theologically or philosophically justified, the Jewish essence was relegated to *"pure* Evil," irremissible and beyond the categories that now shaped reality, as Joel Carmichael has observed.[84] Stated differently, once the Jews had become pure evil, they were *essentially* evil, their essence already tainting their existence. Carmichael points out in this regard that "from the very beginning of the Socialist movement in the wake of the French Revolution, it was usual to take over the ancient stereotype of the Jews, rooted in Church doctrine, and dress it up in a more contemporary form as a way of describing the enemy, in this case the 'class enemy.'"[85] In keeping with the Hegelian emphasis on the collective body politic, the political ideologies that glorify the collective necessarily vilify the emphasis on the individual found in the Jewish teaching and tradition. Indeed, nothing is more dangerous to those ideologies than the Midrash that says God chose Moses to lead the

---

[84] Carmichael, *The Satanizing of the Jews*, 133.   [85] Ibid., 115.

Israelites out of Egypt because, as a shepherd, Moses left his flock to find a single lamb that had lost its way: that is what Moses was doing when he came across the burning bush on Mount Sinai. Thus God knew that, just as he had not forgotten a single lamb, Moses would not forget a single Israelite (*Shemot Rabbah* 2:2).

Because Jewish thought undermines the universalizing thought that leads, for example, to the worldwide workers' movements, not to mention nationalistic collectives, the Jews must be eliminated one way or another: thinking can be neither socialist nor nationalist and at the same time Jewish. Thus we have the famous statement of Count Stanislas de Clermont-Tonnerre (1757–1792) before the French Revolution's National Assembly in 1789: "It will be argued, the Jews have their own judges and particular laws. But, I answer, this is your fault and you should not permit it. Jews, as individuals, deserve everything; Jews as a nation nothing. . . . Within the state there can neither be a separate political body nor an order. There can only be the individual citizen. It is being argued that they themselves refuse to become citizens. Let them say that and they will be expelled: because it is inconceivable that there should be in the state a society of non-citizens, a nation within the nation."[86] As individuals, Jews were to be swallowed up by the collective, one by one, so that they would no longer be a people apart. In short, the Jews would no longer be Jews. Before long, however, even the Jew who disavowed his or her Judaism would be viewed as a threat, since he or she could not disavow his or her essence.

The origin of such "enlightened" anti-Semitic thinking lies in a hatred of the testimonies and traditions that make the Jews who they are, beginning with the testimony to the first utterance from Mount Sinai: "I am God." This social-political stance toward the Jews, like modern philosophical thought, is at once anthropocentric and anthropocratic, to borrow once more from Soloveitchik: the socialist ideologues' elevation and adoration of the collective is humanly determined, absolute, and absolutely bent on the elimination of God through the elimination of the Jews as Jews. The leading socialist ideologues of the post-Enlightenment illustrate this point. In Chapter 1 mention was made of the shift from religious to antireligious Jew hatred revealed in the socialist

---

[86] Quoted in Katz, *From Prejudice to Destruction*, 109; see also Jonathan Frankel, "Assimilation and the Jews in Nineteenth-Century Europe: Towards a New Historiography?," in Jonathan Frankel and Steven J. Zipperstein, eds., *Assimilation and Community: The Jews in Nineteenth-Century Europe* (Cambridge, U.K.: Cambridge University Press, 2004), 11.

anarchist Pierre-Joseph Proudhon, who asserted, "It is not for nothing that the Christians call them deicides. The Jew is the enemy of the human race,"[87] where the "human race" or the social collective is now divine. Consistent with his socialist political views, he also stated that Jews should "be sent back to Asia or exterminated"[88] and that "the Jew is by temperament unproductive,... always fraudulent and parasitical.... He is the evil element, Satan, Ahriman, incarnated in the race of Shem,"[89] where *race* means *essence*. Although Karl Marx (more about Marx in Chapter 8) believed that Proudhon's understanding of Hegel was flawed, the French socialist thinker was nevertheless highly influenced by the German Idealists; Marx, in fact, called him "the French Kant."[90]

Among the other socialist thinkers who shared Proudhon's hatred of the Jews was Alphonse Toussenel (1803–1885), author of *Les Juifs rois de l'époque* (The Jews, Kings of the Era, 1847),[91] where he asserts, "I understand the persecution that the Romans, the Christians and the Moslems made the Jews suffer. The prolonged universal repulsion inspired by the Jew is nothing but just punishment for his implacable haughtiness; and our contempt is a legitimate retribution for the hatred which he seems to bear towards the rest of humanity."[92] Also noteworthy is Charles Fourier (1772–1837), who declared that there had never been a "nation more despicable than the Hebrews."[93] If historian Zosa Szajkowski (1911–1978) claimed that he "could not find a single word on behalf of Jews in the whole of French socialist literature from 1820 to 1920,"[94] it was not because he failed to look hard enough. It was because the totalitarian thinking of the French socialists could allow no room for a Jewish presence. "This convergence of socialism and anti-Semitism," Jacob Katz has shown, "became quite common in France during the mid-nineteenth century. The socialist literature and its propagating agency, the *presse rouge*, thus became an important vehicle for disseminating one version of anti-Semitism – in the same way as the *presse noire*

[87] Pierre-Joseph Proudhon, *Carnets de P.-J. Proudhon*, ed. Pierre Haubtmann (Paris: Marcel Rivière, 1960–1961), 337–338.
[88] Quoted in Dan Cohn-Sherbok, *Anti-Semitism* (Stroud, U.K.: The History Press, 2002), 204.
[89] Quoted in Carmichael, *The Satanizing of the Jews*, 117.
[90] See James H. Billington, *Fire in the Minds of Men: Origins of the Revolutionary Faith* (New Brunswick, N.J.: Transaction Publishers, 1999), 297–98.
[91] See Cohn-Sherbok, *Anti-Semitism*, 204.
[92] Quoted in Katz, *From Prejudice to Destruction*, 123.
[93] Quoted in Carmichael, *The Satanizing of the Jews*, 116.
[94] See Prager and Telushkin, *Why the Jews?*, 128.

became an instrument for spreading other versions."[95] Yet, the socialists used the same religious symbols invoked in the *presse noire* to express their contempt for the Jews; the two may represent different versions of anti-Semitism, but for both of them the Jews constitute a single metaphysical category that undermines the longing to deify either the collective or the church. And if they make the Jews into a metaphysical category, it is because their anti-Semitism has a metaphysical origin.

Just as the nineteenth century's social-political movements were steeped in a metaphysical anti-Semitism, so were its cultural-national manifestations, particularly in Germany and specifically in Richard Wagner (1813–1883), who coined the term *Verjudung*, or "Jewification."[96] Heavily influenced by the Kantian association of freedom with self-legislating autonomy, Wagner understood the national autonomy of the *Volk* in terms of a fervent patriotism. "In this way," Michael Mack explains, "a member of the *Volk* does away with all concerns about his or her own welfare and offers his or her life as a sacrifice for the 'non-egoistic' good of a redemptive body politic."[97] Mack goes on to elucidate the transition from the modern philosophical animosity toward the Jews to Wagner's nationalistic Jew hatred: "If Kant saw the origin of the Jews in their superstition, if Hegel made the Jewish God responsible for the fear for material possessions, and if Feuerbach called Jehovah 'the principle of power,' then Wagner equated the God of the Jews with heteronomy as such," so that "Wagner saw his art in terms of a revenge on Jehovah that consists in taking power away from the Jews."[98] In this revenge taken on the God of Abraham we glimpse once again the metaphysical origin of anti-Semitism; the desire to be as God generates a desire for vengeance against the God who declares that I am not God. If I cannot be as God, then I shall seek a deification of the *Volk* with whom I identify, and the deification of the *Volk* requires the demonization of the Jews, whose essence is antithetical to the *Volk*.

Not surprisingly, the theological discourse comes into play, despite the waning of Christian dogma: in an expression of his true desire to see the German nation unseat God, Wagner charges the Jews with deicide.[99] Also, in keeping with the theological anti-Semitism that precedes him,

[95] Katz, *From Prejudice to Destruction*, 128.
[96] Richard S. Levy, *Antisemitism in the Modern World: An Anthology of Texts* (Lexington, Mass.: D. C. Heath and Company, 1991), 49.
[97] Mack, *German Idealism and the Jew*, 66.   [98] Ibid., 70.
[99] Richard Wagner, *Art and Politics*, trans. William Ashton Ellis (Lincoln: University of Nebraska Press, 1995), 364.

he demonizes the Jews and Judaism, declaring, "Judaism is the evil conscience of our modern Civilization."[100] Steeped in the nationalistic mythology of his art, Wagner, like the German Idealists, took the Jewish contamination of the *Volk* to lie in the Jewish emphasis on the concrete, material reality of this world, rather than the etherealized abstraction of a spiritual, mythical realm. The persona of the artist in his essay "On State and Religion," for example, mouths the words of Jesus, proclaiming, "My kingdom is not of this world."[101] Like the philosophers who influenced him, Wagner borrowed from the anti-Semitic theological valorization of the otherworldly. Thus, he announced the "necessity for fighting for emancipation from the Jews,"[102] who would sanctify and elevate this world through the commandments of Torah. Embracing the idea of an "Aryan Christianity" freed from the contagion of Judaism, notes Robert Wistrich, Wagner would prove to be "a crucial link between the Christian Judeophobic tradition and the 'redemptive' anti-Semitism of Nazism. His vision looked toward the future transformation of European man and the salvation of humanity through the radical solution of the 'Jewish question.'"[103] For Wagner, the "Jewish question" is a question not about what must be done with the Jews but about how to eliminate the source of evil inherent in the Jews, that is, how to silence the Voice of revelation that issues from Mount Sinai and into the world through the Jewish people.

Because evil is associated with essence, and not with action, for the anti-Semite it is rooted in a Jewish essence, that is, in the Jewish *race*.[104] For the racist anti-Semite, race is not an anthropological category but a metaphysical category; thus, Mack points out, Wagner "connected the immutability of race with the 'inseparable link' between the Jews and their God."[105] The Jews cannot be assimilated into the spiritual body of the *Volk* any more than Satan can be assimilated into the spiritual body of the Church. Just as Wagner's demonization of the Jewish people ascribes to the Jews the attributes of evil, so does his deification of the

---

[100] Richard Wagner, *Judaism in Music and Other Essays*, trans. W. Ashton Ellis (Lincoln: University of Nebraska Press, 1995), 100.

[101] Wagner, *Art and Politics*, 9.   [102] Wagner, *Judaism in Music and Other Essays*, 81.

[103] Robert Wistrich, *A Lethal Obsession: Anti-Semitism from Antiquity to the Global Jihad* (New York: Random House, 2010), 103.

[104] Jacob Katz points out that the notion of race in the Jewish context was introduced by the anti-Semitic liberal Christian thinker Ernst Renan (1823–1892); see Katz, *From Prejudice to Destruction*, 135.

[105] Mack, *German Idealism and the Jew*, 69.

Volk invest the Aryan race with divine attributes. Here too, in its racist
form, we see a concrete manifestation of the metaphysical aspect of
anti-Semitism. Mack makes an important observation to underscore
this point: "Racist discourse depicts both nation and 'national blood'
with the language of absolute self-sufficiency that has traditionally
been employed to characterize the divine."[106] Racist discourse, therefore, is the discourse of the modern idolatry. The racist worships the
idol of race as a divinely determined First Cause underlying everything,
so that the Jews must be identified as the most heinous perversion of all
human races; indeed, teaching that all humans stem from a single
human, the Jews pose a fundamental threat to the very notion of race.
Wagner's biographer Houston Stewart Chamberlain (1855–1927)
extended this deification of race as a reflection of metaphysical anti-
Semitism.[107] He transformed Christ into an Aryan,[108] deemed the
German people to be the true heirs of Greek wisdom and the saviors
of humankind,[109] and labeled the Jews the devil and arch enemy of the
German race.[110]

Proceeding from an anti-Semitic outlook, the race theorists are far
more interested in first principles than in anthropology or biology, physi-
ology or physiognomy. If their race theory is tied to Wagner's mythology
of the *Volk*, it is traceable to Hegel's apotheosis of the German, as
Edward Flannery has observed.[111] Which means: anti-Semitism is not a
subset of racism. The philosophical eclipse of God must be established in
order to arrive at the first principles of a racist mode of thought. The
assault on God is always tied to an assault on humanity, that is, an assault
on the Jewish teaching concerning the sanctity and the interconnectedness
of every human being, a teaching that undermines the very notion of race.
"Never was a more exalted view of man conceived," Fackenheim comments on the teachings of Torah, "than that of the divine image, and
never one more radically antiracist. . . . It was therefore grimly logical – if

---

[106] Ibid., 128.
[107] See Houston Stewart Chamberlain, *Richard Wagner*, trans. G. Ainsle Hight (London:
J. M. Dent, 1900).
[108] Houston Stewart Chamberlain, *The Foundations of the Nineteenth Century*, vol. 2,
trans. John Lees (London: John Lane, 1911), 36.
[109] Ibid., 221–222.
[110] See Houston Stewart Chamberlain, *The Foundations of the Nineteenth Century*, vol. 1,
trans. John Lees (London: John Lane, 1911), 494ff.
[111] Edward H. Flannery, *The Anguish of the Jews: Twenty-three Centuries of Anti-Semitism*
(New York: Macmillan, 1965), 178.

to be sure uniquely horrifying – that the most radical racists of all time decreed a unique fate for the Jewish people."[112]

It is important to bear in mind that, as a metaphysical category, race is *invisible*: just as the assault on God is an assault on the metaphysical, so is the assault on the Jew an assault on the invisible, on a presence that is as monolithic and ubiquitous as it is sinister and indiscernible. It is the presence invoked by the reference to the Jews as a "nation within a nation" or a "state within a state," a phrase that dates back to 1784, when it was first used by the German Lutheran preacher Johann Heinrich Schultz (1739–1823).[113] It gained philosophical and cultural currency when in 1793 Fichte declared, "A mighty state stretches across almost all the countries of Europe, hostile in intent and engaged in constant strife with everyone else.... This is Jewry."[114] Such thinking provides the precedent for one of the most notorious documents warning humanity of the world Jewish conspiracy, *The Protocols of the Elders of Zion*.

The Protocols first saw the light of day in 1903 in *Znamya* (The Banner), an anti-Semitic newspaper published in St. Petersburg. "Russian secret service agents under the leadership of Pyotr Ivanovich Rachkovsky," explains Stephen Atkins, "plagiarized two works – Hermann Goedsche's *Biarritz* (1868) and Maurice Joly's *A Dialogue in Hell: Conversations between Machiavelli and Montesquieu about Power and Right* (1864) – to produce the final version of *The Protocols of the Learned Elders of Zion* sometime between 1897 and 1899."[115] Shortly after its appearance in *Znamya* Russian jurist Sergei Alexandrovich Nilus (1863–1929) took over its publication and dissemination. The notorious forgery has its precedents, however, not only in nineteenth-century literature, but also in Christian theological manifestations of anti-Semitism. In the twelfth century Theobold of Cambridge (ca. 1090–1161) maintained that each year the Jews convene a secret council of rabbis to select a Christian child for sacrifice.[116] In 1307, it was claimed that the Jews conspired with King Muhammad I of Tunis to exterminate the Christians by poisoning all the wells.[117] The Jews, in other words, represented a pervasive, invisible evil that threatened all of humanity.

[112] Emil L. Fackenheim, *What Is Judaism?* (New York: Macmillan, 1987), 109.
[113] See Katz, *From Prejudice to Destruction*, 59.   [114] Quoted in ibid., 60.
[115] Stephen E. Atkins, *Holocaust Denial as an International Movement* (Westport, Conn.: Praeger, 2009), 16.
[116] See Prager and Telushkin, *Why the Jews?*, 82.
[117] See Flannery, *The Anguish of the Jews*, 107–108.

The First Protocol in *The Protocols of the Elders of Zion* reveals that, as the embodiment of evil, the Jews are bent on the eradication of "high moral character – openness, honor, honesty," both religious and secular.[118] The Jews carry out this nefarious project not by committing crimes but by corrupting culture and shaping public opinion. "Through the press," it is written in the Second Protocol, "we come into influence yet remain in the shadows,"[119] heinous and hidden. Lurking in the shadows, the Jews manipulate the ledgers of the world: "With the help of gold, which we control entirely, and with the underhanded ways at our disposal, we shall call forth a universal economic crisis."[120] Interested only in their own power, the Jews are the true racists, viewing non-Jews as "a herd of castrated sheep" and themselves as "the wolves," who naturally prey on the sheep – not openly but secretly by infiltrating governments and secret organizations such as the freemasons.[121] Once they have control, their plan is to eliminate anyone who opposes them.[122] Thus in the *Protocols* we see projected on the Jews all the classic evils: they are the greatest threat to moral society, bent on totalitarian rule, out to accumulate the wealth of the world, the sinister manipulators of thought itself. And all of these evils are born of their ineluctable *essence*.

Although such seemingly paranoid thinking appears to border on insanity, the vast majority of Germany's promoters of the *Protocols* were university professors and cultural intellectuals.[123] Why? Not because they were uneducated or stupid but because their thinking stemmed either from German Idealism or from German Volkism, guided by an abstract mode of thought that could not but categorize the Jews as the greatest of all possible threats. Whether it is the charge of killing God, having a slave mentality, or plotting to rule the world, this anti-Semitism rests on an utter unreality because the God that the ego would become is utterly unreal; it has little to do with the idiocy or blindness of the anti-Semite. In its philosophical, political, and cultural manifestations, anti-Semitism rests on thinking in terms of essence, and not in terms of a name or a time-bound fact. "The terms of life," says Rosenzweig in this connection, "are not 'essential' but 'real'; they concern not 'essence' but 'fact.' In spite of this the philosopher's word remains 'essential.' By giving in to wonder,

---

[118] "Protocols of the Elders of Zion," in Levy, *Antisemitism in the Modern World*, 152.
[119] Ibid., 156.   [120] Ibid., 159.   [121] Ibid., 161.   [122] Ibid., 164.
[123] See Mack, *German Idealism and the Jew*, 170.

by halting in his tracks and neglecting the operations of reality, he forces himself to retreat and is restricted to facing essence,"[124] which is faceless. The universal spirit begets a collective that is blind to the face and is therefore totalitarian. And there is no greater threat to the collective than the Jew, who affirms the Name and whose thinking is precisely concrete and time-bound.

SOME IMPLICATIONS

Arthur Cohen (1928–1986) offers an insight into the reversal that has taken place in modernity's project to rid the world of the Holy One and His witnesses: "We of the modern age no longer can deal with the holy, cannot perceive it . . ., but most contrary and fractious, regard ourselves as alone and autonomous in the universe, unbound by laws except as conventions of power, unhedged by moralities except as consent and convenience dictate; is it not the case that in such a civilization all that was once permitted to the infinite power of God and denied to the finite and constrained power of men is now denied to the forgotten God and given over to the potency of infinite man?"[125] Such is the outcome of thinking God out of the picture and installing man as the Most High, a process that demands the elimination of the Jew. And so we have the chief implication of the foregoing reflection on the philosophical manifestation of anti-Semitism, as well as its political and cultural manifestations: the Jew is the enemy of thought, that is, of thought that would eliminate God by thinking Him into irrelevance. The project of modern thought lies in the apotheosis of self-legislating autonomy, of the body politic embodied in the state, of the myth embodied in the *Volk*, of the collective that embraces a socialist or communist ideology – all of which characterize the modern idolatry. Fackenheim understood very well at least one implication: "The God of traditional Judaism can be present *to* man. If man is autonomous, then God can be present only *in* man, as 'conscience' or 'insight' or 'creative genius.' But to accept this is in the end to fall prey to idolatry."[126] And the original, primal, and perennial enemies of idolatry are the Jews.

---

[124] Rosenzweig, *Understanding the Sick and the Healthy*, 42.
[125] Arthur A. Cohen, "Thinking the *Tremendum*," in Michael L. Morgan, ed., *A Holocaust Reader: Responses to the Nazi Extermination* (New York: Oxford University Press, 2001), 192.
[126] Fackenheim, *Quest for Past and Future*, 139.

The modern idolatry promoted by modern thought twists finite onto-logical contingencies – such as natural accidents, ethnic identities, social structures, and sheer power – into abstract absolutes. The true object of worship in these instances is the self that would be as God – that would be free of God and the absolute responsibility that He summons, to and for the other human being. Tragically, as in biblical times, there are Jews who would trade the Torah for the false promises of the idolaters. Looking back from the depths of the Warsaw Ghetto, Rabbi Kalonymos Kalmish Shapira came to a dark realization of the implications of the modern idolatry for Jews who had been so duped: "Before Amalek came to fight with you, there were among you servile people who esteemed the very thinking championed by Amalek. You were impressed with the superficial culture in which Amalek takes such pride. . . . You were sure that Amalek was very cultured, that his philosophy was quite as good as anything. To be sure, it had its ethics, and there is profit to be had from it in this world. What did God do? He brought you face to face with Amalek. And now you see the evil, murderous character of German philosophy, Western philosophy."[127] Looking back as he did, Rabbi Shapira recognized another implication of modern thought: "Even such 'self-evident' laws as those prohibiting robbery and murder are not logical, rational, or natural 'laws' – for as we see now, there are nations whose objective and self-evident reality necessitates and clearly proves that it is right to rob any man of his wealth, and even to murder people."[128] What began as the age of rationalism morphed into the reign of a new and murderous spirit embodied in National Socialism. Here too philosophy had its accomplices.

---

[127] Shapira, *Sacred Fire*, 56. In this translation the word *ethics* might be granting the "wisdom" of Amalek more than its due; in the original text the term is *midot tovot*, which means "good qualities"; see Kalonymos Kalmish Shapira, *Esh Kodesh* (Jerusalem: Vaad Chasidei Pisetsenah, 1997), 24.

[128] Ibid., 65.

5

National Socialist Anti-Semitism

Our race has been poisoned by Judaism.
  Alfred Rosenberg, "*Kultur*: The *Volkish* Aesthetic"

As National Socialism emerged from the convergence of philosophical and political, cultural and religious expressions of Jew hatred, the anti-Semitism rooted in the soul's totalitarian longing to be as God manifested itself more radically than ever before. The Nazis' anti-Semitism was exterminationist not just because they were more evil than other anti-Semites, but because they had the means and the will to follow their first principle to its logical end. That meant the annihilation not only of the Jews but also of the teaching and testimony of Judaism that the Jews represent through their very presence in the world. Steven Katz elaborates on the metaphysical dimensions at work here: "The conflict of Aryan and Jew is an inner-historical actualization of normative, metahistorical antitheses. As such, the struggle between Aryan and Jew is not only necessary and inevitable but also a clash of world-historical (*because more than historical*) significance. Though actualized through blood in time, the depth of the historical encounter is rooted in eternity. In conformity with the recognition of this ontological truth, killing Jews, or, more precisely, eliminating 'the Jews' becomes a sacred obligation."[1] Because it is a "sacred obligation," it is a metaphysical imperative with a metaphysical origin. More learned and more systematic than their predecessors, the Nazis understood that the presence of the Jews in the world *is*

---

[1] Steven Katz, *The Holocaust in Historical Context*, vol. 1 (New York: Oxford University Press, 1994), 6; emphasis added.

the presence of the Holy One in the world; it was a presence that they could not abide. The Nazis "aimed to make the world *rein* of *Juden*, but also of *Judentum*," says Emil Fackenheim,[2] adding that *Judentum* is not exactly the equivalent of the English word *Judaism*; rather, it means "what Jews do collectively"[3] – in other words, what Jews do as *Knesset Yisrael*, as the "Community of Israel," which the Zohar equates with the *Shekhinah*, that is, with the presence of the Holy One in this realm (*Zohar* II, 93a). Fackenheim was quite familiar with this teaching from the Zohar.[4]

Central to the Jewish tradition that the Nazis set out to eradicate is a certain understanding of the human being; indeed, the assault on God always assumes the form of an assault on the very notion of a human being. At the heart of Judaism is the view that the human being is an insertion of something greater than all there is into the midst of all there is. Therefore, a human being is not reducible to the accidents of race, gender, culture, or ethnicity; nor is the human being justified by an inner reason, resolve, or power or even by morality. Created in the image and likeness of the Holy One, the human being harbors the presence of what sanctifies all of being from beyond being. In a word, the human being is a breach of being, defined by the commandment from beyond being, summoned to an uncompromising love for the *other* human being, for the widow and the orphan, the stranger and the beggar, the weak and the infirm. Visiting the sick, *bikur cholim*, in fact, is among the highest of the commandments a Jew can observe; the Nazis, by contrast, do not visit the sick – they murder them, as they did in the T-4 or "euthanasia" program of 1939–1941. These people who have nowhere to turn except to other people are the ones who are closest to the God in whose image they are created; they are the ones through whom God's commandment devolves on me, repeating through His commandment the first utterance from Mount Sinai: "*Anokhi HaShem*, I am the Lord!"

According to Judaism, *every* human being is my fellow human being, indeed, is part of my family, descended as we are from a single human being. Rabbi Shimon ben Azzai maintained that the origin of all humanity from one human being is the most fundamental of all Jewish teachings

---

[2] Emil L. Fackenheim, *Jewish-Christian Relations after the Holocaust: Toward Post-Holocaust Theological Thought* (Chicago: The Joseph Cardinal Bernardin Jerusalem Lecture, 1977), 10.

[3] Ibid., 14.

[4] See Emil L. Fackenheim, *To Mend the World: Foundations of Post-Holocaust Jewish Thought* (New York: Schocken Books, 1989), 327–331.

(see *Talmud Yerushalmi, Nedarim* 9:4). Recall, too, what was noted in the Introduction regarding why God begins humanity with just one human being, and not two: it is so that no one may say to another, "My side of the family is better than your side of the family" (see *Tosefta Sanhedrin* 8:4). There is only one side of the family, and each one, beginning with the first one, comes from the hand and the mouth of the Holy One. Thus all of humanity is interrelated, physically through Adam, metaphysically through the Creator. There is no teaching more inimical to National Socialism, which affirms that there is no connection between the Aryan and the non-Aryan, than this teaching that defines Judaism. In keeping with the paganism of the Nazis, as expressed by Nazi biologist Ernst Lehmann, humanity has its origin not in God but in nature.[5] For the Nazis, the extermination of the Jews was an ontological and ideological necessity.

Henri Crétella states one implication of Jewish thinking about God and humanity: "The adjective *Jewish* does not designate an ethnic group. On the contrary, it signifies that there is no true humanity without being related to divinity – as the Jews have shown us. In other words, it is not blood and soil [*Blut und Boden*] which properly define us, but rather the possibility of emancipating ourselves from this very blood and soil."[6] From a Jewish standpoint, freedom from the accidents of nature is attained not through the autonomy of a self-legislating ego but through a devotion to the commanding God. It lies in the heteronomous "responsibility" expressed by the Hebrew word *acharayut*, whose root is *acher*, meaning "other," indicating an orientation toward and care for the other person. To be created in the divine image is to be summoned to this very care for the other human being. There lies the liberation from *Blut und Boden*, from "blood and soil," as defined by Nazi race theorist Richard Walther Darré, who in 1930 declared that the challenge facing the German people was the restoration of "the unity of blood and soil."[7] What affects one, according to Darré, affects the other, so that the Jewish pathogen endangers not only the blood of the German people but also the very earth they tread. It is a threat,

---

[5] Ernst Lehmann, *Biologischer Wille: Wege und Ziele biologischer Arbeit im neuen Reich* (Munich: Zentralverlag der NSDAP, 1934), 10–11.

[6] Henri Crétella, "Self-Destruction," in Alan Milchman and Alan Rosenberg, eds., *Martin Heidegger and the Holocaust* (Atlantic Highlands, N.J.: Humanities Press, 1996), 159.

[7] Richard Walther Darré, *Um Blut und Boden: Reden und Aufsätze* (Munich: Zentralverlag der NSDAP, 1940), 28.

in other words, to the Aryan *essence*, which in Christianity is the same threat that Satan poses for the human soul.

In the previous chapter we saw how modern philosophy paved the way to social, cultural, and political manifestations of anti-Semitism. Under the Third Reich the Nazis continued to build on those philosophical foundations. At the June 1939 meeting of the National Socialist Association of University Lecturers, its head Dr. Walter Schultze declared before the assembly, "What the great thinkers of German Idealism dreamed of, and what was ultimately the kernel of their longing for liberty, finally comes alive, assumes reality.... Never has the German idea of freedom been conceived with greater life and greater vigor than in our day."[8] A leading intellectual of his day, Professor Schultze saw as clearly as any of Nazi Germany's philosophers the link between the German philosophical tradition and National Socialism. Indeed, it is perhaps startling but not surprising to discover that by 1940 nearly half of the philosophers of Germany were members of the Nazi Party.[9] In 1923 Herman Schwarz, a German thinker influenced by Meister Eckhart and Jacob Boehme, distinguished himself by becoming the first philosopher to publicly support the Nazis. He was followed by Bruno Bauch, Max Wundt, Hans Heyse, and Nicolai Hartmann, all of whom were Kantian Idealists; then there was the noted Hegelian Theodor Haerung, as well as the Nietzscheans Alfred Bäumler and Ernst Krieck. All of these Nazi party members embraced a philosophical tradition that was bent on the elimination of the God of Judaism, who, as a commanding Voice, undermines individual, self-legislating autonomy as the measure of human freedom and authenticity.

The most renowned of them all, of course, is Martin Heidegger. In 1922, Heidegger proclaimed that what attracted him to philosophy was "the full-blown anti-religious attitude of the German *Geist* ripened from German Idealism."[10] By "anti-religious" he meant anti-Semitic, complaining as he did of the "Jewification" of German thought.[11] In his *Introduction to Metaphysics* he maintained that "it was not German Idealism that collapsed; it was the era that was not strong enough to

---

[8] Quoted in George L. Mosse, *Nazi Culture* (New York: Grosset & Dunlop, 1966), 316.

[9] See Hans Sluga, *Heidegger's Crisis: Philosophy and Politics in Nazi Germany* (Cambridge, Mass.: Harvard University Press, 1993), 7.

[10] See Theodore Kisiel, "Heidegger's Apology: Biography and Philosophy and Ideology," in Tom Rockmore and Joseph Margolis, eds., *The Heidegger Case: On Philosophy and Politics* (Philadelphia: Temple University Press, 1992), 34.

[11] Reported in *Die Zeit*, 29 December 1989; see Kisiel, "Heidegger's Apology," 12.

match the stature, the breadth, and the originality of that spiritual world."[12] In the Nazis he saw the triumph of the will necessary to match the will to power of the original idea, an idea that could not abide in the same universe as the Jews and Judaism. If Heidegger was a philosopher who happened to be a Nazi, he was also a Nazi who happened to be a philosopher. Indeed, in his association with the Nazis, the existentialist genius Heidegger simply followed his premise to its logical conclusion. And he knew it.

MARTIN HEIDEGGER: THE NAZI METAPHYSICIAN

Emmanuel Lévinas accurately states the implications of the ontological thinking that finds its apex in Heidegger: "Heideggerian ontology, which subordinates the relationship with the Other to the relation with Being in general, remains under obedience to the anonymous, and leads inevitably to another power, to imperialist domination, to tyranny."[13] In the modern period tyranny is first of all tyranny over the Jew, whose thinking represents the most fundamental threat to totalitarian ontological thought; it is no accident that there are very few, if any, totalitarian states that are not anti-Semitic. Grounding freedom in autonomy and authenticity in resolve, this strain of German philosophy that culminates in Heidegger is, as Lévinas argues, "the outcome of a long tradition of pride, heroism, domination, and cruelty" that "continues to exalt the will to power."[14] One of the pinnacles in this exultation of the will to power came on 27 May 1933, when Heidegger delivered his infamous address "The Self-Assertion of the German University" as Rector of the University of Freiburg. By that time Hitler had assumed dictatorial powers, Dachau was in operation, and books had been burned on university campuses.

In his remarks the greatest philosopher of the twentieth century extolled the "magnificence and greatness" of National Socialism[15] and declared that "all abilities of will and thought, all strengths of the heart,

---

[12] Quoted in Victor Farías, *Heidegger and Nazism*, trans. Paul Burrell (Philadelphia: Temple University Press, 1989), 219.

[13] Emmanuel Lévinas, *Totality and Infinity*, trans. Alphonso Lingis (Pittsburgh, Pa.: Duquesne University Press, 1969), 46–47.

[14] Emmanuel Lévinas, *Collected Philosophical Papers*, trans. Alphonso Lingis (Dordrecht: Martinus Nijhoff, 1987), 52.

[15] Martin Heidegger, "The Self-Assertion of the German University," in Guenther Neske and Emil Kettering, eds., *Martin Heidegger and National Socialism*, trans. Lisa Harries (New York: Paragon, 1990), 13.

and all capabilities of the body must unfold *through* battle, heightened *in* battle, and presented *as* battle."[16] Hearing the repetition of the word *battle*, or *Kampf*, any German listener would immediately think of Hitler's manifesto *Mein Kampf*, the text that laid the foundations for the extermination of the Jews: *the* battle, as outlined in *My Battle*, was the perennial battle against the Jews, and Heidegger was intelligent enough to understand its metaphysical implications. Both Otto Pöggler (b. 1928) and Karl Jaspers (1883–1969) have seen in the Rector's address an expression of Heidegger's aspiration to lead the Nazi revolution;[17] indeed, Hans Sluga argues convincingly that Heidegger considered himself "the born philosopher and spiritual leader of the new movement."[18] Bringing to bear the weight of his metaphysics, both in his address and in his philosophy, Heidegger revealed the metaphysical origin of National Socialist anti-Semitism: it lay in the will and the resolve, the *Entschlossenheit*, to make one's own resolute self, one's own determined *Volk*, the absolute ground of authentic being. Thus the *Volk* and the Führer become the godlike ground of German reality and its law, as Heidegger declared in a statement published a statement in the *Freiburger Studentenzeitung* on 3 November 1933: "The Führer himself and he alone *is* the present and future German reality and its law,"[19] where reality and law are grounded in the will to power.

When Heidegger thus "endorsed in advance the Führer's actions as German 'reality' and 'law,'" says Fackenheim, "he did so not, like countless others, impelled by personal fear, opportunism, or the hysteria of the time, but rather deliberately and *with the weight of his philosophy behind it.*"[20] And the weight of his philosophy was considerable. Although some would excuse the Nazi philosopher by claiming that he later "reappraised" Nazism,[21] he "in no way reappraised his own philosophy," as Fackenheim points out.[22] Not only is there no inconsistency between Heidegger's actions and his thought, there is a certain logical demand that the two converge. He is the existentialist par excellence.

---

[16] Ibid., 12.
[17] See Tom Rockmore, *On Heidegger's Nazism and Philosophy* (Berkeley: University of California Press, 1992), 60.
[18] Sluga, *Heidegger's Crisis*, 4.
[19] See Neske and Kettering, *Martin Heidegger and National Socialism*, 45.
[20] Fackenheim, *To Mend the World*, 169.
[21] See, e.g., Jacques Derrida, *De l'esprit* (Paris: Éditions Galilee, 1987), 11, 12, 64, 65, 155, 156.
[22] Fackenheim, *To Mend the World*, 169.

As an existentialist, Heidegger sought a "secure grounding not in values but in a new unconcealment of Being, a new truth of Being,"[23] which is realized in a Nietzschean merging of knowledge with the will and of the will with knowledge.[24] The issue of that union is the "new man," the mangod or the *Übermensch*, that the Nazi anti-Semite aspires to become. Thus, Heidegger saw in National Socialism the new unfolding of Being as such, neutral and valueless, that finally frees itself from the onto-theological appeal to an infinite or divine being, from all revelation of values. Over against an "inauthentic" appeal to the ethical he posited an authentic "existential ontology," which "has as its sole objective the explication of the primordial transcendental structure of the *Dasein* in man," where the aim of Dasein is "the comprehension of Being."[25] This comprehension of Being is an encompassing of Being through thought and will; it alone – and not any revealed "truth" – will set you free as only God can be free.

Comprehension here is to be taken literally: from the Latin *comprehendere*, it is the "grasping" or "seizing" of being exemplified, for instance, in the notion of *Lebensraum*, which the Nazis invoked in order to justify their program of territorial seizure and occupation. It brings to mind the name of Cain, or *Kayin*, which is seizing in the sense of acquisition, a seizing and appropriation through murder. Such an expansion of the being of the *Volk* over creation is necessary to the primordial usurpation of God as the creator. The Nazi usurpation of God is the ultimate aim of the Heideggerian Dasein, the neutral, ineluctable, and resolved "being there" of man. As an extension of Dasein, the *Volk* appropriates the other, both physically and spiritually, both politically and philosophically, both physically and metaphysically. And the "other" includes God, or at least the dimension of height signified by God, evidenced by a statement that Julius Streicher made in 1936: "Who fights the Jews fights the devil, and who masters the devil conquers heaven."[26] There we have the Nazis' object of conquest through

[23] Martin Heidegger, "Martin Heidegger: A Philosopher and Politics: A Conversation," in Neske and Kettering, *Martin Heidegger and National Socialism*, 217.

[24] See Martin Heidegger, *Poetry, Language, Thought*, trans. Albert Hofstadter (New York: Harper & Row, 1971), 67.

[25] Martin Heidegger, *Kant and the Problem of Metaphysics*, trans. J. S. Churchill (Bloomington: Indiana University Press, 1962), 244.

[26] Quoted in Emil L. Fackenheim, *Jewish Philosophers and Jewish Philosophy*, ed. Michael L. Morgan (Bloomington: Indiana University Press, 1996), 122.

the will to power, beyond Paris or Moscow: it is the conquest of heaven through the conquest of the earth and all that is in it.

Understanding what is required for the fulfillment of the "transcendental structure of the *Dasein* in man," Heidegger understood perhaps better than anyone Nietzsche's assertion that what is needful is "a race . . . with an excess of strength for beauty, bravery, culture . . ., *strong enough to have no need of the tyranny of the virtue-imperative* . . ., beyond good and evil."[27] The "virtue-imperative" is precisely what the God of Judaism would impose on humanity and what the new order, the new man, must overcome, which in concrete terms meant the elimination of the Jews by any means necessary. Karl Löwith (1897–1973) understood this point when in 1936 he suggested to his teacher that there might be an essential, defining connection between Heidegger's philosophy and his embrace of the Nazis. "Heidegger agreed with me," says Löwith, "and elucidated that his concept of 'historicity' was the basis of his political 'engagement.' He also left no doubt about his belief in Hitler."[28] Heidegger's Nazism was not a personal shortcoming or a character flaw but a central feature of a mode of thought driven by the will to power, which is the will to resist the "Jewification" of thought, a will to become as God.

If the will to power defines the *character* of beings, as Heidegger asserts,[29] then the sanctity or holiness of my being lies not in the emanation of the Creator or in my affirmation of the sanctity of the other human being; rather, it lies in my will to assume a divine character, a will to become as God. For Heidegger, what is required for such an apotheosis is *Entschlossenheit*, or "resolve," which he defines as "the loyalty of existence to its own self."[30] The resolve that determines authentic being-there is a resolve for being-guilty for being there, where the guilt is not *incurred* but rather, in a way reminiscent of Christian teaching, existentially *inherited*.[31] In contrast to the responsibility to and for the other that lies at the core of Jewish thought, therefore, resolve is something that concerns only the self: "Dasein *is its own self* in the original isolation

---

[27] Friedrich Nietzsche, *The Will to Power*, trans. Walter Kaufmann and R. J. Hollingdale, ed. Walter Kaufmann (New York: Random House, 1968), 478; emphasis added.

[28] Karl Löwith, "Last Meeting with Heidegger," in Neske and Kettering, *Martin Heidegger and National Socialism*, 158.

[29] Martin Heidegger, *Nietzsche*, vol. 1, trans D. Krell (San Francisco, Calif.: Harper & Row, 1979), 18.

[30] Martin Heidegger, *Sein und Zeit*, 2nd ed. (Tübingen: Max Niemeyer, 1963), 391; my translation.

[31] See ibid., 305.

of silent resolve."[32] Not just resolve but the *isolation* of resolve; instead of the Jewish emphasis on relation, we have the existentialist emphasis on isolation. Neither the new unconcealment of Being nor the comprehension of Being has anything to do with the other human being. "Love ... and friendship," Edith Wyschogrod observes, "play no part in Heidegger's analysis,"[33] because such categories are either irrelevant or threatening to one's existential authenticity. In contrast to the Jew who affirms that a commanded, loving relation to the other human being determines who I am, for Heidegger, other people are *das Man* or "the They," who undermine my authenticity.[34] Here authenticity means a sufficiency of the Same unto itself, as well as the radical appropriation of the other by the Same, a move essential to the transformation of the man into the mangod. It means that what is mine is mine, and, if I have the will, what is yours is mine, which, says the Talmud, is a manifestation of evil (see *Pirke Avot* 5:10). It is the Nazi evil. It is the Heideggerian evil. It is the evil of anti-Semitism.

Eliminating the other human being from his sphere of concern, Heidegger declares, "*Dasein* exists for the sake of itself alone."[35] Ideologically extended, this existence for the sake of oneself alone becomes an existence for the sake of one's *Volk* alone; one can be only with others who are like oneself, that is, who are German, in service to the Führer, as Fackenheim realized: "The *Führer*, no emperor-god, embodies the *Volk*, and the *Volk*, no worshipping community, realizes its selfhood in blind obedience and total sacrifice. Because Nazism internalizes divinity, it is an idealism. Yet, since it idolatrously identifies finiteness and infinitude, it is an idealism *totally without ideals*."[36] And therefore totally inhuman: after the human appropriation of the divine, humanity's savior – the Führer – is inhumanity incarnate. Here we have a clue to a defining feature of National Socialist anti-Semitism: the anti-Semite who would be as God is not only inhumane – he is inhuman. Thus, the apotheosis of the Dasein that is forever engaged in the care of itself alone and that wills itself alone leads to the death of the other. The *Sein-zum-Tod*, or

[32] Ibid., 323; my translation.

[33] Edith Wyschogrod, *Spirit in Ashes: Hegel, Heidegger, and Man-Made Death* (New Haven, Conn.: Yale University Press, 1985), 166.

[34] See Heidegger, *Sein und Zeit*, 254.

[35] Martin Heidegger, *Vom Wesen des Grundes*, 5th ed. (Frankfurt am Main: Klostermann, 1965), 38; my translation.

[36] Emil L. Fackenheim, *Encounters between Judaism and Modern Philosophy* (New York: Basic Books, 1993), 194.

"being-toward-death," that Heidegger takes to be central to authentic existence is a concern for *my* death.[37] The death that concerns the Jew is the death of the *other* human being, the widow, the orphan, and the stranger, who are of no concern to Heidegger. What must be opposed to the evil of Heidegger's ontology is precisely the imposed ethical demand revealed through the Jews: not the autonomy of the self but the sanctity of the other, not the universal maxims of reason but the uncompromising commandments of God – from *on high*.

Here we see one of the chief aspects of the Heideggerian horror: it is the erasure of the dimension of height that would enable us to speak of anything holy or evil, so that what is "there" is *merely* there. Opposing this dimension of height, a Heideggerian mode of thought has to be anti-Semitic, inasmuch as it diametrically opposes the ethical concern for the other human being that has characterized Jewish thought from the time of the Torah. "If one takes the expression 'concern,'" says Heidegger, "in the sense of an ethical and ideological evaluation of 'human life' rather than as the designation of the structural unity of the inherently finite transcendence of *Dasein*, then everything falls into confusion and no comprehension of the problematic which guides the analytic of *Dasein* is possible."[38] For thought to avoid such confusion, it must think God out of the picture, and with God the Jew. It must stop its ears to the outcry of the other human being; otherwise Dasein's capacity to will itself alone is undermined. Indeed, what is most exalting in Jewish thought, being there for the sake of another, is most undermining in Heideggerian thought, being there for one's own sake. Heidegger wrote no treatise on ethics or morality because such matters were not only immaterial but were dangerous to his project. Neither he nor his Nazi colleagues had a different "value system" if *value* pertains to the *ethical*. No, they took themselves to be pursuing not an ethical good but an existential good, beyond good and evil.

By now it is clear that with the Heideggerian valorization of the will as the ground of being comes a collapse of all inherent meaning and value in human life, an erasure of the dimension of height through which any holiness of the human being might be revealed. This absorption of all into the same characterizes the appropriation of all by the Same, by the mangod; it is characteristic of the anti-Semitic thinking that went into the making of the "concentrationary universe." In his

[37] See Heidegger, *Sein und Zeit*, 245, 262–263.
[38] Heidegger, *Kant and the Problem of Metaphysics*, 245.

most infamous comment on the Holocaust Heidegger levels all into the same by equating technologically driven agriculture with the technologically driven murder of the Jews.[39] Similarly, in a letter to Herbert Marcuse (1898–1979) dated 20 January 1948 Heidegger claimed that the Allies' treatment of "Eastern Germans" was precisely the same as Hitler's treatment of the Jews,[40] a position grounded not in evidence but in hatred. This is an important ramification of the anti-Semitic thinking that went into the extermination of the Jews: once everything is all the same, any human being can take the place of another, and every human being is expendable. Once expendable, the human being is rendered faceless. And since, in the words of Lévinas, "the face is what forbids us to kill,"[41] with the Heideggerian obliteration of the dimension of height comes the obliteration of the prohibition against murder.

This is the meaning of the Heidegger's *Seinsverlassenheit*,[42] which is an "abandonment of being," leaving behind the care and anxiety for the other that might disturb the soporific complacency of "letting things be." As Fackenheim points out, however, this abandonment of being amounts to an abandonment not only of the living but also of the dead and the suffering humanity swallowed up by Auschwitz; it is deaf to "the screams of the children and the silence of the *Muselmänner*,"[43] the walking dead who were the iconic inhabitants of the concentration camps. The unsettling nature of those screams and that silence lies at the core of the unsettling presence – the undermining presence – of the Jews. For the "being there" of the Jews is neither neutral nor composed: invoking a common descent from Adam, the very presence of the Jews cries out that those children are your children, the *Muselmann* is your brother – because and in spite of the fact that he is the unique creation of the Nazi worldview as articulated by the ideologues of National Socialism.

---

[39] Heidegger made this move in a lecture given in 1949; see John D. Caputo, "Heidegger's Scandal: Thinking and the Essence of the Victim," in Rockmore and Margolis, *The Heidegger Case*, 266.

[40] Quoted in Domenico Losurlo, "Heidegger and Hitler's War," in Rockmore and Margolis, *The Heidegger Case*, 157.

[41] Emmanuel Lévinas, *Ethics and Infinity*, trans. Richard Cohen (Pittsburgh, Pa.: Duquesne University Press, 1985), 86.

[42] See, e.g., Martin Heidegger, *Beiträge zur Philosophie*, in *Gesamtausgabe*, vol. 65 (Frankfurt: Vittorio Klostermann, 2003), 110.

[43] Fackenheim, *To Mend the World*, 190.

THE FIRST PRINCIPLES OF NATIONAL SOCIALIST
ANTI-SEMITISM

"Just as fleas and elephants have different spiritual constitutions," wrote Nazi Nobel Laureate Philipp von Leonard (1862–1947) in 1936, "so the spirits of different human races and ethnic groups are totally different from each other."[44] Hence "Nordic man," declared the Nazi anthropologist Ludwig Clauss (1892–1974), "can overcome almost anything in the world save the distance separating man from man."[45] Why does bridging this gap lie outside the power of even the Master Race? Because, from a Nazi standpoint, the distance separating man from man is infinite: human beings contain no divine spark that might bind them together, nor do they derive from a single origin, as Judaism teaches. Therefore, Judaism represents a view of God, world, and humanity that is diametrically opposed to the Nazi *Weltanschauung*. Comprehending every aspect of life, both within and without, the *Weltanschauung* is a complete, all-encompassing worldview. As the Nazi economist Peter Heinz Seraphim (1902–1979) insisted, National Socialist anti-Semitism is not reducible to racism or ethnic differences; it has nothing to do with xenophobia, economic envy, or scapegoating.[46] The Nazis were not anti-Semites because they were racists; they were racists because they were anti-Semites. Anti-Semitism was at the defining core of their metaphysics: for the Nazis, the anti-Semitic outlook had to be determined in order to arrive at a racist way of thinking. The Nazi philosopher Max Wundt (1879–1963) was quite right, then, when he asserted that the Jewish view of God, world, and humanity "stands opposed to the folkish world view as its total antithesis."[47] Which is to say: the Jew is not the "other" – the Jew is the *evil* that must be removed from the world, for the sake of the *Volk*, indeed, for the sake of all humanity.

From these statements on the part of the Nazi intellectual elite one sees the soul's primal desire to be as God unfolding as a metaphysical system. More than a biological or anthropological category, "race" in this instance is a *metaphysical* category that reveals the metaphysical origin

---

[44] Quoted in Mosse, *Nazi Culture*, 202; Leonard won the Nobel Prize in physics in 1905.

[45] Ibid., 70.

[46] See Max Weinreich, *Hitler's Professors: The Part of Scholarship in Germany's Crimes against the Jewish People* (New Haven, Conn.: Yale University Press, 1999), 78.

[47] Max Wundt, *Deutsche Weltanschauung* (Munich: J. F. Lehmans, 1928), 75; see also Sluga, *Heidegger's Crisis*, 113.

of Jew hatred. In the Nazi worldview the notion of race is rooted neither in color nor physiognomy nor even in the genes, but in a concept of human essence that fuses biology and being into a single category. The category has a name: it is *Rassenseele*. Explaining the concept of *Rassenseele*, or "race-soul," chief Nazi ideologue Alfred Rosenberg writes, "Soul means race viewed from within. And, vice-versa, race is the externalization of a soul."[48] If race may be viewed from within, then it is not reducible to any outward manifestation such as skin tones or hair texture; rather it is a conceptual, abstract category. The abstraction assumed a concrete form in the extermination of the Jews. Which means that the Nazis did not target the Jews in order to rise to power; rather, they rose to power in order to target the Jews.

Betraying a Nietzschean influence, Rosenberg accentuates the "totality of life" embodied in "spirit and will."[49] Spirit and will – and not, for example, righteousness and justice – constitute the "heroic attitude" of National Socialism, which, he avers, "departs from the *single* but *completely* decisive avowal, *namely from the avowal that blood and character, race and soul are merely different designations for the same entity.*"[50] If race, character, and soul are in the blood, then so is the mode of thought, the teaching and testimony, that characterize a certain way of understanding reality. For the Nazi, the most insidious of all such modes of thought is rooted in the Jewish *Rassenseele*. The Jew, therefore, is an *essential* threat to the Aryan *essence*. According to Rosenberg, the Nazis fought the Jews because the Aryan *Geist*, the Aryan "mind" or "spirit," "has been poisoned by Judaism," and not merely by Jewish blood, for the -ism is in the blood.[51] Therefore, he insisted, all Jews are prone to think talmudically, "whether they are atheistic Bourse-speculators, religious fanatics, or Talmudic Jews of the cloth."[52] The Jewish threat to humanity "would not be altered if the Jew denied the Talmud, because the national character, which remains the same, would continue to represent an equally inflexible, dogmatic viewpoint in other areas."[53] Thus, the

[48] Alfred Rosenberg, *Race and Race History and Other Essays*, ed. Robert Pois (New York: Harper & Row, 1974), 34. The original is "*Seele aber bedeutet Rasse von innen gesehen. Und umgekehrt ist Rasse die Außenseite einer Seele*"; see Alfred Rosenberg, *Der Mythus der 20. Jahrhunderts: Eine Wertung der seelisch-geistigen Gestaltenkämpfe unserer Zeit* (Munich: Hoheneichen Verlag, 1934), 4.

[49] Rosenberg, *Race and Race History*, 95.

[50] Quoted in Weinreich, *Hitler's Professors*, 26; emphasis in the original.

[51] Rosenberg, *Race and Race History and Other Essays*, 131–132.   [52] Ibid., 181.

[53] Ibid., 183.

avenues of conversion and assimilation were permanently closed to the Jew. Indeed, given the metaphysical origin of anti-Semitism in the soul's longing to be as God, neither conversion nor assimilation can possibly be an option for the Jew: as the Nazis realized, once taken to its extreme, the metaphysical origin of Jew hatred demands the complete extermination of the Jews, and nothing less.

In keeping with these metaphysical roots of National Socialist anti-Semitism, Hitler viewed the Jews as "an abstract race of the mind [that] has its origins, admittedly, in the Hebrew religion."[54] Affirming the metaphysical ground of his own anti-Semitism, "Hitler hated *metaphysical* Jewishness," as Robert Michael observes. "He objected to the 'Jewish mind' and to the Jewish religious and cultural values that permeated Jewish thought and behavior. Far from being a prophet of race, Hitler did not see the Jews as flesh and blood. Jews were mere symbols of the Jewish spirit he despised. Hitler suggested that beneath the surface of biological racism, a more essential 'spiritual racism' existed: individual Jews embodied an inherently evil Jewish spirit."[55] Nowhere is this outlook articulated more thoroughly than in *Mein Kampf* (volume one published in 1925, volume two in 1926).

One of the most terrifying of Hitler's assertions in his manifesto comes early on, where he declares that the Nazis' "struggle" is "a struggle for the soul of the child, and to the child its first appeal is addressed."[56] And as we shall see below, the Nazis undertook a systematic assault on the soul of the Jewish child as an integral part of their assault on God. To be sure, laying claim to the soul of the child is a first step in the usurpation of God, for in the soul of the child the Divine Presence burns most intensely. There, in the child, the truth of the verse from the Proverbs is most evident: the soul is the candle of God (see Proverbs 20:27). It is a truth self-evident to anyone who has gazed into the eyes of a child who is five seconds old, as those eyes take their first look at this world. One cannot help but shudder when reading the Nazi German primer for third- and fourth-grade children that included the prayer, "May we become strong and pure ... German children of our Führer."[57] Instead of the refrain from the Jewish prayers, "Our Father, our King," we have the usurpation

[54] Quoted in Robert Michael, *Holy Hatred: Christianity, Anti-Semitism, and the Holocaust* (New York: Palgrave Macmillan, 2006), 181.
[55] Ibid.; emphasis added.
[56] Adolf Hitler, *Mein Kampf*, trans. Ralph Manheim (Boston: Houghton Mifflin, 1971), 12.
[57] See Lisa Pine, *Nazi Family Policy, 1933–1945* (Oxford, U.K.: Berg Publishers, 1999), 60.

of God in the refrain, "Our Father, our Führer." The appropriation of God manifest in the appropriation of the souls of the children was consummated as soon as decent German parents grew afraid of their own children, whose souls had been captured by the Nazi Party,[58] a development set into motion from the founding of the Hitler Youth in 1922. Hitler had the children in mind when he asserted, "Only the greatness of the sacrifices will win new fighters for the cause."[59] Thus, he articulated the premise for placing the children of Germany on the altar to pass them through fire as a sacrificial offering to himself.

The sacrifice of the children lay not only in offering them up to die for the sake of the Germany but, perhaps even more heinously, in transforming them into murderers in the National Socialist project of extermination. The "complete annihilation" of a teaching and tradition, the Führer states as his ultimate aim, "can be carried out only through a process of extermination."[60] The teaching and tradition he would exterminate, of course, is Judaism. Hitler goes on to assert, "The fight against a spiritual power with methods of violence remains defensive until the sword becomes the support, the herald and disseminator, of a new spiritual doctrine."[61] An absolute can be eradicated only with another absolute: here it is the absolute of Judaism's teachings, beginning with the prohibition against murder, over against the absolute of National Socialism, which insists on the necessity of murder. It is the absolute commandment of the God of Abraham to choose life (see Deuteronomy 30:19) over against the absolute injunction of the Führer to inflict death, beginning with the children of Abraham.

Hitler understood the importance of the usurpation of the word in the Nazis' effort to lay claim to the soul, and so he laid out the formula for the assault on the word in his formula for propaganda: "If propaganda is to be effective for the movement, it must be addressed to only one quarter [of the people].... If propaganda renounces primitiveness of expression, it does not find its way to the feeling of the broad masses."[62] Propaganda is intended not to convince but rather to *"reimplant the spirit of proud self-reliance, manly defiance, and wrathful hatred."*[63] Yes, *wrathful hatred,* *"zornigen Hasses"*[64]: the hatred that leads to the extermination of the

---

[58] See Simon Wiesenthal, *The Sunflower: On the Possibilities and Limits of Forgiveness,* trans. H. A. Piehler (New York: Schocken Books, 1998), 31–32.

[59] Hitler, *Mein Kampf,* 103.   [60] Ibid., 170–171.   [61] Ibid., 172.

[62] Ibid., 341–342.   [63] Ibid., 632; emphasis in the original.

[64] Adolf Hitler, *Mein Kampf* (Munich: Zentralverlag der NSADP, 1927), 714.

Jews must be *wrathful*. Any means can be justified to attain this ideological end, including and above all, falsehood and deception. Just so, Hitler understood deception to be an important part of the strategy of any propaganda campaign, because "something of the most insolent lie will always remain and stick."[65] That is how you breed "wrathful hatred." The Nazis were masters of "the most insolent lie," accusing the Jews of everything from the age-old Blood Libel to secretly plotting to take over the world. Thus the calumny that justifies and demands spilling the blood of Jewish children becomes an ideological first principle.

Because all evil is Jewish, Hitler explained, "no one need be surprised if among our people the personification of the devil as the symbol of all evil assumes the living shape of the Jew."[66] And when it comes to fighting the devil incarnate in the Jew, there can be no half measures. "If *der Nationalsozialismus* was the acting out of a *Weltanschauung*," Fackenheim elucidates this point, "and if antisemitism was the 'granite-like' core of it, then neither the Führer nor his 'decent' followers could be satisfied with a *Halbheit* [half measure] that would have *Geschlossenheit* [unity] but stop short of confirming its truth. The 'solution' of the 'problem' posed by the Jewish 'poisoners' of the world, in that case, had to have *Ganzheit*, i.e. be 'final,' and remain so to the end."[67] Therefore the Nazis' determination was without measure, as infinite as the Infinite One whom they sought to eliminate in the extermination of the Jews. What they did was not unimaginable – it was everything imaginable, because the only limitation to their actions lay in the will and the imagination.

There lies the fanaticism of National Socialism, as Hitler understood very well. "The future of a movement," he insisted, "is conditioned by the fanaticism [*Fanatismus*], yes, the intolerance, with which its adherents uphold it as the sole correct movement."[68] National Socialism requires fanatics who "must not fear the hostility of their enemies, but must feel that it is the presupposition for their own right to exist. They must not shun the hatred of the enemies of our nationality and our philosophy and its manifestations; they must long for them."[69] Not only engendering hatred, but also seeking to be hated, the Nazis fed their fanaticism by casting themselves in the role of victims of the world Jewish conspiracy – which is

---

[65] Hitler, *Mein Kampf*, trans. Ralph Manheim, 232.   [66] Ibid., 324.

[67] Fackenheim, "Holocaust and *Weltanschauung*," 206.

[68] Hitler, *Mein Kampf*, trans. Ralph Manheim, 349–350; see also the German edition, Hitler, *Mein Kampf*, 385.

[69] Ibid., 351.

a manifestation of the projected Jewish desire to be as God – so that they, the victims, alone can oppose the absolute evil embodied in the Jew. "The greatness of every mighty organization embodying an idea in this world," writes Hitler, "lies in the religious fanaticism and intolerance with which, fanatically convinced of its own right, it intolerantly imposes its will against all others."[70] And it *is* religious, as any endeavor to usurp God must be. It is religious because it is an idolatry that installs the ego as the new god, not just knowing but determining good and evil. But the god that the fanatic would become is not the God of Abraham, who is "compassionate and gracious, slow to anger, abundant in loving kindness and truth," and so on (Exodus 34:5–7). No, it is the false, idolatrous god, for whom power is the only reality and weakness is the only sin. It is the god of National Socialism, who declares, as Hitler did, "Today I believe that I am acting in accordance with the will of the Almighty Creator: *by defending myself against the Jew, I am fighting for the work of the Lord.*"[71] And the Lord is the Führer.

Making himself into a god, Hitler had to make his enemy into the devil and therefore the most heinous of all threats to humanity: if "the Jew is victorious over the other peoples of the world," he writes, "his crown will be the funeral wreath of humanity."[72] To fight for God and humanity is to fight against the devil, the Jew. Like the devil, the Jew, says Hitler, is an "invisible wirepuller."[73] Rendering the Jew invisible, the Nazi transforms the Jew into an ominous, universal threat, and the effort to eradicate the evil must be equally universal. Finally, given the ubiquitous invisibility of the evil, one cannot be certain of its defeat until the Nazis have become the rulers of all humanity. It must be stressed that the evil is not just the *Jew* – it is *Judaism*. For Jew hatred is always and everywhere a hatred of the Judaism that defines the Jew as a Jew. When, for example, Hitler refers to "the inner grounds which cause the disease in question,"[74] he is referring to Judaism. The savior who does the work of the Lord, waging a holy war against Satan for the sake of redemption, battles the Jew and Judaism. That battle is Hitler's *Kampf*. It is a holy war waged against the Holy One Himself.

THE NAZI WAR AGAINST GOD

In an interview with German journalist Josef Hell in 1922 Hitler told Hell, "Once I really am in power, my first and foremost task will be the

---

[70] Ibid.   [71] Ibid., 65; emphasis in the original.   [72] Ibid.
[73] See, e.g., ibid., 493, 523, 526.   [74] Ibid., 233.

annihilation of the Jews."[75] He later confided to German politician Hermann Rausching (1887–1982) that, as Führer, his mission in life was to destroy the "tyrannical God of the Jews" and His "life-denying Ten Commandments."[76] Kalonymos Kalmish Shapira realized as much when, on 15 December 1941, he wrote in his Warsaw Ghetto diary, "It is not because we robbed or did anything wrong to anyone that we are being persecuted, but because we are Jews – children of Israel, bound to God and to His holy Torah. [This explains] why our enemies are not satisfied with just killing us or extinguishing the divine spark inside us but feel they have to annihilate simultaneously both body and soul of the Jews."[77] Richard Rubenstein agrees: "The aim of creating a world in which God is dead (or, more precisely, in which the Judeo-Christian God is *negated*) was at the heart of the Nazi program."[78] Because an exterminationist anti-Semitism formed the metaphysical core of National Socialism, the Nazi war against the Jews was a war against God.

That is what the Holocaust is about: the Nazi endeavor to obliterate the Holy One in the extermination of the Jews and to exterminate the Jews in the obliteration of the Holy One, a project that betrays the metaphysical origin of anti-Semitism. "Why did they do it?" Fackenheim asks. And he answers: "Perhaps this was the purpose: to kill God."[79] For killing God is ultimately necessary for becoming as God and requires the extermination of the Chosen of God. If one should object that the Nazis targeted both religious and nonreligious Jews for annihilation, we need only recall Rosenberg's assertion that *all* Jews are prone to think "talmudically."[80] Nothing else can explain why the Nazis trekked to Tromsø, Norway, well north of the Arctic Circle, to murder the seventeen Jews residing there; one does not venture into the Arctic out of economic envy, xenophobia, racial animosity, ethnic prejudice, or the longing to find a scapegoat. Because the God of Abraham is omnipresent, the assault on the God of Abraham has to be omnipresent, even if it means venturing

[75] Quoted in Stephen E. Atkins, *Holocaust Denial as an International Movement* (Westport, Conn.: Praeger, 2009), 29.

[76] Quoted in Dennis Prager and Joseph Telushkin, *Why the Jews? The Reason for Antisemitism* (New York: Simon & Schuster, 2003), 16.

[77] Kalonymos Kalmish Shapira, *Sacred Fire: Torah from the Years of Fury 1939–1942*, trans. J. Hershy Worch, ed. Deborah Miller (Northvale, N.J.: Jason Aronson, 2000), 253.

[78] Richard L. Rubenstein, *After Auschwitz: History, Theology, and Contemporary Judaism*, 2nd ed. (Baltimore: Johns Hopkins University Press, 1992), 54.

[79] Fackenheim, *Jewish-Christian Relations after the Holocaust*, 20.

[80] Rosenberg, *Race and Race History and Other Essays*, 181.

into the Arctic. Jewish teaching and testimony had to be the designated target of the extermination project, for Jewish tradition is itself a manifestation of the God of Abraham, Isaac, and Jacob. Recall the words of the Koretzer Rebbe: "God and Torah are one. God, Israel, and Torah are one."[81]

Vilna Ghetto diarist Herman Kruk (1897–1944) confirms that the Nazis were perfectly aware of this metaphysical dimension of their assault on the Jews. In his diary he often refers to the Gestapo's "Jew Specialists," such as the infamous Dr. Johannes Pohl (1904–1960), director of the Gestapo section known as *Judenforschung ohne Juden*, that is, "Research on Jews without Jews."[82] It was their responsibility to thoroughly familiarize themselves with the texts and teachings of Judaism and to use that information to destroy Jewish testimony. To be sure, under the Nazi occupation the Polish and German press referred to the war as the "Jew War" or the "War against the Jews," demonstrating that the Nazis understood themselves to be waging a war against the singled-out witnesses of the divine Covenant and thereby against God Himself. The words of Zelig Kalmanovitch (1885–1944), written from the depths of the Vilna Ghetto, attest to this point: "A war is being waged against the Jews. But this war is not merely directed against one link in the triad [of Israel, God, and Torah] but against the entire triad: against the Torah and God, against the moral law and Creator of the universe."[83] In her Holocaust memoir, to take another example, Judith Dribben (b. 1924) relates the following: "One morning some Germans saw me on the stairs. Richard, a blond and fresh young man who spoke Ukrainian, stopped me. 'Last night we set your synagogue afire! Didn't it burn wonderfully? The Jewish God is burnt to ashes.'"[84] This brief scene is emblematic of the mission of the millennial German Reich.

The Nazis' assault on God as part of their systematic usurpation of God assumed other forms, such as an assault on the Eternal One's entry into time through the holy days. And so the Nazis planned their actions against the Jews – the liquidations of the ghettos and the mass selections in the camps – according to the Hebrew holy calendar. In the chronicles

[81] Louis I. Newman, ed., *The Hasidic Anthology* (New York: Schocken Books, 1963), 147.

[82] See Herman Kruk, *The Last Days of the Jerusalem of Lithuania: Chronicles from the Vilna Ghetto and the Camps, 1939–1944*, ed. Benjamin Harshav, trans. Barbara Harshav (New Haven, Conn.: Yale University Press, 2002), 311.

[83] Zelig Kalmanovitch, "A Diary of the Nazi Ghetto in Vilna," trans. and ed. Koppel S. Pinson, *YIVO Annual of Jewish Social Studies* 8 (1953): 52.

[84] Judith Dribben, *And Some Shall Live* (Jerusalem: Keter Books, 1969), 24.

he kept at the time, Oneg Shabbat[85] member Rabbi Shimon Huberband (1909–1942) jotted down a grim bit of humor that circulated throughout the Warsaw Ghetto: "If we can endure for twenty-one days, then we'll be saved. Namely, eight days of Passover, eight days of Succos, two days of Rosh Hashanah, two days of Shavuos, and one day of Yom Kippur."[86] But endure they did not.

During Rosh Hashanah in Auschwitz it was not God but chief physician Dr. Josef Mengele (1911–1979) who decided who would live and who would die, and, as one can see from Elie Wiesel's *Night*, he knew exactly what he was doing.[87] In his entry for Yom Kippur 1942, to take another example, Emmanuel Ringelblum (1900–1944) simply jots down, "The practice of torturing Jews in the cities on Yom Kippur."[88] The Nazis planned the final liquidation of the Warsaw Ghetto for 19 April 1943, the eve of Passover, which for the Jews is the *zman charuteinu*, the "time of our liberation," a teaching that was not wasted on their murderers; of course, they met with the resistance that was to be the Warsaw Ghetto Uprising. Relating the events of Shavuot 5702 (1942), Hersh Wasser (1912–1980), another member of the Oneg Shabbat circle, wrote, "All the Jews were driven out of Wojsławice, Sielec, Kumów, and Wólka Leszczańska, to Chełm, and on the way masses were 'rendered cold' – shot down by machine guns. The Jewish blood contribution to world slaughter surpasses understanding and measure."[89] Indeed, assaulting the Infinite One, the Nazis' war against God was without measure. Finally, and not surprisingly, we recall that the day of horror that bore particular significance for the Jews of the Shoah was Tisha B'Av, the ninth day of the Hebrew month of Av: on Tisha B'Av 1942 the first of the mass transports to Treblinka pulled out of Warsaw.

---

[85] The Oneg Shabbat circle was a group of people from all walks of life assembled by Emmanuel Ringelblum to keep diaries and to gather other accounts of the Nazis' activities in the Warsaw Ghetto, as well as throughout Poland. The term *Oneg Shabbat* means "delight in the Sabbath," which is a delight in the entry of the Eternal One into time.

[86] Shimon Huberband, *Kiddush Hashem*, trans. David E. Fishman, ed. Jeffrey S. Gurock and Robert S. Hirt (Hoboken, N.J.: Ktav and Yeshiva University Press, 1987), 118.

[87] See, e.g., Elie Wiesel, *Night*, trans. Marion Wiesel (New York: Hill and Wang, 2006), 71–72.

[88] Emmanuel Ringelblum, *Notes from the Warsaw Ghetto*, trans. and ed. Jacob Sloan (New York: Schocken Books, 1974), 314.

[89] Hersh Wasser, "Daily Entries of Hersh Wasser," trans. Joseph Kermish, *Yad Vashem Studies*, 15 (1983): 275.

What is the significance of Tisha B'Av? It is the day of the destruction of both Temples, as well as numerous other catastrophes in Jewish history.[90] In the time of the Shoah, the Jews themselves took the place of the Temple. Like the Temple, they signify the presence of the Holy One in the world; like the Temple, they were consigned to the flames. In the words of Elie Wiesel, "with each hour, the most blessed and most stricken people of the world numbers twelve times twelve children less. And each one carries away still another fragment of the Temple in flames."[91] Indeed, children were the designated first targets in the Nazi war against God.

"It was as though the Nazi killers knew precisely what children represent to us," says Wiesel. "According to our tradition, the entire world subsists thanks to them."[92] I have just one correction to his insight: it was not *as though*. In the Midrash it is written, "R. Judah said: Come and see how beloved are the children by the Holy One, blessed be He. The Sanhedrin were exiled but the *Shekhinah* did not go into exile with them. When, however, the children were exiled, the *Shekhinah* went into exile with them" (*Eichah Rabbah* 1:6:33). The Talmud teaches that all of Creation endures thanks to the breath of little children (*Shabbat* 119b), and not by the pillars of power, as invoked by the Greek image of Atlas holding up the world on his shoulders. If the child sustains creation, the murder of the child is central to the war against the Creator. And in the death of the child we see Him in the throes of death. Wiesel drives home this point with devastating pathos in *Night*, where we encounter one of the most dreadful of all the memories that now haunt Jewish memory: the hanging of a child. In the assembly of prisoners forced to witness the hanging the young Eliezer hears a Jew next to him asking, "Where is God? Where is He now?" And from within his soul comes the terrifying reply: "Where is He? Here He is – He is hanging here on these gallows."[93] It is not for nothing that this horrific scene appears at the center of Wiesel's memoir: it is pivotal to the Shoah itself. If, as it is written in the *Tikunei HaZohar*,

[90] Other catastrophes that took place on that date include the Roman massacre of the Jews of Betar in 133 and the expulsions of the Jews from England in 1290 and from Spain in 1492.

[91] Elie Wiesel, *Ani Maamin: A Song Lost and Found Again*, trans. Marion Wiesel (New York: Random House, 1973), 27, 29.

[92] Elie Wiesel, *A Jew Today*, trans. Marion Wiesel (New York: Random House, 1978), 178–179.

[93] Wiesel, *Night*, 65.

children are "the face of the Shekhinah,"[94] it is because, gazing into the eyes of a child, we catch a glimpse of the Divine Countenance and the commanding Voice that the Nazis systematically set out to annihilate.

Because children are the face of the Divine Presence, the Nazis rooted out that presence by creating realms that were void of Jewish children. "In the ghetto streets no children played," writes Yehiel Dinur (1909–2001), the survivor and novelist known as Ka-tzetnik 135633. "In the ghetto there were no children. There were small Jews and there were big Jews – all looking alike."[95] In his memoir George Lucius Salton (b. 1928) recalls the moment when, on his liberation from Wöbbelin, he saw children for the first time "in years." They were German children: "The Jewish children had all been gassed."[96] And who can forget Sara Nomberg-Przytyk's (1915–1990) memory of *a transport* of Jewish children burned alive: "Suddenly, the stillness was broken by the screaming of children,... a scream repeated a thousand times in a single word, 'Mama,' a scream that increased in intensity every second, enveloping the whole camp. Our lips parted without our being conscious of what we were doing, and a scream of despair tore out of our throats.... At the end everything was enveloped in death and silence."[97] With this silencing of the screams of the children, God Himself is rendered silent. The Nazis set out to tear meaning from the word in a tearing of human from human, and the word from which meaning was most radically torn is *Mama*. No one ever uttered a prayer that came more profoundly from the depths than this child's scream of "Mama!" According to Jewish tradition, only the prayers of our children reach the ears of God, "for the outcry of children," says Jacob ben Wolf Kranz (ca. 1740–1804), the Maggid of Dubno, "is formed by the breath of mouths unblemished by sin."[98] But one wonders whether this outcry ever reached the ears of the Holy One; with the extermination of the children it is as though God had been

---

[94] Cited in Nehemia Polen, *The Holy Fire: The Teachings of Rabbi Kalonymus Kalman Shapira* (Northvale, N.J.: Jason Aronson, 1999), 102; the *Tikunei HaZohar* is an appendix to the *Zohar* consisting of seventy commentaries on the opening word of the Torah, *Bereshit*.

[95] Ka-tzetnik 135633, *Kaddish*, trans. Nina De-Nur (New York: Algemeiner Associates, 1998), 30.

[96] George Lucius Salton, *The 23rd Psalm: A Holocaust Memoir* (Madison: University of Wisconsin Press, 2002), 218.

[97] Sara Nomberg-Przytyk, *Auschwitz: True Tales from a Grotesque Land*, trans. Roslyn Hirsch (Chapel Hill: University of North Carolina Press, 1985), 81.

[98] Quoted in Eliyahu Kitov, *The Book of Our Heritage*, vol. 1, trans. Nathan Bluman (New York: Feldheim Publishers, 1973), 75–76.

rendered deaf. And once rendered deaf, He is rendered irrelevant. Thus in the assault on the children the Nazis attain their deicidal aim.

From the foregoing we realize that if the annihilation of the children is central to the Nazis' deicidal aim, so too is the obliteration of prayer. Indeed, just as the *Shekhinah* is associated with the community of Israel, so is she associated with prayers of Israel. The Baal Shem teaches that "when a man begins the Amidah and says the opening verse: 'O Lord, open Thou my lips!' [Psalms 51:17] the *Shekhinah* immediately enters within his voice, and speaks with his voice."[99] Therefore the annihilation of the Indwelling Presence required the annihilation of prayer. "Never before was there a government so evil that it would forbid an entire people to pray," Chaim Kaplan (1880–1942) records in the diary he kept in the Warsaw Ghetto.[100] Never before had a government undertaken such an assault on the Holy One *as a policy of state*. Central to that assault is the assault on the testimony to the Holy One manifest in prayer. "Only when you are My witnesses," it is written, "am I God, but when you are not My witnesses, I – if one dare speak thus – am not God" (*Pesikta de-Rab Kahana* 12:6; see also *Sifre* on Deuteronomy 33:5).[101] In keeping with their horrifying logic, the Nazis understood that both the Source and its seekers, both God and His witnesses, had to be destroyed.

We understand, then, why the Nazis transformed places of prayer into latrines, stables, scrap depots, and other such facilities. Often they were not content, however, merely to desecrate the places of prayer; they put them to the torch, with praying Jews inside, and thus consigned God Himself to the flames. The assault on the place of prayer is an assault not on a building or a space but on the encounter between God and the soul that characterizes prayer: in order to assail God, the Nazis launched an attack on the prayer that is itself divinity. Chaim Kaplan bears witness to this assault. On the eve of Tisha B'Av 5700 (1940), for example, he writes, "Public prayer in these dangerous times is a forbidden act. Anyone caught in this crime is doomed to severe punishment. If you will, it is even sabotage, and anyone engaging in sabotage is subject to execution."[102] Note well: the Nazis deemed prayer *an act of sabotage*. Why? Because

---

[99] See Newman, *The Hasidic Anthology*, 337.

[100] Chaim A. Kaplan, *The Warsaw Diary of Chaim A. Kaplan*, trans. and ed. Abraham I. Katsh (New York: Collier, 1973), 202.

[101] The *Pesikta de-Rab Kahana* is a collection of midrashic teachings dating from sometime between the fifth and seventh centuries CE; there were several great sages known as Rav Kahana from the earlier centuries.

[102] Kaplan, *The Warsaw Diary of Chaim A. Kaplan*, 179.

prayer, and prayer alone, affirms the divine, transcendent authority behind the commandments of Torah, beginning with the prohibition against murder. Only where there is a place for this absolute, divine prohibition does the Divine Presence find a dwelling place in the world, and only where there is a dwelling place for the Divine Presence is there a place for prayer.

According to Jewish teaching, humanity's task is revealed in the first letter of Torah, in the letter *beit*, which means "house" or "home": we are to create a dwelling place for the Creator in the midst of His creation, and His dwelling place lies in the between space of human relation. Therefore the Nazi assault on God took the form of an assault on human relation. The head of a block in Buchenwald, in one of the most chilling lines in all of Holocaust literature, informed the young Eliezer in Wiesel's *Night* that in the camp "there is no such thing as father, brother, friend. Each of us lives and dies alone."[103] Primo Levi describes the antiworld by saying, "The struggle to survive is without respite, because everyone is desperately and ferociously alone."[104] Yes: *ferociously* alone! For the Jews the Lager, or camp, was *not a punishment*, as Levi realized, but a level of being – or of non-being – to which the Jews were relegated as part of the assault on God and the soul created in His image and likeness.[105] The annihilation of the soul through the destruction of human relation is the destruction of the divine image that constitutes the *holiness* of the human being, which is a fundamental principle of the Jewish teaching that the Nazis set out to exterminate in the extermination of the Jews. Thus, we glimpse the soul of an anti-Semite, who would destroy Jewish souls, and not just Jewish bodies, and whose primary fear, as Eichmann expressed it, was not that Germany might lose the war but that Germany might lose the war before all the Jews could be exterminated.[106]

If what took place at Auschwitz was an "anti-creation," as Levi describes it,[107] it was the anticreation of the "non-man," of the Muselmann, formed in the image and likeness of one who would be as God, in the image and likeness of the quintessential anti-Semite. The lifeless, soulless Muselmann is the mirror image of the anti-Semite who has slain the

---

[103] Wiesel, *Night*, 110.

[104] Primo Levi, *Survival in Auschwitz*, trans. Stuart Woolf (New York: Simon & Schuster, 1996), 88.

[105] See ibid., 82–83.

[106] See Haim Gouri, *Facing the Glass Booth: The Jerusalem Trial of Adolf Eichmann*, trans. Michael Swirsky (Detroit, Mich.: Wayne State University Press, 2004), 92.

[107] See Primo Levi, *The Reawakening*, trans. Stuart Woolf (Boston: Little, Brown, 1965), 128.

Creator and Sustainer of the soul. Levi describes the Muselmänner as "the backbone of the camp, an anonymous mass, continually renewed and always identical, of non-men who march and labour in silence, the divine spark dead within them, already too empty to really suffer. One hesitates to call them living: one hesitates to call their death death."[108] From these lines Fackenheim draws a startling conclusion: "The divine image in man *can* be destroyed. No more threatening proof to this effect can be found than the so-called *Muselmann* in the Nazi death camp."[109] If Auschwitz epitomizes the assault on God, the Muselmann embodies the essence of that assault. The Muselmann is the manifestation of an evil that is ultimate, singular, and incarnate in a creature who silently announces the meaning of National Socialist anti-Semitism. For the Muselmann is not merely the outcome of torture, exposure, and deprivation. Far more than the victim of starvation and brutality, the Muselmann is *the Jew* whose very existence was deemed criminal, whose prayers were regarded as an act of sedition, whose holy days were turned over to desecration. He is *the Jew* for whom marriage and childbirth were forbidden, for whom schooling was a crime, for whom there was neither punishment nor protection under the law. He is *the Jew* widowed and orphaned, destitute and homeless, rendered ferociously alone and utterly nameless: the endless stream of the Muselmänner formed an *anonymous* mass.

"They will even take away our name," Levi writes with his usual depth and insight, "and if we want to keep it, we will have to find ourselves the strength to do so, to manage somehow so that behind the name something of us, of us as we were, still remains."[110] For the Jews, the struggle to keep their names was a struggle to keep their souls. From 1938, when the Nazis added the name *Israel* to every Jewish male and the name *Sarah* to every Jewish female, the erasure of the name of the Jew was central to the assault on the soul. Indeed, Jewish tradition teaches that the name and the soul are of a piece.[111] Recall from the Introduction the teaching from Nachman of Breslov concerning what befalls us when we die.[112] As we lie

---

[108] Levi, *Survival in Auschwitz*, 90.

[109] See Emil L. Fackenheim, *The Jewish Return into History* (New York: Schocken Books, 1978), 246.

[110] Levi, *Survival in Auschwitz*, 27.

[111] See, e.g., Yehuda HeChasid, *Sefer Chasidim*, trans. Avraham Yaakov Finkel (Northvale, N.J.: Jason Aronson, 1997), 244.

[112] See Nathan of Nemirov, *Rabbi Nachman's Wisdom: HaRan and Sichos HaRan*, trans. Aryeh Kaplan, ed. Zvi Aryeh Rosenfeld (New York: A. Kaplan, 1973), 148.

in the grave, says Rabbi Nachman, the Angel of Death comes to us to take us into the presence of the Holy One. In order to enter into His presence, however, we must be able to answer a question: What is your name? But the Muselmann is denied the question put to every human being, his name having been eclipsed by a number. That is why his death is not death: the Angel of Death, now the minion of the Nazis rather than the servant of God – has nothing to ask him.

The number tattooed on the arm transforms the being of the human being into an indifferent nothingness that marks the Jew for his descent into the mute indifference of the Muselmann. Confronted with the image of the Muselmann and the tattoo that eclipses his name, we collide with the essence of the Nazi assault on the One who is known as *HaShem*, "the Name." Ka-tzetnik's outcry to the Rabbi of Shilev comes to mind, from one of his harrowing visions in *Shivitti*: "At last you must admit, Rabbi, that the God of the Diaspora himself is climbing into this truck [on His way to the gas chamber] – a Muselmann."[113] This terrifying image captures the singularity of National Socialist anti-Semitism as a systematic assault on the One who declared from Mount Sinai, "Thou shalt not murder." The Nazi creation of the anti-man – of the Muselmann – defines the Nazi, just as much as God's revealed creation of man defines the Jew. Thus Fackenheim sees in the Muselmann the Nazis' "most characteristic, most original product."[114] In this denizen of the Nazi antiworld we discover the singularity of National Socialist anti-Semitism.

THE SINGULARITY OF NATIONAL SOCIALIST ANTI-SEMITISM

Once we have identified the metaphysical origins of anti-Semitism and recognized the Nazis' assault on God in their extermination of the Jews, we realize that the Holocaust is not only "phenomenologically unique," as Steven Katz has demonstrated,[115] but also metaphysically unique. As an attempt to annihilate *more* than a people, the Holocaust is not reducible to one case of genocide among many; indeed, to label it a genocide and leave it at that is very misleading. Beyond the Jewish people, the Nazis set out to eradicate from creation not only the millennial teachings

---

[113] Ka-tzetnik 135644, *Shivitti: A Vision*, trans. Eliyah De-Nur and Lisa Herman (New York: Harper & Row, 1989), 7.
[114] Fackenheim, *To Mend the World*, 100.
[115] Katz, *The Holocaust in Historical Context*, 28.

of the Jewish people but also the living God of Abraham, Isaac, and Jacob embodied by the Jews *in particular*. All explanations of Nazi anti-Semitism based on the usual cultural, sociological, religious, and other ontological categories fail to address two *defining* features of the Shoah: the essence of the *Nazi* project of extermination and the essence of the *Jew* targeted for extermination. The unique horror of the Holocaust is that it was an assault on the very principle – the first principle of the *holiness* of the human being – that makes other horrors horrible and not just "tragedies" or matters of academic curiosity. The singularity of the Holocaust, then, lies in its assault on the *singular sanctity* of every human being created in the image and likeness of the Holy One.

Because singling out the Jews and Jewish testimony bears this implication for all of humanity, the Holocaust illustrates the essential connection between Jewish particularity and Jewish universality. "It is precisely *because* of the uniqueness of Auschwitz, and *in* his particularity," Fackenheim states it, "that a Jew must be at one with [a universal] humanity."[116] This being at one with humanity is rooted in the testimony to all humanity for which the Jews are chosen: it is a proclamation that every human being is chosen for a unique responsibility to and for his neighbor, that each is accountable for a specific task that no other can perform, and that every soul is indispensable to all of creation – a teaching that is blatantly contrary to the foundations of National Socialism. The Jewish presence in the world is at odds with the modern inclination toward generalities that cannot abide the notion of a people apart. To be sure, entire books on the Holocaust have been written by very distinguished scholars with little or no mention of the Jews as a singled-out people. "Men shun the scandal of the particularity of Auschwitz," writes Fackenheim. "Germans link it with Dresden; American liberals, with Hiroshima. Christians deplore antisemitism-in-general, while Communists erect monuments to the victims-of-Fascism-in-general, depriving the dead of Auschwitz of their Jewish identity even in death. Rather than face Auschwitz, men everywhere seek refuge in generalities."[117] Generalities are always about *them*; thus generalities free me of any implication and all accountability. Indeed, to think

---

[116] Emil L. Fackenheim, *God's Presence in History* (New York: Harper & Row, 1970), 87–88.

[117] Emil L. Fackenheim, "Jewish Faith and the Holocaust," in Michael L. Morgan, ed., *A Holocaust Reader: Responses to the Nazi Extermination* (New York: Oxford University Press, 2001), 116.

anti-Semitically is to think in generalities that render us blind to the face and deaf to the outcry of the flesh-and-blood human being.

The particularity of Auschwitz, however, is about *me*, as one who must confront the desire to be as God within his own soul. That desire implicates me as it implicated Adam, who, on succumbing to the temptation, confronted the question from on high: "Where are you?" (Genesis 3:9), a question that fundamentally defines the Torah revealed for the sake of all humanity, the very Torah that the Nazis set out to obliterate. Here the link between modern philosophical anti-Semitism and the rise of National Socialist anti-Semitism becomes even more evident. Once the *I* of the Cartesian *I think* or the ego of Kantian autonomy becomes the commanding authority, it eclipses the image of the divine, both in oneself and in the other human being, making the other into an *experience* of the I. In the previous chapter we saw how this philosophical premise played out in political collectivism, cultural ethnocentrism, and sheer racism. In National Socialism we collide with a radical demonstration of the truth that when the voice of the autonomous I becomes the commanding voice, murder can be justified. As an assault on the commandment of Torah, the Nazis' singular assault on the Jew is a singular assault on the word: there is no word for what is done to the Jew, no word "to express this offense," as Levi says, no word for "the demolition of a man."[118] For the demolition of a man – the demolition of the *medaber*, or the "speaking being" – *is* the demolition of the word. It is what Winston Churchill deemed "a crime without a name," saying more than perhaps he himself realized.[119] The demolition of the word is the demolition of what imparts meaning and value to a human being, and it begins with the demolition of the Jew.

This undermining of language is another aspect of the singularity of the Shoah, something that Primo Levi understood very well. In his memoir the Lager's perversion of the human image is reflected in the perversion of language, symbolized by the Carbide Tower at Buna, the tower they referred to as the *Babelturm*, or "Tower of Babel." Like the Tower of Babel, it represents not only the confusion of tongues but the collapse of humanity. "Its bricks," says Levi, "were called *Ziegel, briques, cegli,*

---

[118] Levi, *Survival in Auschwitz*, 26.

[119] Churchill used the phrase in a speech he delivered on 24 August 1941, when reports on the Nazi killing units were coming in; see Markus P. Beham, "'Borrowed' Concepts: The Pitfalls of 'Atrocity Labeling' in Contemporary Historiography," in Marija Wakounig and Markus Peter Beham, eds., *Transgressing Boundaries: Humanities in Flux* (Berlin: Lit Verlag, 2013), 76.

kamenny, mattoni, téglak, and they were cemented by hate."[120] As in the time of Babel, the tower's bricks were not bricks, and the men were not men. Says the Midrash, "If a man fell [from the Tower] and died they paid no heed to him, but if a brick fell they sat down and wept, and said: Woe is us! When will another come in its stead?" (*Pirke de Rabbi Eliezer* 24).[121] Another word torn from meaning in a tearing of human from human was *bread.* In the antiworld of nonmen, says Levi, bread was nonbread, the "grey slab" of "bread-brot-Broid-chleb-pain-lechem-keynér" that in this realm was their "only money."[122] Once the meaning of *bread* is thus torn from the word, human is torn from human and the soul rent asunder. Bread is bread only when it is offered to another; a human being is not what he eats – he is what he offers another to eat. Thus, after the Nazis had abandoned the camp, Levi recalls the moment when one person offered another something to eat: "It really meant that the Lager was dead. I believe that that moment can be dated as the beginning of the change by which we who had not died slowly changed from Häftlinge [camp inmates] to men again."[123] The act of offering bread to another, therefore, is a fundamental signifier of a humanity created in the image of the divine.

This brings us to just one more singularity that defines the Holocaust born of National Socialist anti-Semitism, one that may forever change the meaning of *bread.* The Nazi assault on the God of Abraham cast its shadow over all humanity created in the image and likeness of the Holy One; indeed, its shadow is within us, cast to the inside. In an effort to grasp the graphic meaning of this point, remember the disaster that occurred in Chernobyl on 26 April 1986, when a cloud of radioactive material was released into the air from one of the chimneys at a nuclear power plant. Two weeks later radiation levels in Montana were elevated. In fact, earth scientists claim that one can determine air pollution levels over the years by taking a plug of snow and ice from Antarctica. In the time of the Shoah the remains of the Jewish people bellowed into the air in columns of fire and smoke and ash, not for one day but for a thousand days, not from one chimney but from dozens. Then there are the tens of thousands of Jews exhumed from their mass graves and burned in an

---

[120] Levi, *Survival in Auschwitz,* 72–73.
[121] The *Pirke de Rabbi Eliezer* is a collection of teachings attributed to the great sage of the early second century CE Rabbi Eliezer ben Hyrcanus, with the text itself probably dating from the seventh century.
[122] Levi, *Survival in Auschwitz,* 39.   [123] Ibid., 160.

effort to hide the evidence of the crime without a name. The winds have spread the ashes of untold millions of Jews over the face of the earth, east to west, pole to pole. They inhabit the soil from which we harvest our bread. They abide in the bread we put into our mouths, in a dark eucharistic union that binds us to the body of Israel. As we are made of that bread, so are we made of those ashes: we are the grave to those denied a grave. Thus we understand an insight from Czech survivor and novelist Arnošt Lustig (1926–2011):

These ashes would be indestructible and immutable, they would not burn up into nothingness because they themselves were remnants of fire.... No one living would ever be able to escape them.... These ashes will be contained in the breath and expression of every one of us and the next time anybody asks what the air he breathes is made of, he will have to think about these ashes; they will be contained in books which haven't been written and will be found in the remotest regions of the earth where no human foot has ever trod; no one will be able to get rid of them, for they will be the fond, nagging ashes of the dead who died in innocence.[124]

And in their nagging abides a nagging question: What is your name?

That is the Jewish Question for which the National Socialist anti-Semites sought a Final Solution, the question they snatched from the mouth of the Angel of Death. It is a variation of the first question put to the first human being – "Where are you?" (Genesis 3:9) – which in turn is embodied in the questions put to Cain – "Where is your brother?" (Genesis 4:9) and "What have you done?" (Genesis 4:10). In the post-Holocaust era it is the question denied by those who would deny the Holocaust. Here, then, we discover one more singularity of the Holocaust: it is Holocaust denial. While certain governments deny the atrocities in their own history and others ignore or minimize the horrors they have perpetrated, this *worldwide* phenomenon attaches to no other historical event. Holocaust denial, then, is not about history; rooted in the same metaphysical origins as National Socialism, it is about anti-Semitism.

---

[124] Arnošt Lustig, *A Prayer for Katerina Horovitzova*, trans. Jeanne Nemcova (New York: Harper & Row, 1973), 50–51.

6

Antihistorical Anti-Semitism: Holocaust Denial

> The enemy killed the Jews and then he made them disappear in smoke, in ashes, so every Jew was killed twice.... Now he tries to kill them for the third time by depriving them of their past; ... nothing could be as ugly, as inhuman, as the wish to deprive the dead victims of their death.
>
> Elie Wiesel, "The Holocaust as Literary Inspiration"

What do Holocaust deniers deny? Simply stated, they deny that the Nazi assault on the God of Abraham manifest in the extermination of the Jews ever took place. Are they saying, therefore, that there was no assault on God? Not exactly. The most rabid of the Holocaust deniers most fervently wish that the extermination of the Jews, and with them the God of Torah, had taken place. Simply stated, the reason for the denial of Hitler's slaughter of the Jews of Europe is that Hitler was unable to go far enough: there is more work to be done. As always, this desire is rooted in the soul's desire to unseat the Holy One and set up another god in His place, whether ideological or theological. Because the desire to usurp God burns in each of us with varying intensity, Holocaust denial is a phenomenon that runs a spectrum, ranging from the outright claim that there was no extermination to a willing, if at times unwitting, trivialization and evasion of the subject. Because Holocaust denial concerns an event that took place in history, the denial of the event has implications not only for how we understand what took place but also for how we understand history itself – there, in our relationship to history, lies the key to what Holocaust denial has to do with the metaphysical origin of anti-Semitism. Inasmuch as this denial of both history and the essence of history is rooted in anti-Semitism, it is characterized by what I call antihistorical anti-Semitism.

As I explain below, the view of history denied by Holocaust deniers is a specifically Jewish view of history, which is grounded in a certain understanding of the God of history. Like all other manifestations of anti-Semitism, antihistorical anti-Semitism is not about prejudice, racism, or ethnic bias. Running much deeper than such social or psychological phenomena, it arises from a primal longing within the soul and a fundamental mode in which we think: antihistorical anti-Semitism has a metaphysical origin.

Although existing approaches to Holocaust denial correctly under-score its anti-Semitic essence, they tend to reduce it to a case of either bigotry-in-general or a perversion of the scientific principles on which historical research is founded. Kenneth Stern, for example, maintains that "anti-Semitism is a form of human bigotry" and a "subset of human hatred."[1] Stern may be correct in his assertion that Holocaust denial is not about the Holocaust, but his claim that it is in fact "about politics, ideology and power" does not go far enough.[2] Such things come into play, but they are surface manifestations of a more profound problem. Similar to Stern, Deborah Lipstadt falls short in her analysis when she writes, "Just as *the Holocaust was not a tragedy of the Jews but a tragedy of civilization* in which the victims were Jews, so too denial of the Holocaust is not a threat just to Jewish history but a threat to all who believe in the ultimate power of reason."[3] Like Lipstadt, Michael Shermer and Alex Grobman see Holocaust denial as "an attack on all history and on the way we transmit the past to the future."[4] Not only the shortcoming but also the danger in these assessments of Holocaust denial is that they tend to marginalize the Jews and thus may unwittingly play into the hands of the deniers. How? By making Holocaust denial about ethnic hatred *alone* and not about a certain mode of thought or a usurpation of the God of history.

Anti-Semitism is not a subset of human hatred – it is the ground of human hatred. With anti-Semitism at its core, Holocaust denial is not a threat to our belief in human reason – it is a threat to the divine revelation of human sanctity, to which the Jews are the world's most ancient and

---

[1] Kenneth S. Stern, *Holocaust Denial* (New York: American Jewish Committee, 1993), 91–92.

[2] Ibid., 94.

[3] Deborah E. Lipstadt, *Denying the Holocaust: The Growing Assault on Truth and Memory* (New York: The Free Press, 1993), 19–20; emphasis added.

[4] Michael Shermer and Alex Grobman, *Denying History: Who Says the Holocaust Never Happened and Why Do They Say It?* (Berkeley: University of California Press, 2000), 16.

enduring witnesses. It is an attack on the God of history, who is revealed to the world through the Jewish people, and an evasion of the ramifications of that revelation for how we understand history itself. Because it is driven, either explicitly or implicitly, by such an ultimate aim, it is calculated and systematic, with an internal logic of its own. Therefore Lipstadt is misleading, if not mistaken, when she writes, "Holocaust denial is the apotheosis of irrationalism."[5] Like other movements driven by anti-Semitism, Holocaust denial is a manifestation of a certain movement toward an apotheosis of the self, and there is little of the irrational about it. It is true that wherever the topic arises, someone is quick to ask, "How can anyone believe the Holocaust did not happen?" Taking this to be a question about evidence, Shermer and Grobman maintain that Holocaust deniers deny three things that are in evidence: (1) the use of a high-tech program, including gas chambers, to kill the Jews; (2) the estimate of six million Jews killed; and (3) the intention on the part of the Nazis to exterminate the Jews.[6] While their assessment is true on the surface, it does not go very far beyond the surface. Subsequently, they adopt precisely the wrong approach in their response to the denial of these three things: they set out to disprove the deniers' claims by presenting more evidence.[7]

When speaking of Holocaust denial many recall the words of an SS minion who mocked a starving remnant of the Jews as the war neared its end: "However this war may end, we have won the war against you; none of you will be left to bear witness, but even if someone were to survive, the world will not believe him. There will perhaps be suspicions, discussions, research by historians, but there will be no certainties, because we will destroy the evidence together with you. And even if some proof should remain and some of you survive, people will say that the events you describe are too monstrous to be believed."[8] The SS man's taunt is vicious, cruel, and calculated as part of the assault on the souls of the Jews. But it has little to do with Holocaust denial. Anyone whose mind reels at the specter of Auschwitz accepts its possibility only because of its actuality: more was real than was possible, but it *was* real. Anyone who denies the Holocaust, however, flees from reality's swoon, both despite and because of the overwhelming evidence. Because it is a

---

[5] Lipstadt, *Denying the Holocaust*, 20.
[6] Shermer and Grobman, *Denying History*, 100.   [7] Ibid., 2.
[8] Quoted in Primo Levi, *The Drowned and the Saved*, trans. Raymond Rosenthal (New York: Vintage Books, 1989), 11–12.

manifestation of blatant anti-Semitism, Holocaust denial arises neither from a lack of evidence nor from the monstrosity of the events; Holocaust denial is itself part of the singular monstrosity of the Holocaust. Other horrors in history have been ignored and even denied, as the Turkish government denies the Armenian genocide, but they have not been explicitly and systematically denied on a worldwide scale of humanity. And how we understand our humanity is directly tied to how we understand our history, as well as the essence of history itself.

We begin our examination of Holocaust denial as an antihistorical manifestation of anti-Semitism with a consideration of a Jewish understanding of history. This is not to say that only Jews have a correct understanding of history, nor is it to suggest that the view presented below is the only way Jews understand history. What is presented, however, is based on traditional Jewish teaching, and the Holocaust deniers' denial of Jewish history entails a denial of that teaching. An explication of how Jews traditionally view history, therefore, is essential to an understanding of Holocaust denial as an instance of antihistorical anti-Semitism.

A JEWISH UNDERSTANDING OF HISTORY

Emil Fackenheim has explained that in Judaism "the divine Presence occurs *within* history, not as its consummation or transfiguration."[9] From a Jewish perspective, history is the presence of God in the realm of space. Inasmuch as those who deny the Holocaust continue the Nazi assault on the divine Presence, Holocaust denial entails an assault on history understood as the presence of God in the realm of space, just as the Holocaust was an assault on the Jews in the realm of space – the space called *Europe*. To be sure, Holocaust denial brings under assault the whole testimony of Jewish tradition, where "tradition" is understood as *masoret*, from the verbal root *masar*, which means to "transmit" or "hand down." Jewish history entails handing down a teaching and a testimony, a *meser*, or "message," concerning the infinite dearness of human relation as an expression of a higher relation. Thus a cognate of *masoret* is *mesirut*, which is "devotion" or "dedication," a responsibility to and for the other person, including the unborn, that transcends the horizons of one's own life. It is devotion rooted in a wisdom characterized

---

[9] Emil L. Fackenheim, *God's Presence in History: Jewish Affirmations and Philosophical Reflections* (New York: Harper & Row, 1970), 18.

by our capacity to "behold the unborn," as stated in the Talmud (*Tamid* 32a). A Jewish understanding of history, then, lies in an understanding of time that Emmanuel Lévinas describes when he writes, "Time is precisely the fact that the whole of existence of the mortal being – exposed to violence – is not being for death, but the 'not yet' which is a way of being against death,"[10] that is, against the death of the *other* human being. This way of being against the death of the other human being, even if it means my own death, lies at the crux of history, understood from the Jewish perspective, because it lies at the crux of the divine prohibition against murder. If history is about the divine Presence in this world, it is about our response to this most basic of the divine commandments: do not murder.

Bearing in mind that a "message," or *meser*, is also the moral of a story, we realize that the link between tradition and history opens up a tale that contains a teaching essential to life: history is *about* something. To be sure, telling tales that harbor teachings – relating history – is a central feature of a Jewish understanding of history. Relating the tale of history is a calling of deep unto deep; it entails the transmission of the word from mouth to mouth, generation to generation, and memory is at its core: as oblivion is tied to exile, says the Baal Shem Tov, so is memory tied to redemption.[11] So we realize why the Holocaust, as both Elie Wiesel and Primo Levi have said, was a war against memory, against the history and memory of the Jews.[12] If the Holocaust entails an assault on God and the soul, that assault demands an assault on memory as the root of redemption and therefore on the meaning of history itself. And the assault on memory is at the core of the antihistorical anti-Semitism of Holocaust denial. The teachings transmitted through tales that bear the memory of a people address not only the course of human events but also the truths of the first things that come to us from the Most High: aggadah, the tales that form the time of tradition, opens up a dimension of height that comes under assault both in the Holocaust and in the denial of the Holocaust. The One who spoke and brought the world into being not only spoke – He *related*: in the beginning is the tale, which is the tie that binds us to the first things, to the eternal things, to the Holy One, and to one another. The narration of tradition, therefore, is the ground of meaning in history.

[10] Emmanuel Lévinas, *Totality and Infinity*, trans. Alphonso Lingis (Pittsburgh, Pa.: Duquesne University Press, 1969), 224.
[11] See Elie Wiesel, *Souls on Fire: Portraits and Legends of Hasidic Masters*, trans. Marion Wiesel (New York: Vintage, 1973), 227.
[12] Elie Wiesel, *Evil and Exile*, trans. Jon Rothschild (Notre Dame, Ind.: University of Notre Dame Press, 1990), 155, and Levi, 31.

From a Jewish standpoint, then, there is a divine narrative that the historian aspires to transmit and a divine commandment that the chronicler aspires to fulfill, the commandment to remember through telling the tale. "To the modern historian," Abraham Joshua Heschel explains, "history is not the understanding of events, but rather the understanding of man's experience of events. What concerns the prophet is the human event as a divine experience."[13] At the center of the divine narrative is an ethical narrative: if tradition is the history of the eternal in time, it is the history of the ethical in time, so that, in the words of Leo Baeck (1873–1956), "through the unity of the ethical is realized the unity of history."[14] Instead of the "narratives" or "texts" of postmodernism, we have what Lévinas refers to as "the Book" when he laments, "We are no longer acquainted with the difference that distinguishes the Book from documentation. In the former there is an inspiration purified of all the vicissitudes and all the 'experiences' that had been its occasion, offering itself as Scripture whereby each soul is called to exegesis, which is both regulated by the rigorous reading of the text and by the unicity – unique in all eternity – of its own contribution, which is also its discovery, the soul's share."[15] Proceeding from the Book, history summons the soul not only to exegesis but also to accountability.

So understood, history is the history of humanity's struggle to create a realm in which the good that God demands may be realized. That struggle is a struggle for memory, which is a struggle for the future. As a denial of Jewish history, then, Holocaust denial is a denial not only of the Jewish past but also of the ethical demand that shapes the Jewish future. It is a denial of the Jewish child whom the Nazis sought to exterminate and of the ethical message transmitted through that child, beginning with the commandment to treat our neighbor in a loving manner. Indeed, the child is at the center of a Jewish understanding of history – the very child whom the Nazis singled out for extermination in their assault on the God of Israel. Here we are reminded that the Hebrew word often translated as "history" is *toledot*, which has the same root as *yeled*, the word for "child." History is not reducible to generating this narrative or that; rather, it is about bringing into the world children to whom we transmit

---

[13] Abraham Joshua Heschel, *The Prophets*, vol. 1 (New York: Harper & Row, 1962), 172.
[14] Leo Baeck, *The Essence of Judaism*, revised ed., trans. Victor Grubenweiser and Leonard Pearl (New York: Schocken Books, 1948), 236
[15] Emmanuel Lévinas, *New Talmudic Readings*, trans. Richard A. Cohen (Pittsburgh, Pa.: Duquesne University Press, 1999), 75–76.

the meaning and the message of the Covenant. Thus, we realize that in creating realms utterly void of children, the Nazis set out to create realms devoid of history, starting with Jewish covenantal history: killing covenantal history begins with killing children.

According to the Midrash, the children at Mount Sinai, even the infants in the womb, agreed to serve as sureties for the future of the Covenant and, by implication, for the continuation of history (*Tanchuma Vayigash* 1; *Shir Hashirim Rabbah* 1:4:1; *Midrash Tehillim* 1.8.4). At Auschwitz, however, the children had no voice in the matter of whether they might serve as sureties for the Covenant. Therefore the question that arises in a post-Holocaust context is infinitely more pressing: what shall we make of the Covenant placed in our hands when our sureties have been confiscated? It is a question that comes to us from the face of history. For history has a face: it has the face of a child. That face asks us how we shall answer for what has been placed in our care. As the guarantor of the Covenant of Torah, the child is the guarantor of history – the *yeled* is the guarantor of *toledot*. As a "guarantor," or *arev*, the child situates us at the *erev*, or at the "eve," of history, making history into what is *about* to transpire but is *not yet* decided, and not simply what has already unfolded. History moves along the edge of this *not yet*. That edge – that eve – has a name: it is *birth*. What the Covenant means to a Jewish understanding of history, therefore, can be seen from another meaning of *toledot*: it is "generations," which are "brought forth," from the verb *yalad*, meaning to "give birth."

Here we realize, on a deeper level, why history is something to which God and humanity *give birth* in a covenantal union: history in this sense is *sacred* history. Only where there is a sense of sacred history is there a sense of meaning in history, for the realization of meaning in history, as Fackenheim has argued, "requires the incursion of God,"[16] who commands us to seek justice (Deuteronomy 16:20). As an interweaving of the ethical and the existential, history is the history of justice, or of our striving for justice. Once we have lost a sense of justice, we have lost a sense of sacred history. And once we have lost a sense of sacred history, we have lost a sense of justice.[17] As a pursuit of justice, the movement

---

[16] Emil L. Fackenheim, *Quest for Past and Future: Essays in Jewish Theology* (Bloomington: Indiana University Press, 1968), 89.

[17] Franklin Littell raises a key question in this connection: "On what basis do we affirm that the Exodus, Sinai, the return from the first exile,... the destruction of the Temple,... the Holocaust,... a restored Israel, and a united Jerusalem ... [are] more important to our view of history than, say, the Battle of Waterloo or Custer's Last Stand?" See Franklin

toward the future draws on the history of the past, as Elie Wiesel has suggested. "The opposite of the past," he writes, "is not the future but the absence of future; the opposite of the future is not the past but the absence of past."[18] Therefore, history is not just a narrative of the past; it is an orientation toward the future that derives its meaning from a redemption yet to unfold: *toledot* is *messianic*.

The Holocaust, then, may constitute a breach in history, but it is Holocaust denial that divorces us from our past. Divorcing us from the past, it divorces us from our covenantal relation to the Holy One and the divine commandment to pursue justice (Deuteronomy 16:20), a commandment that gives meaning to our future, which in Hebrew is *acharit*. It is a cognate of *acharei*, meaning "after," so that the Holocaust deniers who would deny the Jews a future deny the *after* of the Holocaust: if there was no Holocaust, there is no *after*, and if there is no after, there is no history, no future, for the Jews. The Hebrew *acharit* also shares a root with the word *acher*, meaning the "other" human being, who in turn is at the center of our *acharayut*, or "responsibility." If, according to a Jewish understanding, history is about the future, it is about our infinite and absolute responsibility to and for the other human being.

Articulating a connection between above and below, between God and Israel, the covenantal bond makes manifest the metaphysical origin of history itself. Viewed in terms of Torah, history unfolds in the between space of the intimate, covenantal relation between God and humanity, beginning with the Jews, whereby humanity receives from the Father a "memorial and a Name," a *yad vashem*, that it must weave into the fabric of time itself. Hence "the human situation in history," says the French thinker André Neher (1914–1988), "begins with the covenant,"[19] which in turn receives its meaning from the merging of the ethical and the existential into a single injunction: "I have set before you this day life and good, death and evil . . . , blessing and curse: therefore choose life, that you and your children may live" (Deuteronomy 30:15–19). Oblivious to the ethical, Holocaust deniers opt for death, curse, and evil. The evil lies in the obviation of the first utterance from Mount Sinai: "I am the Lord your God"; the curse is the eternal execration leveled at the Jews; and the death

Littell, *The Crucifixion of the Jews: The Failure of Christians to Understand the Jewish Experience* (Macon, Ga.: Mercer University Press, 1986), 10.

[18] Elie Wiesel, *From the Kingdom of Memory: Reminiscences* (New York: Summit Books, 1990), 239.

[19] André Neher, *The Prophetic Existence*, trans. William Wolf (New York: A. S. Barnes, 1969), 142.

emerges in the obviation of the sixth commandment of the divine revelation: "You shall not murder." The shock and the outrage that most people feel toward blatant Holocaust denial are rooted in such Holocaust denial's implicit obliteration of the prohibition against murder.

THE DENIERS' DENIAL OF THE COMMANDING VOICE

The first person to publish a piece denying the Holocaust was Alexander Ratcliffe (1888–1947), leader of the British Protestant League; as early as 1943 (first edition in March, second edition July), in a pamphlet titled *The Truth about the Jews*, he wrote, "The various press reports about Hitler's persecution of the Jews mostly are written up by Jews and circulated by Jews. Mostly such reports are the invention of the Jewish mind. For the historian immediately after the war will prove that 95% of the Jews' 'atrocity' stories and 'photographs' of such atrocities appearing in the press, magazines and journals are mere inventions."[20] As soon as the extermination of the Jews had finally come to an end, the perpetrators began to vehemently deny that it happened. Among the more notorious Nazi deniers were General Otto Ernst Remer (1912–1997) and Dr. Heinrich Malz (1910–?); Malz served as a personal advisor to Ernst Kaltenbrunner (1903–1946), Chief of the *Reichssicherheitshauptampt* (RSHA, Reich Main Security Office).[21] They were followed by Wilfred von Oven (1912–2008), an SS officer who worked closely with Joseph Goebbels (1897–1945) and who claimed there were no crematoria,[22] and Wehrmacht officer Wilhelm Stäglich (1916–2006), author of *Der Auschwitz-Mythos* (The Auschwitz Myth, 1973).[23]

Among the most influential authors of more than one hundred books denying that the Holocaust took place are the following, listed in the order of their publishing activities:

[20] Quoted in Colin Holmes, "Alexander Ratcliffe: Militant Protestant and Antisemite," in Tony Kushner and Ken Lunn, eds., *Traditions of Intolerance: Historical Perspectives on Fascism and Race Discourse in Britain* (Manchester, U.K.: University of Manchester Press, 1989), 207.

[21] See Stephen E. Atkins, *Holocaust Denial as an International Movement* (Westport, Conn.: Praeger, 2009), 3, 103.

[22] See Stern, *Holocaust Denial*, 42; see also Wilfred von Oven, *Mit Goebbels bis zum Ende* (Buenos Aires, 1949; Tübingen: Rudolf Grabert-Verlag, 1974).

[23] See Wilhelm Stäglich, *Der Auschwitz-Mythos* (Torrance, Calif.: Historical Review Press, 1984).

1. Paul Rassinier (1906–1967), author of *Le passage de la ligne* (Crossing the Line, 1948),[24] the first in a series of denial books that he would write over the next two decades; in *Le drame des Juifs européens* (The Drama of European Jewry, 1964), long before Hamas and PLO propaganda, he argued that the Zionist establishment invented the lie about the extermination of the Jews in gas chambers. For example, commenting on Hannah Arendt's coverage of the Eichmann trial, he describes her by saying, "She is obviously a Zionist agent, that is, a propagandist, since propaganda is apparently [Zionism's] only means of existing."[25]

2. French fascist Maurice Bardèche (1907–1998), author of *Nuremberg ou la terre promise* (Nuremberg or the Promised Land, 1948), where he maintains that the Jews were guilty of the atrocities of which the Nazis had been accused, saying that they "orchestrated the program."[26]

3. Francis Parker Yockey (1917–1960), American author of *Imperium: The Philosophy of History and Politics* (1948), a book dedicated to Adolf Hitler and published under the pseudonym of Ulick Varange. In it he blames the "Culture-distorters," a code name for the Jews, for the Second World War and for the Holocaust propaganda that followed it, which "was on a world-wide scale, and was of a mendacity that was perhaps adapted to a uniformized mass, but was simply disgusting to discriminating Europeans."[27]

4. Harvard graduate David Hoggan (1923–1988), author of *The Myth of the Six Million* (1969), in which he maintains, "There has never been even the slightest conclusive proof for such a campaign of promiscuous slaughter on the part of Germany, and, in the meantime, all reliable evidence continues to suggest with increasing volume and impact that this genocide legend is a deliberate and brazen falsification" perpetrated by the Jews.[28] Lipstadt counts

---

[24] See Paul Rassinier, *Le passage de la ligne* (Paris: Éditions Bressanes, 1948).

[25] Paul Rassinier, *Le drame des Juifs européens* (Paris: Le Sept Couleurs, 1964), 59; my translation.

[26] Maurice Bardèche, *Nuremberg ou la terre promise* (Paris: Le Sept Couleurs, 1948), 8; my translation.

[27] See Francis Parker Yockey, *Imperium—The Philosophy of History and Politics*, 4th ed. (Los Angeles, Calif.: Noontide Press, 2008), 233.

[28] David Hoggan, *The Myth of the Six Million* (Los Angeles, Calif.: Noontide Press, 1969), 104.

him, along with Austin J. App, among "the most significant figures in the evolution of Holocaust denial" in America.[29]

5. Austin J. App (1902–1984), professor of English at the University of Scranton and LaSalle College and author of *The Six Million Swindle: Blackmailing the German People for Hard Marks with Fabricated Corpses* (1973). There he repeats the deicide charge.[30] He insists that "the charge that Hitler and the Third Reich wanted to exterminate all Jews is a totally fabricated, brazen lie"[31] and that "the Talmudists have from the beginning used the six million swindle to blackmail West Germany into 'atoning' with the twenty billion dollars of indemnities to Israel."[32]

6. Richard Verrall (b. 1948) of the neo-Nazi British National Front; he wrote *Did Six Million Really Die? The Truth at Last* (1974) under the name of Richard Harwood. Relying heavily on Rassinier, he argues that the claims that the Holocaust took place rest on completely fraudulent evidence.[33]

7. Robert Faurisson (b. 1929), professor of French literature at the University of Lyon who "openly joined the ranks of the Holocaust deniers on July 27, 1974, by publishing a letter in the weekly newspaper *Le Canard Enchaîné* (Paris) in which he challenged the claim that the Nazis had planned the genocide of the Jews."[34] He later published the infamous *The Problem of the Gas Chambers* (1980).[35]

8. Arthur R. Butz (b. 1933), a Northwestern University engineering professor and author of *The Hoax of the Twentieth Century: The Case against the Presumed Extermination of European Jewry* (1976), in which he argues that the Jews invented the Holocaust in order to further their Zionist aims.[36] In 1985, Louis

---

[29] Lipstadt, *Denying the Holocaust*, 102.

[30] See Austin J. App, *The Six Million Swindle: Blackmailing the German People for Hard Marks with Fabricated Corpses* (Tacoma Park, Md.: Boniface Press, 1973), 2.

[31] Ibid., 3.   [32] Ibid.

[33] See Richard Verrall, *Did Six Million Really Die? The Truth at Last*, 2nd rev. ed. (Torrance, Calif.: Historical Review Press, 2011), 37–41.

[34] Atkins, *Holocaust Denial as an International Movement*, 97.

[35] See Robert Faurisson, *The Problem of the Gas Chambers* (Newport Beach, Calif.: Institute for Historical Review, 1980).

[36] See Arthur R. Butz, *The Hoax of the Twentieth Century: The Case against the Presumed Extermination of European Jewry* (Torrance, Calif.: Historical Review Press, 1976), 87.

Farrakhan (b. 1933) invited Butz to speak at the Nation of Islam's Saviour's Day celebration.[37]

9. Willis A. Carto (b. 1926), who with William David McCalden (1951–1990) founded the Institute for Historical Review (IHR) in 1978, an organization devoted to the publication of material denying the Holocaust and inciting Jew hatred; the Anti-Defamation League labeled him "the most important and powerful antisemite in the United States."[38] Among the stated aims of the IHR is to expose the truth about a world Jewish conspiracy.[39]

10. David Irving (b. 1938), a British historian who filed a libel suit against Deborah Lipstadt in 1996 for exposing him as a Holocaust denier; his activity as a denier dates from 1982, when he delivered a series of speeches in Germany denying the Holocaust. His affiliation with Carto's IHR dates from 1983, and in 1988 he testified for the defense at the trial of Holocaust denier Ernst Zündel in Canada.

11. Roger Garaudy (1913–2012), member of the French Communist Party, Marxist philosopher, and author of *The Founding Myths of Modern Israel* (1985).[40] When he was charged on 27 February 1998 with "complicity in contesting crimes against humanity," notes Robert Wistrich, "Palestinian professors, religious leaders, and journalists publicly protested," and "Lebanon's Arab Journalists Union called on fellow Arab intellectuals to rally to the man 'who had the courage to divulge Zionist lies.' All of Jordan's political parties issued a statement claiming that 'Zionists have fabricated the falsehoods about the extermination of the Jews in Germany to mislead the world and blackmail Western governments.'"[41]

12. Ernst Nolte (b. 1923), a German philosopher and historian who launched the *Historikerstreit*[42] in 1986 and wrote *Der europäische*

---

[37] See Stern, *Holocaust Denial*, 20.   [38] Lipstadt, *Denying the Holocaust*, 144–145.

[39] See ibid., 143.

[40] See Roger Garaudy, *The Founding Myths of Modern Israel* (Newport Beach, Calif.: Institute for Historical Review, 2000).

[41] Robert S. Wistrich, *A Lethal Obsession: Anti-Semitism from Antiquity to the Global Jihad* (New York: Random House, 2010), 648.

[42] The *Historikerstreit* or "historians' struggle" (1986–1989) was characterized by a debate in Germany over the uniqueness of the Nazi fascism and how the Holocaust compared with other catastrophes; see Charles S. Maier, *The Unmasterable Past: History, Holocaust, and German National Identity* (Cambridge, Mass.: Harvard University Press, 1998), 1–8, 47–56.

Bürgerkrieg, 1917–1945: Nationalsozialismus und Bolschewismus (The European Civil War, 1917–1945: National Socialism and Bolshevism), in which he maintains that the Wannsee Conference did not take place and that the actions of the Einsatzgruppen killing units were merely justifiable security measures.[43]

13. Bradley R. Smith (b. 1930), who with Mark Weber (b. 1951) formed the Committee on Open Debate on the Holocaust (CODOH) in 1987; they were responsible for Holocaust denial ads in college newspapers. Smith's primary influences were Faurisson and Butz.[44]

14. Ernst Zündel (b. 1939), who in 1988 published *The Leuchter Report: An Engineering Report on the Alleged Execution Gas Chambers at Auschwitz, Birkenau, and Majdanek, Poland* by Fred A. Leuchter (b. 1944),[45] which was also published by David Irving's publishing house Focal Point Publications. In 1985, the Canadian government charged him with a hate speech crime for publishing Richard Verrall's *Did Six Million Really Die? The Truth at Last*; among his defense witnesses were Robert Faurisson, Bradley Smith, Mark Weber, and David Irving.

15. Gerd Honsik (b. 1941), the Austrian neo-Nazi author of *Freispruch für Hitler?: 36 Ungehörte Zeugen wider die Gaskammer* (Acquittal for Hitler?: 36 Unheard Witnesses against the Gas Chambers, 1988).[46]

16. Henri Roques (b. 1920), who in *The Confessions of Kurt Gerstein* (1989) set out to discredit Kurt Gerstein (1905–1945), a German SS officer who gave information to Swedish diplomat Göran von Otter (1907–1988) about the extermination camps.[47]

17. German-born Germar Rudolf (b. 1964), author of *The Rudolf Report: Expert Report on Chemical and Technical Aspects of*

---

[43] See Ernst Nolte, *Der europäische Bürgerkrieg, 1917–1945: Nationalsozialismus und Bolschewismus* (Berlin: Propyläen Verlag, 1987), 509–513, 592–593; see also Lipstadt, *Denying the Holocaust*, 214.

[44] See Shermer and Grobman, *Denying History*, 61.

[45] See Fred A. Leuchter, Robert Faurisson, and Germar Rudolf, *The Leuchter Reports: Critical Edition* (Chicago, Ill.: Theses and Dissertations Press, 2005).

[46] See Gerd Honsik, *Freispruch für Hitler?: 36 Ungehörte Zeugen wider die Gaskammer* (Vienna: Burgenländischer Kulturverband, 1988).

[47] See Henri Roques, *The Confessions of Kurt Gerstein* (Newport Beach, Calif.: Institute for Historical Review, 1989).

the "Gas Chambers" of Auschwitz, written in 1993 as part of the defense of Otto Ernst Remer.[48]

18. Carlo Mattogno (b. 1951), Italy's foremost denier and author of *The Myth of the Extermination of the Jews* (2000).[49]

From this list it is evident that, as a manifestation of anti-Semitism, Holocaust denial is global. Indeed, Japan's leading denier is Masami Uno (b. 1942); Brazilian industrialist Siegfried Ellwanger (b. 1928) and Australians John Tuson Bennett (b. 1944) and Frederick Töben (b. 1944), could be added to the list, not to mention Iranian President Mahmoud Ahmadinejad (b. 1956).

All of them subscribe to the eight "principles," articulated by Austin J. App and adopted by the IHR:

1. The Reich's plan for solving Germany's Jewish problem was emigration, never annihilation.
2. The gas chambers never existed.
3. Most Jews who disappeared remained in Soviet territory.
4. Jews who died were subversives, partisans, spies, saboteurs, and criminals who deserved to die.
5. If six million were actually murdered, world Jewry would demand subsidies to conduct research on the topic, and Israel would open its archives to historians.
6. The Jews and the media have no evidence to support their claims.
7. The accusers, not the accused, must bear the burden of proof.
8. Jewish scholars themselves have "ridiculous" discrepancies in their numbers.[50]

Similar to App, Maurice Bardèche drafted his own articles of the deniers' faith, which have also been widely used among these anti-Semites:

1. Jews are responsible for World War II.
2. Eyewitnesses are unreliable.

---

[48] See Germar Rudolf, *The Rudolf Report: Expert Report on Chemical and Technical Aspects of the "Gas Chambers" of Auschwitz* (Chicago, Ill.: Theses and Dissertations Press, 2003).

[49] See Carlo Mattogno, *The Myth of the Extermination of the Jews* (Chicago, Ill.: Theses and Dissertations Press, 2009); see also Carlo Mattogno and Germar Rudolf, *Auschwitz-Lies: Legends, Lies, and Prejudices on the Holocaust* (Chicago, Ill.: Theses and Dissertations Press, 2005).

[50] Lipstadt, *Denying the Holocaust,* 99–100.

3. The horrors of the communist regime should not be forgotten.
4. Atrocities committed in the camps were committed by the Jews.
5. The Nazis never wanted to exterminate the Jews.
6. The only use of gas in Auschwitz was to prevent disease.[51]

Like the affirmation of any creed, none of these premises is subject to proof; rather, they form the ground from which the deniers proceed in their assault on the place of the Jews in history. They constitute the *ani maamin*, the "I believe," of the idolatry couched in this mode of antihistorical anti-Semitism. French historian Pierre Vidal-Naquet (1930–2006) exposes both the core of the deniers' doxology and the method they adopt in his list of eight fundamental ramifications of their axiomatic lies:

1. All testimony presented by a Jew is either a lie or a fantasy.
2. Any testimony or document from the war years is a forgery.
3. Documents supposedly based on firsthand information concerning Nazi methods are either forgeries or have been tampered with.
4. Nazi documents written in coded language are taken at face value, but those that are written plainly are unacknowledged.
5. Post-war testimony from the Nazis was obtained under torture or by intimidation.
6. A vast arsenal of pseudo-technical evidence is used to demonstrate the impossibility of mass gassings.
7. The gas chambers did not exist because nonexistence was one of their attributes.
8. Anything that might render the Holocaust believable is either ignored or falsified.[52]

Once again, one immediately realizes that what we have here is not historical revisionism, laying bare the misnomer of "Holocaust revisionism," but a blatantly antihistorical anti-Semitism. And so the wheel turns. Maurice Bardèche looks to the Holocaust, sees the Jews as the true perpetrators of the horrors, and confirms it to be evidence of the evil of the Jews. And because the Jews are evil, Robert Faurisson looks to the Holocaust and confirms that the Jews have forged all evidence of its occurrence. In short, the Jews are evil and must be eliminated.

[51] Atkins, *Holocaust Denial as an International Movement*, 89.
[52] Pierre Vidal-Naquet, *Assassins of Memory: Essays on the Denial of the Holocaust*, trans. Jeffrey Mehlman (New York: Columbia University Press, 1992), 21–23.

Further, like Satan, world Jewry is ubiquitous, invisible, and behind every evil, including the horrors of the camps and the war itself. Indeed, all Jews who were murdered deserved to be murdered because they embody the essence of evil. They control information and the media and keep secret any evidence that might exonerate the Nazis. Because the Jews are evil *by definition*, only evidence exonerating the Nazis can be true; the Nazis are *by definition* innocent, since they are the true victims, the victims of the Jews. Indeed, for the antihistorical anti-Semite, *the Jews are the Nazis*. As for the gas chambers, there is no evidence of their existence – and if they did exist, there is no evidence that they were used for mass killing – because, in keeping with the deniers' ontological argument, they do not exist *by definition*. If the horrors of the communist regime should not be forgotten, it is because the Jews are behind those horrors: for the Holocaust deniers, as for the Nazis, the terms *communist*, *Bolshevik*, and *Marxist* are synonymous with the word *Jew*.

Most important, what is to be noted in all of this is that the "testimony" of the deniers is a countertestimony not to the "Holocaust narrative" of the Jews but to the Torah made manifest through the Jews and to the Commanding Voice of the Holy One that shapes history itself. Thus, the Holocaust deniers set out not to "revise" but to appropriate history *and its essence*: if history consists of a struggle between the forces of good and evil – with good and evil being determined by the autonomous will of the ego – then the force of evil confronting humanity is embodied in the prevaricating, manipulating, and ever conspiring Jew. Therefore, as a manifestation of anti-Semitism, Holocaust denial has an implicitly religious underpinning, the idolatrous underpinning that belongs to any effort to unseat the God whose commanding Voice determines good and evil from Mount Sinai and reverberates from the depths of the silence of Auschwitz. Holocaust denial is a denial of that Voice, what Emil Fackenheim calls "the Commanding Voice of Auschwitz." It is a voice that cries out both to humanity in general and to the Jews in particular.

"Jewish opposition to Auschwitz," Fackenheim argues, "cannot be grasped in terms of humanly created ideals but only as an *imposed commandment*. And the Jewish secularist, no less than the believer, is *absolutely singled out* by a Voice as truly *other* than man-made ideals – an imperative as truly *given* – as was the Voice of Sinai."[53] What do Sinai and Auschwitz have in common? Both are moments of the revelation of a

---

[53] Fackenheim, *God's Presence in History*, 83.

singular Ultimate that informs all understanding of history. If the religious Jew submits to the Voice of Sinai after Auschwitz, it is because Auschwitz demonstrates what becomes of a world that has grown deaf to the Voice of Sinai. If the secular Jew – simply by identifying him- or herself as a Jew – submits to the Voice of Auschwitz, it is because he or she cannot escape the Voice of Sinai, which, according to one tradition, says just one thing: "I am God" (Exodus 20:2), which, again, means: "Thou shalt not murder" (Exodus 20:13). The Holocaust denier's hatred is aimed at the elimination of both, which is required for the elimination of the Torah that "goes forth from Zion" (Isaiah 2:3). Radical Holocaust deniers, therefore, are necessarily anti-Zionists. For Zionism is above all about Torah (a point I explore in the next chapter). As the Jews – all Jews – act on the "Zionist impulse" and return to Zion, so does the Torah go forth from Zion with the Jewish return to Zion. Here we discover a basic link between the Holocaust deniers in the West and the Holocaust deniers in the Muslim world; the two are driven by the same ultimate aim, their differences notwithstanding. To be sure, some Holocaust deniers, such as Roger Garaudy and Swiss denier Ahmed Huber (1927–2008), converted to Islam.

HOLOCAUST DENIAL IN THE MUSLIM WORLD

There is at least one basic reason for distinguishing between Holocaust denial in the West and the same denial in the Muslim world: in the West the phenomenon is relatively marginal, and there are numerous universities where one can research and even earn a degree or a certificate in Holocaust studies. The Catholic University of Leuven in Belgium, in fact, requires their theology students to take a course on the Holocaust. Does the renowned Al-Azhar University in Cairo have a similar requirement for their future imams, or even offer a course on the Holocaust as a mere elective? Is there *any* university in the Muslim world where one can study this upheaval in history or even take a single course on it? No.

Antihistorical anti-Semitism in Islam is as old as the Quran, where, as noted in Chapter 3, it is affirmed that Abraham was not a Jew but a Muslim (3:67) and that the Jews falsified Scripture (2:59; 3:78), which consists largely of the history of the Jewish people. Just as the appropriation of God entails the appropriation of the Word, so does the appropriation of the Word entail the appropriation of history by subverting the place of the Jews in history. Thus, from the time of Islam's inception, the Jews have been cast in the mold of falsifiers of history.

In keeping with that tradition several Muslim countries have hosted conferences surrounding the theme of Holocaust denial. In April 2001, Lebanon provided a venue in Beirut for such a conference in partnership with the IHR and its Swiss counterpart, the L'Association Vérité et Justice. Featured speakers included Roger Garaudy, Robert Faurisson, and Mark Weber, with sessions in Arabic, French, and English.[54] A month later the Jordanian Writers' Association held a conference in Amman along the same lines; among its speakers was Jordanian university professor Dr. Ibrahim Alloush, who brought with him all of the authority of his academic standing. Then there is the International Conference to Review the Global Vision of the Holocaust held in Tehran in December 2006 and sponsored by the Iranian government. Among its attendees were Ku Klux Klansman David Duke, Robert Faurisson, and Ahmed Rami (b. 1946), a writer and radio broadcaster whom Stephen Atkins describes as "the leading denier in the Muslim world."[55]

In addition to the involvement of Muslim countries in the organization of "scholarly" conferences that would lend some sort of legitimacy to Holocaust denial, there is the active support of Holocaust "revisionism" on the part of other Muslim governments. Saudi Arabia is a glaring example. Atkins points out that the "Saudi regime has long been a financial supporter for the Holocaust denial movement,"[56] and Lipstadt notes that "Saudi Arabia financed the publication of a number of books accusing the Jews of creating the Holocaust hoax."[57] That this is the official position of the Saudi government is confirmed by the fact that Gamal Baroodi, their representative to the U.N., has denied that the Holocaust ever occurred.[58] Then there is Saudi-born Abdullah Mohammad Sindi (b. 1944), who has been as a professor of political science at several universities in California.[59]

Egypt is another case in point, going back to Holocaust denier Gamal Abdel Nasser. On 29 April 2002, Egyptian journalist Fatma Abdullah Mahmoud published an article in the Egyptian newspaper *Al-Akhbar* proclaiming that "French studies have shown that [the Holocaust] is nothing more than a fabrication," adding, "I, personally, complain to Hitler ..., 'If only you had done it, brother, if only it had really happened, so that the world could sigh in relief without their evil and sin.'"[60] And in

---

[54] See Atkins, *Holocaust Denial as an International Movement*, 133.   [55] Ibid., 129.
[56] Ibid., 214.   [57] Lipstadt, *Denying the Holocaust*, 14.
[58] Stern, *Holocaust Denial*, 49.
[59] See Atkins, *Holocaust Denial as an International Movement*, 214.
[60] Quoted in Matthias Küntzel, *Jihad and Jew-Hatred: Islamism, Nazism and the Roots of 9/11*, trans. Colin Meade (New York: Telos Press, 2007), 61.

December 2005, Hisham Abd al-Rauf wrote in the Egyptian newspaper *Al-Masaa*, "These massacres, which Israel alleges the Nazis perpetrated against the Jews, never happened."[61] Thus, in many quarters of the Muslim world Holocaust denial is not a marginal phenomenon found only among marginalized fanatics but is rather part of mainstream society, both popular and professional.

The anti-Semitism underlying Holocaust denial is also a defining feature of Muslim theo-political movements, particularly those that fall into the category of Islamic Jihadism. Wistrich points out, for instance, that "Iran is the first example of a modern state since Hitler's Germany that has *officially* adopted an active policy of anti-Semitism as a means to promote its national interests.... This is the context in which one must consider the relentless denial of the Nazi Holocaust that is so rampant in Iran and much of the Arab world. Such a denial is inextricably linked to the planned annihilation of Israel."[62] The Iranian-spawned terrorist organization Hezbollah has embraced the same position. True to the established pattern, Hezbollah leader Hasan Nasrallah first demonizes the Jews by labeling them Nazis and then denies that the Nazis ever launched a program of extermination against them. In a speech given during an Ashura flagellation ceremony on 9 April 2000 he cried out that "the Jews invented the legend of the Nazi atrocities."[63] Later, in a speech aired on Al-Jazeera Television on 3 February 2006, he invoked the infamous denier Roger Garaudy, describing him as "a great French philosopher" who "proved that this Holocaust is a myth."[64] Here we have yet another example of the process of wedding Western anti-Semitism with traditional Islamic Jew hatred to form Islamic Jihadism, as noted in Chapter 3.

That the Holocaust was either perpetrated by the Jews or is a hoax promulgated by the Jews (with their compartmentalized thinking, Jihadist deniers hold both positions simultaneously) is the official stance of the

---

[61] Quoted in Atkins, *Holocaust Denial as an International Movement*, 207.

[62] Wistrich, *A Lethal Obsession*, 909.

[63] Hassan Nasrallah, "Excerpts from Speech by Hizbullah Secretary-General Nasrallah," Israel Ministry of Foreign Affairs, 9 April 2000, available at http://www.mfa.gov.il/MFA/MFAArchive/2000_2009/2000/4/Excerpts%20from%20Speech%20by%20Hizbullah%20Secretary-Genera.

[64] Hassan Nasrallah, "Hizbullah Leader Nasrallah: Great French Philosopher Garaudy Proved Holocaust a Myth," MEMRI, 7 February 2006, available at http://www.memri.org/bin/articles.cgi?Page=archives&Area=sd&ID=SP108806.

Muslim Brotherhood and its offshoot Hamas. In 2003, former Hamas leader Dr. Abdel Aziz al-Rantisi (1948–2004) published an article in the Hamas weekly *Al-Risala* arguing that the Holocaust was "the greatest of lies" spread by the Jews, and, if there was a Holocaust, the Jews were the true perpetrators.[65] Said al-Rantisi, "It is no longer a secret that the Zionists were behind the Nazis' murder of many Jews, and agreed to it, with the aim of intimidating them [other Jews] and forcing them to immigrate to Palestine. Every time they failed to persuade a group of Jews to immigrate, they unhesitatingly sentenced [them] to death. Afterwards, they would organize great propaganda campaigns, to cash in on their blood."[66] The Holocaust did not happen, and the Jews did it.

Like other Holocaust deniers, the Jihadist deniers embrace the axiom that the Jewish witnesses are either liars or murderers or both, bent on the establishment of a Jewish state to be used as a base of operations to take over the world. Therefore the God of history is not God – the Jihadist deniers are the gods of history. As the embodiment and origin of evil, the Jews lie about the Holocaust, or if it happened they did it, and if Hitler did it he was the instrument of Allah who meted out a just punishment, because the Jews are evil incarnate – like the Nazis. Thus Article Twenty of the Hamas Charter of Allah describes the Jews as Nazis, a ploy used, as noted above, among other Holocaust deniers to veil the Nazi-like nature of their own ideology and to further incite hatred of the Jews. As Matthias Küntzel points out, the projection of "Nazi" on the Jew is "a specific form of Holocaust denial, one which legitimates the pursuit of an anti-Jewish extermination policy, while projecting these murderous intentions onto the chosen victim."[67] Indeed, having come to signify the most heinous of evils, the term *Nazi* is a designation attached to anyone who deserves annihilation. Whereas for the non-Muslim deniers the annihilation of the Jews is an ontological demand, for the Jihadists deniers it is a religious duty.

Holocaust denial is also an official position of the Palestinian Authority. In 1983, Palestinian head Mahmoud Abbas published a book based on his doctoral dissertation titled *The Other Side: The Secret Relationship*

---

[65] "Hamas Leader Rantisi: The False Holocaust," MEMRI, 27 August 2003, available at http://www.memri.org/bin/articles.cgi?Page=subjects&Area=antisemitism&ID=SP55803.
[66] Quoted in David Aaron, *In Their Own Words: Voices of Jihad* (Santa Monica, Calif.: Rand Corporation, 2008), 137.
[67] Küntzel, *Jihad and Jew-Hatred*, 118.

between Nazism and the Zionist Movement.[68] Also typical is the sermon broadcast on Palestinian Authority television on 21 September 2001 by Sheikh Ibrahim Madhi, in which the cleric proclaimed, "One of the cursed actions of the Jews is called the Holocaust, that is to say, the massacre of the Jews by Nazism. But revisionist historians have proved that this crime rumoured against some Jews was manipulated by Jewish leaders and became a political tactic."[69] And in 1975 Palestinian author Ahmad Hussein published *Palestine My Homeland*, in which he denies that the Holocaust ever happened.[70]

Underlying this antihistorical anti-Semitism in the Muslim world is a decidedly anti-Zionist aim: if the Jews established a Jewish state as a haven in a world that is hostile toward them and if the Jews never suffered from such hostility, then there is no need for such a haven. As a manifestation of the desire to eliminate the Jewish state, "Holocaust denial," as Stern has observed, "not only attacks Jewish history, its inherent anti-Zionism also targets the Jewish present and the Jewish future."[71] Later he adds, "Like the 'Zionism is racism' canard, Holocaust denial provides a reason for disliking the mere existence of Israel."[72] As we have seen, an assault on history always entails an assault on the future, so that the anti-Semites may proceed with the project to usurp God unencumbered by the unsettling presence of the Jews.

Because that presence undermines the religious imperative to bring the world under the rule of Islam,[73] the Jihadist deniers slip into what Neil Kressel calls "*Protocols* thinking," that is, the thinking that proceeds from the world Jewish conspiracy premise that the Jewish state is nothing more than a base of operations from which the Jews intend to nefariously rule the world.[74] Such a view is confirmed by Shermer and Grobman's observation that "embedded in the anti-Jewish agenda of Holocaust denial is a strong conspiratorial streak."[75] And as Stern states it,

---

[68] See Anti-Defamation League, *Holocaust Denial in the Middle East: The Latest Anti-Israel Propaganda Theme* (New York: Anti-Defamation League, 2001), 5–6.

[69] Quoted in David Matas, *Aftershock: Anti-Zionism and Anti-Semitism* (Toronto: Dundurn, 2005), 32.

[70] See Stern, *Holocaust Denial*, 49.   [71] Ibid., 52.   [72] Ibid., 86.

[73] See Majid Khadduri, "The Law of War: The Jihad," in Andrew G. Bostom, ed., *The Legacy of Jihad: Islamic Holy War and the Fate of Non-Muslims* (Amherst, N.Y.: Prometheus Books, 2005), 307; see also Bostom, "Jihad Conquests and the Imposition of *Dhimmitude* – A Survey," 98.

[74] See Neil J. Kressel, *"The Sons of Pigs and Apes": Muslim Antisemitism and the Conspiracy of Silence* (Washington, D.C.: Potomac Books, 2012), 41.

[75] Shermer and Grobman, *Denying History*, 80.

"the Holocaust-as-hoax belief is rooted in the idea of a world Jewish conspiracy. Israel, of course, would have to be a key part of any such conspiracy."[76] For the Jihadists, history is the history of the Islamic struggle against a Jewish conspiratorial evil striving to rule the world, in opposition to the Jihadist design to do the same. It is therefore the history of a metaphysical conflict between Jihadist good and Jewish evil. Hence Jihadist antihistorical anti-Semitism has a clear metaphysical origin.

Not all forms of Holocaust denial are so fanatic as those we have considered so far. It happens that, rather than trying to remove Jews from history, we simply invite them to leave the room. There may be no rabid hatred of the Jew, but there is a real resentment, not because of some heinous world Jewish conspiracy but because of a higher ethical injunction that the Jews represent by their very presence. It is an injunction that implicates us even in our relationship with the dead.

SUBTLE MANIFESTATIONS OF HOLOCAUST DENIAL

Although outright Holocaust deniers continue the work of the Nazis' assault on God, one does not have to be a Nazi or a Jihadist to flee from the ethical implications couched in a collision with the Holocaust. The more subtle forms of Holocaust denial are akin to denial in a psychological sense, that is, the avoidance of confrontation or the evasion of a grim truth described in *The Freud Encyclopedia* as "acting to ward off perceptions of external reality that would be upsetting. . . . Or the anxiety-arousing experience may be minimized, or ridiculed, or otherwise distorted so that the arousal of negative affect is diminished. . . . [Denial also arises in] situations in which external reality is overwhelmingly painful and immutable."[77] The Holocaust is undoubtedly painful and immutable. What makes it painful and immutable is not only the empathy for human suffering but also the ethical outcry that implicates all of us. Taking flight from the ethical implication, the ego curls up in the cave of its complacency, which becomes the cave of its complicity. Such a flight from accountability is a temptation that lies within any soul; while it may not be steeped in a conscious hatred of the Jews, it is the temptation that underlies anti-Semitism.

I have witnessed this phenomenon personally and professionally. I have had colleagues say to me, "You're going to teach a course on

---

[76] Stern, *Holocaust Denial*, 53.

[77] Edward Erwin, ed., *The Freud Encyclopedia: Theory, Therapy, and Culture* (New York: Routledge, 2002), 142–143.

the Holocaust *again*? Can't we get over it? It happened so long ago! People are tired of it!" I have never heard anyone declare to a colleague, "You're going to teach a course on the Civil War *again*? Can't we get over it? It happened so long ago!" During the years when I sat on a state Holocaust commission, to take another example of subtle denial, a professor from a leading university declared that in our discussions of the Holocaust we must avoid the word *evil* because of its "religious baggage." Religious baggage always comes with ethical implications. And the ethical implications, above all, must be avoided.

An incident even more disturbing occurred at a conference on the Holocaust that I attended. As we were leaving a plenary session, a friend who is a survivor told me that she had come to a horrifying realization about the relation between Holocaust scholars and Holocaust survivors. Speaking in a whisper, as though afraid of her own words, she said to me, "I know now what they want us to do: they want us to die." I was shocked. And then it hit me: we scholars who pretend to deal with the Holocaust do not want to deal with the surviving Jews because we do not want to deal with the flesh and blood of Jewish life, which is rooted in Judaism. We do not want to look into the faces that put to us the question of what is ultimate in life, from beyond life. Whether or not this or that Jew believes in the sacred tradition is irrelevant; the very presence of the Jews signifies the teachings of that tradition, and the presence of the surviving Jews signifies the radical assault on those teachings during the Holocaust. It tells the Jews that they do not have the luxury of regarding their tradition as a cultural curiosity; it tells the Christians that their Christianity is, at least in its traditional forms, a scandal; and it tells the scholars that their postmodern relativism is a disgrace. That is why we scholars want the survivors to go away. In their presence we collide with the cry of an absolute commandment that, like the shofar of Mount Sinai, shakes us from our egocentric slumber.

Thus my friend's words shook me from my own shameful slumber. She opened my eyes to a pervasive pattern in Holocaust studies, both in teaching and in scholarship, a pattern characterized by the elimination of the Jews from a consideration of the Holocaust. It is tied to the phenomenon that Alvin Rosenfeld describes as "the end of the Holocaust," something that can be found not only in the popular culture that would trivialize the event but also in the halls of the academy and the exhibits of the museums that would relativize it: to relativize is to trivialize. Says Rosenfeld, "As the mass murder of millions of innocent people is trivialized and vulgarized, a catastrophic history, bloody to its core, is lightened of its historical burden and gives up the sense of scandal that necessarily should attend it. . . . The more successfully it enters the public mainstream, the more commonplace it becomes. A less taxing version of a tragic history begins to emerge – still full of suffering, to be sure, but a suffering relieved of its weightiest moral and intellectual demands."[78] Relieved of its weightiest moral and intellectual demands, the Holocaust is relieved of its Jewish demands. The Nazis' victory turns out to be more pervasive than we think. More and more – in academia and in the public mainstream, on museum boards and Holocaust commissions – we do not speak of Jews at all. If we happen to comment on the Jews, we generally say nothing of what it means to be a Jew. But what can it mean to speak of the murder of the Jews without addressing the Judaism that makes them who they are?

One postmodernist scholar, Robert Eaglestone, understands that "Holocaust denial can most simply and clearly be understood as a form of anti-Semitism."[79] At the same time, he explains, postmodernism questions the "empiricist view of history," that is, the view that "objective observation" is possible,[80] adding that "historical knowledge is produced, and history books are written, as a genre."[81] History, in other words, is nothing more than a kind of fictional narrative. According to Eaglestone, the problem with Holocaust denial is that it "doesn't obey the rules of the genre."[82] And yet, what absolute principle enables the postmodernist to declare one set of generic rules to be privileged over another? What is the ethical demand attached to following the rules of the genre? Insisting that postmodernism provides "very strong weapons in the fight against Holocaust denial,"[83] but without addressing the question of why it matters, Eaglestone relies heavily on Jean-François Lyotard's *The Differend*. Lyotard begins his reflection by saying, "Human beings ... were placed in a situation such that none of them is now able to tell about it. . . . Either the situation did not exist as such. Or else it did exist, in which case your informant's testimony is false, either because he or she should have disappeared, or else because he or she should remain silent . . .; he or she can bear witness only to the particular experience he had."[84] After citing Robert Faurisson's assertion that he had never found a deportee who had

---

[78] Alvin Rosenfeld, *The End of the Holocaust* (Bloomington: Indiana University Press, 2011), 11.

[79] Robert Eaglestone, *Postmodernism and Holocaust Denial* (Duxford, U.K.: Icon Books, 2001), 9.

[80] Ibid., 21.   [81] Ibid., 39.   [82] Ibid., 50.   [83] Ibid., 7.

[84] Jean-François Lyotard, *The Differend: Phrases in Dispute*, trans. Georges Van Den Abbeele (Minneapolis: University of Minnesota Press, 1988), 3.

actually seen a gas chamber with his own eyes, Lyotard expounds, "To have 'really seen with his own eyes' a gas chamber would be the condition which gives one the authority to say that it exists and to persuade the unbeliever. Yet it is still necessary to prove that the gas chamber was used to kill at the time it was seen. The only acceptable proof that it was used to kill is that one died from it. But if one is dead, one cannot testify that it is on account of the gas chamber."[85] This is like saying that the only legitimate testimony in a murder trial is the testimony of the victim. Although Lyotard makes this point to expose Faurisson's sophistry, there is a certain sophistry in his own claim that being able to testify only to one's own experience somehow calls into question the testimony, if that is indeed his claim. If it is not his claim, there is no escaping the postmodernist position that the survivor's "narrative" is no more than one narrative among many; indeed, one's status as a survivor is determined by the narrative. Once we are left only with the narrative, we are left without the Jew. Left without the Jew, we are left without the ethical demand. And so we slip into the spectrum of Holocaust denial.

One understands, then, Lipstadt's complaint that among postmodernists, "it became more difficult to talk about the objective truth of a text, legal concept, or even an event. In academic circles some scholars spoke of relative truths, rejecting the notion that there was one version of the world that was necessarily right while another was wrong."[86] She adds in this vein that "because deconstructionism argued that experience was relative and nothing was fixed, it created an atmosphere of permissiveness toward questioning the meaning of historical events and made it hard for its proponents to assert that there was anything 'off limits' for this skeptical approach."[87] One wonders whether postmodernism and deconstructionism might have at their core a certain antihistorical anti-Semitism that undergirds the anti-Semitic historical revisionism of Holocaust denial.

The process of de-Judaizing the Holocaust has crept into various quarters of academia to produce what I call "Holocaust studies without the Holocaust." In the postmodern era the other who unsettles and troubles the good conscience of those engaged in Holocaust studies is the Jew. That is why many of us seek to eliminate the Jew from our thinking about the Holocaust. We do not deal with the Jews because, in our effort to get rid of God and the absolute responsibility that He imposes on us, we do not want to have to respond to the first question

---

[85] Ibid., 3.   [86] Lipstadt, *Denying the Holocaust*, 18.   [87] Ibid.

put to the first human: "Where are you?" We do not want to look into the faces of slaughtered Jews through whom the question resounds. Instead, we hide the Jews by burying them in the meaningless category of victims-in-general. In doing so, we play into the hands of Holocaust deniers by rendering the study of the Holocaust *Judenrein*. Rather than speak of Jews and Judaism, we speak of coping and trauma, dialogue and healing, representation and remembrance, textual analysis and ethnic tolerance, even bullying – everything except the singular assault on the testimony, tradition, and teachings that emanate from Mount Sinai.

An example can be found in Dominick LaCapra's concern with ways of "working through" the Holocaust so as to avoid the pitfalls of "acting out." In his book *Writing History, Writing Trauma*, he adapts "psychoanalytical concepts to historical analysis as well as sociocultural and political critique in elucidating trauma and its aftereffects in culture and in people."[88] If he invokes the traumatic "absence of a radically transcendent divinity,"[89] he reads such an absence as a psychological condition, and not as an evil that threatens humanity. For LaCapra, there is only me and my trauma. The fact that it was *Jews* who were exterminated is incidental, and he is careful to avoid any "superordinate master language,"[90] such as one finds in the Torah. What must be avoided above all, he says, is any "sacralization of the event,"[91] which would include any attempt to situate the Shoah within Jewish sacred history. If Jews want to see the event in such religious terms, it is merely an indication of a neurosis that they have yet to "work through." Not surprisingly, therefore, LaCapra reduces anti-Semitism to a psychological subset of "other forms of racism and victimization,"[92] a case of "quasi-sacrificial acting out," which also applies to the victimization of Gypsies, Bolsheviks, Slavs, and homosexuals.[93] His basic answer to the Jews who have been "traumatized" by the Holocaust is that they should "put it behind them." The "it," however is not just the Holocaust but, more important, the centuries of teaching and testimony that form the Judaism marked for annihilation.

Another subtle form of Holocaust denial can be found in the effort to get rid of it by explaining it away, a phenomenon that Fackenheim understood very well:

---

[88] Dominick LaCapra, *Writing History, Writing Trauma* (Baltimore, Md.: Johns Hopkins University Press, 2001), ix.

[89] Ibid., 23.   [90] Ibid.. 62.   [91] Ibid., 92–93.   [92] Ibid., 129.   [93] Ibid., 132.

Before Nazism happened, we thought it could not happen. Now that it has happened, we resort to explanations that explain it away. We take it, in the style of Enlightenment liberalism, as a mere lapse into atavistic prejudice, superstition, or neurosis, ills that should not happen in this day and age and for which – soon if not now – there will be a cure. Or we take it, in neo-Lutheran style, as a mere case of national pride, lust for power, or xenophobia, sins will always happen because we are all sinners. Possibly we take it as a mixture of the two. In any case we resist confronting it as a modern idolatry – one might say, as *the* modern idolatry, because, being unsurpassable, it reveals all that idolatry can be in the modern world.[94]

Because from the beginning Jews have most vehemently opposed idolatry, the idolaters most vehemently oppose the Jews: it is perhaps the most fundamental form of anti-Semitism. It lies in the investiture of the finite in the garb of the infinite, a move that is essential to the anti-Semite's effort to be as God.

Just as the Jew vanishes into general explanations, so the Jew disappears into other agendas that appropriate the Holocaust to serve their own ends; these other agendas are found, for example, in race, class, and gender studies, as well as in areas such as postcolonial and cultural studies. Often the Jews themselves are deemed complicit in their own murder, as they get blamed for positing the absolutes that underlie racism, sexism, and colonialism. In the high-school textbook *World Geography: Building a Global Perspective*, for instance, the authors maintain that the Nazis started killing the Jews in the Warsaw Ghetto when the Jews rebelled,[95] as if it were the fault of the Jews that the Nazis murdered them. In fact, it was the other way around: the Warsaw Ghetto Fighters rose up on 19 April 1943, when the Nazis came to liquidate the ghetto after having already sent close to half a million Jews to their deaths at Treblinka. The authors go on to say that in the six extermination camps "people from many nations suffered horribly or were brutally murdered,"[96] with no specific mention of the Jews. Similarly, in their textbook *World History* Elizabeth Gaynor Ellis and Anthony Esler state that Hitler wanted to "pursue a vicious program to kill all people he judged 'racially inferior,'"[97] ignoring the fact that only the Jews were the designated targets of the Final Solution.

---

[94] Emil L. Fackenheim, *Encounters between Judaism and Modern Philosophy* (New York: Basic Books, 1993), 192–193.

[95] Thomas J. Baerwald and Celeste Fraser, *World Geography: Building a Global Perspective* (Upper Saddle River, N.J.: Prentice Hall, 2007), 390.

[96] Ibid.

[97] Elizabeth Gaynor Ellis and Anthony Esler, *World History* (Upper Saddle River, N.J.: Prentice Hall, 2007), 936.

The point here is not to put such individuals into the category of Holocaust deniers; they would never deny that the Holocaust took place. Rather, it is to show that Holocaust denial has its roots in the soul's tendencies to turn away from the Jews and the unsettling pronouncements of Jewish teaching and testimony. In its most extreme and insidious forms, as we have seen, Holocaust denial is not so subtle. But the seeds that produce the denial of the Holocaust can be found in the desire to relativize, trivialize, and generalize it.

A CLOSING THOUGHT ON THE WHY OF HOLOCAUST DENIAL

Antihistorical anti-Semites, from many who turn away from the horror to all who deny that it ever took place, see the world Jewish conspiracy as a move to take over not only the world but also history itself – which is precisely the aim of the Holocaust deniers in their effort to usurp the God of history. In the end, radical Holocaust deniers, like those who fall into a psychological denial, deny the Holocaust not because they believe it never happened but precisely because they know it happened. The deniers' issue with Holocaust testimony, then, is not an issue with evidence; nor is it about this narrative or that. As for the denial phenomenon itself, it is not about undermining the scientific methods of historical research, and least of all is it about following the rules of the narrative genre called "history." This form of anti-Semitism is antihistorical because it is about silencing the divine testimony that issues from Mount Sinai and enters the world through the Jewish people to weave the fabric of history itself. The why of Holocaust denial lies in either silencing or turning away from the Jewish Question for which the Nazis sought a Final Solution. And yet the real Jewish Question is not: What is to be done with the Jews? Rather, the Jewish Question is the first question put to the first human being: Where are you? It is couched in the two questions put to the first murderer: Where is your brother? And what have you done? The question implicates each of us in our responsibility to and for our fellow human being. It is the question of what we stand for, why we live, and why we die. No one wants to have his or her sleep interrupted by such a disturbing question. But the question will not go away, any more than the ashes will go away. Holocaust denial is an attempt to silence the question that comes both from within and from beyond the Jewish people by turning them over to the silence of the grave.

On second thought: not the silence of the grave. Those turned over to the silence of the grave at least have a grave. The Holocaust deniers would remove the Jewish people from history altogether and turn them over to the silence of nonbeing: the Holocaust is nothing but a rumor – it never happened. The Jews never happened. Mount Sinai never happened. And there is no ethical absolute.

And so we see why Holocaust denial is inextricably and invariably tied to a denial of the Jewish state, as the Jewish return to the Jewish state signifies the Jewish return to history. Thus, the deniers of the Holocaust join together with the anti-Zionists in a chorus calling for the destruction of the Jewish state, and the subsequent extermination of the Jews to erase them not only from the face of the earth but from history itself. Thus the same Palestinians who deny that the Holocaust took place also deny that the Jews ever had a place in Palestine, as it is written in Article Twenty of the PLO Charter: "The claim of historical or spiritual links between the Jews and Palestine is neither in conformity with historical fact nor does it satisfy the requirements for statehood."[98] There is no place in history, no place in geography, for Jews and Judaism. They are to be expunged from both time and space. Those who never died in Auschwitz should never live in Jerusalem. Indeed, from a Jewish standpoint, history is the history of the Holy City, because history is the history of the holy. And, like history, once Jerusalem is purged of its Jewish presence, it is purged of the divine Presence and the commanding Voice that disturbs the sleep of the anti-Semite.

---

[98] "The Palestine National Charter," in Itamar Rabinovich and Jehuda Reinharz, eds., *Israel in the Middle East: Documents and Readings on Society, Politics, and Foreign Relations, Pre-1948 to the Present*, 2nd ed. (Lebanon, N.H.: University Press of New England, 2008), 245.

7

Anti-Zionist Anti-Semitism

Zion is absolute in the world. It is the life of all countries.

Maggid of Mezeritch

Elhanan Yakira, a philosophy professor at Hebrew University, underscores the link between Holocaust denial and anti-Zionism. Says Yakira,

Both in Rassinier and his faithful followers on the radical French left one can find this syndrome: one must not allow the crime that was committed at Auschwitz, as it were, to blind us to the main thing, which is the suffering of those who are truly exploited – the workers, people of the Third World, the Palestinians. What happened at Auschwitz was, in the last analysis, just another instance, among many, of the true source of all crimes: colonialism, imperialism, capitalism, and Zionism. Thus, one cannot avoid the conclusion that nothing unique happened at Auschwitz. Its uniqueness can be negated by the claim that there was no systematic, planned extermination of the Jews or, alternatively, by the claim that systematic, planned extermination, real or symbolic, is what the Israelis are doing to the Palestinians.[1]

This is the circular logic that paints the Jewish state into the corner of something abhorrent and worthy of extinction, the same corner into which the Nazis painted the Jews. Identified as colonialists and imperialists, who, by implication, are out to rule the world, the Zionists are worthy of nothing less than annihilation.

---

[1] Elhanan Yakira, *Post-Zionism, Post-Holocaust: Three Essays on Denial, Forgetting, and the Delegitimation of Israel*, trans. Michael Swirsky (Cambridge, U.K: Cambridge University Press, 2010), 41.

Here we have an archetypical instance of what was identified in the previous chapter as "*Protocols* thinking," a thinking rooted in the world Jewish conspiracy canard; it is emblematic not only of antihistorical anti-Semitism but also of anti-Zionist anti-Semitism, and it is symptomatic of anti-Semitism's metaphysical origins. Why? Because, as we have seen, it casts the Jews in the mold of an ominous, invisible presence lurking throughout creation, sowing havoc and evil, when the real evil lurks within our own soul. To be sure, world Jewish conspiracy thinking vis-à-vis Zionism was in place long before the Zionists' establishment of a Jewish state. In 1922, Alfred Rosenberg published his diatribe *Der staatsfeindliche Zionismus* (Zionism: Enemy of the State), in which he argues that Zionism is a Jewish strategy for world domination.[2] And in *Mein Kampf* Hitler relates that during his years in Vienna (1907–1913) he discovered the "national character of the Jews" – that is, their *essential* evil – "in the Zionists,"[3] asserting, "While the Zionists try to make the rest of the world believe that the national consciousness of the Jew finds its satisfaction in the creation of a Palestinian state, the Jews again slyly dupe the dumb *Goyim*. It doesn't even enter their heads to build up a Jewish state in Palestine for the purpose of living there; all they want is a central organization for their international world swindle."[4] Therefore, "the Jewish state," according to the Führer, "is completely unlimited as to territory."[5] Nor was such thinking confined to Nazi Germany. In 1924, Polish politician Roman Dmowski maintained that the aim of Zionism was to create "the operational basis for action throughout the world."[6] Such thinking would pervade the Muslim world as well.

The Islamic actions taken against the Jews prior to the advent of the Jewish state were not reactions to Jewish "occupation"; rather, they were initiatives taken to destroy the Jewish state before it could be born – not because the Jews had no rightful claim to the land but because they intended to use it as a base of operations for international Jewry's rule of the world, as outlined in the *Protocols of the Elders of Zion*, a work that the Muslim Brotherhood and many others in the Muslim world

---

[2] Alfred Rosenberg, *Der staatsfeindliche Zionismus* (Hamburg: Deutsch Völkische Verlagsanstalt, 1922), 62–63; see also Francis R. Nicosia, *Zionism and Anti-Semitism in Nazi Germany* (Cambridge, U.K.: Cambridge University Press, 2008), 67–68.

[3] Adolf Hitler, *Mein Kampf*, trans. Ralph Manheim (Boston: Houghton Mifflin, 1971), 56.

[4] Ibid., 325.   [5] Ibid., 301.

[6] Roman Dmowski, "The Jews and the War," trans. Richard S. Levy, in Richard S. Levy, ed., *Antisemitism in the Modern World: An Anthology of Texts* (Lexington, Mass.: D. C. Heath and Company, 1991), 184.

regard as Gospel. At the Parliamentary Conference for Arab and Muslim Countries convened in Cairo in October 1938, for example, the Brotherhood distributed copies of *Mein Kampf* and the *Protocols*.[7] And Article Thirty-two of the Hamas "Charter of Allah" confirms that the Jihadists take the world Zionist conspiracy to be axiomatic truth; the proof text is the *Protocols*.[8] The global domination that the anti-Semite fears, however, is neither political nor financial; rather, it is the all-encompassing ethical demand that emanates from Mount Sinai through the Jews and into the world. Indeed, there is a midrash that says God revealed His Torah outside the Holy Land, so that the Jews would not be so conceited nor the nations so complacent as to think that it applied only to the Jews (*Mekilta Bachodesh* 5). In this teaching we see once again the metaphysical origin of anti-Semitism: the anti-Semite within each of us fears nothing more than this transcendent, absolute ethical demand that devolves on us, both from within and from beyond, prior to every ontological contingency.

"There is no doubt," observes Rosemary Radford Ruether, "that anti-Zionism has become a way of reviving the myth of the 'perennial evil nature of the Jews.'"[9] Similarly, Walter Laqueur has argued that "there is no clear borderline" between anti-Semitism and anti-Zionism.[10] The truth of these statements is, however, contextual. Prior to the Holocaust – before the unthinkable was thinkable – Franz Rosenzweig (d. 1929) could cling to the post–World War I hope that perhaps the Jews could find a place in the world after all, that perhaps there was no need for a Jewish state.[11] In the post-Holocaust era there can be no such hope. Inasmuch as the aim of Zionism is to establish a haven for the Jewish people, in a post-Holocaust world the anti-Zionists must either deny that the Holocaust happened or desire that it happen again. To deny the Jewish state the right to exist is to deny the Jewish people the right to live. Even in its affirmative form the statement that "Israel has a right to exist" smacks of

---

[7] See Matthias Küntzel, *Jihad and Jew-Hatred: Islamism, Nazism and the Roots of 9/11*, trans. Colin Meade (New York: Telos Press, 2007), 25.

[8] See Dimitry Kapustyan and Matt Nelson, *The Soul of Terror: The Worldwide Conflict between Islamic Terrorism and the Modern World* (Washington, D.C.: International Affairs Press, 2007), 147–148.

[9] Rosemary Radford Ruether, *Faith and Fratricide: The Theological Roots of Anti-Semitism* (New York: Seabury Press, 1974), 227.

[10] Walter Laqueur, *The Changing Face of Antisemitism: From Ancient Times to the Present Day* (Oxford, U.K.: Oxford University Press, 2006), 7.

[11] See Franz Rosenzweig, *On Jewish Learning*, ed. N. N. Glatzer (New York: Schocken Books, 1955), 64.

anti-Semitism, almost as much as the smug pronouncement, "I have nothing against the Jews; it's the Zionist state that I have a problem with." Does China, India, or Canada have a "right to exist"? The question is absurd not because these countries have a "right to exist" but because it is unintelligible. There is a similar problem with the language of secure borders: why should Israel have to negotiate or justify wanting secure borders? No other country has to constantly defend the need and see to the assurance of having secure borders. Why the need for secure borders? The explanation is simple: among all the nations of the world only the Jewish state is surrounded by countries that are bent on its annihilation, which is the aim of anti-Zionism.

"Can one be an ardent Israel-hater while, at the same time, bearing no ill will toward Jews?" asks Neil Kressel. "The answer, I think, is no."[12] And yet "to hide their antisemitism," Dennis Prager and Joseph Telushkin point out, "enemies of the Jews nearly always use the word 'Zionist' when they mean Jews."[13] More than twenty-five years before them Franklin Littell wrote, "The new code word for Antisemitism is *Anti-Zionism*, whether the slogan is uttered by Communists, Arab League propagandists, adherents of the 'New Left,' or liberal Protestants."[14] One exception to the disingenuous masking of anti-Semitism with anti-Zionism can be found as early as 1969, when Jordanian minister for social affairs Emile al-Ghori frankly declared, "It is our firm belief that there is no difference at all between Jews and Zionists. All Jews are Zionists and all Zionists are Jews."[15] Among the anti-Zionist anti-Semites, however, al-Ghori's honesty is as unusual as it is refreshing. In most cases the anti-Zionist manifestation of anti-Semitism is perhaps the most perfidious because, as Prager and Telushkin point out, it "is the first form of Jew-hatred to deny that it hates Jews."[16] If the Holocaust deniers deny the Jews their deaths and their past, the anti-Zionists deny the Jews their lives and their future. Because existence is made of death and life, past and future, both deprive the Jews of their existence: the two are inextricable. The difference

[12] Neil J. Kressel, *"The Sons of Pigs and Apes": Muslim Antisemitism and the Conspiracy of Silence* (Washington, D.C.: Potomac Books, 2012), 187.

[13] Dennis Prager and Joseph Telushkin, *Why the Jews? The Reason for Antisemitism* (New York: Simon & Schuster, 2003), 157.

[14] Franklin H. Littell, *The Crucifixion of the Jews: The Failure of Christians to Understand the Jewish Experience* (Macon, Ga.: Mercer University Press, 1986), 97.

[15] See Kressel, *"The Sons of Pigs and Apes,"* 23.

[16] Prager and Telushkin, *Why the Jews?*, 155.

between the Holocaust deniers and the anti-Zionists is that many of the anti-Zionists deny their own denial.

Jonathan Sacks identifies three levels of anti-Zionism: first, "Jews are not entitled to a nation-state of their own, a denial, in other words, of the right of Israel to exist." Second, "the existence of Israel is merely an aberration. It is responsible for all the evils of the world." Third, what Sacks calls "the bridge from anti-Zionism to anti-Semitism" is that "all Jews are Zionists; therefore all Jews are responsible for the sufferings caused by Israel; therefore all Jews are legitimate targets of attack."[17] He argues that anti-Zionism does not wax anti-Semitic until the anti-Zionist refuses "the Jewish people their right to self-determination, e.g., by claiming that the existence of the state of Israel is a racist endeavor, applying double standards by requiring of it a behaviour not expected or demanded of another democratic nation, using the symbols and images associated with classic antisemitism (e.g., claims of Jews killing Jesus or blood libel) to characterise Israel or Israelis, drawing comparisons of contemporary Israeli policy to that of the Nazis, or holding Jews collectively responsible for the actions of the state of Israel."[18] Sacks's view is insightful but, I think, mistaken in one respect: in the post-Holocaust context there is no "bridge" from anti-Zionism to anti-Semitism – the anti-Zionist is anti-Semitic from the outset, both for reasons already stated and for reasons elucidated below.

Still, Sack succinctly articulates the insidious genius of anti-Zionist anti-Semitism, or what he calls "the new antisemitism": "The new antisemitism emerged by a strategy of devastating simplicity and effectiveness. It goes as follows. Antisemitism is evil. The Holocaust is the worst crime of human being against human being.... Israel behaves towards the Palestinians as the Nazis behaved towards Jews.... If, therefore, you oppose antisemitism – which, as a civilised human being, you must – you must oppose the state of Israel and all those who support it, who happen to be Jews."[19] The comparison of Israel to the Nazis is a key to understanding the pernicious nature of anti-Zionist anti-Semitism. Making such a comparison, notes Robert Wistrich, "one is finally free to express in politically correct anti-Zionist language those sentiments that have not been entirely respectable among educated people since

---

[17] Jonathan Sacks, *Future Tense: Jews, Judaism, and Israel in the Twenty-first Century* (New York: Schocken Books, 2010), 97–98.
[18] Ibid., 98.   [19] Ibid., 101.

1945 – namely dislike of Jews."[20] What must be made clear, however, is that the amalgamation is prior to the accusation. "Anti-Zionists," David Matas explains, "move from opposition to Israel to charges against Israel rather than from wrongdoing by Israel to anti-Zionism. . . . What matters is the condemnation itself. For anti-Zionists, the more repugnant the accusation made against Israel the better."[21] In other words, like all anti-Semites, the anti-Zionists oppose the Jewish state *not for any action* but for its *presence*. Indeed, whatever the current evil might be – racism, colonialism, imperialism, apartheid, ethnic cleansing, crimes against humanity, or genocide – one can be sure that the anti-Zionists will hang the label on the Jewish state. Like the religious and secular anti-Semites of the nineteenth century, the religious and secular anti-Zionists, from rabid Jihadists to radical liberals, share a self-righteous indignation over the very existence of the Jewish state precisely because they themselves would be the moral measure of humanity.

Just as the Jew hatred that characterizes Holocaust denial opposes itself to a Jewish understanding of time, so the Jew hatred that characterizes anti-Zionism opposes itself to a Jewish understanding of space. Just as the Covenant is tied to a sanctification of time as sacred history, so is it tied to a sanctification of space in the Holy Land, which is, indeed, the Land of the Covenant. From this Jewish standpoint, the Holy Land is holy not because certain events have transpired there; rather, certain events have transpired there because the Holy Land is holy. This means that, from a metaphysical standpoint, the sanctity of the Jewish state transcends historical contexts, even as the establishment of the Jewish state signals a Jewish return to history. After the Holocaust, however, the holiness of the Holy Land assumes a deeper dimension. "What would be the face of Western history today," asks Abraham Joshua Heschel, "if the end of twentieth-century Jewish life would have been Bergen-Belsen, Dachau, Auschwitz? The State of Israel is not an atonement. It would be blasphemy to regard it as a compensation. . . . No act is as holy as the act of saving human life. The Holy Land, having offered haven to more than two million Jews ... has attained a new sanctity."[22] The Holy Land has attained a renewed holiness because, as Emmanuel Lévinas states it,

[20] Robert S. Wistrich, *A Lethal Obsession: Anti-Semitism from Antiquity to the Global Jihad* (New York: Random House, 2010), 630–631.
[21] David Matas, *Aftershock: Anti-Zionism and Anti-Semitism* (Toronto: Dundurn, 2005), 53.
[22] Abraham Joshua Heschel, *Israel: An Echo of Eternity* (New York: Farrar, Straus and Giroux, 1969), 113.

"the Shoah re-establishes the link – which up until then had been incomprehensibly hidden – between present-day Israel and the Israel of the Bible."[23] These insights, of course, are steeped in a Jewish mode of thought. As has been the case throughout this volume, we shall undertake a consideration of the anti-Zionist manifestation of anti-Semitism from the standpoint of the Jewish testimony that the anti-Semites would obliterate from the world.

Just as the previous chapter rested on a Jewish understanding of history, so this chapter proceeds from a Jewish understanding of geography, of the Land of Israel, the land that the anti-Zionists would erase from the map (indeed, many of them do not show Israel on their maps). Next, transitioning from the previous chapter, we shall consider the spectrum of seemingly well-intentioned anti-Zionist anti-Semitism found primarily among liberal Christians and liberal intellectuals. Finally, the chapter takes up an examination of the exterminationist anti-Zionism found among the Islamic Jihadists.

THE HOLINESS OF THE HOLY LAND: A JEWISH UNDERSTANDING

"We must ask," writes Emil Fackenheim, "whether this ever happened that, after two millennia, a people was returned to its language, its state, its land. *Without a Book – this Book – this return could not possibly have taken place.* This is the shared astonishment behind all religio-secular diversities. This is the shared experience that makes possible a bond between all Israel and Torah. These are the gates of *Teshuva* open to the whole Jewish people today."[24] The anti-Semitic determination to erase the People of the Book from the face of the planet is a determination to erase the Book itself; without the People there is no Book, and without the Book there is no People. The Book referred to here is, of course, the Torah that emanates into the world not from Mount Sinai but from the Land of Israel, as it is written: "For the Torah goes forth from Zion and the word of HaShem from Jerusalem" (Isaiah 2:3). Why Zion, and not Sinai? Because Zion is where the Torah is *lived*. What the anti-Zionists would obliterate is precisely the voice of the Torah – and with

---

[23] Emmanuel Lévinas, *Difficult Freedom: Essays on Judaism*, trans. Sean Hand (Baltimore, Md.: Johns Hopkins University Press, 1990), 12.

[24] Emil L. Fackenheim, *To Mend the World: Foundations of Post-Holocaust Jewish Thought* (New York: Schocken Books, 1989), 328.

the Torah, God and Israel as well. Because the Torah determines the covenantal relation to the land, without which there is no *teshuvah*, no movement of return to *this* land, the Jewish presence in Israel far transcends any political agenda, where power can justify anything. If the Israelis' struggle for their very survival amounts to something more than a power struggle, it is because the Jewish state, in the words of Lévinas, "stems from the religion which modern political life supplants,"[25] which is the religion of creation and covenant, of revelation and redemption.

André Neher comprehended very well the metaphysical scope of Zionism, as well as the metaphysical origins of anti-Semitism, when he wrote, "Is not the State of Israel, in its very existence, a meta-state? And surely the war launched against Israel on Yom Kippur, October 6, 1973, was not only horizontal.... Zion, which is only a fragment of Jerusalem and the Land of Israel, is a word one can neither play around with, nor play tricks with, nor beat around the bush with. It is the key word of the 'meta' of Jewish history. Through Zion, Zionism becomes bi-dimensional. The vertical is interlocked with the horizontal."[26] This interlocking of the vertical with the horizontal is signified by the very presence of the Jewish people in the Land of Israel. For the Jewish return to history through their return to the Land of Israel is a return of Torah to history. This incursion of the vertical into the horizontal is precisely what the anti-Zionists are against. If the advent of the State of Israel has no metaphysical meaning – if the Land of Israel is not the Holy Land – then the revelation at Mount Sinai has no meaning, the Torah has no meaning, and the Jewish people have no meaning, which is the contention of the anti-Zionists. If that is the case, however, then the absolute nature of the prohibition against murder has no meaning.

The prohibition against murder is the most fundamental of the commandments, of the *mitzvot*, that connect humanity both to God and to Zion (recall that the root of *mitzvah* is *tzavta*, which means "connection," as noted in the Introduction). Indeed, Rabbi Yehuda Loeve (1513–1609), the renowned mystic known as the Maharal of Prague, maintains that "God's Name is identified with the Land of Israel," because God is known through His commandments.[27] The commandments of Torah that

[25] Lévinas, *Difficult Freedom*, 217.
[26] André Neher, *They Made Their Souls Anew*, trans. David Maisel (Albany: SUNY Press, 1990), 58.
[27] Yehuda Loeve, *Maharal of Prague: Pirke Avos*, trans. and ed. R. Tuvia Basser (Brooklyn, N.Y.: Mesorah, 1997), 322.

radiate from Zion and into the world form what the Maharal calls "the life force of holiness" that illuminates creation by affirming the holiness of life.[28] This Jewish view of the Land of Israel and the Torah that issues from it is central to a Jewish understanding of the Jewish state – and to the impetus to destroy the Jewish state, an impetus to power alone, the power to usurp God. Because the holiness of the land is central to the notion of human sanctity, without that holiness, power is the only reality and weakness is the only sin. From a traditional, halakhic standpoint, the holiness of the Land does not mean I can justify any action to maintain possession of the Land; rather, it means that if I am to dwell in the land, then I must justify *every* action before God and humanity, in accordance with the commandments of the Torah. Because the Jewish testimony of the Torah originates from Zion, a Jewish haven for that testimony is to be found only in Zion. For the Jews and the Land *together* signify the Covenant that commands love and forbids murder.

The Covenant and its commandments are what make Israel the *Eretz HaKodesh*, the "Holy Land." Therefore, Lévinas insists, the state of Israel, "in accordance with its pure essence, is possible only if penetrated by the divine word," which always speaks in the imperative.[29] A Voice resounds from the Land of Israel to undermine the anti-Semitic pretense to power precisely because the Jews once again dwell in the Land. Because the state of Israel is "penetrated by the divine word," it has an inescapable, metaphysical significance, both for the Jews and for the nations. "Israel, though chosen by God," says Leo Baeck of the Jewish people, "can remain so only if it practices righteousness; sin separates it from God. Its only possible existence is religious: either it will live as God has commanded or it will not live at all."[30] Hence, as Lévinas states it, "the State of Israel will be religious because of the intelligence of its great books which it is not free to forget. It will be religious through the very action that establishes it as a State. It will be religious or it will not be at all."[31] Israel's great books – the *sifre kodesh*, or holy books that the anti-Semites consign to the flames – are the vessels of the testimony that enters the world through the Jewish people, a testimony through which all the nations of the world are blessed (see, e.g., Genesis 12:3). Which means:

[28] Ibid., 355.
[29] Emmanuel Lévinas, "Zionisms," trans. Roland Lack, in Sean Hand, ed., *The Levinas Reader* (Oxford, U.K.: Basil Blackwell, 1989), 271.
[30] Leo Baeck, *The Essence of Judaism*, trans. Victor Grubenweiser and Leonard Pearl, revised ed. (New York: Schocken Books, 1948), 67.
[31] Lévinas, *Difficult Freedom*, 219.

neither the Jews nor the nations are free to turn away from Israel. As with God, one can either embrace Israel or oppose it, but one cannot ignore it. Because there are powerful people who continue to harbor extermina- tionist designs on the Jews, the holiness of the Land can endure only through a Jewish presence in the Land. And just as the Land is the center of Jewish life, so is Jerusalem the center of the Land.

To say that Jerusalem bears a particular significance for anti-Zionists of every ilk is to state the obvious; it shows up along a spectrum ranging from objections to the Israelis' building schools, homes, or hospitals *within* Jerusalem to the call for Jews to be purged *from* Jerusalem. But why Jerusalem? The meaning of Jerusalem in Jewish religious conscious- ness provides a key, both to the question and to anti-Zionist anti-Semit- ism. The notion that there is something holy about the city of Jerusalem is part of the consciousness of much of humanity. If you should announce to your friends that you are planning a trip to the Holy City, they probably will not ask, "Which city is that?" Many traditions speak of a heavenly Jerusalem, once again denoting the interlocking of the vertical with the horizontal, but there is no heavenly New York, no heavenly Paris, nor even a heavenly Dallas. Why? Because, according to the Midrash, "the gate of heaven is in Jerusalem" (*Midrash on Psalms* 4:91:7). Jewish tradition, which both includes and extends the biblical tradition, provides a clue as to why this is the case, regardless of whether or not one subscribes to the tradition.

According to the Talmud, God, Torah, and Jerusalem are among the ten things that are distinguished by the word *living* (*Avot d'Rabbi Nathan* 34:11).[32] They are among the things necessary for *life*. As the site where the Temple stood, Jerusalem signifies the presence of Torah in the world, and Torah signifies the sanctity of life in the world. Thus, the Midrash teaches that the windows of the Temple were designed not to let light in but to allow the light of Torah to radiate from the Temple and into the world for the sake of all humanity (*Tanchuma Tetzaveh* 6). Indeed, the third-century sage Rabbi Joshua ben Levi taught that the Temple was a greater blessing to the nations than it was to Israel (*Bamidbar Rabbah* 1:3). The nations, and not just the Jews, can no more live without Jerusalem than they can live without God and Torah. Indeed, Jerusalem is not only the capital of Israel – it is the *Umbilicus Urbis*, the center of the

---

[32] Although the text says ten things, it actually lists eleven; the other eight things distin- guished by the word *living* are Israel, the righteous, the Garden of Eden, a tree, the Land of Israel, loving kindness, the wise, and water.

world.[33] The holy texts articulate this significance of the Holy City by saying, "This world is likened to a person's eyeball: the white of the eye [corresponds to] the ocean which surrounds the whole world; the iris to the [inhabited] world; the pupil of the eye to Jerusalem; the face in the pupil to the Temple" (*Derekh Eretz Rabbah* 9:13).[34] Which means: Jerusalem is the lens through which God gazes on the world and puts to humanity the perennial question from which the adamic anti-Semite in each of us is forever fleeing: "Where are you?" According to this tradition, Jerusalem is the source of life's holiness because it signifies the Creator of life, the Holy One Himself. Thus it is written in the Talmud: "R. Shmuel bar Nachman said in the name of R. Yochanan: 'Three are called by the Name of the Holy One, and they are: the righteous, the Messiah, and Jerusalem'" (*Bava Batra* 95b). In keeping with this tradition, Joseph Albo identifies the name *Jerusalem* as one of the names of God (*Sefer HaIkkarim* 2:28). Which means: Jerusalem and the Shekhinah, or the Divine Presence, are of a piece.[35] Which means: anyone who would usurp God must lay claim to Jerusalem – a claim that Jews and Judaism precisely *do not* make.

The Jews do not lay claim to Jerusalem – Jerusalem lays claim to the Jews. When Jews pray to the Holy One they never refer to Jerusalem as "our city," but rather as *irkha*, "Your city," that is, God's city, invoking God as the *Boneh Yerushalayim*, the "Builder of Jerusalem." As the Boneh Yerushalayim God is the *Shokhen Yerushalayim*, "the One who dwells in Jerusalem" (see, e.g., Psalms 135:21). Signifying the light of God and Torah, Jerusalem signifies a *metaphysical height*, the very dimension of height that the anti-Zionist anti-Semites would expunge from this world. Whereas the anti-Zionists would ban the Jews from Jerusalem, as they were banned from the Old City prior to the Six-Day War, a Jewish understanding of the meaning of Jerusalem demands an openness to every human being. That openness has been attained only since Jerusalem became reunified as the capital of the Jewish state in 1967: since that time, everyone who comes in peace has been free to pray in the Holy City.

---

[33] See Abraham Ezra Millgram, *Jerusalem Curiosities* (Skokie, Ill.: Varda Books, 2002), 50–54.

[34] The *Derekh Eretz Rabbah* is one of the minor tractates of the Talmud.

[35] According to a kabbalistic interpretation based on Gematria, or interpretation based on numerical values of Hebrew words, when written out the names of the letters that spell *Shekhinah* have a total of 596, which is the numerical value of *Yerushalayim* or *Jerusalem*; see Matityahu Glazerson, *Building Blocks of the Soul: Studies on the Letters and Words of the Hebrew Language* (Northvale, N.J.: Jason Aronson, 1997), 175.

The prayers of humanity, and not just the Jews, draw the holiness of the Holy One into the Holy City. Indeed, through Jerusalem each of us is tied to the origin of humanity, to Adam, and, through Adam, to each other. "In the place whence Adam's dust was taken," it is written in the *Tanna debe Eliyahu*, "there the altar was built."[36] As the Holy City's Holy of Holies, the altar signifies the link between God and humanity; as the place from which Adam's dust was taken, it signifies the bond between human and human. By contrast, one need only look to Mecca to see what the notion of a "holy city" means in the Muslim world: it is closed to all except Muslims. Whereas Mecca signifies the truth of Islam, Jerusalem signifies the holiness of humanity – that is what makes Jerusalem God's dwelling place. That is what makes Jerusalem the Holy City.

Of course, since exile is a metaphysical and not just a geographical condition, one can be in exile even within the walls of Jerusalem. Just as the Jewish people have undertaken a movement of return from Auschwitz to Jerusalem, so does Jerusalem itself struggle to undertake a movement of return. In the Book of Lamentations, which is chanted on the Ninth of Av, the anniversary of the destruction of the two Temples, the city itself is said to have become a *nidah*, or a "wanderer" (Lamentations 1:8): Jerusalem itself follows the Jews into exile. And Jerusalem itself returns to the Land with the return of the Jews to Jerusalem, to the extent that the Jews allow the Holy One entry into Jerusalem by living according to the commandments of Torah. In the Talmud Rabbi Yochanan teaches, "The Holy One, blessed be He, said: 'I will not enter the heavenly Jerusalem until I can enter the earthly Jerusalem'" (*Taanit* 5a). When can God enter the earthly Jerusalem? When every human being can enter the earthly Jerusalem. And only the Jews, since their return from Auschwitz to Jerusalem, have taken a step toward that end with the reunification of the Holy City.

The Talmud relates that on the destruction of the Second Temple in 70 CE, God exacted one oath from the gentiles and two oaths from the Jews. The gentiles swore that they would not excessively oppress the Jews. And the Jews swore that they would neither resist their persecutors nor would they prematurely "climb the wall" to return to Jerusalem (*Ketuvot* 111a). Fackenheim invoked this passage whenever he spoke about the Jewish return to the Land of the Covenant, particularly about the return from

---

[36] *Tanna debe Eliyahu: The Lore of the School of Elijah*, trans. William G. Braude and Israel J. Kapstein (Philadelphia: Jewish Publication Society, 1981), 411; this midrashic collection of teachings ascribed to the prophet Elijah was probably compiled in the tenth century.

Auschwitz to Jerusalem. That the gentiles have excessively oppressed the Jews is self-evident, as is the fact that many of them continue to harbor exterminationist designs against the Jews. Therefore, the Jews' "premature" climb over the walls of Jerusalem comes not in an evasion of their persecutors but simply in an evasion of being murdered. The walls that the Jews have climbed in their return to Jerusalem are the walls that the Holocaust deniers would deconstruct and that the anti-Zionists would reconstruct: they are the walls whose gates are embossed with the words *Arbeit Macht Frei*, the walls that would wall the Jews out from the world and into a graveyard without a single grave. Therefore the Jewish return to Jerusalem is nothing less than a resurrection.

And yet, it is a resurrection threatened with annihilation from all who oppose the existence of the Jewish state, from the "benign" left-wing liberal to the murderous fanatic Jihadist. So what should be the Jewish response to the anti-Zionist anti-Semitism that would inevitably mean the end of the Jewish people? The Torah itself warns us that "the sword shall bereave you of children without, as shall the terror from within" (Deuteronomy 32:25). In a commentary on this biblical passage, the Talmud urges us to move to the inside, even if there, too, terror threatens to bereave us of our children (see *Bava Kama* 60b). Lévinas elaborates: here, he says, we "see the entire problem of present-day Israel appear, with all the difficulties of the return. One must withdraw into one's home.... And even if 'at home' – in the refuge or in the interiority – there is 'terror,' it is better to have a country, a house, or an 'inwardness' with terror than to be outside."[37] The point in having a home and a haven for the Jewish people is not mere survival: it means having a community, an *edah*, in Hebrew, which is also a "testimony," the testimony that the anti-Zionist, whether liberal intellectual or radical Jihadist, would purge from the world. It means bearing witness to the holiness of the human being from within the center that commands that testimony. It means a Jewish presence in Jerusalem and in the Land of Israel.

Lévinas articulates the implications of this internal terror for a Jewish understanding of anti-Zionist anti-Semitism by saying, "Do we not smell here ... the odor of the camps? Violence is no longer a political phenomenon of war and peace, beyond all morality. It is the abyss of Auschwitz or the world at war.... One must go back inside, even if there is terror inside. Is the fact of Israel unique? Does it not have its full meaning

---

[37] Emmanuel Lévinas, *Nine Talmudic Readings*, trans. Annette Aronowicz (Bloomington: Indiana University Press, 1990), 190.

because it applies to all humanity? All men are on the verge of being in the situation of the State of Israel. The State of Israel is a category."[38] Hence, after the Shoah, says Lévinas, "Judaism is no longer just a teaching whose theses can be true or false; *Jewish existence itself is an essential event of being; Jewish existence is a category of being.*"[39] Applying to all humanity, the state of Israel is more than a "category of being" – it is a *metaphysical* category that bespeaks the metaphysical origin of anti-Semitism in its anti-Zionist manifestation. The diatribes of the anti-Zionist anti-Semites reek of the odor of the camps, and they reek most disgustingly in the sanctimonious denunciations of the Israelis that erupt from the mouths of well-meaning liberal Christians and not-so-well-meaning liberal intellectuals. In both we discover that time-worn manifestations of Jew hatred turn out to be timeless. Liberal Christian anti-Zionism has implications that play into the hands of supersessionist theology. Left-wing intellectual anti-Zionism is the fashionable expression of Jew hatred traceable to what we have seen in the Enlightenment and the socialist liberalism that followed in its wake.

LIBERAL ANTI-ZIONISM

Franklin Littell writes, "The rage for universal truths, accompanied by abandonment of holy events and the Scriptures that record them, came to dominate university thinking following the Enlightenment. It is this style of thinking that is the most fertile single source of liberal Antisemitism – whether religious or secular."[40] The liberal on the far left, whether religious or secular, has to be anti-Zionist for the same reason that a liberal intellectual of the Enlightenment has to be anti-Semitic: both dress their Jew hatred in the guise of tolerance, declaring that the Jewish individual deserves the same consideration as any other human being, but the Jewish people deserve nothing, least of all a Jewish state. "One form of antisemitism," explains Matas, "denies Jews access to goods and services because they are Jewish. Another form of antisemitism denies the right of the Jewish people to exist as a people because they are Jewish. Anti-Zionists distinguish between the two. To the anti-Zionist, the Jew can exist as an individual as long as Jews do not exist as a people."[41] And yet without the Jewish people and the Torah that

---

[38] Ibid., 190–191.   [39] Lévinas, *Difficult Freedom*, 183; emphasis in original.
[40] Littell, 38–39.   [41] Matas, *Aftershock*, 113.

defines them there is no Jewish individual: if the Jewish state has no "right to exist," then neither may the individual exist as a Jew.

In the post-Enlightenment era the "emancipation" of the Jews came, if at all, at the cost of their Judaism: in order to assimilate into society and find a seat at the banquet, the Jews had to check their Judaism at the door, and with it their definitive tie to the Jewish people. What is not so commonly known is that the Christians of an enlightened Europe adopted a similar stance, with the result that, for the liberal Protestant, "the lines of the baptized blur into the patterns and values of the dominant society," as Littell puts it, until "Christianity becomes, not the commitment of a peculiar people, but rather a thin veneer over the real and controlling ethnic or national thrust."[42] And as we have seen, the dominant, nationalistic thrust of nineteenth-century Europe was invariably anti-Semitic; "emancipated" thought was and is almost always contemptuous of what the liberal takes to be a constraining Jewish thought. "Emancipated thought," Littell explains, "whether liberal Protestant or Marxist or other, has always had difficulty with the Old Testament and the Jews,"[43] since the Hebrew Bible and its witnesses attest to an imposed accountability that is always a threat to autonomous self-justification, either by faith or by will. In the modern age, says Littell, "blending into the dominant culture, accommodating to the spirit of the times, has virtually become the major enthusiasm of Christian political and social establishments."[44] Such an accommodation is fertile ground for anti-Semitism, and today it manifests itself as an accommodation of anti-Zionism.

One area in which this thinly veiled Jew hatred finds expression among liberal Protestants and intellectuals lies in the persistent call for divestments and economic boycotts of Israel, the so-called Boycott, Divestment, and Sanction (BDS) movement. "The Unitarian Universalist program 'Toward Peace and Justice in the Middle East' [from 2002]," Kressel notes, "strongly condemns Israel in very specific terms for its 'occupation' and specifically calls for various acts against the Jewish state, including divestment and withholding of weaponry key to its defense."[45] This should come as no surprise, since Unitarian Universalism must *ipso facto* reject the notion of a state consisting of a people apart, even if it means rendering them defenseless in the face of enemies who have vowed to wipe them out.

---

[42] Littell, *The Crucifixion of the Jews*, 36.   [43] Ibid.   [44] Ibid., 39.
[45] Kressel, *"The Sons of Pigs and Apes,"* 80.

In another notorious example, at its 216th General Assembly in Richmond, Virginia, 26 June–3 July 2004, the Presbyterian Church, U.S.A., decided to initiate a process of phased selective divestment from corporations operating in Israel. Although they softened the language of divestment in 2006, here, as in other calls for punishing Israel economically, the anti-Zionist anti-Semites are so blinded by their hatred that they fail to see the obvious, namely, that the Palestinian economy is interwoven with the Israeli economy: to damage one is to damage the other. With Israel's innovations in high technology, agricultural production, and medicine, moreover, one wonders whether these liberal Protestants' hatred of the Jewish state trumps their love of humanity. If boycott means a refusal to use Israeli products or inventions, it would require a refusal to use Windows computer systems, Centrium processors, voice mail, AOL Instant Messenger, and cell phones, to name just a few Israeli innovations. Israelis are also known for their advancements in the treatment of multiple sclerosis, paralysis due to stroke, breathing disorders, depression, Alzheimer's disease, smallpox, immune deficiency syndromes, movement disorders, and uterine fibroids. Other Israeli developments in medicine have come in the wake of hundreds of terrorist attacks against the Jews. As a result of the Palestinians' bombing of their buses, for instance, the Israelis have become the world's experts in the treatment of burn victims. If a Presbyterian has a child who has suffered serious burns, would he or she really want to boycott the Israelis' latest advancements in the treatment of burn victims?

The Catholic Church has proven to be no better when it comes to an institutional support for the Jews seeking a haven in the Land of the Covenant. Fackenheim makes the following observation: "When in 1903 Herzl visited Pope Pius X the latter declared that whereas the Church could not prevent a Jewish return to Jerusalem, it could never sanction it. When in 1967 the old city returned to Jewish control, the Vatican began to issue a series of calls for its internationalization; this had never happened during the nineteen years that the city was under Jordanian control."[46] In fact, the Vatican did not grant the State of Israel official recognition until 1993 (yet they were the first to give Nazi Germany diplomatic recognition, with the signing of the Reichskonkordat on 20 July 1933, a deal brokered by Cardinal Eugenio Pacelli, the future Pope Pius XII). In April–May 2002 the Palestinian terrorists' occupation

---

[46] Emil L. Fackenheim, *What Is Judaism?* (New York: Macmillan, 1987), 231–232.

of the Church of the Nativity in Bethlehem presented the Catholics with a dramatic opportunity to show the world that they had freed themselves from their centuries-old hatred of the Jews. Hiding behind the sanctuary provided by the church, the terrorists desecrated the holy site, as they used a baptismal font for a sink, an altar for a dining table, and the grotto where the birth of Jesus is venerated as sleeping quarters.[47] They knew that they would be safe inside the church because they knew that, unlike themselves, the Israelis would respect the holiness of the ancient place of worship.

When the standoff came to an end, what was the Catholic comment? Accusations were leveled at the Jews by Michel Sabbah, the Latin Patriarch in Jerusalem, who called on the Israelis to "stop talking about terrorism to hide the root evil,"[48] which, in his mind, is the Jewish state. Sabbah's invectives parallel the Vatican's silence over another incident that happened a year earlier. When Pope John Paul II was in Syria on 5 May 2001, the mass murderer Bashar al-Assad greeted him by declaring that the Jews are bent on destroying the principles of religion "with the same mentality with which they betrayed Jesus Christ." Just weeks prior to his meeting with the Pontiff, al-Assad had declared the Israelis to be worse racists than the Nazis. On both occasions the Pope said nothing.[49] On both occasions Fackenheim drafted letters to Cardinal Edward Idris Cassidy, the man to whom John Paul II wrote his famous letter on the atrocity of the Holocaust and someone whom Fackenheim knew well. In response, however, the Cardinal offered little more than excuses.

Ironically, there was a certain parallel between the Roman Church and the Soviet Union, which had been one of Syria's allies, just as the Russians continue to be allies of the Syrian regime. With the emergence of the Marxist left, the Soviets came to serve a function similar to the one that the Church had provided, as Joel Carmichael has pointed out. Among the elites of the intellectual left, he notes, the Zionists became "the quintessential expression of an Evil People ..., both universally potent and satanically evil, powered by a demented urge for world rule.... The only bulwark against the satanic array was the Soviet Union, like the Church in

---

[47] See Sergio Minerbi, "The Vatican and the Standoff at the Church of the Nativity," Jerusalem Center for Public Affairs, 15 March 2004, available at http://jcpa.org/jl/vp515.htm.

[48] Quote in Joseph D'Hippolito, "Patriarch of Terror," FrontPageMag.com, 4 January 2005, available at http://archive.frontpagemag.com/readArticle.aspx?ARTID=10031.

[49] See Eric J. Greenberg, "Open Season on Jews," *The Jewish Week*, May 11, 2001.

classical Christian theology."[50] The Soviets were among the first to propagate the lie that the Zionists were the instigators of the Holocaust, with figures such as historian Vladimir Begun (d. 1989) declaring that the Zionists' evil is based on the Torah, which, he says, is full of "bloodthirstiness and moral degeneracy."[51] Recall also a statement made on 21 October 1973 by the Soviet ambassador to the U.N. Yakov Malik: "The Zionists have come forward with the theory of the chosen people, an absurd ideology. That is religious racism."[52] The Soviet Union's campaign against the Zionists was most profoundly reflected in its vicious oppression of Soviet Jewry, cementing the tie between anti-Zionism and anti-Semitism. As Wistrich has pointed out, "the orchestrated [Soviet] campaign [against the Jews] that unfolded in 1982, and the unexpected resonance it found in the West, eroded the already flimsy distinctions between anti-Zionism and anti-Semitism."[53] Not surprisingly, the primary quarter in which this anti-Zionist Jew hatred found some resonance in the West was among left-wing intellectuals.

Just as religious and secular anti-Semites could find common cause in the nineteenth century, so do the religious and secular anti-Zionists come together now. Here Laqueur is mistaken in his claim that "the anti-Zionism of the far left is ... mainly motivated by anti-Americanism and America's support for Israel,"[54] as if it were a matter of a displaced hatred of the United States and not directly targeted against the Jews. No, anti-Zionist anti-Semitism has its metaphysical aspect and origin, a point perfectly illustrated by remarks by Portuguese author José Saramago (1922–2010), winner of the 1998 Nobel Prize in literature, who in an interview with *El Pais* on 21 April 2002 referred to Israel as "a racist state by virtue of Judaism's monstrous doctrines – racist not just against the Palestinians, but against the entire world, which it seeks to manipulate and abuse." He went on to state that "Israel's struggle against its neighbors had 'a unique and even metaphysical quality of genuine evil.'"[55] A thoroughgoing liberal, Saramago's invocation of the metaphysical evil is a reflection of the metaphysical origin of his own evil. It is an instance of left-wing "negationist anti-Zionism," as Wistrich names it; a mode of

---

[50] Joel Carmichael, *The Satanizing of the Jews: Origin and Development of Mystical Anti-Semitism* (New York: Fromm International Publishing Corporation, 1992), 192.
[51] See Dan Cohn-Sherbok, *Anti-Semitism* (Stroud, U.K.: The History Press, 2002), 317.
[52] Quoted in Prager and Telushkin, *Why the Jews?*, 26.
[53] Wistrich, *A Lethal Obsession*, 495.
[54] Laqueur, *The Changing Face of Antisemitism*, 17.
[55] Quoted in Wistrich, *A Lethal Obsession*, 7.

anti-Semitism "that delegitimizes and dehumanizes Israel is not only Manichean in the philosophical sense, but totalitarian in its political essence, and *theological* in its insistence that Israel was 'born in sin.'"[56] Cognizant of its metaphysical origin, we realize that this anti-Semitic position is a manifestation of the primal temptation within the soul, the temptation to be as God.

Among the most notorious icons of the liberal left was Edward Said (1935–2003) of Columbia University. With Said, says Martin Kramer, "Middle Eastern studies became a field where scholarship took a backseat to advocacy, where a few biases became the highest credentials, where dissenting views became thought-crimes.... For Prof. Said, no understanding of the Middle East had validity unless it was joined at the hip with political sympathy for the cause and the struggle. The cause was the empowerment of Palestinians, Arabs, and Muslims. The struggle was against an axis of evil comprised of Western orientalism, American imperialism, and Israeli Zionism."[57] Other noteworthy examples of such intellectuals include the following:

- Ibrahim Aoude of the University of Hawaii: "Israel is a colonial project and no colonial project has a basis for existence."
- Joseph Massad of Columbia University: Israel has perpetrated "racist colonial violence for the last century against the Palestinian people.... The ultimate achievement of Israel [is the] transformation of the Jew into the anti-Semite and the Palestinian into the Jew."
- Nicholas De Genova of Columbia University: "The heritage of the Holocaust belongs to the Palestinian people. The state of Israel has no claim to the heritage of the Holocaust."
- Marc Ellis of Baylor University: "The Palestinians are comparable to the Jews in the Warsaw Ghetto, awaiting annihilation."
- Joshua Schreier of Vassar College: "Israel is engaged in a low-grade war of genocide against the Palestinians."[58]

Then there is Gil Anidjar of Columbia University, who, perfectly aware of Aoude's assertion that "no colonial project has a basis for existence,"

---

[56] Ibid., 62; emphasis in original.

[57] Martin Kramer, "Columbia University: The Future of Middle Eastern Studies at Stake," in Manfred Gerstenfeld, ed., *Academics against Israel and the Jews* (Jerusalem: Jerusalem Center for Public Affairs, 2007), 103.

[58] Edward S. Beck, "Scholars for Peace in the Middle East (SPME): Fighting Anti-Israelism and Anti-Semitism on the University Campuses Worldwide," in Gerstenfeld, ed., *Academics against Israel and the Jews*, 134–135.

insists that Zionism is "colonial in the strict sense" and that "Israel is absolutely a colonial enterprise, a colonial settler state."[59] All of these anti-Zionist anti-Semites accuse Israel of the going evil of the day, from colonialist oppression to National Socialist extermination. They do not argue, they incite. "The outright denunciation of Israel," David Mamet has observed, "as 'acquisitionist, bloodthirsty, colonial, et cetera' is to me simply a modern instance of the blood libel – that Jews delight in the blood of others."[60] And if the Jewish state is inherently evil, it is because the Jews are the very embodiment of evil.

These examples from the American intelligentsia have their European counterparts, where "the elimination of the Jews," as Richard Rubenstein points out, is "a nonnegotiable aspect of the political program of the European left."[61] Michael Sinnott, former professor of "paper science" at the University of Manchester, for example, promoted the world Zionist conspiracy lie, saying, "With the recent crop of atrocities the Zionist state is now fully living down to Zionism's historical and cultural origins as the mirror image of Nazism."[62] Kressel has an interesting observation on one thing that may be driving such left-wing anti-Semitism among the Europeans: "When one looks at the psychological and political implications, hostility toward Israel and insensitivity to antisemitism make a neat package, especially for Europeans. Liberal Europe proves its superiority to America; shows that its own Jewish victims, by extension, couldn't have been all that blameless; rescues its religious tradition; and proves that it is now more moral than ever by helping the Palestinian victims. . . . If facts about antisemitism get in the way, the facts be damned."[63] More than a sign of emotional hysteria or rank irrationalism, the insignificance of facts is yet another indicator of the metaphysical origins of anti-Semitism in its anti-Zionist form. What the anti-Semite sees, European and otherwise, is owing to his metaphysics.

Similar to their anti-Zionist Christian cohorts, European academics openly call for the boycott of Israeli scholars and universities.

---

[59] Quoted in Nermeen Shaikh, *The Present as History: Critical Perspectives on Global Power* (New York: Columbia University Press, 2007), 247.

[60] David Mamet, *The Wicked Son: Anti-Semitism, Self-Hatred, and the Jew* (New York: Schocken Books, 2006), 11.

[61] Richard L. Rubenstein, *After Auschwitz: History, Theology, and Contemporary Judaism*, 2nd ed. (Baltimore, Md.: Johns Hopkins University Press, 1992), 121.

[62] Quoted in Manfred Gerstenfeld, "Academics against Israel and the Jews," in Gerstenfeld, ed., *Academics against Israel and the Jews*, 26.

[63] Kressel, *"The Sons of Pigs and Apes,"* 151.

On 22 April 2005, Britain's Association of University Teachers passed a motion to boycott Haifa University and Bar-Ilan University, a move initiated by Sue Blackwell of Birmingham University.[64] And on 6 June 2005, Mona Baker of the University of Manchester dismissed two Israeli academics from the editorial board of the British journal *The Translator* solely because they were from Israel; the two scholars in question were Miriam Schlesinger of Bar-Ilan and Gideon Toury of Tel Aviv.[65] When were German, Soviet, Chinese, Iraqi, Iranian, Syrian, or Palestinian scholars ever dismissed because of where they were born? Only the Israelis enjoy the distinction of a boycott demanded by left-wing intellectuals because of who they are and not because of what they espouse.

Comprising much of the professoriate, anti-Zionist intellectuals infect numerous university campuses with their Jew hatred. In 2006 the U.S. Commission on Civil Rights published a report titled *Campus Antisemitism*; it said, "Anti-Israeli or anti-Zionist propaganda has been disseminated on many campuses that include traditional antisemitic elements, including age-old anti-Jewish stereotypes and defamation." It also said that "antisemitic bigotry is no less morally deplorable when camouflaged as anti-Israelism or anti-Zionism." The report found substantial evidence that "many university departments of Middle East studies provide one-sided, highly polemical presentations and some may repress legitimate debate concerning Israel."[66] Manfred Gerstenfeld has identified twelve characteristic manifestations of the anti-Zionist anti-Semitism found on university and college campuses:

1. Promoting classic anti-Semitism
2. Academic boycott of Israeli universities
3. Preventing Israeli academics from receiving grants
4. Convincing academics not to visit Israel
5. Refusing to invite Israelis to conferences to give lectures
6. Preventing publication of research by Israeli scholars
7. Refusing to review the work of Israeli scholars
8. Refusing to contribute to Israeli publications
9. Promoting divestment of Israeli securities
10. Expelling Jewish organizations from campus

---

[64] Ronnie Fraser, "The Academic Boycott of Israel: Why Britain?," in Gerstenfeld, ed., *Academics against Israel and the Jews*, 198.
[65] Ibid., 199.   [66] Gerstenfeld, "Academics against Israel and the Jews," 40.

11. Hampering careers of pro-Israeli academics
12. Refusing to give recommendations to students who want to study in Israel.[67]

The list of campuses that have such a history is long, and it continues to grow, ranging from Concordia University in Montreal to the Ca' Foscari University in Venice, from the University of California at Berkeley to the Australian National University in Canberra. In his study of the phenomenon Alain Goldschläger asserts, "In the name of tolerance, understanding, and concern for the weak, many intellectuals defend racist and anti-Semitic statements and even acts of violence and terror."[68] Just as the desire to damage the Israeli economy through boycotts trumps the concern for the Palestinian economy, so does the demonization of Israel trump the ostensible liberal defense of women's rights, gay rights, and a whole range of civil rights routinely violated by the Muslim nations that are bent on the destruction of the Jewish state. Why? Could it be that many, if not most, of the left-wing intellectuals of academia harbor the same exterminationist longing as Israel's enemies?

JIHADIST EXTERMINATIONIST ANTI-ZIONISM

Kressel shows that, due to this desire shared between many left-wing intellectuals and the Islamic Jihadists, "for many self-designated members of the antiracist community, Muslim antisemitism has become an unmentionable prejudice."[69] Subsequently, "those who take the lead in calling attention to the rise in contemporary Jew-hatred, especially its manifestation in the Muslim world, very frequently draw the scorn of a subset of self-defined progressive and anti-Israel intellectuals."[70] And so we come to the realization that, as in the case of the left-wing intellectuals, the Islamic Jihadists do not hate the Jews because of the "Zionist entity" that has taken root in the Middle East; rather they hate the "Zionist entity" because they hate the Jews: the anti-Semitism precedes the anti-Zionism.

As Salafist Sheikh Muhammad Hussein Yaqoub (b. 1956) declared in a broadcast aired on Egypt's Al-Rahma TV, on 17 January 2009, "If the Jews left Palestine to us, would we start loving them? Of course not.... They are enemies not because they occupied Palestine. They would have

---

[67] Ibid., 50–52.
[68] Alain Goldschläger, "The Canadian Campus Scene," in Gerstenfeld, ed., *Academics against Israel and the Jews*, 161.
[69] Kressel, *"The Sons of Pigs and Apes,"* 56.   [70] Ibid., 71.

been enemies even if they did not occupy a thing. . ... Our fighting with the Jews is eternal, and it will not end . . ., until not a single Jew remains on the face of the Earth."[71] This visceral hatred of the Jews is not rooted in any ontological circumstance, such as the immigration of the Jews to Palestine and the subsequent establishment of the Jewish state. Rather, this hatred of Jews, Judaism, and the Jewish state is a hatred grounded in a metaphysical first principle that defines the entire Jihadist worldview. Indeed, Lévinas's assertion that "the State of Israel is a category"[72] obtains as much for the Jihadist anti-Zionists as it does for the Jews, since for both the Jewish state signifies the testimony embodied in the Jewish people.

Stemming from a metaphysical origin, the Jihadists' hatred of the Jewish state is a hatred of the teachings of Judaism that undermine their project of the usurpation and appropriation of God. Thus, says Wistrich, "Judaism, Zionism, and Israel are virtually synonymous in Hezbollah's vocabulary."[73] Indeed, they are not "virtually" synonymous – they are synonymous. Hezbollah's Sheikh Taha al-Sabounji understood as well as the Koretzer Rebbe that God, Israel, and Torah are one, as demonstrated in a statement he made in April 2002: "Judaism is a project against all humanity. ... Those who are fighting Israel are not just defending themselves; they are defending the whole world. . ... *There is no such thing as Zionism. . ... There is only Judaism.*"[74] This principle affirmed by the Jihadists of Hezbollah can also be found in the Arab Muslim press: Saudi journalist Ashraf al-Faqi declared in the newspaper *Al-Watan* in 2009 that the insidious policies of the Jewish state have their origins in the Torah, and in the pan-Arab newspaper *Al-Hayat* Royal Jordanian CEO Abd al-Rahmanal-Khatib insisted that the ideology reflected in the *Protocols* comes from the Torah and Talmud.[75] As Wistrich has understood, among the Muslims "the Zionist 'monster,' embodied in the State of Israel, is regarded as the very 'essence of Judaism.'"[76] If the word *Zionist* is synonymous with *Jew*, so is *Zionism* synonymous with *Judaism*: anti-Zionism is anti-Judaism, and anti-Judaism is anti-Semitism.

Inasmuch as this equation of Zionism with Judaism imparts to anti-Zionist thinking a metaphysical aspect, it is tied to the demonization of

---

[71] Muhammad Hussein Yaqoub, "We Will Fight, Defeat, and Annihilate Them," Al-Rahma TV, 17 January 2009, available at http://memri.org/bin/latestnews.cgi?ID=SD227809.
[72] Lévinas, *Nine Talmudic Readings*, 190–191.
[73] Wistrich, *A Lethal Obsession*, 770–771.   [74] Quoted in ibid., 775; emphasis added.
[75] Kressel, "*The Sons of Pigs and Apes*," 102.
[76] Wistrich, *A Lethal Obsession*, 806.

the Jewish state. More than tagging Israel with whatever evil is currently fashionable, the demonization of the Jewish state is calculated to label Israel as the *source* of every evil. And the source of evil falls into a metaphysical category that transcends ontological contingency. It is a move that the Islamic anti-Semites learned very well from the National Socialists, as Wistrich has observed: "The demonization of the Jews provides a unifying thread for an Islamist ideology in which the word 'Zionist' fulfills exactly the same function as did the word 'Jew' for Hitler and the Nazis."[77] Because the Jewish state is demonic in its essence, it is universal in its scope; hence the determination among Jihadists that, far from being a mere haven for a persecuted people, Israel is the epicenter of a satanic plot to take over the world and is therefore the enemy of all humanity – a view that Jihadists also inherited from the Nazis. Adopting the Nazis' representation of the Zionist movement, Muslim Brotherhood ideologue Sayyid Qutb viewed the Jewish state, according to Ronald Nettler, as just a small part of a "universal Zionist conspiracy; indeed, like Hitler, he took Marxism and Zionism to be part of a single conspiracy."[78] Another example of the Islamic anti-Zionist imitation of the Nazis is a familiar image employed by Nazi propagandists to illustrate the Zionist threat; it shows an octopus with its deadly tentacles wrapped around the entire globe and a Star of David inscribed on its head. The same image can be found among many of the Jihadist illustrations of nefarious "world Zionism."

The Islamic demonization of the "Zionist entity," however, goes beyond taking the Zionist discourse of haven and homeland to be nothing more than a ploy in the Jewish plot to rule the world. It would seem, in fact, that the Jews have already taken over the world, even as they were struggling to bring the Jewish state into being. When in December 1948, for example, the Muslim Brotherhood was banned in Egypt, their leader Hasan al-Banna blamed International Zionism.[79] In 1950, Islamic scholar Abd al-Rahman Sami Ismat wrote, "The Jews and Zionism are like an evil tree. Its root is in New York, its branches all over the world, its leaves the Jews – all of them, old and young, male and female, without exception, are its thorny leaves and poisoned thorns, and the poison is swift and

---

[77] Ibid., 651.
[78] See Ronald L. Nettler, *Past Trials and Present Tribulations: A Muslim Fundamentalist's View of the Jews* (Oxford, U.K.: Pergamon, 1987), 49, 55.
[79] Küntzel, *Jihad and Jew-Hatred*, 54–55.

deadly."[80] Years later Hezbollah's Al-Manar television broadcast system would portray "the Israeli-Palestinian conflict as a key part of a larger effort to halt the 'cancer' of Zionism" that spreads throughout the world, a view also espoused by Hamas leader Ismail Haniya.[81] In a recurring projection of their own evil on the Jews, the Jihadist anti-Zionists accuse the Jews of their own stated designs of world domination.

Of course, they cast their designs in terms of saving the world. As Qutb stated it, "The Muslim war aims at converting all humans on the entire earth [to Islam].... Islam ... is an expansionist militancy which aims at liberating the whole of mankind."[82] Such a project begins with the extermination of the demonic "Zionist entity." Commenting on Qutb's anti-Zionist anti-Semitism, Ronald Nettler notes that from Qutb's

judicious use of ancient sources applied imaginatively to contemporary crises, there arose familiar ideas: the Jews as inherently decadent and anti-religious; the Jews as being driven by an obsessive urge to destroy the only true religion, Islam; the Jews as the organizers and agents of the Western political threat to Islam; the Jews as the main purveyors of the cultural Westernization which has so damaged Islam; the Jews as the modern "Hypocrites" continuing the work of their ancient predecessors; and the Jews as the power behind the Westernizing "Muslim" politicians. The monstrous evil exemplifying these specific Jewish evils was the Jewish Satan of Zionism and Israel.[83]

Promulgating the "world Jewish conspiracy" calumny, Qutb deems the Jews' passion to control others as a "driving force in their national character,"[84] which is a demonic character.

Nor is Qutb an isolated example among the Jihadist anti-Zionists. Consider the Ayatollah Ruhullah Khomeini's assertion in his "Message to the Pilgrims to Mecca for the Haj" (6 February 1971) that Zionism is "the enemy not only of Islam but of all humanity."[85] In other words, Israel – both the people and the country – is an absolute evil that must be annihilated. In his "New Year's Message" delivered on 21 March 1980, Khomeini shouted that Israel and its puppet-state America are "global

---

[80] Quoted in Bernard Lewis, *Semites and Anti-Semites: An Inquiry into Conflict and Prejudice* (New York: W. W. Norton, 1999), 15.

[81] Avi Jorisch, *Beacon of Hatred: Inside Hizballah's Al-Manar Television* (Washington, D.C.: Washington Institute for Near East Policy, 2004), 68.

[82] Quoted in Laurent Murawiec, *The Mind of Jihad* (Cambridge, U.K.: Cambridge University Press, 2008), 98.

[83] Nettler, *Past Trials and Present Tribulations*, 69.   [84] Ibid., 37–38.

[85] Ruhullah Khomeini, *Islam and Revolution: Writings and Declarations of Imam Khomeini (1941–1980)*, trans. Hamid Algar (Berkeley, Calif.: Mizan Press, 1981), 195

plunderers"[86] interested in ruling far more than the Middle East. The Islamic Jihadist hatred of the American "puppet" of the Jews has little to do with Iraq, Afghanistan, or the American support of Israel; because the United States is viewed as kind of Israeli colony, the hatred of America is a hatred of Israel itself. In a speech delivered to the pilgrims setting out for Mecca on 12 September 1980 Khomeini referred to the United States as "the number-one enemy in the world" precisely because their actions "are coordinated" by "international Zionism."[87] If there is a "Little Satan" and "Big Satan," the Big Satan is Israel.

Like the Muslim Brotherhood and its Hamas offshoot, like Qutb and Khomeini, the Palestine Liberation Organization demonizes the Jewish state as the headquarters of the "world Jewish conspiracy." Article Twenty-two of the PLO Charter states, "Israel is the instrument of the Zionist movement, and geographical base for world imperialism placed strategically in the midst of the Arab homeland to combat the hopes of the Arab nation for liberation, unity, and progress. Israel is a constant source of threat vis-à-vis peace in the Middle East and the whole world."[88] Given this view of the Jewish state, the only logical position that the PLO can promote is the annihilation of Israel and the Jews, an aim spelled out in Article Fifteen of the PLO Charter.[89] Thus Sakhr Habash (b. 1939), a member of Fatah's central committee and a PLO ideologue, commented on the Oslo agreement of 1993 by saying that once the Palestinians had control of Gaza and the West Bank, they would proceed to the "final solution."[90] Just so, Habash described the PLO's position by saying, "There can be no coexistence between Zionism and the Palestinian national movement,"[91] any more than there can be any coexistence between God and Satan.

What must be stressed once again about these murderous manifestations of Jihadist anti-Zionism is the diametric opposition to Judaism and the Torah's teaching concerning the holiness of the other human being, as well as its caution about succumbing to the temptation to be as God. Judaism singles out the Jewish people to bear a singular witness to all of humanity concerning the infinite sanctity of every human being. Islamic Jihadism sets out to affirm the infinite expendability of every human being

---

[86] Ibid., 286.   [87] Ibid., 305.

[88] See Kapustyan and Nelson, *The Soul of Terror*, 139–140.

[89] See Küntzel, *Jihad and Jew-Hatred*, 113.

[90] Efraim Karsh, *Arafat's War: The Man and His Battle for Israeli Conquest* (New York: Grove Press, 2003), 62.

[91] Quoted in ibid., 199.

in the name of Allah; hence Ayman al-Zawahiri's argument that Muslims may be killed in the effort to murder Jews.[92] Such is the thinking – such is the evil – that morphs murder into martyrdom, even to the point of training one's own children to kill themselves in the process of murdering Jews. As Zaki Chehab points out, "it is imperative for the family of a Hamas fighter to be seen in front of the world's media as proud of their beloved son rather than bitter or tragic and they should extol Hamas's belief in the battle and the glorious afterlife their son is destined to experience."[93] The Jihadist anti-Zionist evil represents a radical perversion of the most ancient, most fundamental evil – murder – into the highest good that brings with it the highest reward. In this appropriation of God, not only is the prohibition against murder eliminated, it is twisted into a commandment to murder.

Thus, we see how the Jihadist appropriation of God's word is tied to the tearing of meaning from the word. Where meaning is torn from the word, holiness is torn from the human, and this perversion of the word is a defining feature of Islamic anti-Zionism. It entails not only the appropriation of the word of Torah and the elimination of its absolute prohibition against murder, but also the undermining of the Holy Quran. In 1899, when the Zionist movement began to gain momentum, a major political figure of the Ottoman Empire named Yusuf al-Khalidi (1829–1907) affirmed that the Zionist idea was "completely natural, fine and just," adding, "Who can challenge the rights of the Jews on Palestine? Good Lord, historically it is really your country."[94] How can a faithful Muslim support a Jewish presence in Israel? Why would he make such a statement? Because, as a faithful Muslim, he embraces the Quran's designation of the Land of Israel as a dwelling place for the Jews, to which the Jews in exile will be returned when the last days approach (17:104). The fact that this verse is seldom mentioned by the Jihadists underscores their rebellion against God and what they view as "the Holy Quran," a rebellion against the spirit and the meaning of Islam itself, which they do not follow but rather exploit to suit their own ends. In a sense, then, anti-Zionism is anti-Islamic. Here the Islamic anti-Zionists part ways with their left-wing secular counterparts. The left-wing intellectual who opposes the "Zionist

---

[92] See Ayman al-Zawahiri, "*Jihad*, Martyrdom, and the Killing of Innocents," in Raymond Ibrahim, ed., *The Al Qaeda Reader*, trans. Raymond Ibrahim (New York: Doubleday, 2007), 113, 142.

[93] Zaki Chehab, *Inside Hamas: The Untold Story of the Militant Islamic Movement* (New York: Nation Books, 2007), 97.

[94] Quoted in Wistrich, *A Lethal Obsession*, 685.

entity" is merely remaining true to the first principles of his or her enlightened liberalism and the universalism it entails: there can be no people apart, hence no Jewish state. The Jihadist who sacrifices his or her children in the war against the Zionist entity betrays the very text that he or she so often invokes to justify such murderous actions.

CLOSING REFLECTION

Two events in the last century have shaken Jewish history, as well as the history of humanity, to its core: the Holocaust and the advent of the Jewish state. From the standpoint of Jewish sacred tradition, both events are situated within Jewish sacred history. If the tales that came out of the Shoah might be viewed as the tales of a new Bible, as Primo Levi has stated,[95] the same might be said of the tale of the Jewish state that was born *in spite of* the Holocaust. "*The messianic hope died during the Holocaust,*" Fackenheim articulates one implication of this turn of events. "*The post-Holocaust State of Israel has resurrected it.*"[96] If this history has shown anything, it has shown that a Jewish state is indispensable to any hope for a future for the Jewish people. This shift in the Jewish condition is a defining feature of the post-Holocaust era, an era darkened by the anti-Zionist anti-Semitism that casts its shadow over all of humanity. That shadow is the shadow of Auschwitz itself. Just as the denial of Auschwitz is a denial of the Jewish people as a people with a past, so is the opposition to the existence of the Jewish state an opposition to the Jewish people as a people with a future. And the future of humanity hinges on the future of the Jewish people as a people chosen for a testimony to the sanctity of every human being.

One group of anti-Zionist anti-Semites that may be conspicuous by its absence from the foregoing discussion consists of Jews who oppose the existence of the Jewish state, among whom are Israelis, primarily, but not entirely, from the far secular left. Here too Jew hatred makes for strange bedfellows. That group, however, comes under extensive discussion in the next chapter.

[95] Primo Levi, *Survival in Auschwitz*, trans. Stuart Woolf (New York: Simon & Schuster, 1996), 66.

[96] Fackenheim, *What Is Judaism?*, 268–269.

8

Jewish Jew Hatred

Judaicide is the ultimate conclusion of the Jew wanting his Jewishness to be "like the others," for the others draw the Jew into their nets in order to make him disappear from the scene of history.

André Neher, *They Made Their Souls Anew*

There is a story about a Jew sitting on a park bench in New York reading his newspaper. He looks up and notices a man in a black coat, black hat, and beard sitting on a bench across from him. After staring for a moment the Jewish gentleman puts down his newspaper and says to the black hat, "You Chasidic fanatics make me sick! You give all of us a bad name, with your backward dress, your ridiculous superstitions, and your sycophantic rebbe worship!"

A bit taken aback, the man in black replied, "I am sorry, sir, but I think you have mistaken me for someone else. I am Amish."

Overcome with embarrassment, the Jew who had railed at him quickly apologized and said, "Oh, I have such admiration for you people! You live such a simple and pure life, free from all the craziness of the world. And you are so moral, so upright! You set a good example for all of us!"

We are all familiar with "secular" Jews who are embarrassed by the traditions of their grandfathers, whose bar mitzvahs were their last imitation of any religious observance and whose worst nightmare is that one of their children might marry an ultra-Orthodox Jew. They are the Jews who, David Mamet complains, "nod when Tevye praises tradition but fidget through the seder; who might take their curiosity to a dogfight, to a bordello or an opium den but find ludicrous the notion of a visit to the synagogue; whose favorite Jew is Anne Frank and whose second-favorite does not exist; who are humble in their desire to learn about Kwanzaa and proud of their ignorance of Tu B'Shvat; who dread endogamy more than incest; who bow the head reverently at a baptism and have never attended a bris."[1] They are the Jews who might declare, "I am Jewish but not *too* Jewish," which, says Mamet, translates into "because my ancestors suffered persecution and *prevailed*, I will renounce their struggle and call my ingratitude enlightenment; my ignorant scorn of the Israelis and their struggle will be called championship of the oppressed, my ignorance of religion common sense; and my supercilious superiority to its practices a licensed diversion."[2] They are the Jews whose Jewish guilt is not about being Jewish but about failing to be Jewish.

Focusing on Jews who are more calculating and systematic in their thinking, however, this chapter is generally concerned with more heinous manifestations of the most heinous form of anti-Semitism: Jewish Jew hatred. "Among no group in the world," Dennis Prager and Joseph Telushkin have observed, "are there so many individuals who single-mindedly attempt to damage the group into which they were born."[3] And the damage is severe. If in the post-Holocaust era anti-Zionism is an especially egregious form of anti-Semitism, Jewish anti-Semitism is even more so. It is one thing for a Jew to play into the hands of the Christians, who, after all, have a limiting principle that may curb their actions against the Jews, as well as an ostensible interest in "saving" the Jews. But in the post-Holocaust context, the anti-Semitic Jew aids and abets the extermi-nationist agenda and the eclipse of God that the Nazis undertook, and for the Nazis there is no going too far, no limiting principle. The assault on God within oneself invariably generates a hatred of oneself, not just as a Jew but as a human being. In the words of Holocaust diarist Yitzhak Katznelson, "When you remove from a child his 'Jewish gene,' you remove from him the 'human gene.'"[4] And that was the Nazis' highest aim in their determination that the Jew is not a human being. The systematic removal of the human gene from the Jew was central to the systematic assault on his soul. And the Jew who hates Jews can do so only by removing his human gene.

---

[1] David Mamet, *The Wicked Son: Anti-Semitism, Self-Hatred, and the Jew* (New York: Schocken Books, 2006), xi–xii.

[2] Ibid., 119–120.

[3] Dennis Prager and Joseph Telushkin, *Why the Jews? The Reason for Antisemitism* (New York: Simon & Schuster, 2003), 53.

[4] Yitzhak Katznelson, *Vittel Diary*, trans. Myer Cohn, 2nd ed. (Tel-Aviv: Hakibbutz Hameuchad, 1972), 152.

As Emil Fackenheim has argued, "Nazism can seek nothing higher from the 'non-Aryan' 'race'-enemy than self-destruction, preceded by self-transformation into the loathsome creature which, according to Nazi doctrine, he has been since birth."[5] And so it came to pass in those days of destruction. "Instead of loathing and despising those foulest dregs of humanity, the accursed German nation," Katznelson records in his diary, "we have begun to hate ourselves."[6] Whom do the Jews hate when they hate themselves? They hate themselves as the people of the Covenant, chosen to bear witness to the revelation of Torah, to be a light unto the nations, and to announce to the world the ineluctable "chosenness" of every human being. It is a hatred that leads them not only to abandon who they are but to assume the identity of their murderers; in the end, there is no middle ground. Like the Nazi assault on the Jewish people, this assault on the Jews' regard for themselves begins with the children. "In a refuge center an eight-year-old child went mad," Emmanuel Ringelblum attests in his diary. "Screamed, 'I want to steal, I want to rob, I want to eat, I want to be a German.' In his hunger he hated being Jewish."[7] Madness, Ringelblum calls it. And so it is: it is the madness that underlies the elimination of the prohibition against murder. It is the madness of anti-Semitism. While this surely does not apply to the case of an eight-year-old – he can be viewed only as another victim – it surely does apply to the adult whose Jewish Jew hatred is calculated.

The hunger that leads the Jew to slip into the madness of Jew hatred is a hunger in the soul: like any soul, his soul hungers for meaning, relation, and belonging in a world that refuses the Jew and his testimony. In his madness he turns his hatred for the world onto the Jews, whose teaching and tradition transform him into an unwilling witness. And yet there is no meaning, no relation, no belonging outside the teaching and tradition that make him a Jew. Mamet offers a penetrating insight in this connection: "The apostate or assimilated Jew, who might express delight and wonder at the Japanese tea ceremony and retain these impressions throughout a lifetime, is hard pressed to remember if Rosh Hashanah precedes or follows Yom Kippur. This is not a 'lack of interest.' It is panic."[8] It is panic in the face of the Holy One whose Voice reverberates throughout

---

[5] Emil L. Fackenheim, *To Mend the World: Foundations of Post-Holocaust Jewish Thought* (New York: Schocken Books, 1989), 209.

[6] Katznelson, *Vittel Diary*, 94.

[7] Emmanuel Ringelblum, *Notes from the Warsaw Ghetto*, trans. and ed. Jacob Sloan (New York: Schocken Books, 1974), 39.

[8] Mamet, *The Wicked Son*, 164.

the High Holy Days, from Rosh Hashanah to Yom Kippur, from Yom Kippur to Sukkot and beyond, crying out to us as He cried out to Adam, "Where are you?" This is why "self-hate," as Elie Wiesel says, "is more harmful than hate toward others. The latter questions man's relationship with man; the first implicates man's relationship to God."[9] What is called "self-hatred" is a hatred of the soul created in the image and likeness of the Holy One. It is a resentment of the meaning and mission imposed on the soul. It is an abhorrence of the absolute ethical demand that devolves on us from on high. In the end, it is a hatred not of the self, which is a self-deception, but of the other human being. The hatred of the soul always manifests itself as a hatred of the other human being, for the soul lives precisely in relationship to another.

Attempting to fathom why a Jew would want to become part of a world that he holds in contempt, Mamet writes, "The acquiescent apikoros [a Jew who has left the fold] basks in sloth. This person is not righteous but cowardly, and neither sloth nor cowardice will protect him if, God forbid, the hammer of the Crusades, the Inquisition, the Holocaust, the jihad falls toward him. Who will protect him? His fellow Jews."[10] And he wonders: "How, please, are the self-absorbed, deceitful, busy-unto-death, distracted, irreverent, and unschooled (according to your and my constant gossip) mob who make up the totality of humankind suddenly transformed into a wise council of the Just, waiting to embrace the quondam Jew who has seen the light?"[11] There is, however, an answer. It lies in the metaphysical origin of anti-Semitism. Trading the Torah for the promise of a seat at the table of an anti-Semitic society, the Jew-hating Jew buys into a promise as deadly and deceptive as the temptation of the serpent: you will be like God, or at least like those of us who would be as God.

The self-hating soul is a soul in exile, and for the Jews the paradigm of exile is the ancient exile in Egypt, a realm ruled by a Pharaoh who thinks he is God and plagued by a darkness in which "a man cannot not see his brother" (Exodus 10:23). The true horror of the Egyptian exile, as Adin Steinsaltz expresses it, "was that the slaves gradually became more and more like their masters, thinking like them and even dreaming the same dreams. Their greatest sorrow, in fact, was that their masters would not let them fulfill the Egyptian dream."[12] And their greatest wretchedness

---

[9] Elie Wiesel, *The Oath* (New York: Avon, 1973), 88.
[10] Mamet, *The Wicked Son*, 140.   [11] Ibid., 54.
[12] Adin Steinsaltz, *On Being Free* (Northvale, N.J.: Jason Aronson, 1995), 22.

was that they saw no harm in dreaming the Egyptian dream, a dream of power and possessions, of pleasure and prestige, a nightmare in which more is better but never enough. Examining the Hebrew word for "Egypt," *Mitzraim*, Steinsaltz notes that it is a cognate of *metzar*, which means "narrowness" or "anguish." Therefore "Egypt symbolizes narrow-mindedness. Ancient Egypt and its paganism form the model for the individual who fabricates an entire system to refute real knowledge. The system upholds its false reality in the face of Divine reality. Egypt is the prototype of a world that proclaims itself to be autonomous and announces that it owes nothing to others because it is self-sufficient."[13] This announcement is precisely the lie of the serpent.

In his analysis of anti-Semitism, psychiatrist Theodore Isaac Rubin observes that Jews who have converted to Christianity "can develop dangerous symbol sickness; symptoms may include the need to burn Jewishness out of their beings by burning Jews."[14] If they do not demand the burning of Jews, they certainly demand the burning of the books that make the Jews who they are. Of course, when we begin by burning books, we end by burning people, as Heinrich Heine foretold.[15] As Jew-hating Jews, Jewish anti-Semites are Torah- and Talmud-hating Jews. Such Jews, Cynthia Ozick observes, "are not what is commonly called self-haters, since they are motivated by the preening self-love that congratulates itself on always 'seeing the other side.' Not self-haters, no; low moral cowards, rather, often trailing uplifting slogans."[16] Trading the Torah for cultural convention, the Jew begins by rejecting his people and ends by imitating the very ones who would consign his people to the flames. To such a Jew Mamet poses a telling question: "To you, the wicked son, does it seem logical that the creators, receivers, interpreters and protectors of the Bible for millennia, somehow had it wrong? – that the rabbis, mystics, and prophets who lived to give sense to immemorial memory were somehow deluded?"[17] Of course, it is neither logical nor rational: the Jew who in

---

[13] Adin Steinsaltz, *The Seven Lights: On the Major Jewish Festivals* (Northvale, N.J.: Jason Aronson, 2000), 126.

[14] Theodore Isaac Rubin, *Anti-Semitism: A Disease of the Mind* (New York: Continuum, 1990), 121.

[15] See Heinrich Heine, *The Complete Poems of Heinrich Heine: A Modern English Version*, trans. Hal Draper (Boston: Suhrkamp/Insel, 1982), 187.

[16] Cynthia Ozick, "The Modern 'Hep! Hep! Hep!,'" in Edward Alexander and Paul Bogdanor, eds., *The Jewish Divide over Israel: Accusers and Defenders* (New Brunswick, N.J.: Transaction Publishers, 2008), 6.

[17] Mamet, *The Wicked Son*, 178.

the age of modernity would trade his or her Judaism for modernity's rationalism is here exposed as utterly irrational. But reason is only half the person; in the soul there stirs a longing, a fear, and a temptation that exceed reason.

Sander Gilman notes in this connection an observation of the German Hebraist Johann Reuchlin (1455–1522), who "divides the Jews into two classes: the educated, intelligent Jews, who remain with their religion and are knowledgeable of the Talmud; and the ignorant, crude converts. The first are devoted to their children, their books; the latter destroy them."[18] In my view, however, Jew-hating Jews set out to burn the books of the sacred tradition not because they were ignorant of them but because they knew them, at least on some level; they knew the absolute ethical injunction that devolves on the world through the Torah and the Talmud, an injunction in the face of which no one is innocent. "What is the fear that the Jew engenders and that manifests itself as hatred?" asks Mamet. And he answers: "Perhaps it is caused by his historical, absolute terrifying certainty that there is a God."[19] And where there is a God – the God of Abraham and Moses – there is an absolute commandment that undermines the human being's longing to be as God.

The initial purging of the Talmud undertaken in Christendom came at the instigation of a Jewish Dominican convert named Nicholas Donin; it was he who urged Pope Gregory IX to examine the Talmud for its anti-Christian teachings. The result was the Disputation of Paris in 1240 held under the auspices of King Louis (1214–1270), who was later canonized as a saint.[20] Soon after the disputation the folios were consigned to the flames. Another Dominican convert, Pablo Cristiani (d. 1274), instigated the famous Disputation of Barcelona in 1263, which featured the renowned Jewish scholar Nachmanides; when the sage published his account of the exchange, he was immediately exiled.[21] One of the most spectacular of the Christian efforts to turn the Jews against themselves was the Tortosa Disputation of 1413. Forcing the Jews of Aragon and Catalonia to attend, antipope Benedict XIII (1328–1423) called on Jewish convert Geronimo of Santa Fé to represent the Christians against fourteen rabbis. After a year and nine months of arguments, three thousand Jews

---

[18] Sander L. Gilman, *Jewish Self-Hatred: Anti-Semitism and the Hidden Language of the Jews* (Baltimore, Md.: Johns Hopkins University Press, 1986), 43.

[19] Mamet, *The Wicked Son*, 60.

[20] Edward H. Flannery, *The Anguish of the Jews* (New York: Paulist Press, 1965), 104.

[21] Ibid., 129; see Nachmanides, *The Disputation at Barcelona*, trans. Charles B. Chavel (New York: Shilo, 1983).

converted, including all but two of the rabbis.[22] For these Jewish anti-Semites, the aim of the disputations forced on the Jews was neither to convince nor to edify but to destroy the teachings of the Torah that the Jews represent by their very presence in the world.

In modern times "the first of the great modern anti-Semites of the rationalist school," as Edward Flannery puts it, "was himself a Jew, Baruch Spinoza [1632–1677]," who "discarded traditional Judaism as a gross superstition and believing Jews as worshipers of a God of hate."[23] Indeed, Emmanuel Lévinas observes that "Spinoza is the first messenger of the death of a God bearing the well-known resemblance to man spoken of in Genesis."[24] Thus, with the onset of the Enlightenment heralded by the likes of Spinoza, there came a new form of the conversion phenomenon in the secularization of the Jew and in the liberalization of Judaism, both of which issued largely from the German Idealism of the Enlightenment. Fackenheim refers to this turnabout among the "enlightened" Jews as an "empty abstraction" that "mistakes Jews for members of the *Kant-Gesellschaft*."[25] He registers a complaint concerning this abandonment of traditional Judaism on the part of these Jews who bartered the God of Abraham, Isaac, and Jacob for the God Idea of Idealism:

Jewish prayer, once *between* a "subjective" self and an "objective" God, is viewed as the self's disport with its own feelings, conducive to aesthetic or therapeutic benefit. Halakhah, once a way walked *before* God, is reduced to "custom and ceremony," performed for the sake of warm emotions within or wholesome relations without. Judaism, once a covenant involving a singling-out God and a singled-out Israel, is seen as a man-made civilization, created by Jewish genius in its human solitariness. And the human person, who once believed he *actually* mattered to God, is now engineered into the mere *feeling* that he matters, on the ground that such feelings banish anxiety and alienation.[26]

Of course, the result is just the opposite: the more Jews have tried to "fit in" socially and culturally, the more alienated and anxiety-ridden they have become. For no one matters to the *idea* of God.

---

[22] Ibid., 134; see, e.g., Baruch Spinoza, *Theological-Political Treatise*, trans. Samuel Shirley and Seymour Feldman, 2nd ed. (Indianapolis, Ind.: Hackett, 2001), 35–47.

[23] Ibid., 174.

[24] Emmanuel Lévinas, *Proper Names*, trans. Michael B. Smith (Stanford, Calif.: Stanford University Press, 1996), 84.

[25] Emil L. Fackenheim, *Quest for Past and Future: Essays in Jewish Theology* (Bloomington: Indiana University Press, 1968), 14.

[26] Ibid., 178.

It could not be otherwise. This "fitting in" is a bailing out that requires a Jew to renounce his or her essence and identity as a Jew. Jewish alienation and anxiety are not so much the outcome of the gentile's rejection of the Jew as the Jew's rejection of what lies at the core of his or her own being. While it has been the bane of the Jewish people since the exile in Egypt, modern times have witnessed an epidemic of Jew hatred among the Jews, ranging from complacency to apostasy, from smug silence to diatribes against the Jewish people. In this chapter, then, we examine Jewish Jew hatred as a feature of modernity, with a consideration of the phenomenon in its post-Holocaust manifestations, including the anti-Zionist anti-Semitism that so many Jews have espoused in an embrace of the serpent itself.

THE SEDUCTION OF MODERNITY

In Chapter 4 we examined the philosophical and ideological anti-Semitism that characterizes much of the thinking in the modern world. If the Holocaust proves anything, it is the utter bankruptcy of that thinking and the emptiness of its promises, particularly to the Jews. As Elie Wiesel once wrote, Hitler "alone has kept his promises, all his promises, to the Jewish people."[27] Among the broken promises to the Jews was the promise that, if they should abandon their Judaism, then they would be allowed entry into the banquet halls of modernity. Abandoning their Judaism, however, was not enough. If the Jews were to be allowed to pass through those hallowed gates, they had to embrace modernity's contempt for the teachings and traditions of Judaism. And so it is, in Mamet's words, that "Jewish self-loathing and Jewish anti-Semitism" became "the theoretical aspects of an empty modern life. The mind finds phobia preferable to free-floating anxiety, so it creates or accepts the idea of an enemy."[28] Of course, if one is a Jew, the enemy turns out to be oneself. Recall in this connection Franz Rosenzweig's realization that in the end the only thing that the Western ontological tradition can recommend is suicide,[29] a horrifying conclusion that

---

[27] Elie Wiesel, *Night*, trans. Marion Wiesel (New York: Hill and Wang, 2006), 81.

[28] Mamet, *The Wicked Son*, 177.

[29] See Franz Rosenzweig, *The Star of Redemption*, trans. William W. Hallo (Boston: Beacon Press, 1972), 4. Schopenhauer is famous for offering this recommendation; see Arthur Schopenhauer, *Parerga and Paralipomena: Short Philosophical Essays*, vol. 2, ed. E. F. J. Payne (Oxford: Clarendon Press, 2000), 306–311. And in *The Possessed* Dostoyevsky's character Kirilov understood it very well: "God is indispensable and therefore must

thinkers such as Søren Kierkegaard[30] and Leo Tolstoy (1828–1910)[31] had reached well before him. It is surely why Albert Camus (1913–1960) opens *The Myth of Sisyphus* with one of the most famous lines in modern philosophy: "There is but one truly serious philosophical problem, and that is suicide."[32] Having thought God out of the picture, modern philosophy thinks itself into suicide: to think God out of the picture is to think humanity out of the picture, beginning with one's own soul.

In contrast to the themes of suicide that haunt modernity,[33] in biblical Hebrew there is no precise equivalent for "suicide." Although we have the modern Hebrew word *hitratzach*, which, like the Latin-based word *suicide*, means to "murder oneself," this verb does not appear in the holy tongue that informs Jewish thought. Nevertheless, there are Hebrew terms for suicide that are quite revealing. In the *Kitzur Shulchan Arukh*,[34] for example, the phrase meaning to "commit suicide" is *ibed atzmo* (201:3), literally to "lose oneself" or to lose one's "substance," one's "strength," the very "bone" of one's being. And what is the substance of the human being? It is the soul that emanates from the divine being. Another phrase for "suicide" in the *Kitzur Shulchan Arukh* is *ibed atzmo ladaat*, which is literally to "lose knowledge of one's essence" (201:1), as if a person could take his or her own life only if he or she had lost all knowledge or understanding of who he or she is. And as soon as a Jew forsakes the Torah, he or she loses a sense of who he or she is, which is to say, he or she loses his or her senses. The result is a certain spiritual suicide.

exist.... But I know there is no God and can't be.... Can't you really see that that alone is a sufficient reason to shoot oneself?" See F. M. Dostoevsky, *The Possessed*, trans. Andrew R. MacAndrew (New York: New American Library, 1962), 634.

[30] See Søren Kierkegaard, *Concluding Unscientific Postscript*, trans. David Swenson and Walter Lowrie (Princeton, N.J.: Princeton University Press, 1941), 273.

[31] See Leo Tolstoy, *Confession*, trans. David Patterson (New York: W. W. Norton, 1983), 27–55.

[32] Albert Camus, *The Myth of Sisyphus*, trans. Justin O'Brien (New York: Random House, 1955), 3.

[33] Recall the lead characters in such literary works as Leo Tolstoy, *Anna Karenina*, trans. Constance Garnett (New York: Random House, 1994); Joseph Conrad, *The Secret Sharer* (New York: St. Martin's Press, 1997); Gustave Flaubert, *Madame Bovary*, trans. Geoffrey Wall (New York: Penguin Books, 2002); and Arthur Miller, *The Death of a Salesman* (New York: Penguin Books, 1998).

[34] Compiled in the nineteenth century by Shlomo Ganzfried, the *Kitzur Shulchan Arukh* is a summary of the famous code of Jewish law, the *Shulchan Arukh*, which was compiled in the sixteenth century.

The loss of such knowledge characterizes the madness of modernity, a madness whereby we begin by killing God, proceed to killing our neighbor, and end with killing ourselves. The Talmud, in fact, sees the denial of God and God's commandments as a form of madness (see *Sotah* 3a). And yet this distinctively modern condition is anticipated in the ancient story of Cain, who set out to kill both himself and God by killing his brother; murdering his brother, Cain murdered his own name, and with it the Holy Name, as suggested in the Midrash (see *Bereshit Rabbah* 1:11).[35] This single, suicidal movement – in which God, the soul, and the other human being are consumed by a counterfeit "I" – is rooted in the desire to be as God or, in modern times, as the mangod. In the Talmud it is written that the heart cannot contain the ego and the *Shekhinah*, God's Indwelling Presence, at the same time (*Pesachim* 66b), a view that undermines the autonomous, ego-based thinking of modernity. In contrast to the Cartesian *cogito*, the "I think" that establishes itself as the illusory ground of being, we have in Judaism the notion of *bitul hayesh*, which is the "annulment of the self" that produces a "'vessel' for truth to enter."[36] The self that would be all proves to be nothing, so that the madness of modernity lies in its pursuit of an apocalypse without redemption. It is the apocalypse of the eclipse of God, the chaos of the collapse of the soul. And the Jew-hating Jew succumbs to it in an act of Judaicide, which is a suicide of the soul.

Here a language in which we may speak of suicide becomes even more significant. Indeed, in his seminal study of Jewish self-hatred Sander Gilman sees the issue of language as a key to understanding modern Jewish anti-Semitism. "The thinkers of the Enlightenment," he observes, "desired the Jews to convert, not to Christianity, but to the new religion of rationalism. This conversion was also represented by the abandonment of the Jews' language, which, as with the converts of the early eighteenth century, was conflated with the discourse of the Jews."[37] For a Jew, to abandon the Jewish language is to abandon the holy tongue of the Torah and the mode of thought it engenders. Above all, it means abandoning one's name, the Hebrew name of which the Jewish soul is made, the name that announces the meaning and mission of our lives, for Jewish tradition

[35] For a good discussion of this point, see Elie Wiesel, *Messengers of God*, trans. Marion Wiesel (New York: Random House, 1976), 60–62.

[36] See Yitzchak Ginsburgh, *The Alef-Beit: Jewish Thought Revealed through the Hebrew Letters* (Northvale, N.J.: Jason Aronson, 1991), 72; see also Louis Jacobs, *Hasidic Prayer* (New York: Schocken Books, 1972), 21.

[37] Gilman, *Jewish Self-Hatred*, 81.

teaches that the name and the soul, the name and the person, are of a piece.[38] Suddenly we realize the wisdom of the teaching from the Midrash that says the Hebrews in Egypt were able to emerge from their exile for four reasons: (1) they did not change their language; (2) they did not change their names; (3) they did not intermarry; and (4) they did not inform on one another (*Mekilta Pischa* 5). It is no accident that Jews who hate Jews almost invariably engage in all of these actions.

If it should be objected that the Jews who ushered in the Haskalah, the "Jewish Enlightenment," adopted Hebrew as their language of discourse, the Hebrew that they promoted, Gilman points out, "was the antithesis of Talmudic language. It is rather the Hebrew of the Christian Orientalists and grammarians, such as Michaelis."[39] Inspired by Moses Mendelssohn (1729–1786), who sought a way for the Jews to live as Jews in an enlightened Europe, the Jews of the Haskalah adopted Hebrew in such a way as to usurp the holiness of the holy tongue and with it the essence of the Jew. Although Mendelssohn asserts that "without God, providence and a future life, love of our fellow man is but an innate weakness,"[40] he nonetheless insists that we need not recognize any *"eternal truths other than those that are not merely comprehensible to human reason but can also be verified by human powers."*[41] Making a distinction between religion and legislation,[42] Mendelssohn declares that the laws of God "did not have to be given by direct revelation."[43] Of course, once "human powers" are sufficient for the derivation of "eternal truths," there is no need for "direct revelation." And once there is no need for revelation, what need is there for the Holy One and the language of revelation? Indeed, what need is there for the Jews?

Mendelssohn was followed by others who sought to accommodate not their "enlightened" thinking to their Judaism but their Judaism to enlightened thinking by "reforming" their Judaism. In 167 BCE, Fackenheim points out, Antiochus' decree prohibiting Jewish observances "owed its inspiration to Hellenizing Jewish leaders who, long bent on

---

[38] See, e.g., the *Sefer Chasidim* (244) of the medieval sage Rabbi Yehuda HeChasid; see also Nachman of Breslov, *Tikkun*, trans. Avraham Greenbaum (Jerusalem: Breslov Research Institute, 1984), 103.

[39] Gilman, *Jewish Self-Hatred*, 105; the reference is to Johann David Michaelis (1717–1791), German Protestant scholar of the Hebrew language.

[40] Moses Mendelssohn, *Jerusalem or On Religious Power and Judaism*, trans. Allan Arkush, introduction and commentary by Alexander Altmann (Hanover, N.H.: Brandeis University Press, 1983), 63.

[41] Ibid., 89; emphasis in the original; see also 93–94.   [42] Ibid., 97.   [43] Ibid., 126.

'accommodating traditional Judaism to the times,' at length enlisted non-Jewish government force. In their own eyes, these leaders were not traitors or apostates. They were a 'reform party,' concerned not to destroy Judaism but rather to preserve it. Yet had their efforts succeeded, they would have destroyed Judaism from within far more thoroughly than any external enemy."[44] And so the wheel turns. The most prominent figure in the early years of Reform Judaism was Abraham Geiger (1810–1874), who "fashioned his image of Judaism along the lines of the concepts of freedom and of reason as formulated in the pseudotheological strands of German idealism. Indeed, he took up the Kantian notion of freedom from the heteronomous rules of Jewish ceremonies."[45] Insisting on the autonomy of the thinking ego, Geiger asserted that the Torah, the Bible, and other texts of the sacred tradition "can no longer be viewed as of Divine origin. . . .. By driving such falsehoods into a corner," he believed, Jews would "bring about the great cave-in which will bury the old world beneath its ruins and open a new world for us in its place."[46] As it turned out, it would be the Jews who were buried beneath the ruins of modernity.

Another result of the Jewish accommodation of German Idealism was the emergence of *die Wissenschaft des Judentums*, that is, "the scientific study of Judaism," a movement whose leading figure was Leopold Zunz (1794–1886). The aspiration was to make Judaism more "reasonable" and therefore more attractive to the many "educated" Jews who were abandoning the tradition of their fathers and mothers.[47] Other Jews who promoted this accommodation include the Galician philosopher Nachman Krochmal (1785–1840), the French thinker Salomon Munk (1803–1867), and the German rabbis Solomon Formstecher (1808–1889) and Samuel Hirsch (1815–1889). All of them, to varying degrees, fit Mamet's description of Jews who "identify with their oppressors – the slave with their strength, the apostate Jew with their reason";[48] he adds that the apostate

---

[44] Emil L. Fackenheim, *Encounters between Judaism and Modern Philosophy* (New York: Basic Books, 1993), 107.

[45] Michael Mack, *German Idealism and the Jew: The Inner Anti-Semitism of Philosophy and German Jewish Responses* (Chicago, Ill.: University of Chicago Press, 2003), 92.

[46] Abraham Geiger, "Jewish Scholarship and Religious Reform," in Paul Mendes-Flohr and Jehuda Reinharz, eds., *The Jew in the Modern World: A Documentary History*, 2nd ed. (Oxford, U.K.: Oxford University Press, 1995), 233.

[47] For a valuable insight into Leopold Zunz, see Luitpold Wallach, *Liberty and Letters: The Thought of Leopold Zunz* (London: East and West Library, 1959); see also Peter Wagner, *Wir werden frei sein: Leopold Zunz, 1794–1886* (Detmold: Gesellschaft für Christlich-Jüdische Zuzammenarbeit, 1994).

[48] Mamet, *The Wicked Son*, 147.

"is ensnared in a delusion. His delusion is that he is thinking rationally."[49] Buying into the philosophical system of enlightened modernity, many of these Jewish thinkers are like the man who saw a "For Sale" sign in front of a beautiful establishment and went inside to inquire, only to discover that it was merely the sign itself that was for sale.

Perhaps the most prominent of the Jews of accommodation was Hermann Cohen (1842–1918), the founder of the neo-Kantian Marburg School. His reflections on Judaism initially came as a reply to the noted historian Heinrich von Treitschke's essay "A Word about Our Jews" (1879), where Treitschke declared, "The Semites bear a heavy share of guilt for the falsehood and deceit, the insolent greed of fraudulent business practices, and that base materialism of our day."[50] In his response to Treitschke Cohen argued (as if it were a defense of Judaism) that Reform Judaism was essentially the same as German Protestantism; rooted as they were in the basic principles of the Enlightenment, both Reform Judaism and German Protestantism had overcome the dark irrationalism of religious myth to become a rational, civilized *Kulturreligion*.[51] His most profound work is *Religion of Reason out of the Sources of Judaism* (published posthumously in 1919). Here Cohen views his task to be similar to the one that Maimonides supposedly undertook in *The Guide for the Perplexed*, namely, the marriage of philosophy and Judaism, that is, the marriage of Kantian philosophy and Judaism.

Although Jews such as Mendelssohn, Geiger, Zunz, and Cohen turned away from traditional Judaism, they did not go so far as to become anti-Semites; indeed, Cohen was responding to the anti-Semite Treitschke. Other Jews, however, both overtly and more subtly, would take that step. The key figures to be examined in this connection are Karl Marx, Otto Weininger, and Sigmund Freud, despite and because of his psychoanalytical method.

FROM ACCOMMODATION TO ABANDONMENT

Karl Marx is one of the modern Jews who most notoriously vilified the language of the Jewish religious discourse. Marx viewed the language of

---

[49] Ibid., 157.
[50] See Heinrich von Treitschke, "A Word about Our Jews," trans. Richard S. Levy, in Richard S. Levy, ed., *Antisemitism in the Modern World: An Anthology of Texts* (Lexington, Mass.: D. C. Heath and Company, 1991, 72.
[51] See the introduction to Herman Cohen, *Reason and Hope: Selections from the Jewish Writings of Hermann Cohen*, trans. Eva Jospe (Cincinnati, Ohio: Hebrew Union College Press 1993), 17.

questioning and argument that characterizes Jewish talmudic and midrashic tradition as nothing but the language of "haggling." Marx's new "language of revolution, the language of the prophet,"[52] is not only a language different from that of the Jews, it is the language of Jewish Jew hatred. Gilman points out, however, that Marx's "Jewish identity even appears when he is damning the Jews,"[53] because the language of opposition and prophecy characterizes much of the talmudic and biblical language. Indeed, one finds in Marx a projection on the Jew of all that he or she despises about him- or herself as a Jew. One example of this projection is his condemnation of the Jews as people who embody the "egoistic principle of dominating all," not as a human flaw, as Jacob Katz has said, "but as an essentially Jewish characteristic."[54] What else but a totalitarian "egoistic principle of dominating all" lies at the root of the famous lines from the *Manifesto of the Communist Party*: "The proletarians have nothing to lose but their chains. They have a world to win. Working men of all countries, unite!"?[55] Not only do we see something of the prophetic in these lines, but we also find something messianic: Communism is indeed a kind of messianism that promises a utopian deliverance from the suffering and injustice inflicted on the world by capitalism.

It is, however, a messianism that replaces God with the mangod, the revolutionary who dares to confront the evil that is capitalism. And what is that evil? It is, according to Marx, Jews and Judaism. Listing his complaints against the capitalists in "On Bruno Bauer's *The Jewish Question*," Marx names the sins of the Jews: "What is the profane basis of Judaism? *Practical* need, *self-interest*. What is the worldly cult of the Jew? *Huckstering*. What is his worldly god? *Money*."[56] And: "The emancipation of the Jews is the *emancipation of mankind from Judaism*."[57] He did not simply hate capitalism – he hated the Jews and Judaism, the embodiment of the metaphysical evil manifest in capitalist materialism. Following in his footsteps, as Edward Alexander and Paul Bogdanor point out, almost all the modern anti-Semitic Jewish intellectuals "identify

---

[52] See Gilman, *Jewish Self-Hatred*, 204.   [53] Ibid., 297.

[54] Jacob Katz, *From Prejudice to Destruction: Anti-Semitism, 1700–1933* (Cambridge, Mass.: Harvard University Press, 1980), 174.

[55] Karl Marx and Friedrich Engels, *Manifesto of the Communist Party*, authorized English translation (Radford, Va.: Wilder Publications, 2007), 45.

[56] Quoted in Robert Wistrich, *A Lethal Obsession: Anti-Semitism from Antiquity to the Global Jihad* (New York: Random House, 2010), 110.

[57] Ibid.

with the political left and take Karl Marx as an exemplar of wisdom on a large range of issues, including the Jewish one."[58] And the Jewish issue is always an issue concerning Judaism.

Gilman notes that among "the most classic examples of Jewish self-hatred" on the part of the modern Jews is aspiring Austrian philosopher Otto Weininger (1880–1903).[59] Michael Mack suggests the reason: Weininger, he writes, "combined the Kantian and Hegelian denigratory assessment of Jewish religiosity as intrinsically materialist (seeking 'earthly well-being') with the Wagnerian fear of Judaism as a demonic world power.... Weininger established a sense of an eternal Jewish character by tying the Jewish people to an omnipotent and inevitable deity that held them eternally in thrall with promises of earthly happiness and world domination."[60] He maintained that, "devoid of a soul,"[61] the Jew "is eminently the unbeliever. Faith is that act of man by which he enters into relation with being.... The Jew is really nothing, because he believes in nothing."[62] Of course, like all Jews who hate Jews, Weininger must engage in a bit of mental sleight-of-hand in order to maintain such a view. "Directing his anger against the Jews," Mamet points out, "the enlightened Jew is debarred from identifying himself as 'Other'.... But he is not free to fully identify the Jews as others unless he can purge 'the Jew in himself.'"[63] Thus, says Weininger, "to defeat Judaism, the Jew must first understand himself and war against himself."[64] He confirmed this observation by pursuing the war against himself to its logical end in 1903: shortly after completing his notorious volume *Sex and Character*, Weininger "performed a dramatic suicide in the Vienna house where Beethoven had died."[65] Because, like Marx, he understood Jewish evil in terms of Jewish *essence*, there could be no other way to rid himself of his own Jewishness, which was rooted in Judaism.

The suicide of this Jew may be seen as a case of *ibed atzmo ladaat*, a "loss of knowledge of his [true] essence" as a Jew. Reflecting a Freudian

---

[58] Alexander and Bogdanor, *The Jewish Divide over Israel*, xvi.

[59] Gilman, *Jewish Self-Hatred*, 244.   [60] Mack, *German Idealism and the Jew*, 106.

[61] Otto Weininger, *Sex and Character*, authorized English translation from the German 6th ed. (New York: G. P. Putnam's Sons, 1907), 313.

[62] Ibid., 321.   [63] Mamet, *The Wicked Son*, 178.

[64] Weininger, *Sex and Character*, 312.

[65] Ritchie Robertson, "Historicizing Weininger: The Nineteenth-Century German Image of the Feminized Jew," in Bryan Cheyette and Laura Marcus, eds., *Modernity, Culture, and "the Jew"* (Stanford, Calif.: Stanford University Press, 1998), 23.

influence,[66] Weininger views Judaism not as a religion, but rather "as a tendency of the mind, a psychological constitution which is a possibility for all mankind, but which has become actual in the most conspicuous fashion amongst the Jews."[67] Judaism is, in other words, a mental disorder, and the Jews are the embodiment of the illness – an illness that poses a threat to the body politic. Exhibiting a Hegelian influence, like many of the modern Jewish anti-Semites, Weininger maintains that, like women, Jews lack a capacity for reason and have an "aversion to the state as an association of rational beings. Jews are not individuals. The Jew has no self and hence no self-respect: hence there cannot be a Jewish gentleman, just as women have no real dignity. Instead, Jews display insecurity and pushiness."[68] Like Hegel,[69] he associates the family with women, saying, "The family is feminine and maternal in its origin, and has no relation to the State or to society. The fusion, the continuity of the members of the family, reaches its highest point amongst the Jews."[70] Therefore "the true conception of the State is foreign to the Jew, because he, like the woman, is wanting in personality; his failure to grasp the idea of true society is due to his lack of a free intelligible ego. Like women, Jews tend to adhere together, but they do not associate as free independent individuals mutually respecting each other's individuality."[71] Entrenched in the heteronomy of the Covenant of Torah, the Jews undermine the modern inclination toward the autonomy of the individual who would be as God. Rejecting the project of modernity, they are deemed inherently flawed.

In this gendering of the Jew we see a trace of the metaphysical origin of anti-Semitism on the part of one who would join the ranks of the moderns by feminizing the Jews. It is, at any rate, a clear case of projection, as Gilman has observed. "It is not the Eastern Jew," he writes, "but rather the Westernized Jew who is sick, and the illness is one of the psyche. Here the process of projection is complete."[72] Once the Jew is feminized,

[66] Weininger took his dissertation to Freud in 1901 for advice on seeking a publisher, but Freud was not impressed. See Barbara Hyams and Nancy Anne Harrowitz, "A Critical Introduction to the History of Weininger Reception," in Nancy Anne Harrowitz and Barbara Hyams, eds., *Jews and Gender: Responses to Otto Weininger* (Philadelphia: Temple University Press, 1995), 7–8.

[67] Weininger, *Sex and Character*, 303.   [68] Robertson, "Historicizing Weininger," 24.

[69] See Georg W. F. Hegel, *Phenomenology of Spirit (The Phenomenology of Mind)*, trans. J. B. Baillie (Digireads.com Publishing, 2009), 205.

[70] Weininger, *Sex and Character*, 310.   [71] Ibid., 307–308.

[72] Gilman, *Jewish Self-Hatred*, 297.

the Jew becomes like Eve, the source of the original sin that threatens humanity. It happens, however, that where there is projection, there is inversion, so that instead of being the sin that issues from the female, modernity's endeavor to become as God is the redemption that issues from the male. Once the inversion is achieved, the feminized Jew is deemed incapable of the task of consuming the fruits of modernity that would effect the apotheosis of the body politic in the form of the state.

The metaphysical origin of Jewish anti-Semitism is even more evident in Sigmund Freud, who, as we saw in Chapter 1, believed that anti-Semitism is rooted in a fear of castration – which may be construed as a fear of being feminized – on the part of uncircumcised non-Jews.[73] With Freud, the fear may lie in his own fear not of castration or of circumcision exactly, but of *brit milah*, the "covenant of circumcision," which would draw the soul out of the confines of the Freudian psyche and into a higher relation to One who is beyond the psyche. "Freud's scientific German," writes Gilman, "is a language tainted by Weininger's anti-Semitism. Thus, even in this seemingly neutral medium of writing about Jews, Freud finds himself confronted with a new, hidden language of the Jew, the language of the Jew as anti-Semite, in which all of the charges brought against the Jew come home to haunt the author and lead him to the only possible escape, self-destruction."[74] Freud proceeds down that path, falling into the category of "anti-Semitic thinkers" who, Gilman observes, "presuppose the self-sufficiency of human consciousness and project human shortcomings onto the Jews."[75] Presupposing the self-sufficiency of consciousness couched in the psyche, Freud engages in this psychological projection most blatantly in *Moses and Monotheism*. There we see a metaphysical origin of Jewish anti-Semitism exposed in the psychoanalytical usurpation of the God of Moses accomplished by altering the figure of Moses himself. This may be the reason why Freud confessed that he had "great difficulties" and "inner misgivings" about his attack on Judaism's founding figure.[76]

---

[73] Sigmund Freud, *Moses and Monotheism*, trans. Katherine Jones (New York: Vintage Books, 1955), 116.

[74] Gilman, *Jewish Self-Hatred*, 268. Ironically, Freud viewed Weininger as the classic self-hating, diseased Jew; see Sander L. Gilman, "Otto Weininger and Sigmund Freud: Race and Gender in the Shaping of Psychoanalysis," in Harrowitz and Hyams, *Jews and Gender*, 104.

[75] Mack, *German Idealism and the Jew*, 138–139.

[76] Freud, *Moses and Monotheism*, 69.

Freud reveals a connection between his contempt for the sign of the Covenant and his eradication of God the Father in his account of what circumcision signifies: "When we hear that Moses 'sanctified' his people by introducing the custom of circumcision, we now understand the deep-lying meaning of this pretension. Circumcision is the symbolic substitute of castration, a punishment which the primeval father dealt his sons long ago out of the fullness of his power; and whosoever accepted this symbol showed by doing so that he was ready to submit to the father's will."[77] The sign of the Covenant, however, is a symbol not of submission but of a higher relation, a relation manifest at times in confrontation. Abraham's first conversation with God after his circumcision was an argument over the fate of Sodom and Gomorrah (Genesis 18:23–33), an argument that God Himself invites. Freud appears to be utterly ignorant of this Jewish tradition. Rejecting the Jewish view of the soul as a relationship and understanding the individual in terms of the inner workings of the psyche, he sees circumcision only in terms of a power struggle. When the struggle goes awry, it unfolds as trauma, defense, latency, and finally neurosis – which is precisely how Freud views the unfolding of Judaism.

He begins his assault on the God of the Jews by de-Judaizing the man whom God chose to bring the Jews out of Egypt and to whom He would reveal His Torah. Claiming that "the man Moses, the liberator and lawgiver of the Jewish people, was not a Jew, but an Egyptian,"[78] Freud voids the Torah revealed at Mount Sinai and with it the foundational utterances of "I am God" and "Thou shalt not murder" – the very utterances that the anti-Semite in each of us fears most. He maintains that the God of Moses was not the God of Abraham, Isaac, and Jacob but the God of the Egyptian Ikhnaton, who conceived a kind of monotheism around 1375 BCE.[79] Not only did the Egyptian Moses give the Jews a new religion, says Freud, but he also introduced the custom of circumcision,[80] so that the one thing that marks the Jew as a Jew does not mark the Jew as a Jew at all – it is the mark of the new Egyptian. Thus, delegitimizing the covenant of circumcision as the sign of the Jews' relation to God, Freud obviates the covenant of Torah that circumcision signifies. In doing so he obviates the most fundamental signifier of Jewish identity. Arguing further that the "real" father of Judaism, Ikhnaton, was killed and replaced by a Midianite Moses,[81] Freud reveals his own assault on God the Father. For, like many Jewish anti-Semites, he realized

---

[77] Ibid.,156 [78] Ibid., 16. [79] Ibid., 27. [80] Ibid., 29. [81] Ibid., 57–58.

that only by getting rid of his Judaism, which meant getting rid of God, could he free himself from the stigma of being a Jew in a world that hates the Jews. In such a world one is either "in or out," as Mamet puts it.[82] And Freud wanted to be in.

Thus, the father of psychoanalysis fits the profile of "the apostate" who "feels himself superior to that Other which is his race and clan, and glorifies in his profession of exile," as Mamet describes it, "seeking notoriety and endorsement for their magnificent detachment. Such 'fair-mindedness' contains a refusal to recognize, in their brothers and sisters, the anguish of their situation and the imperfection of their solutions as they engage in a literal battle for their lives."[83] Freud justifies his assault on the God of the Midianite Moses, who revived the God of the Egyptian Moses, by blaming the Midianite for the hatred aimed at the Jews. "When one is declared favourite of the dreaded father one need not be surprised that the other brothers and sisters are jealous," he avers, and "it was the man Moses who stamped the Jewish people with this trait [of being the favorite son].... It was one man, the man Moses, who created the Jews. To him this people owes its tenacity in supporting life; to him, however, also much of the hostility which it has met with and is meeting still."[84] Thus the anti-Semites, including Freud himself, are absolved of the sin of Jew hatred; it is the fault of Moses, who led the Jews to suppose that they are "nobler, on a higher level, superior to the others."[85] And yet it is precisely Freud who, like other anti-Semitic Jews, takes himself to be superior to the Jews precisely because he has transcended the trauma that lies at the core of Judaism.

Although, as noted in Chapter 1, Jean-Paul Sartre's assessment of anti-Semitism has anti-Semitic overtones, he makes a point that may apply here. "In anti-Semitism," Sartre writes, the self-hating Jew "denies his race in order to be no more than a pure individual, a man without blemish in the midst of other men; in masochism, he repudiates his liberty as a man in order to escape the sin of being a Jew."[86] In the case of Freud, the man without blemish is the man free of the neurosis, not to say the sin, of being Jewish. Here it is noteworthy that Freud had to interrupt the writing of his work when the Nazis moved into Austria on 12 March 1938 precisely because he himself had been branded with this ultimate, original

---

[82] Mamet, *The Wicked Son*, 7.   [83] Ibid., 10–11.
[84] Freud, *Moses and Monotheism*, 135–136.   [85] Ibid., 134.
[86] Jean-Paul Sartre, *Anti-Semite and Jew: An Exploration of the Etiology of Hate*, trans. George L. Becker (New York: Schocken Books, 1976), 109.

sin. Forced to flee his home in Vienna on 4 June, he wrote the third and final section of *Moses and Monotheism* in London, as he notes in the work itself.[87] At a time when the Nazis were formalizing their murderous designs against the Jews, Freud was formulating his own assault on Judaism. If, however, he can be excused because the extermination project had not yet commenced, such an excuse does not extend to the Jewish anti-Semites of the post-Holocaust era, particularly those who turn their Jew hatred toward a hatred of what might have been a haven to Jews subject to mass murder: the Jewish state.

JEWISH ANTI-SEMITISM AS JEWISH ANTI-ZIONISM

Neil Kressel has observed that outside Israel, Jews are acceptable only as long as they publicly condemn the Jewish state.[88] Many if not most anti-Semitic Jews who succumb not only to this pressure but to this temptation are to be found in the halls of academia and among what passes for the Jewish intelligentsia. Historian Joel Beinin of Stanford University, for example, once declared, "In my view the state of Israel has already lost any moral justification for its existence," adding that Israel's "claim to represent all Jews throughout the world endangers even Jews who totally reject Zionism."[89] Indeed the very *existence* of the Jewish state is somehow criminal, and all Jews are accused of the crime. Thus, American political activist and editor Michael Lerner has proclaimed that the anti-Zionist call for the annihilation of Israel is "correct in its fundamental impulses,"[90] because its fundamental impulses are morally sound. Similarly, British historian Tony Judt has said that because of the existence of the Jewish state, "non-Israeli Jews feel themselves once again exposed to criticism and vulnerable to attack."[91] Translation: Israel is an evil that must be purged from the earth – for the sake of the Jews. If Israel is bad for Jews, however, it is bad for Jews who wish to rid themselves of their Jewishness. And a Jew can rid him- or herself of Jewishness only by getting rid of other Jews. Therefore, the Jewish anti-Semite must also be an anti-Zionist: only with the elimination of the Jewish state can there be an elimination of the *other* Jews.

[87] Freud, *Moses and Monotheism*, 69.
[88] Neil J. Kressel, *"The Sons of Pigs and Apes": Muslim Antisemitism and the Conspiracy of Silence* (Washington, D.C.: Potomac Books, 2012), 103.
[89] Quoted in Alexander and Bogdanor, *The Jewish Divide over Israel*, xii.
[90] Ibid., xiii.   [91] Ibid., xv.

The Jewish "intellectuals" who indulge in Jewish anti-Zionism are legion. Among those in North America are Daniel Boyarin of Berkeley and Norman Finkelstein, formerly of DePaul University, who, according to Paul Bogdanor, "considers friends of Israel the moral equivalent of Gestapo torturers and mass murderers."[92] Michael Neumann, a philosophy professor at Trent University, is a particularly interesting example. Operating from the axiomatic assumption that the Jewish state is a criminal enterprise, he affirms that any Jew who does not explicitly condemn Israel is complicit in its crimes, and its primary crime, presumably, is its existence.[93] Reasoning rather like a Holocaust denier, Neumann declares, "I am not interested in the truth, or justice, or understanding, or anything else, except so far as it serves [the Palestinian cause]. If an effective strategy means that some truths about the Jews don't come to light, I don't care. If an effective strategy means encouraging reasonable anti-Semitism, or reasonable hostility to Jews, I also don't care. If it means encouraging vicious racist anti-Semitism, or the destruction of the State of Israel, I still don't care."[94] In Neumann's "I don't care" we see the mythologizing of the Palestinian that reflects a metaphysical facet of the Jewish anti-Zionist's anti-Semitism. As Mamet has said, "this engagement with the mythic (as opposed to the real) Palestinians allows ... an otherwise unpermitted race-hatred: anti-Semitism."[95] Not only is anti-Semitism now permitted, it is morally required. Afraid of being counted among the "evil Jews," says Manfred Gerstenfeld, the anti-Zionist Jews of academia "identify with the suffering of the Palestinians and belittle or explain their major crimes.... In effect these Jews say to the non-Jewish world: 'We are among the examples of the Jews you should like. We are the good Jews.'"[96] And since we are Jews we cannot be anti-Semitic.

Alexander and Bogdanor see a link between this mode of Jewish anti-Semitism and the age-old Jewish conversion to Christianity. "If conversion to Christianity is no longer ... required of Jews eager to play a special role as accusers of Jews," they explain, "the supersessionist Christian

---

[92] Paul Bogdanor, "Norman G. Finkelstein: Chomsky for Nazis," in Alexander and Bogdanor, *The Jewish Divide over Israel*, 135.

[93] See Alain Goldschläger, "The Canadian Campus Scene," in Manfred Gerstenfeld, ed. *Academics against Israel and the Jews* (Jerusalem: Jerusalem Center for Public Affairs, 2007), 157.

[94] Quoted in ibid., 157–158.   [95] Mamet, *The Wicked Son*, 84–85.

[96] Manfred Gerstenfeld, "Academic against Israel and the Jews," in Gerstenfeld, *Academics against Israel and the Jews*, 27.

worldview nevertheless lurks in the recesses of their brains. The mental universe of Israel's fiercest Jewish accusers is permeated by a messianic utopianism that depicts Israel as the Devil's very own experiment station, the one stumbling block impeding the arrival of a post-national new heaven and new earth, the one nation in the world whose 'right to exist' is considered a legitimate subject of debate."[97] The reference to conversion here is more revealing than Alexander and Bogdanor may realize, for it tells us that Jewish anti-Zionism is a matter that concerns the soul, and not just some sort of political or social positioning. In a word, it points toward the metaphysical origin of this manifestation of anti-Semitism as a longing for the purity, innocence, and redemption that come with being as God. Inasmuch as the Jewish state signifies a vertical dimension of history, as discussed in the previous chapter, it signifies the dimension of Torah. And if the soul is made of the commandments of Torah, as Jewish tradition maintains,[98] then Jewish anti-Zionism, like conversion to Christianity, is expressive of the Jew's hatred of his or her soul and the words of Torah that it contains, beginning with the warning that on the day we succumb to the temptation to be as God we surely die. For on that day we set out down the path to murder: if I am to be like God, then the other Jews must be like the devil, and the devil must be eliminated.

The metaphysical traces of Jewish anti-Zionism are especially evident in the systematic demonization of the Jewish state by the likes of Noam Chomsky, the author of the introduction to Robert Faurisson's *The Problem of the Gas Chambers*, who deems Israel "the devil state in the Middle East."[99] Thus, Chomsky projects on the Jew his own surrender to the devil's temptation to be as God. Promoting the anti-Semitic lie of a nefarious world Jewish conspiracy, Chomsky maintains that the Jewish state has been "part of an international terror network that also included Taiwan, Britain, Argentine neo-Nazis, and others"[100] and declares that the Jewish state is bent on a world domination that will surely lead to "a final solution from which few will escape."[101] In the post-Holocaust

---

[97] Alexander and Bogdanor, *The Jewish Divide over Israel*, xxi.
[98] See, e.g., Isaiah Horowitz, *The Generations of Adam*, trans. and ed. Miles Krassen (New York: Paulist Press, 1996), 99.
[99] See Paul Bogdanor, "The Devil State: Chomsky's War against Israel," in Alexander and Bogdanor, *The Jewish Divide over Israel*, 77.
[100] Noam Chomsky, *Middle East Illusions* (Lanham, Md.: Rowman & Littlefield, 2003), 179.
[101] See Noam Chomsky, *Fateful Triangle: United States, Israel and the Palestinians* (London: Pluto Press, 1999), 467–469.

context any reference to the final solution is an invocation not only of the Nazis' project to exterminate the Jews but also of the mythologized, transcendent Nazi evil that shows itself in their assault on God. And Chomsky's comparisons of Israel with Nazi Germany are numerous and unrelenting.[102] "In Chomsky's mental universe," Bogdanor observes, "there are few questions about Israel and the Middle East that cannot be resolved by equating Jews with Nazis,"[103] which amounts to equating Jews with the children of Satan, as anti-Semites have done over the centuries, from John Chrysostom to Sayyid Qutb.

Not surprisingly, Chomsky has his allies among the Israelis themselves. "I am indebted to several Israeli friends," he effuses, "for having provided me with a great deal of material."[104] Those friends include Marxist activist Dov Yirmiah, who says Israel is "a nation of vicious thugs, whose second nature is fire, destruction, death and ruin," and sociologist Baruch Kimmerling, who describes Israel as a *"Herrenvolk* Republic."[105] Then there is Jacob Talmon of the Hebrew University, who may have been Chomsky's inspiration for the demonization of Israel. He is "Israel's most respected historian," as Israeli philosopher and founder of the Shalem Center in Jerusalem Yoram Hazony describes him; Talmon is the man who asserted that "Israeli leaders who justified warfare on the grounds of national interest [survival of the Jews and the Jewish state] or historical rights were a throwback to the 'Devil's accomplices in the last two generations.'"[106] Perhaps the most notorious of Chomsky's Israeli cohorts, however, is Israel Shahak, the Hebrew University chemistry professor who refers to the late Lubavitcher Rebbe Menachem Mendel Schneerson (1902–1994) as the "Führer of Chabad."[107] He deems the Jewish state "the true successor of the Third Reich" and maintains that "most Jews throughout the world are undergoing a process of Nazification."[108] Note that it is not the Israeli but the Jew who embodies the Nazi evil. The point, therefore, is not

---

[102] See ibid., 141, 217, 230, 233, 240, 307, 333, 335, 390, 398, 404, 417.
[103] Bogdanor, "The Devil State: Chomsky's War against Israel," 78.
[104] Chomsky, *Fateful Triangle*, 3n.
[105] Paul Bogdanor, "Chomsky's Ayatollahs," in Alexander and Bogdanor, *The Jewish Divide over Israel*, 115–116.
[106] Yoram Hazony, *The Jewish State: The Struggle for Israel's Soul* (New York: Basic Books, 2001), 7.
[107] Israel Shahak, *Jewish History, Jewish Religion: The Weight of Three Thousand Years* (London: Pluto Press, 1997), 27.
[108] Quoted in Bogdanor, "Chomsky's Ayatollahs," 117.

political or national but metaphysical. Like the Christians who accused the Jews of being the devil's spawn, these anti-Zionist, Israeli anti-Semites mythologize the Jews into something monstrous. Like the Christian anti-Semites of old, Shahak accuses the Jews of worshiping Satan,[109] signaling the sort of conversion mindset that Alexander and Bogdanor refer to above.

Shahak's most well-known work is *Jewish History, Jewish Religion: The Weight of Three Thousand Years* (1997); in his endorsement on the cover of the book Chomsky writes, "Shahak is an outstanding scholar, with remarkable insight and depth of knowledge."[110] In the opening pages of his volume Shahak states that, like any imperialist state, "Israel aims at imposing a hegemony on other Middle Eastern states."[111] Therefore "Israel as a Jewish state constitutes a danger not only to itself and its inhabitants, but to all Jews and to all other peoples and states in the Middle East and beyond.... The danger [is] inherent in the Jewish character of the State of Israel."[112] *Inherent in the Jewish character*: whatever is inherent to the Jewish character belongs to the essence of the Jew, and essence cannot be altered. If both the Jewish character and the Jewish state are *inherently* imperialist and therefore *inherently* evil, then what must be done with them?

We have seen the profound influence that German Idealism has had on Jewish Jew hatred in the modern era; Hazony maintains that such an influence extends to Israeli anti-Zionist intellectuals, whose thinking is rooted in concepts that "have deep roots in German-Jewish anti-Zionist philosophy"[113] as found, for example, in this philosophy of the Kantian Hermann Cohen.[114] It is one thing, however, to be an anti-Zionist German Jew in the nineteenth century; it is quite another to be an anti-Zionist Israeli Jew in the post-Holocaust period. While the former seeks a place where the Jewish people may live among the nations, the latter espouses a view that aids and abets the destruction of the Jewish nation. Consistent with the thinking of the Enlightenment and Kant's assertion that "the euthanasia of Judaism is the pure moral religion,"[115] the discourse of the Israeli anti-Zionists is tinged with the moral indignation that characterizes the diatribes of other anti-Semites, even as they

---

[109] Shahak, *Jewish History, Jewish Religion*, 34.
[110] Quoted in Bogdanor, "Chomsky's Ayatollahs," 123.
[111] Shahak, *Jewish History, Jewish Religion*, 11.   [112] Ibid., 2.
[113] Hazony, *The Jewish State*, xxv.   [114] See Cohen, *Reason and Hope*, 33–35.
[115] Immanuel Kant, *Conflict of the Faculties*, trans. Mary J. Gregor (New York: Abaris, 1979), 95.

"wallow in a carnival of self-loathing," as Hazony puts it.[116] In an article published in *Haaretz* in 1994 Aharon Megged called it "the Israeli urge to suicide."[117] It is indeed a case of *ibed atzmo ladaat*.

The Jew hatred found in the work of those such as Hassan Nasrallah and Ruhullah Khomeini, who long for the destruction of the Jewish state, can be found among Jews who enjoy the protection of the Jewish state, as Megged laments: "Since the Six Day War, and at an increasing pace, we have witnessed a phenomenon which probably has no parallel in history: an emotional and moral identification by the majority of Israel's intelligentsia with people openly committed to our annihilation."[118] Openly committed to Israel's annihilation, they are devoutly committed to Israel's demonization. In his study Hazony points out, for example, that the renowned mathematician and scientist Yeshayahu Leibowitz of the Hebrew University "had no difficulty calling the Israeli armed forces 'Judeo-Nazis,' and declared that Israel would soon be engaging in the 'mass extermination and slaughter of the Arab population' and 'setting up concentration camps.'"[119] In a similar move, Yosef Agasy of Tel Aviv University compares Israel to Nazi Germany because, like the Nazis, Israel's interests are tied to a "phantom nation."[120] In other words, the notion of "the Jewish people" is just as empty and contrived as the notion of "the Aryan people." Not only does Israel operate under such an illusion, but, like Nazi Germany, it invokes the illusion to justify murderous actions. And, like Nazi Germany, the Jewish state is evil from its very inception and therefore *in its very essence*.

The demonization of the Jewish state takes other forms. From the beginning, says Israeli historian Benny Morris, "Zionism was a colonizing and expansionist ideology and movement" that stemmed from "the European colonist's mental obliteration of the 'natives'" and reduced the Arabs to "objects to be utilized when necessary," so that the entire Zionist enterprise was "tainted by a measure of moral dubiousness."[121] Zeev Sternhell, author of *The Founding Myths of Israel* (1986), and Yehuda Shenhav, a sociologist at Tel Aviv University, hold the same view.[122] Baruch Kimmerling equates Zionism with other forms of nineteenth-century colonialism driven by a kind of white supremacism.[123]

---

[116] Hazony, *The Jewish State*, 339.
[117] See ibid., 3–6.   [118] Alexander and Bogdanor, *The Jewish Divide over Israel*, xviii.
[119] Hazony, *The Jewish State*, 6.   [120] Ibid., 11–12.
[121] Benny Morris, *Righteous Victims: A History of the Zionist-Arab Conflict, 1881–1998* (New York: Vintage Books, 2001), 676–678.
[122] See Hazony, *The Jewish State*, 8–9.   [123] Ibid., 10.

As for Hebrew University sociologist Moshe Zimmermann, he pursues his anti-Semitic anti-Zionism further to maintain that (1) accusations leveled against the Jews in the Middle Ages, such as the blood libel and charges of desecrating the host, had some justification; (2) Zionism is responsible for bringing anti-Semitism to the Middle East; and (3) Zionists exploit Holocaust victims for their own purposes.[124] Like his academic compatriots, Israeli sculptor Yigal Tumarkin has said, "When I see the black-coated *haredim* with the children they spawn, I can understand the Holocaust."[125] Tanya Reinhart, professor emeritus from Tel Aviv University, describes Israeli policy in the territories as "slow and steady genocide,"[126] once again accusing the Jews of perpetrating the very horrors that they suffered.

In the diatribes of these great minds we see the sophisticated demonization of Israel and the Jews through the pretentious machinations of an academic jargon calculated to project every evil on the Jews. To equate Zionism with colonialism and expansionism, with the "obliteration" of natives, and with the reduction of others to little more than raw material is to cast it in the mold of irremissible evil. Indeed, what evil is more heinous than the white supremacism known as apartheid? Here the Jews are not the victims of anti-Semitism – they are the source of it, and these intellectuals will have no part of anti-Semitism, any more than they will have any part of genocide! For the genocidal, racist, colonial anti-Semites are surely to be counted among the damned. Much of the world – including and especially the academic world – divides humanity into the damned and the saved, with the Jews and all things Jewish invariably relegated to the former category. Realizing this, the anti-Semitic Israeli academics clamber to find their place among the saved by turning their country and their fellow Jews over to the self-righteous vitriol of an anti-Semitic world.

When Lévinas states that the Jewish state "will be religious or it will not be at all,"[127] he is affirming a metaphysical dimension of the Jewish state that has a bearing on the metaphysical aspect of the human being,

[124] Ibid., 11.

[125] Quoted in Edward Alexander, "Israelis against Themselves," in Alexander and Bogdanor, *The Jewish Divide over Israel*, 36.

[126] See Tanya Reinhart and Jon Elmer, "A Slow, Steady Genocide," *Z Magazine/Z Net*, 11 September 2003, available at http://cosmos.ucc.ie/cs1064/jabowen/IPSC/php/art.php?aid=4278.

[127] Emmanuel Lévinas, *Difficult Freedom: Essays on Judaism*, trans. Sean Hand (Baltimore, Md.: Johns Hopkins University Press, 1990), 219.

beginning with the Jew. The Jew's anti-Zionism is rooted in a certain rebellion against the Zion from which the Torah goes forth, against the Torah that comes from the Holy One, and against the holiness that lies at the core of the Jew's humanity. In its anti-Zionist mode Jewish anti-Semitism is characterized not only by a usurpation of the One who chose the land for His people, but also by a rejection of everything that goes into making the Jew who he or she is: a human being created in the image and likeness of the Holy One and chosen for the task of attesting to the sanctity of every human being. Thus, the one who succumbs to this anti-Zionist Jewish Jew hatred renders his or her soul *Judenrein* – purified of the taint of Jewishness and Judaism. And of all the Jews, none is more tainted than the Israeli Jew. Yet the latter's "taint" is in truth his or her salvation. It is the salvation of all Jews and, through the Jews, of all humanity.

A CLOSING THOUGHT: THE SUICIDAL INSANITY OF JEWISH JEW HATRED

It may seem at first glance that Israeli anti-Zionists are as delusional as Holocaust deniers in their denial of the Palestinians' avowal of a desire to annihilate the Jewish state. Indeed, there appears to be something delusional, if not psychotic, about Jewish Jew hatred. But the reasons behind their denial of the danger are much the same as the reasons behind the denier's denial of the Holocaust. Both are rooted in the deicidal desire to rid the world of Jewish teaching, testimony, and tradition, a desire that lurks in the soul of each of us. While the existence of the Jewish state may place the Jews of the world in a certain danger, the Jews of the world need the Jewish state as much as they need the Sabbath in order to be who they are. For Jerusalem is to space what the Sabbath is to time. And in a very important sense, a Jew can desecrate, as well as consecrate, both as no other can. Jewish Jew hatred is Sabbath hatred; it is Jerusalem hatred. Both *Sabbath* and *Jerusalem* are counted among the names of God (see *Zohar* II, 88b; *Talmud Bavli, Bava Batra* 75b). Jews who trade the Torah and the Sabbath for the delusions of modernity engage in a desecration not only of Torah and the Sabbath but also of the divine image within their own souls. Therefore those who endure the dangers that come with the rejection of modernity's promises must take up the task of the consecration of the Torah and the Sabbath.

For a Jew, God and Torah and Covenant are most fundamentally remembered in the remembrance of the Sabbath, where the commandment first to remember (Exodus 20:8) and then to observe (Deuteronomy 5:12) is actually a single commandment, as the Talmud teaches: *zakhor veshamor bedibur echad* – "remember and observe – remember and watch over – were given in a single word" (*Rosh Hashanah* 27a). According to the Midrash, the observance of this commandment is equivalent to the observance of all the commandments (*Shemot Rabbah* 25:12; see also *Zohar* II, 47a). Why? Because, says the eighteenth-century sage Chayim ben Attar, Sabbath observance is the highest repudiation of idolatry (*Or HaChayim* on Exodus 34:18). If, as Nehemia Polen has argued, the Nazis' idolatry was manifest in their determination to destroy the Sabbath,[128] the same may be said of modernity's idolatry. One way, then, for Jews to most fundamentally oppose Jewish Jew hatred is to remember and watch over the Sabbath. For the point of this remembrance and observance is to make room for holiness in the world. Abraham Joshua Heschel states it well when he says, "To the philosopher the idea of the good is the most exalted idea. But to the Bible the idea of the good is penultimate; it cannot exist without the holy."[129] As the Maharal of Prague has taught, the six days of creation correspond to the six directions of space in the material world; the seventh day corresponds to the holy, which gives meaning to the other six.[130]

Perhaps here we have the key to a prayer that Jews recite every Sabbath during the morning services. Praying Psalm 34, they recall the time when King David feigned madness in order to save himself from the Philistine king Avimelekh. The Psalm opens with the words *leDavid, beshanoto et tamo*, that is, "A Psalm of David, when he feigned madness." The literal translation of *beshanoto et tamo*, however, is "when he changed his understanding," that is, when he altered his "judgment" or "discernment." David feigned madness in order to escape being trapped and murdered by the Philistines. In the modern and postmodern world, we too may feign madness or alter our discernment in order to make our way in a world gone mad. Indeed the word for "weekday," *chol*, is also the word for "sick." But on the Sabbath we recite King David's psalm

[128] Nehemia Polen, *The Holy Fire: The Teachings of Rabbi Kalonymus Kalman Shapira* (Northvale, N.J.: Jason Aronson, 1999), 20.

[129] Abraham Joshua Heschel, *God in Search of Man* (New York: Farrar, Straus and Giroux, 1955), 17.

[130] From *Gevurot Hashem*, 46, cited in Pinhas H. Peli, *The Jewish Sabbath: A Renewed Encounter* (New York: Schocken Books, 1988), 11–12. See also Avraham Yaakov Finkel, *Kabbalah: Selections from Classic Kabbalistic Works from Raziel HaMalach to the Present Day* (Southfield, Mich.: Targum Press, 2002), 152.

so as to remind ourselves of that madness. Otherwise we may slip into the suicidal insanity of Jewish Jew hatred. Indeed, there are times when we have gone mad without realizing it – that is the difference between us and King David: we have come to think like the Egyptians, the Philistines, the Greeks, and the Romans – like the anti-Semites – without noticing it. Taking on their cleverness, we suppose we are crazy like a fox, when in fact we are merely crazy.

It is not for nothing that central to the remembrance of the Sabbath is the remembrance not only of the creation but also of the deliverance from Egypt. The difficulty facing a Jew today is to emerge from the Egyptian darkness, a wood that is lovely, dark, and deep in its seductions. Jews who have succumbed to the seductions of Jewish Jew hatred live in a realm in which they have lost the Sabbath, and the madness that overcomes them is no longer feigned. They have become "like the others," enamored of the modern and postmodern deception. It is the suicidal insanity of "Judaicide," as André Neher calls it, which they can no longer recognize, as they are no longer a people apart.[131] It is a dismantling of the Jewish soul, a purging of the soul of its "Jewish gene," which in the end is a purging of the soul of its "human gene." What being Jewish has to do with being human I examine in the next and final chapter.

[131] André Neher, *They Made Their Souls Anew*, trans. David Maisel (Albany: SUNY Press, 1990), 33.

9

Sounding the Depths of the Anti-Semitic Soul: Arthur Miller's *Focus*

There comes a time when one cannot be a man without assuming the Jewish condition.

Elie Wiesel, *A Beggar in Jerusalem*

While acknowledging some of the distinctive features of the self-hatred reflected in Jewish anti-Semitism, Sander Gilman also notes that "its deep structure is universal."[1] Indeed, it is as deep and as universal as the human soul in which anti-Semitism has its metaphysical origins. From Bernard Lazare to Hannah Arendt, from Jean-Paul Sartre to Perez Bernstein, one reason many of the analyses of anti-Semitism thus far have proven to be less than adequate is that its metaphysical origins elude a speculative analysis rooted in ontological contingencies. A sense of the metaphysical origins of anti-Semitism requires symbol and simile, so that where the life of the soul is concerned, artistic renditions are often called for, and, arguably, the most adequate art form to meet this particular task is literature. In the *Sifre* on Deuteronomy 11:22 it is written: "If you wish to recognize the One who spoke and brought the world into being, learn Aggadah for in Aggadah you will find God." Similarly, if we wish to sound the depths of the metaphysical origins of anti-Semitism, in the end we must turn to a kind of aggadah or storytelling: we must turn to literature. In literature we may discover what eludes philosophical investigation or psychological examination. Guided by the poetics of myth and metaphor, literature has the capacity

---

[1] Sander L. Gilman, *Jewish Self-Hatred: Anti-Semitism and the Hidden Language of the Jews* (Baltimore, Md.: Johns Hopkins University Press, 1986), 1.

for opening up the metaphysical. In the case at hand it has the capacity for sounding the depths of the anti-Semitic soul.

And so in this final chapter we turn to the literary representation of the anti-Semite in Arthur Miller's novel *Focus*. In doing so, we move from the confines of the theologians, philosophers, and ideologues – from the echelons of the intellectual elite in society – to the deep structure of the universal in which every soul shares in the soul of Adam. Thus we address a question that may have already occurred to the reader: "I can see that in certain cases various highly sophisticated thinkers may have indulged in Jew hatred from a desire to get rid of God in order to become as God. But what about the everyday anti-Semite who lacks such erudition? Do his or her thoughts, desires, and ambitions really run as deep as those of John Chrysostom or Immanuel Kant? Might not his or her anti-Semitism simply be the product of base envy or bad upbringing?" The question is altogether legitimate. In *Focus* Arthur Miller (1915–2005) provides a most profound response.

Focus is Miller's only novel. It was originally published by Reynal and Hitchcock, a publishing house based in New York, on 30 October 1945; in 2001 the film version starring William Macy appeared. Miller relates that when he was working in the Brooklyn Navy Yard during the war, he heard fellow workers blame the Jews for dragging the United States into the conflict,[2] which disturbed him deeply and led him to reflect on why this was the case. With a deep "sense of emergency,"[3] he says, he wrote the novel at a time when "a sensible person could wonder" whether the Jews had a right to exist.[4] The anti-Semites "fear the Jew, as they fear the real," says Miller. "And perhaps this is why it is too much to expect a true end of anti-Semitic feelings. In the mirror of reality, of the unbeautiful world, it is hardly reassuring and requires much strength of character to look and see oneself."[5] Why does looking into our own soul require so much strength? Because in each of us there is a trace of the anti-Semite who fears to see that he or she is implicated in relation to his or her neighbor. We fear that gaze as Dorian Gray fears to gaze on his portrait. Therefore the implications run far deeper than the social, deeper even than Miller himself may have realized: to look into the mirror and thus confront the real is to behold the metaphysical origins of anti-Semitism within each of us.

[2] Arthur Miller, *Focus* (New York: Penguin Books, 2001), v.   [3] Ibid., vi.
[4] Ibid., vii.   [5] Ibid., x.

This is not to suggest that delving into the soul of the anti-Semite means slipping into the ethereal realm of abstraction; just the opposite. Understood from a Jewish perspective, the soul is not distinct from the body but has its concrete, flesh-and-blood aspect at the level of *nefesh*, which is the physical aspect of the soul, where the soul merges with the body. It is written in the Torah, for example, that the *nefesh* is in the blood (Leviticus 17:11), so that "the Bible," Abraham Joshua Heschel explains, "knows neither the dichotomy of body and soul nor the trichotomy of body, soul, spirit, nor [even] the trichotomy within the soul [as per the Greek tripartite model]."[6] Because *nefesh* is just such a fusing of body and soul, Job could cry out, "From my flesh shall I behold Godliness" (Job 19:26); indeed, if we cannot see Godliness from the flesh and in the flesh, we cannot see it at all. This concrete understanding of the soul is part of the teaching that the soul has five levels or dimensions (see *Zohar* II, 94b),[7] a teaching that brings together the physical and the metaphysical, maintaining that each requires the other in order to exist. As the physical aspect of the soul, *nefesh* is what imparts to life its gravity. It provides life with ballast, thus enabling us to keep our feet on the ground, lest we forget the plight of our neighbor in some mystical flight of ecstasy. At the level of *nefesh* life grows heavy, but heavy with meaning.

The concrete fusion of the physical and metaphysical aspects of the soul takes place in the human face, as the great sage of the Talmud, Rabbi Akiva, maintained; in the face, he taught, lies the image of the Holy One,[8] a point that should be kept in mind as we examine the significance of the face in Miller's novel, where the face plays a pivotal role. Therefore, before delving into the novel itself, a few words must be said about the face. It will prove to be a key not only to understanding the novel but also to fathoming the metaphysical origins of anti-Semitism.

THE METAPHYSICS OF THE FACE

A good place to begin a Jewish analysis of the metaphysics of the face is with the Hebrew word for "face," *panim*, which is plural. Why is it

---

[6] Abraham Joshua Heschel, *The Prophets*, vol. 2 (New York: Harper & Row, 1975), 37.

[7] The five levels of the soul are *nefesh*, which is the animating spark of life; *ruach*, which is spirit or the emotional level of the soul; *neshamah*, or the level of intellect and understanding; *chayah*, which is the life force of the soul; and *yechidah*, or the point of union between the soul and the Holy One.

[8] See Louis Finkelstein, *Akiba: Scholar, Saint and Martyr* (New York: Atheneum, 1981), 103.

plural? Because, according to one tradition, each of us has two faces: the face of Adam, who came from the hand and mouth of God, and our own individual face. The face, therefore, is both universal and particular, both transcendent and immanent, both hidden and exposed. As the cognate Hebrew word *penim*, which means "inside" or "interior," suggests, the face is the exposure of the utterly interior *as* interior, without the loss of interiority. This exposure is nothing less than the revelation of a fundamental responsibility that cannot be circumvented, and this is what it means to be irreplaceable: only I can meet this concrete responsibility here and now for this human being. Only I can help. Revealed both from within and from beyond the face, it is a responsibility that precedes every response: I am chosen *already* for this responsibility that I have *yet* to meet, so that the face and the future are of a piece. This *already* is precisely what constitutes the *between* space of the human relation: in this between space of human relation the soul draws its breath from the Holy One. To be sure, according to the Torah, God speaks from the depths of the space *between* the two cherubim who sit face-to-face atop the Ark of the Covenant (Exodus 25:20–22): situated above the tablets of Torah, this between space of the face-to-face is higher than even the Torah itself.

Announcing a *between* that is also *within*, the face eludes the projects of comprehension and possession that preoccupy the perceiving self: nothing that meets the eye belongs to the face. As Emmanuel Lévinas states it, "the best way of encountering the Other is not even to notice the color of his eyes!"[9] And yet the Hebrew word for "eye," *ayin*, can also mean "face." If we behold the sanctity of the other human being by looking beyond what meets the eye, it is because that sanctity emanates from the eyes. "Those eyes," writes Lévinas, "which are absolutely without protection, the most naked part of the human body, none the less offer an absolute resistance to possession, an absolute resistance in which the temptation to murder is inscribed: the temptation of absolute negation."[10] This absolute resistance to possession on the part of the most vulnerable is a revelation of the hidden *as* hidden, forever inviolate. If the *in* of the Infinite is "both *non-* and *within*," as Lévinas has said, the face is precisely a manifestation of that Infinite that is "both *non-* and

---

[9] Emmanuel Lévinas, *Ethics and Infinity*, trans. Richard A. Cohen (Pittsburgh, Pa.: Duquesne University Press, 1985), 85.

[10] Emmanuel Lévinas, *Difficult Freedom: Essays on Judaism*, trans. Sean Hand (Baltimore, Md.: Johns Hopkins University Press, 1990), 8.

within."[11] It is *non-* because it is not part of the mute and indifferent landscape of being. It is a *within* that is also an *above*: the height manifest from within the face is the height that "ordains being."[12] Ordaining being, the face imparts meaning to a concrete, flesh-and-blood reality that is otherwise meaningless. That is what makes the appearance of the face a revelation of the otherwise than being: being can be "ordained" only by what is otherwise than being.

The *or panim*, the "light of the face," is precisely the injunction of the *or Torah*, the "light of Torah." To encounter the face, in other words, is to encounter the commanding Voice of Torah and, through Torah, the Holy One Himself. "*The face of man is the proof of the existence of God*," declares Lévinas. "Clearly the concern here is not with deductive proof, but with the very dimension of the divine (the monotheistic divine) disclosing itself in that *odd configuration of lines that make up the human face. It is in the human face that ... the trace of God is manifested, and the light of revelation inundates the universe.*"[13] Through the face of the other, God commands us to be there for the sake of the other, beginning with the prohibition against murder, as we have seen repeatedly. That is why the anti-Semite *must* blind him- or herself to the human face of the Jew in his or her assault on the Jew: obliterating the human face, the anti-Semite obviates the prohibition against murdering the human being, which is perquisite to becoming as the Holy One.

Because the human face signifies the holiness of the Holy One, "the face is signification, and signification *without context*," as Lévinas insists. "I mean that the Other, in the rectitude of his face, is not a character within a context. Ordinarily,... the meaning of something is in its relation to another thing. Here, to the contrary, the face is meaning all by itself."[14] This is what it means to say that the face is not another fixture in the landscape of being; the ontological landscape, rather, is illuminated by the light of the face. Indeed, without this meaning beyond context, without this absolute, that enters this world through the flesh-and-blood soul embodied in the face, this world has no meaning; it is simply there, mute and indifferent. The face breaks through this

[11] Emmanuel Lévinas, *Of God Who Comes to Mind*, trans. Bettina Bergo (Stanford, Calif.: Stanford University Press, 1998), 63.

[12] Emmanuel Lévinas, *Collected Philosophical Papers*, trans. Alphonso Lingis (Dordrecht: Nijhoff, 1987), 100.

[13] Emmanuel Lévinas, *Proper Names*, trans. Michael B. Smith (Stanford, Calif.: Stanford University Press, 1996), 95; emphasis in the original.

[14] Lévinas, *Ethics and Infinity*, 86–87; emphasis added.

mute indifference by commanding us to be there for the sake of another with a cry of "Here I am for you" that *"testifies* to the Infinite."[15] Hence the commandment of the face is the appearance of a metaphysical absolute in the midst of ontological contingency. Because the face thus has meaning without context, it imparts meaning to every context, to every instance, of human relation. When Elie Wiesel's character, the poet Paltiel Kossover, writes, "The hungry child, the thirsty stranger, the frightened old man all ask for me,"[16] we do not have to ask, "Which child, which stranger, which old man?" in order to grasp what is said.

Left only with contextual signs and cultural conventions, we lose both word and meaning and are turned over to a sound and fury signifying nothing. That is where we lose our humanity, our sanctity, and our significance because we lose the absolutely commanded relation that makes us who we are. If, as Lévinas says, "the face as *à-Dieu* is the latent birth of meaning,"[17] it is because with the revelation of the absolute prohibition, the face declares an absolute responsibility that we forever have *yet* to fulfill. Indeed, the more we respond, the more responsible we become: the debt increases in the measure that it is paid. Therefore the face is disarming and unsettling. And the Jew whose very presence affirms this to be so is most unsettling indeed: the Jew disturbs the sleep of our solipsistic indifference. And we must have our sleep, a point that will prove to be especially salient in our analysis of Miller's *Focus*.

Symbolic of the arousal from sleep is the rite of morning prayer, when Jews don their *tallit* and *tefillin*, their prayer shawl and the leather straps around the arm and head, to step before the countenance. At what hour in the morning, the rabbis ask, shall a Jew put on his *tefillin*? The answer: when it is light enough for him to recognize the face of his neighbor (*Kitzur Shulchan Arukh* 10:2). If you cannot behold the face of your neighbor, you cannot enter into a relation with the Holy One. Indeed, before Jews pray each morning, they declare, "I take upon myself the commandment to love my neighbor as myself." To don *tefillin* is to affirm that there is no Torah without the face, no face without the Torah. Putting on *tefillin*, then, is no mere ritual; far more than that, it is, in the words of Lévinas, the confirmation of "the conception of God in which

---

[15] Ibid., 106.

[16] Elie Wiesel, *The Testament*, trans. Marion Wiesel (New York: Summit Books, 1981), 38.

[17] Lévinas, *Of God Who Comes to Mind*, 168.

He is welcomed in the face-to-face with the other, in the obligation towards the other."[18] As it is written in the *Mekilta*, "when one welcomes his fellow man, it is considered as if he had welcomed the Divine Presence" (*Mekilta, Amalek* 3), and to welcome another is *kidem et panim*, literally to "welcome the face." To welcome another is to greet the face with a face, face to face, *nefesh* to *nefesh*. Anything less than a welcome, anything less than kindness shown toward another, is not only a betrayal but a failure to fathom the holiness that the face signifies. Which means: we have failed to be who we are. Who is the anti-Semite? He is one who has failed to be who he is: a human being created in the divine image who is commanded absolutely to *act* on an absolute responsibility to and for the other.

The commanding Voice that reverberates from the face transmits a teaching and a testimony. Hence, in the words of Lévinas, "the presence of the Other is a presence that teaches."[19] In the *Pirke Avot* it is written, "Who is wise? He who learns from every person" (4:1). Everyone who has a face has something to teach, from an infant to an Alzheimer's patient, since in every face there is holiness and commandment. "For Judaism," writes Lévinas, "the world becomes intelligible before a human face, and not, as for a great contemporary philosopher who sums up an important aspect of the West, through houses, temples, and bridges."[20] Only where we come face to face with an inherent dearness in the flesh-and-blood face of the other human being do we discover a presence that transcends our thinking and our being and that lays absolute claim to us. If "Being" is all there is, then only the will to power can determine value, so that we possess the world by conquering, controlling, and building. Here the message is that there is no message; there is only our inner resolve, which alone justifies us, as Heidegger insisted.[21] With such a move, the flesh-and-blood soul of the other is rendered meaningless, except as an object that we appropriate, exploit, and oppress. And our own souls are rendered deaf to the outcry and blind to the face of the

---

[18] Emmanuel Lévinas, "Revelation in the Jewish Tradition," trans. Sarah Richmond, in *The Levinas Reader*, ed. Sean Hand (Oxford: Basil Blackwell, 1989), 204.

[19] Emmanuel Lévinas, *Outside the Subject*, trans. Michael B. Smith (Stanford, Calif.: Stanford University Press, 1994), 148.

[20] Lévinas, *Difficult Freedom*, 23. The "great contemporary philosopher" is, of course, Martin Heidegger; see, e.g., Martin Heidegger, *Poetry, Language, Thought*, trans. Albert Hofstadter (New York: HarperCollins, 2001), 141–160.

[21] See Martin Heidegger, *Sein und Zeit*, 2nd ed. (Tübingen: Max Niemeyer, 1963), 322.

other human being – a point that, as we shall see, is crucial to an understanding of Arthur Miller's *Focus*.

THE LITERARY INSIGHT INTO THE ANTI-SEMITE

When Arthur Miller's novel came out in 1945, it was not particularly well received; Charles Poore reviewed it unfavorably in the *New York Times*, as did Saul Bellow in *The New Republic*.[22] In fact, according to Miller's biographer Martin Gottfried, most academic critics have taken the playwright's attempt to try his hand at a novel to be "unworthy of serious study."[23] One exception is Leonard Moss, who, in his analysis of the novel's main character Lawrence Newman, notes that Miller "focuses upon the individual rather than upon the illusory abstraction."[24] This is, indeed, the strength of Miller's penetration into the soul of the anti-Semite: drawing on everyday contemporary life, he lays bare the face-to-face relation that the anti-Semite fears most. It is a flesh-and-blood relation laden with an ethical injunction that no abstraction can yield and from which the anti-Semite flees in fear. Moss falls a bit short, however, in his view that Miller's aim is to show that even a person "of small intelligence may experience moral regeneration."[25] Moral "regeneration" is not a matter of intelligence; it is a matter of realizing that we are chosen for an absolute ethical responsibility, a matter of assuming the Jewish condition.

C. W. E. Bigsby is closer to the mark when he observes that Newman has "no clear awareness of his own identity, indeed no clear identity. He is self-enclosed, with no great interest in others."[26] This self-enclosure is indicative of the self-centered autonomy that we all crave but in the end proves to be as unreal as the reflection in the pool peering back at Narcissus. In the pages that follow it is shown that, as he is drawn out of his isolation and into a human relation, Newman is drawn ever more deeply into the Jewish condition, where he discovers his true identity as the one who is responsible for the other, *I more than the others*. Bigsby realizes as much when he notes that the character ultimately assumes such a condition "not merely in refusing to dissociate himself from Finkelstein

---

[22] Martin Gottfried, *Arthur Miller: His Life and His Work* (Cambridge, Mass.: Da Capo Press, 2006), 89–90.

[23] Ibid., 90.   [24] Leonard Moss, *Arthur Miller* (Boston: Twayne Publishers, 1980), 15.

[25] Ibid., 17.

[26] C. W. E. Bigsby, *Arthur Miller: A Critical Study* (Cambridge, U.K.: Cambridge University Press, 200), 68.

[the Jew in the novel] but in accepting moral responsibility for a world not of his own making."[27] Accepting that responsibility, Newman comes to realize a condition of chosenness, which is the opposite of the Heideggerian condition of thrownness.[28] Whereas the former summons the soul to an ethical relation to another human being, the latter locks the self into a solipsistic self-deception, where it tries to muster a counterfeit resolve for "being-toward-death," rather than answer to its responsibility for the death of the other human being. I examine in detail what it means for Newman not only to recognize such a responsibility but to realize that he is *already* responsible, whether he recognizes it or not. Although Bigsby rightly refers to *Focus* as "an act of courage,"[29] one shortcoming in his analysis is where he asserts that "Miller was effectively asking whether what happened in Europe could be replicated in America."[30] In my view, Miller raises a question that runs much deeper than the contingencies of American mores. He sets out to determine what the anti-Semite is against and why. In doing so, he sounds the depths of the soul of the anti-Semite in ways that confront each of us with the first question put to the first man, the true Jewish question: Where are you?

This is the unsettling question that shakes us from the sleep of our complacent indifference. Significantly, Miller's novel was originally titled *Some Shall Not Sleep*, calling to mind a teaching from the Midrash: "The beginning of a man's downfall is sleep" (*Bereshit Rabbah* 17:5). The novel opens, in fact, with Lawrence Newman, an average guy in an average New York neighborhood, awakened from his sleep by a woman's cry for help outside his open window; his sleep having been so disturbed, he "regretted having left it open so wide."[31] He had been dreaming about an empty carousel going round and round, moving rapidly yet going nowhere, a dream, no doubt, indicative of the aimlessness of his preoccupation with himself. The woman whose cry woke Newman from his dream was being attacked by a man whom Newman thought he recognized. In a pitiful, frantic attempt to renounce his responsibility, he convinced himself that her Spanish accent meant "that she was abroad at night for no good purpose."[32] Like every anti-Semite, Newman justifies his flight from the demands of the transcendent by turning his own guilt onto the victim who calls out to him: she is a stranger, and a stranger must be up to no good. And yet the Torah that enters the world through

---

[27] Ibid., 71.
[28] See, e.g., Heidegger, *Sein und Zeit*, 337–340.   [29] Bigsby, *Arthur Miller*, 75.
[30] Ibid., 73.   [31] Miller, *Focus*, 1.   [32] Ibid., 3.

the Jews commands us thirty-six times to love and care for the stranger as one of our own, because in truth there are no strangers – there are only children of the Holy One.

Pleading for help, "weeping into the darkness around her," the woman tries to make her way toward Newman's house. Only "twenty yards from her," he "could hear the frantic breath rushing out of her body as she screamed for the police. She turned in the direction of his window now.... Newman quickly stepped back into his room,"[33] terrified by the wordless cry of the soul, the *neshamah*, the frantic *breath* that singled him out. "Awakened rudely from his sleep, he thought he saw her eyes. The whites were bright against the dark skin, and she was darting helpless glances at his and all the other houses from which people were undoubtedly watching her. But he backed away from the window, the woman screaming '*Police! Police!*' in her accent."[34] Recall what Lévinas points out above about the naked vulnerability of the eyes and how the eyes of the other summon me to an absolute responsibility that only I can meet. Thus her helpless eyes gaze into his soul to reveal what Lévinas calls "the exigency of the holy,"[35] which is precisely the need of the other that singles me out. As we probe deeper into the novel, keep in mind that Newman's eyesight is good enough to see the whites of her eyes. He flees from her outcry not because he has poor eyesight, but precisely because his eyesight is quite good. It is good enough to behold the revelation that emanates from her face: that is why he hides, like the first human being who hid from the cry of "Where are you?" In Newman we behold the adamic anti-Semite in each of us who longs to hide, offering the excuse of "I was afraid." Afraid of what? Afraid of the responsibility that devolves on me and thus deposes the sovereignty of my ego.

The next morning the anti-Semite in Newman stirs when he goes to buy his newspaper from Mr. Finkelstein, the Jew who runs the shop down the street. As he paid for the newspaper, he was "careful not to touch the man's hands," as "he fancied a certain odor of old cooking coming from Mr. Finkelstein. He did not want to touch the odor,"[36] indicating the abstraction, the invisibility, of the category *Jew*: just as there is no touching an odor, there is no touching the Jew. Chatting then with his next-door neighbor Fred, Newman listens to him rail against Mr. Finkelstein, thinking, "You wished he would speak more softly, but you somehow wanted him to go on for he said things you felt and dared not say."[37]

---

[33] Ibid., 2.   [34] Ibid., 3.   [35] Lévinas, *Ethics and Infinity*, 105.
[36] Miller, *Focus*, 6.   [37] Ibid., 11.

Fred knows very well that their neighbor Petey was the one who attacked the woman with the "accent." But he informs Newman that first they will "clean out" the Jews and then take care of the "Spics,"[38] confirming that what befalls humanity befalls the Jews first. Taking the subway to work, Newman notices some graffiti inscribed on a pillar in the subway station: *Kikes started the WAR* and *Kill kikes.* "He stood unmoving, caught. Nothing he ever read gripped him so powerfully as did these scrawled threats. To him they were a kind of mute record that the city automatically inscribed in her sleep; a secret newspaper publishing what the people really thought."[39] Yes, caught, seized, and summoned. These words expose anti-Semitism precisely as a call to murder, exposing a secret that resides in the human being who has traded his soul for the promises of the city. Perhaps it is no coincidence that the first murderer was the first to build a city (Genesis 4:17). The city is the embodiment of the new Moloch of modernity, to whom the Jews are offered up.

Newman works in the personnel division of a large business firm; he is a "people person." When he makes the mistake of hiring a woman who appears to be Jewish for the secretarial pool, his boss Mr. Gargan declares that she is "not our type of person" and orders Newman to get himself a pair of glasses, so that he will not make the same mistake again.[40] Fearing for his job security, as the anti-Semite in each of us longs for security, Newman complies and convinces himself that he is safe "because he had toed the line, done his duty, carried off the ceaseless indignities that came from above. He was safe."[41] Safe from what? From the outcry of the other. Safe because he got the glasses that would keep him from repeating the mistake of hiring a Jew, the glasses that blind him to the face of the other. When, however, he happened to gaze into his bathroom mirror – one of a multitude of mirrors in the novel – "he was looking at what might very properly be called the face of a Jew. A Jew, in effect, had gotten into his bathroom. The glasses did just what he feared they would do to his face."[42] And yet, transformed into a Jew, Newman is not simply made into the object of other people's contempt (although he becomes that); rather, he is transformed into a witness summoned to testify to the absolute responsibility that devolves on him from beyond. In a word, he now bears the task for which the Jews are chosen. He, of course, resists the perilous assignation.

[38] Ibid., 12.   [39] Ibid., 7.   [40] Ibid., 17.   [41] Ibid., 19.   [42] Ibid., 24.

Now able to "focus" properly, Newman is determined to demonstrate that he is not a Jew and that he will hire no Jews. Therefore when Gertrude Hart comes in to interview for a job, he decides immediately that she is a Jew, only to find that she has pegged him for a Jew. As he was interviewing her, "a fright was coming over him and he did not know why. There was something ... in the way she sat so angrily confident waiting for him to reply. She was not moving, glaring at him.... The intimacy ... that's what frightened him ... yes, the intimacy was new. Her malevolence was intimate. She sat there as though she knew everything about him, as though ... She was taking him for a Jew."[43] As it always happens, what we most fear will be disclosed about ourselves is not some absurd lie but the most intimate truth of who we are. And we hate anyone who sees who we are in truth; that is why the anti-Semite hates the Jew. Therefore when Gertrude takes him for a Jew, he hates her for it. He hates her because he is, in a sense, a self-hating Jew. "He sat there unable to speak to her through his hate. And yet the perspiration on the palms of his hands was to him the sign of embarrassment also, for he was polite to an extreme and he could not say that he was not Jewish without coloring the word with his repugnance for it, and thus for her. And in his inability to speak, in his embarrassment she seemed to see conclusive proof, and strangely – quite insanely – he helplessly conceded that it was almost proof. For him Jew had always meant imposter."[44] Newman, of course is an imposter, not because he is literally a Jew pretending not to be a Jew, but because he is a human being pretending not to be accountable.

Longing to be pure as only God can be pure (anti-Semitic movements are always purist movements), Newman's hatred of the Jews stirs within him "a sense of power and self-purification. Listening to reports of their avarice insensibly brought him closer to an appreciation of his own liberality, which seemed proven by the simple fact that he was not a Jew. And when he encountered an open-handed Jew his own parsimonious nature was outraged, and since he saw all men only through his own eyes, in the Jew's open-handedness he saw only trickery or self-display. Pretenders, imposters."[45] Thus in the abstract object of his Jew hatred Newman sees only the concrete evil within himself, as he himself secretly realizes: "He was sitting there in the guilt of the fact that the evil nature of the Jews and their numberless deceits, especially their sensuous lust for women – of which he had daily proof in the dark folds of their eyes

---

[43] Ibid., 32.   [44] Ibid., 33.   [45] Ibid.

and their swarthy skin – all were reflections of his own desires with which he had invested them."[46] The power he feels in his Jew hatred is the power to decide good and evil, and the self-purification comes in the projection of all the evil within himself onto the Jew. His hatred grows when he is demoted because he now looks like a Jew; rather than take the demotion, however, he resigns from his position, only to have trouble finding another job because, yes, he looks like a Jew.

Meanwhile, as bent as Newman is on proving he is not a Jew, Fred is bent on driving the Jew Finkelstein from the neighborhood. One morning Newman goes to purchase his newspaper from Finkelstein only to discover that Fred has brought in another vendor across the street. Newman decides to buy from the new vendor, but as he listens to Fred's slurs against the Jews, he cannot bring himself to chime in. "Why couldn't he say something, any of the things he had so often said to himself about the Jews?" he chides himself.[47] Developing his own suspicions about Newman, Fred later asks him if he killed anyone during his service in the First World War. Newman tells his neighbor that, yes, he did kill a man, wondering "why he should feel this fright at Fred's sudden fascination with his killing."[48] Notice that Fred's measure of the fellow anti-Semite is the willingness to engage in killing. Although Fred is far too boorish to know anything of philosophy, the author is not: the Hegelian dialectic that leads to the synthesis of man and God into the mangod requires not only killing but the abrogation of the absolute, divine prohibition against murder. On some level the anti-Semite, including someone as unschooled as Fred, understands this necessity very well.

Buying into this temptation to usurp the absolute, which is a temptation to power, Newman succumbs to a self-righteous hatred of Finkelstein, and as "he felt a strange power flowing into him, it was as though his very body were growing larger."[49] When he once again comes across an anti-Semitic slogan on the subway, "the tinge of embarrassment that would have disturbed him once did not occur this morning. This mute 'scene' – there were several of the Jewish brethren standing right under the card – brewed within him instead a small but undeniable tension of power."[50] To his delight, he spies a Jew, the target of the hatred written on the subway wall. "With an air of chieftaincy he turned his eyes among the passengers and found his Jew, and quite omnisciently raised his brows

[46] Ibid., 34.   [47] Ibid., 47.   [48] Ibid., 53.   [49] Ibid., 57.   [50] Ibid., 58–59.

with the pleasing awareness of man's stupidity – man who could sit so leisurely and calm while his very doom was written on the wall above his head."[51] And so by this time Newman's pitiful appropriation of the supposed "attributes" of God is laid bare: hating Jews gives him a sense of omnipotence, purity, and omniscience.

Ironically, Newman is on his way to a job interview with a certain Mr. Stevens, who will not consider him for an opening because he looks like a Jew. It occurs to him that he could present Stevens with his baptismal certificate, but, of course, Jew hatred has nothing to do with baptism:

In the old days in the glass cubicle no proof, no documents, no words would have changed the shape of a face he himself suspected. A face … His face…. *He* was not this face. Nobody has a right to dismiss him like that because of his face. Nobody! He was *him*, a human being with a certain definite history and he was not this face which looked like it had grown out of another alien and dirty history. They were trying to make two people out of him …! They dare not do that to him because he was no one else but Lawrence Newman …![52]

The face that had "grown out of another alien and dirty history" is the face of the holy transfigured into the demonic by the one who would be as God. If the face of the Jew bears a certain guilt, it is the projected guilt of the one who would be as God and who must therefore murder the Jew. Of course, Newman's preoccupation with the look of his face blinds him to the meaning of the face, as we realize when, instead of presenting a baptismal certificate, the next time Newman dropped by to see Fred he "began talking of the war and how he had killed the German."[53] Just as the German had been demonized and his killing thus justified, so is the Jew now demonized. And he must be killed.

How this projection works is revealed when Newman reflects on the change in his attitude toward Gertrude, who, having found work at another firm, manages to get Newman a job as well: "As a Jewess she had seemed dressed in cheap taste, too gaudily. But as a gentile he found her merely colorful in the same dress…. It was as though now she had a right to her faults…. As a Jewess she had seemed vitriolic and pushy and he had hated himself even as he was drawn fearfully to her."[54] As if seeking the ultimate justification of the anti-Semitism that lurks within him, Newman marries Gertrude, who is herself an anti-Semite. She adores Father Charles Coughlin, for example, the notorious Catholic priest whose virulently anti-Semitic radio broadcasts of the 1930s were

---

[51] Ibid., 59.
[52] Ibid., 66–67.   [53] Ibid., 68.   [54] Ibid., 83.

wildly popular. She also takes a liking to Fred, who is a member of the Coughlin-like Christian Front, and she urges Newman to join the organization in order to allay the growing suspicions among the neighbors that he is a Jew. How murderous her anti-Semitism is comes out when she and Newman are turned away from a restricted hotel, and she spews forth her desire for a Final Solution to the Jewish problem: "Why don't they take everybody and find out who's who and put the damned kikes off to themselves and settle it one and for all!"[55] She blames her husband for their being turned away, saying to him, "Why do you always let them make a Jew out of you?... Why didn't you tell him what you are?" adding, "Nobody makes a Jew out of me and gets away with it."[56] Of course, it is Newman who is making a Jew out of her by her association with him. And he will not get away with it.

When the Christian Front inevitably moves into the neighborhood to cleanse it of its Jews, both Newman and Finkelstein become the targets of their hatred, whereupon Gertrude insists that they either join the Christian Front or leave the neighborhood. The Christian Front has "a lot of good ideas which anybody would agree with,"[57] she affirms, because "everybody, pretty near, has no use for the Jews. ... A depression comes, there's people out on the street, an organization comes along that can get them going and it's the end of the Hebrews."[58] The move against the Jews "is going to happen," she prognosticates, "and when it does I'm going to be on the right side and so are you."[59] The "right side" in this case is not the side of what is right; no, it is the side that flees from what is morally right and ethically demanded. When Newman finds his garbage cans have been overturned because they suspect he is a Jew, his comment is: "Sometimes I feel like I could almost murder them [the Jews]. But I can't seem to say it anymore." Although the anti-Semitic desire for murder still smolders in his soul, here we have the first indication that Newman is slowly becoming a human being: "I don't know what's happening to me." After spending a life of quiet revulsion toward the Jews, "he had come to see how many others shared his feeling, and he had found stimulation around the subway pillars. ... In those earlier impressions of the violence to come, the attackers were ... well, if not gentlemen, certainly amenable to the guidance of gentlemen much like himself."[60] But now he finds himself among the human refuse designated for the cleanup operation to be carried out by, well, if not gentlemen, people who deemed

[55] Ibid., 116.   [56] Ibid., 117.   [57] Ibid., 128.   [58] Ibid., 131.   [59] Ibid., 132.
[60] Ibid., 133.

themselves good, decent Christians whose counterfeit faith assured them of their power and their purity.

Realizing that the redemption of the Christians in the Christian Front requires his sacrifice, Newman "wanted to go back to the old days when his hate had no consequences,"[61] when he could curl up in the egocentric cave of his somnolent complacency. But the questions come, questions that will allow him no sleep: "He had always known it. Every morning on the subway, every night coming home. Why suddenly was it such a horror to him? What was Finkelstein to him? What right had the man here in the first place? Why was he acting as though the man ...?"[62] As though the man what? As though the man were a human being, as though he were somehow at fault for summoning the Jew within him, as though Finkelstein were the one who had robbed him of his slumber. And yet, in a sense, it is indeed Finkelstein the Jew who shakes him from his sleep, as we find Newman awakened once again, disturbed by the dream of the merry-go-round and a distant cry of someone being attacked outside his window, someone whose screams he tries desperately to ignore. "He lay still, fighting to recall the kind of sound it had been, the web of sleep folding away from his mind. Maybe they had come for Finkelstein ... '*Police!*'"[63] And so some shall not sleep.

In a last-ditch effort to convince the members of the Christian Front that he is one of them, Newman attends a gathering of the Front. Hanging in the hall is a fifteen-foot portrait of George Washington: "The cheeks in the picture were colored so brilliant a pink that his face seemed to be gazing out over the audience like one embalmed,"[64] suggesting that the American ideal of openness toward the stranger was dead. It was Washington who wrote to the Hebrew congregation in Newport, Rhode Island: "May the stock of Abraham who dwell in this land continue to merit and enjoy the good will of the other inhabitants; while everyone shall sit in safety under his own vine and fig tree and there shall be none to make him afraid [Micah 4:4]."[65] As a prominent priest makes his way to the stage, "a heaving movement was suddenly sweeping the hall ... *Father!*"[66] – a cry hauntingly reminiscent of *Führer!* He is the Father/Führer, the mangod of the anti-Semites, come to cleanse their

[61] Ibid., 134.   [62] Ibid., 135.   [63] Ibid., 136.   [64] Ibid., 154.
[65] George Washington, "Reply to the Hebrew Congregation in Newport, Rhode Island," in George M. Goodwin and Ellen Smith, eds., *The Jews of Rhode Island* (Hanover, N.H.: Brandeis University Press and the University Press of New England, 2004), 229.
[66] Miller, *Focus*, 155.

neighborhoods of the evil of the Jews – and to make them very afraid. As Newman himself grew more afraid, he looked at "the sharp, excited eyes around him" and "remembered the burly youths shaking out the garbage on his lawn and finally felt wise at having come tonight. It was definitely a wise thing for him to be doing."[67] It was "wise" for one who craves the security of his sleep and the complacency of his blindness to the face of the other human being.

Staking out his invisible enemy, the priest warns the audience that among them there are "internationalists," meaning the Jews who are part of the invisible and nefarious world Jewish conspiracy. At the priest's words of warning about a possible outburst from the sinister trouble-makers, "Mr. Newman's mind floundered in anxiety.... He did not want to be caught without a prearranged plan of action, for he knew that somewhere in the hall Fred was sitting, and in it too the people who had turned over his garbage can, and he would prefer to be seen doing the right thing vigorously. He wanted to be known as one of these people, as in fact he was."[68] But, of course, he was not. Although Newman sought safety in the midst of his would-be murderers, he had already begun have doubts about his own Jew hatred. His sleep had already been disturbed.

The priest no sooner incites the crowd into blaming the Jews for the war than they spot Newman for a Jew simply because he did not join in the clapping that came with declaring the Jews to be the satanic evil behind all the killing.[69] And so the accusations fly, as the anti-Semites invoke the Jew slaughtered at Golgotha in their vitriol aimed at Newman: "He's a Jew, for Christ's sake!... Christ Almighty, can't you see he's a Sammy?... Sammy, God damn! Sammy ya, Sammy ya Sammy!"[70] It is noteworthy that this epithet for a Jew, taken from the common Jewish name Sam or Samuel, is *Shmuel* in Hebrew, which means "name of God," so that when the Jews are identified with the name *Sammy*, they are identified with God. Once again, the assault on the Jew is expressive of the usurpation of God. And the anti-Semite must above all get rid of God if he is to become as God. In this case, they must get rid of Newman, and so they do. All he can manage to do, as they throw him out of the building, is to shout over and over, "I'm not, you damned fools, I'm not!"[71] Significantly, he does not cry out, "I am not a Jew," but just "I'm not!" Why? Because if he does not identify with the Jews – if he is not seeking to become as the Jews, rather than as God – he *is not*: he has

---

[67] Ibid., 156.   [68] Ibid., 158–159.   [69] Ibid., 160.   [70] Ibid., 161–162.
[71] Ibid.

no being, no presence as a human being, for his presence as a human being turns on the testimony to the dearness of the other human being, the testimony for which the Jews are chosen.

The murderous mob into which Newman longed to assimilate out of fear and panic no sooner throws him into the street than he is greeted with a word of kindness from a Jew, his neighbor Mr. Finkelstein. "Despite himself he [Newman] felt drawn to this man. It was not that he thought of himself as being in the same situation as the Jew walking leisurely beside him, for *consciously* he did not think of himself that way. It was only that he saw the man in possession of a secret that left him controlled and fortified, while he himself was circling in confusion in search of a formula through which he could again find his dignity."[72] Any time a soul starts to emerge as who it truly is, it is always despite the egocentric self. The soul that emanates from the Holy One is the opposite of the self that is constructed from the mirrors of the eyes of others, the self that would dominate, control, and be secure in its indifference. If Finkelstein appears to be in control of himself, it is not the control of power but the confidence of someone who knows who he is and what must be done for the sake of the other human being. Finkelstein's self-control is the control of someone who has the wisdom to confront Newman with his own humanity. He asks Newman, "Why do you want I shall get out of the neighborhood?" To which Newman lamely replies, "Well, it's not you particularly." Finkelstein, however, presses him on the matter, saying, "But it is me particularly. . . . If you want the Jews shall get out you want me to get out. I did something you don't like?"[73] Newman answers, "It's not what *you've* done, it's what others of your people have done,"[74] which is an answer that evades the question.

At this point Finkelstein drives home his most crucial point: "In other words, when you look at me you don't see me,"[75] that is to say, when you look at me you see a Jew, not a human being. You see "Jewish features," not a human face. And in your blindness to the human face you lose your humanity. If Newman needs to focus, he needs to focus on what does not meet the eye: he needs to focus on the face. We see that Newman understood very well what Finkelstein was telling him when we read, "The eyes of Mr. Finkelstein were on his back, hurting him more. If the man would just disappear, just go away . . . for God's sake go away and let everybody be the same! The same, the same, let us all be the same!"[76]

[72] Ibid., 165; emphasis added.   [73] Ibid., 167.   [74] Ibid., 168.   [75] Ibid.
[76] Ibid., 170.

For once everyone is the same – once the difference is removed – then all can curl up in the sleep of their indifference, where everything is all the same. Their sleep will not be disturbed by the cry of *Help! Help!* that returns to haunt Newman, as he begins to fear for his own safety. "Who would come out to him from behind venetian blinds? Who?" Then he remembers the night the woman was attacked outside his window, when he failed to respond to her pleas: "She could have been murdered, clubbed to death out here that night. No one would have dared outdoors to help, to even say she was a human being. Because all of them watching from their windows knew she was not white.... But he was white. A white man, a neighbor. He *belonged* here. Or did he?"[77] Yes, she could have been murdered. He could be murdered. Who would come out to help? We shall find that only Finkelstein, the Jew, would come out to help. To belong is to help. To belong is to belong with Finkelstein.

Precisely because he is aware of this truth, Newman is thrown into a state of fear and resentment:

They had him hooked up with Finkelstein. He knew he would never come out and risk a broken nose for Finkelstein. He knew he would remain behind his venetian blinds saying to himself that Finkelstein should have moved away when he knew they were after him, that a beating was not so horrible to the Jew because he had been expecting it. As it was not so horrible for that woman, who was accustomed to attack because she had never in her life been safe. It was not so horrible for them, it was a natural thing for them ... *"In other words when you look at me you don't see me. What do you see?"*[78]

What does Newman see? He sees a Jew or a Spic. Or better: he is *trying* to see a Jew or a Spic. He is trying not to see a human being, because to see a human being is to behold the face, and to behold the face is to help, no matter the cost to oneself, in a moment of absolute forgetfulness of the self, which is demanded by the absolute commandment. Otherwise, we justify the suffering of other people, as Newman does, and thereby dehumanize them. And if they are not human, they do not concern me. In my lack of concern, I lose my own humanity.

Newman now lives the truth that the soul suffers what it inflicts. Dehumanizing the other human being, he experiences the meaning of dehumanization. Blind to the humanity of the other, he collides with the blindness of others to his own humanity, precisely because of his association with the Jews, the millennial witnesses to the sanctity of humanity

---

[77] Ibid., 177.   [78] Ibid., 178.

and the responsibility to and for the other person. "However close to being a human a Jew might seem," Newman reflects on his neighbors' failure to respond if he were attacked, "they would not come out because he would be a Jew in their eyes, and therefore guilty.... They had no evidence that he had ever conspired against them or hurt them, and yet once they were convinced he was a Jew he knew they would feel he had a curse for them in his heart."[79] Notice that, once again, the hatred of the Jew rests on nothing that the Jew has actually *done*. He does not *become* guilty – he is *already* and *essentially* guilty. The object of Jew hatred is what the presence of the Jew signifies, namely, the divine assertions of "I am God" and "Thou shalt not murder." Here too the words of Lévinas come to mind: "The face requires you, calls you outside. And already there resounds the word from Sinai, 'thou shalt not kill,' which signifies 'you shall defend the life of the other....' And *you* are responsible, the only one who could answer, the noninterchangeable, and the unique one."[80] Recall Newman's desire for all to be the same and interchangeable, all expendable, hence worthless and meaningless. It is the anti-Semite's definitive desire for indifference. The Jew announces to the world this unsettling truth that *you* are responsible for *this* human being, unique and indispensable to all creation. And Newman's neighbors had him "hooked up" with the Jew.

Beginning to realize the truth of the testimony that the Jews are chosen to bear, Newman begins to undergo a transformation into who he is in truth, into *Newman*, into a *new man*: "He had changed. In those solemn days between him and his wife, the city kept carving a new shape upon his soul. Like a current along a shore it scoured silently along the sides of his mind."[81] The current that was carving a new shape into his soul leads him to a question: "What did people have a right to do to a Jew? Why was he so crippled in thinking about it? It used to be so clear to him that they simply had to be frightened out of a neighborhood where they didn't belong. But now the picture of it clenched his stomach and he could not even utter it."[82] The change that carves its way into him creates an opening in his soul through which a light may enter, the light of the face, the *or panim*. Having been made into a Jew, he is led to confront that light and behold the truth of what it means to be a human being.

[79] Ibid.
[80] Emmanuel Lévinas, *Is It Righteous to Be? Interviews with Emmanuel Levinas*, ed. Jill Robbins (Stanford, Calif.: Stanford University Press, 2001), 208
[81] Miller, *Focus*, 184.   [82] Ibid., 194.

One evening he and Gertrude decide to take in a movie. A scene from contemporary Europe, from the Holocaust, unfolds on the screen, as "the whole picture there swept into focus." Before him are Jews assembled by the Nazis. The Jews are praying, and among them is a priest who is also praying, facing the audience in the theater, confronting them, confronting Newman. The Nazis march the Jews to a city square, where a gallows has been erected. The rabbi and the priest plead with the German officer, declaring that the Jews must not be killed simply because they are Jews, whereupon a mocking laugh of "Ha!" bursts forth from somewhere in the darkened theater. Before the Nazis can act further, the priest quickly ascends to the platform of the gallows and shouts that it is not Christian to murder these people and that the Christians dare not have any part of it. Needless to say, the Nazis drag him down from the gallows and proceed to murder the Jews.[83] Newman sees before his eyes the needful substitution of the self for the other that imparts meaning to the life of the soul; it is the one-for-the-other of signification, whereby the individual takes on significance by becoming a sign of the dearness of the other. As ever, Lévinas can help here, for the priest's action – which cuts Newman to the quick, cuts through the anti-Semite in his soul – is a perfect example of what Lévinas calls "substitution."

"To substitute oneself," Lévinas explains, "does not amount to putting oneself in the place of the other man in order to feel what he feels. . . . Rather, substitution entails bringing comfort by associating ourselves with the essential weakness and finitude of the other; it is to bear his weight while sacrificing one's interestedness and complacency-in-being, which then turn into responsibility for the other. . . . The in-itself of a being persisting in its being is surpassed in the gratuity of being outside-of-oneself, for the other, in the act of sacrifice or the possibility of sacrifice, in holiness."[84] Substitution has nothing to do with either sympathy or empathy; it is not a matter of knowing how it feels or what it is like to be the other. Nor it is a question of allowing oneself to become a scapegoat; scapegoats do not transcend the complacency of their being in an act of absolute self-abdication. No, it is a matter of taking on the wounds of the other in an affirmation of a profound physical and metaphysical connection to him or her. What Lévinas calls "being outside-of-oneself" is a certain forgetfulness of oneself, an abrogation of the ego, in a renewal of the life of the soul in holiness. There lies the

[83] Ibid., 200–201.   [84] Lévinas, *Is It Righteous to Be?*, 228.

meaning of *Kiddush HaShem*, or "the Sanctification of the Name": sanctification entails substitution. As the face of the other comes into focus, Newman is faced with just such a substitution.

Notice also that in the case of the priest the ascent to the dimension of height opened up by the other human being is an ascent to the gallows. To make that ascent is to bear the weight of this substitution; once again, the heaviness here is the heaviness of meaning, which is elevating. Here we realize that the dimension of height does not signify a position of privilege; rather, it announces a destitution that harbors a demand. Hence the face of the other human being, says Lévinas, "challenges me from his humanity and from his height ... [with] a summons to respond ...; the I is, by its *very position*, responsibility through and through."[85] And yet the summons precedes the position; we are in a position to help because we have *already* been summoned. The challenge put to us is not to obey an order; rather, it is to become who we are in an answering of "Here I am" to the one who calls. In his own way, Newman finally understands this. As they walk home from the theater, he tells Gertrude that he does not believe in anything that the Christian Front stands for. When she tells him it is not a question of what he believes, he insists, "Even if they decided I was all right I couldn't go along with them," whereupon she accuses him of talking too much to Finkelstein,[86] as if the Jew were the source of some sort of contamination. Thus we understand the nature of the purity that the anti-Semite seeks.

Proceeding down the dimly lit sidewalk, Newman is suddenly aware of a group of four young men following them. It strikes him: "They were going for Finkelstein. They must be.... It was Finkelstein tonight. Poor fella ... well, he shouldn't have moved in where he wasn't wanted.... Thank God for Finkelstein. Supposing there wasn't anyone like him on the block.... He would have to run for it now, run as fast as his legs could go ... Poor man, poor Jew...."[87] Although Newman is relieved by the presence of Finkelstein as someone who might take his place when they come for the Jews, there is another, much deeper meaning in the phrase "Thank God for Finkelstein." Suppose there was no one like Finkelstein – no "poor Jew" chosen to declare to humanity the divine revelation of the holiness of the other human being and our infinite responsibility to and for one another, not only on the block but in the world. Then what?

---

[85] Emmanuel Lévinas, *Basic Philosophical Writings*, ed. Adriaan T. Peperzak, Simon Critchley, and Robert Bernasconi (Bloomington: Indiana University Press, 1996), 17.
[86] Miller, *Focus*, 203–204.   [87] Ibid., 205.

Then there would be no soul, no identity, no humanity – no *who* and no *why*, no meaning and no value. For where there is no *why* there is no *who*, no humanity. There is simply what is, with everything locked into the neutrality of being. There would be nothing left but the horror of the "there is," in which power is the only reality and weakness the only sin. Newman needs Finkelstein not to save him from being targeted but to save him from his sleep, to save him from his illusory anti-Semitic self.

It turns out that the four young hoodlums from the Christian Front are not after the Jew Finkelstein – they are after the Jew Newman! As they assault him outside Finkelstein's store, his wife Gertrude flees the scene and heads home. Finkelstein, however, suddenly appears, wielding two Louisville sluggers. Handing one to Newman, he and his neighbor fight off the attackers. After the skirmish, their faces bruised and bleeding, Newman helps Finkelstein back into the store. Having once been repulsed by the touch of Finkelstein's hand when purchasing a newspaper, Newman now collects some ice and attends to Finkelstein's wounded face. Then he looks into a mirror; his own face looks back at him, the face that the anti-Semites had assaulted, now black and blue and oozing blood. Strangely, "in all his life he had never known such calm, despite the torrent of blood rushing through him. Within his raging body a stillness had grown very wide and very deep and he stared at his image feeling the texture of this peace."[88] This peace, this *shalom*, is the *shalem*, or "wholeness" of identity; it is a peace that comes only from on high, with the opening of the dimension of height. The Bahir, an ancient kabbalistic text, teaches that "peace" is a synonym for "truth,"[89] and the Portuguese sage Don Isaac Abrabanel (1437–1508) holds that "peace" is a synonym for the ethical.[90] The truth of who we are as human beings created in the image and likeness of the Holy One – the truth that the anti-Semite next door would obliterate in his or her effort to become as God – lies in the wholeness of the ethical relation to the other human being. As the Jews affirm three times each day in the last of the Eighteen Benedictions, it is a peace that comes only from God. Thus ethics is first philosophy; ethics is metaphysics. In this metaphysics we discover the metaphysical origins of anti-Semitism.

---

[88] Ibid., 212.
[89] *The Bahir*, trans. Aryeh Kaplan (York Beach, Maine: Samuel Weiser, 1979), 75.
[90] Don Isaac Abrabanel, *Abrabanel on Pirke Avot*, trans. Abraham Chill (New York: Sepher-Hermon, 1991), 79.

With his newly found wisdom, Newman sets out for the police station to stand up and attest to the crimes committed in his neighborhood. On his way he reflects on the city of New York and its millions who "were going mad. . . . People were in asylums for being afraid that the sky would fall, and there were millions walking around as insane as anyone could be who fear the shape of a human face."[91] Which is to say: who fear the commandment from on high that issues from "the divine disclosing itself in that *odd configuration of lines that make up the human face.*"[92] It is indeed a kind of madness, the madness of taking ourselves to be otherwise than who we are, as Newman had done throughout the novel.

With this realization reverberating through his head, Newman arrives at the police station and reports the incident. "How many of you people live there?" the policeman asks him, taking Newman for a Jew. It seemed that to deny that he was a Jew would be "to repudiate and soil his own cleansing fury of a few moments ago." And he answers: "'There are the Finkelsteins on the corner. . . .'" The officer asks, "'Just them and yourself?'" "'Yes. Just them and myself,' Mr. Newman said. Then he sat down and the policeman picked up a pencil from among many on the desk, and began to take down his story. Telling it, Mr. Newman felt as though he were setting down a weight which for some reason he had been carrying and carrying."[93] The weight he had been carrying was the emptiness of the ego that had eclipsed his soul as a human being. Declaring himself to be a Jew, Newman answers "Here I am." Thus affirming he is a Jew, Newman affirms who he is *in truth* on a level most profound.

This movement of substitution goes far beyond bearing wounds: it is bearing witness to the truth that, in the words of Lévinas, "it is Me who is a substitution and a sacrifice and not another,"[94] which is the meaning of the commandment "You shall love your neighbor as yourself" (*Veahavta lereakha k'mokha*, Leviticus 19:18), where the "as yourself" (*k'mokha*) means "that is who you are." As the non-Jew Newman becomes Newman the Jew, we encounter what Lévinas calls the "breakup of identity" that characterizes substitution as taking on meaning and therefore bearing witness: "This breakup of identity, this changing of being into signification, that is, into substitution, is the subject's subjectivity, or its subjection to everything, its susceptibility, its vulnerability."[95] In this subjection

[91] Miller, *Focus*, 215.   [92] Lévinas, *Proper Names*, 95.   [93] Miller, *Focus*, 217.
[94] Lévinas, *Basic Philosophical Writings*, 94.
[95] Emmanuel Lévinas, *Otherwise Than Being or Beyond Essence*, trans. Alphonso Lingis (The Hague: Martinus Nijhoff, 1981), 14.

whereby the human being's life takes on meaning Newman discovers the freedom not of doing whatever he wants to do but of doing what *must* be done. Thus understanding that "signification is the ethical deliverance of the self through substitution for the other,"[96] he is finally delivered from the meaninglessness of the carousel that turns round and round and the horror of the solipsistic isolation of the ego. Turning to Lévinas just once more will drive home this important point: "Substitution frees the subject from ennui, that is, from the enchainment to itself, where the ego suffocates in itself due to the tautological way of identity, and ceaselessly seeks after the distraction of games and sleep in a movement that never wears out."[97] Declaring himself to be a Jew, Newman leaps from the merry-go-round to become who he truly is.

A CLOSING THOUGHT: WHERE IS YOUR BROTHER AND WHAT HAVE YOU DONE?

Miller's literary exploration of the anti-Semitic soul reveals not only the metaphysical origin of anti-Semitism as a temptation that lurks in the soul but also the soul's metaphysical liberation from the temptation. It turns out that, as we peer into inner recesses of the anti-Semite, we peer into the mirror that pervades Miller's novel. From the depths of that mirror the soul of every human being, the soul of Adam – *my* soul – gazes back at me to reveal my secret longing to be as God, to expose my hiding from the divine demand that echoes in the human cry for help: "Ayeka! Where are you?!" Anti-Semitism, therefore, is altogether different from the ordinary racism that engenders a sense of racial superiority; it is prior to any racial consideration. As with the human being's flight from the first question put to the first man, the metaphysical origin of anti-Semitism is rooted in a flight from this preoriginary question, this an-archic question, concerning my responsibility to and for my fellow human being – the one who is my brother. To hate the Jew is not only to hate God but also to hate my brother: Jew hatred is hatred of humanity.

Miller's unveiling of the metaphysical aspect of anti-Semitism also clarifies how and why Jew hatred can manifest itself in any place and at any time, high and low, apart from the contingencies of political, economic, or social conditions. If it lies dormant in the soul, then it can flare up in anyone, from Martin Luther to Lawrence Newman, from

[96] Ibid., 164. [97] Ibid., 124.

Manetho to *me*. I am summoned to declare, "Here I am for you," in response to the plea that lays claim to me, both from on high and from outside my window. Anti-Semitism is precisely the abrogation of this responsibility, of this cry of "Here I am for you," for the sake of each and all. It is manifest in the sophisticated treatises of the Church Fathers and the "enlightened" philosophers, in the Nazi ideologues and in Lawrence Newman – and in *me*.

Concluding Reflection

The Messianic Side of the Soul of Adam

> To love one's neighbor is to go to Eternity, to redeem the World or prepare the Kingdom of God. Human love is the very work, the efficiency of Redemption.
>
> Emmanuel Lévinas, *Outside the Subject*

We have traversed a lengthy path, from a consideration of why existing explanations of the origins of anti-Semitism have proven to be inadequate, through its theological and philosophical displays, to its expressions relative to the Holocaust and its manifestations in post-Holocaust contexts. We have seen that it is not the product of historical, social, or political circumstances. Those contingencies, rather, merely provide the occasion for the emergence of a Jew hatred that runs much deeper, that is rooted in the soul of the child of Adam who would be as God, be that person philosopher or dictator, intellectual or ideologue, the next-door neighbor or me. And yet, proceeding from the premise of Jewish tradition as we have done all along, it turns out that in order to oppose anti-Semitism we must indeed be as God – not the God of power and possession but the long-suffering God of loving kindness. We are commanded to be holy as God is holy (see Leviticus 19:2), but this means assuming the attributes of kindness and compassion that go into God's holiness (see Exodus 34:6–7). To be holy is not to be the wisest, most powerful, or even the supreme Good; it has nothing to do with ontological superlatives. To be holy is to be unique, beyond essence; it is to give – *hav* – what only I can give, in an act of love – of *ahavah* – for another.

In this Jewish response to anti-Semitism we discover yet another level of the notion of substitution that proved to be so helpful in our examination of Arthur Miller's character Lawrence Newman. "The psyche in the soul," Emmanuel Lévinas states it, "is the other in me, a malady of identity, both accused and *self*, the same for the other, the same by the other.... It is a substitution."[1] This idea brings to mind Abraham Joshua Heschel's contrast between God and the human being. Whereas God is "I Am That I Am – *ehyeh asher ehyeh*" (Exodus 3:14), says Heschel, the human being is "I am that I am not." He explains: "I am endowed with a will, but the will is not mine; I am endowed with a freedom, but it is a freedom imposed on the will. Life is something that visits my body, a transcendent loan; I have neither initiated nor conceived its worth and meaning.... *I am what is not mine*. I am that I am not."[2] The side of the soul that would be the same as God is what Lévinas calls "the Same," the self that not only knows but pretends to determine good and evil and therefore its own essence, meaning, and value. The aspect of the soul that would be there for the sake of another belongs to another, as if possessed or, in Lévinas's words, held hostage: what is not mine, beyond my grasp, "provokes this responsibility against my will, that is, by substituting me for the other as a hostage. All my inwardness is invested in the form of a despite-me, for-another. Despite-me, for-another, is signification par excellence."[3] To thus have meaning is to be chosen, so that the other who lays claim to me – the one whose presence emanates from the human face – is God, who through the Jew proclaims that every human being is chosen. By extension, then, what Lévinas refers to as "the psyche in the soul" is the Jew in me. Even if I am a Jew, the Jew in me is the "am not" that lies at the core of my identity. For even – or especially – if I am a Jew there is always *more* I must become by meeting one responsibility *more*. Invoking this "more," this "am not," God commands me to love *bekol-meodekha*, "with all your 'more'" (Deuteronomy 6:5). The *more* with which I love – the "am not" that I am – is a messianic more. Thus we have the Jewish teaching, that in addition to a trace of the soul of Adam, every soul harbors a spark of the soul of the Messiah, the Anointed One of the House of David, the Jew.[4]

---

[1] Emmanuel Lévinas, *Otherwise Than Being or Beyond Essence*, trans. Alphonso Lingis (The Hague: Martinus Nijhoff, 1981), 69.

[2] Abraham Joshua Heschel, *Between God and Man: An Interpretation of Judaism* (New York: Free Press, 1997), 62.

[3] Lévinas, *Otherwise Than Being*, 11.

[4] See, e.g., the teaching of the Chasidic master Zadok ha-Kohen in Norman Lamm, *The Religious Thought of Hasidism: Text and Commentary* (Hoboken, N.J.: Ktav, 1999),

Anti-Semitism is to be opposed not merely with something like education in tolerance and certainly not with some form of the assimilation of the Jews, which is itself an anti-Semitic endeavor. No, it is to be opposed with a Jewish conception of Messianism, where Messianism is viewed not as an eschatological abstraction but as a matter of concrete urgency here and now. "Salvation does not stand as an end to History," Lévinas explains, "or act as its conclusion. It remains *at every moment* possible. ... Messianism is no more than this apogee in being, a centralizing, concentration or twisting back on itself of the Self [*Moi*]. And in concrete terms this means that each person acts as though he were the Messiah. Messianism is therefore not the certainty of the coming of a man who stops history. It is in my power to bear the suffering of all. It is the moment when I recognize this power and my universal responsibility."[5] So what about the literal meaning of the Messiah, the scion of David, whose coming we pray for three times a day? According to Lévinas, it is all too literal, more literal than we wish to think: *I* am the one who must take on myself the messianic task and testimony – literally. *I* am the one who must attend to the care of the widow, the orphan, and the stranger – literally. *I* am the one whose bears responsibility for creation and humanity – literally.

The teaching that the advent of the Messiah is at every moment possible stems from the Talmud. When the sage Rabbi Yehoshua ben Levi asked Elijah when the Messiah would come, the prophet directed him to a leper at the gates of Rome, saying, "Ask him yourself." And so Rabbi Yehoshua asked the Messiah, "When will you come?" And the Messiah answered, "Today" – that is, "Today, if you heed the Voice of HaShem" (*Sanhedrin* 98a).[6] And Yehoshua ben Levi walked away in dismay. It is said that if he had simply helped the Messiah with his wounds, the Messiah would have made his appearance. If the advent of the Messiah is at every moment possible, we are the ones who must make it happen. Indeed, according to the Talmud, the question of whether we anticipated and worked for the coming of the Messiah is one of the four questions that God puts to us when we stand before the heavenly

---

576–577; see also the teaching of the Stretiner Rebbe in Louis Newman, ed., *The Hasidic Anthology* (New York: Schocken Books, 1963), 248.

[5] Emmanuel Lévinas, *Difficult Freedom: Essays on Judaism*, trans. Sean Hand (Baltimore, Md.: Johns Hopkins University Press, 1990), 90.

[6] See also Raphael Patai, *The Messiah Texts* (New York: Avon, 1979), 110–111.

tribunal (*Shabbat* 31a).[7] It is a question concerning whether we have kindled the spark of the messianic soul within ourselves.

Such an anticipation and preparation for the coming of the Messiah is rooted in the twelfth of the Thirteen Principles of Judaism outlined by Maimonides in his commentary on the Mishnah (*Sanhedrin* 10): "I believe with complete faith in the coming of the Messiah; even if he may tarry, no matter what, I shall await his coming every day." To understand what this has to do with a response to anti-Semitism, it is important to understand the meaning of *emunah*, here translated as "faith." It is not the "assent of the understanding to what is believed" that Thomas Aquinas defines as faith,[8] nor even the passion that Kierkegaard defines as faith.[9] The opposition to anti-Semitism, understood from the Jewish perspective, requires more *emunah*, not more "faith," if faith simply means "belief." *Emunah* is "conscientiousness," "honesty," and "trust." In the Talmud a person who does not keep his or her word is called a *mechusar amanah*, "one who is lacking in honesty" (see, e.g., *Bava Metzia* 49a). The mystical tradition defines "faith" as *devekut*, that is, as a "clinging" to God that lies in a devotion to one's fellow human being (see, e.g., *Tolodot Yaakov Yosef, Yitro* 6). Because matters of honesty and devotion are matters of action, Jewish teaching recognizes no distinction between faith and deeds; each is a manifestation of the other. Indeed, *doing* is prior to *believing* or *understanding*, as implied in the *naaseh v'nishma*," "we shall do, and we shall hear," of Exodus 24:7. Faith, then, implies a certain character, a certain condition of the soul, which in turn requires living in a loving relation with other people, and not just with God. God is not the object of belief; rather, He is the subject who commands deeds of loving kindness.

Emil Fackenheim describes faith as a "listening openness while yet no voice is heard."[10] This is the divine "Before you call, I shall answer" (Isaiah 65:24) that we are summoned to declare to our fellow human being in our messianic effort to be holy as God is holy. Having faith, then, is not a matter of affirming, "I believe in God," as Lévinas correctly points

---

[7] The other three questions are: Did you try to make time to study Torah? Were you devoted to raising a family? Were you honest in your business affairs?

[8] See Thomas Aquinas, *On Faith*, trans. Mark D. Jordan (Notre Dame, Ind.: University of Notre Dame Press, 1990), 39.

[9] See Søren Kierkegaard, *Fear and Trembling*, trans. Alastair Hannay (New York: Penguin Books, 1985), 95.

[10] Emil L. Fackenheim, *Encounters between Judaism and Modern Philosophy* (New York: Basic Books, 1973), 27.

out, but of declaring, "Here am I, Your servant, ready to serve,"[11] ready
to enter a service that is the opposite of servitude. It is, says Adin
Steinsaltz, "that special quality which goes beyond the mind, which is of
wisdom – that is to say, it is an experience directly connected with the
Divine and not with knowing this or that about Him."[12] We are directly
connected with the divine through the commandment, the *mitzvah*, that
we encounter through the human face. Faith is the opposite not of disbelief but of the failure to answer and to act for the sake of the other; it is a
diametric reversal of the deadly isolation within the illusory ego. Thus
Heschel writes, "Faith is the beginning of the end of egocentricity.
'To have faith is *to disregard self-regard*,' said the Kotzker.... 'I believe
in God' does not mean that *I* accept the fact of *His* existence. It does not
signify that *I* come first, then *God*, as the syntax of the sentence implies.
The opposite is true. Because God exists, I am able to believe."[13] Which
means: I do not "believe" in God, as someone might believe in the tooth
fairy. Rather, God "believes" in me – and through me. Like the messianic
age, faith rests not in my heart but in the work of my hands for the sake of
another. The wisdom that is faith, the wisdom rooted in the messianic side
of the soul, is acquired through the vulnerability we assume for the sake
of the other. The man of faith, then, is the opposite of the anti-Semite.

Notice also that the faith affirmed in the Twelfth Principle is "complete
faith," *emunah shlemah*, where *shlemah*, the "completeness" or "wholeness" of faith, is the *shalom*, the "peace" that we seek in the Messiah. It is
the peace that Lawrence Newman attained when he finally became who
he was in truth. It is not a state of contentment or tranquility, which may
characterize the smug self-righteousness or the complacent "peace" of the
anti-Semite. It lies, rather, in a certain strife of the spirit, in the torrent of
blood racing through us, in a certain wounding, without which we are not
whole. This peace or wholeness is characterized by the tension and the
intensity of anticipation, as suggested by the word *achakeh*; more than
"await," this verb means to "expect," as if my actions were to open
up the gate for the Messiah to enter at any instant, with the performance
of *this* mitzvah. As individuals who bear a trace of the soul of the
Messiah, each of us is responsible for *this* entry of the eternal into time.

[11] Emmanuel Lévinas, *Of God Who Comes to Mind*, trans. Bettina Bergo (Stanford, Calif.:
Stanford University Press, 1998), 75.
[12] Adin Steinsaltz, *The Long Shorter Way: Discourses on Chasidic Thought*, trans. Yehuda
Hanegbi (Northvale, N.J.: Jason Aronson, 1988), 118.
[13] Abraham Joshua Heschel, *A Passion for Truth* (New York: Farrar, Straus and Giroux,
1973), 189–190.

What makes the wait for the Messiah interminable, therefore, is not just that *he* tarries. It is that *I* tarry. Because a trace of the Messiah abides within my soul, the Messiah is precisely the one who has *yet* to come: here the eternity that enters time is the eternal *not yet*.

Because we are prone to tarry, the Talmud teaches that two times are destined for the coming of the Messiah: now and the appointed time (*Sanhedrin* 98a). This teaching is based on the words from the prophet Isaiah: "I HaShem will hasten it in its time" (Isaiah 60:22); that is, either I will hasten it to make it now, or it will be in its appointed time. *Now*, if we perform the task for which we were created. *Now*, if we treat others, especially those who are most defenseless, with loving kindness. In short, now *is* the appointed time for *me* to act for the sake of another. Without the wait for the Messiah, there is nothing to hasten and no time appointed. Waiting for the Messiah, though he may tarry, is just the opposite of the languishing that characterizes so much of our intellectual game playing, which is no more than a means of marking time by killing time.

The time of our lives, of striving to be who we are in our own unique being there for the sake of another, is rooted in the interminable waiting and working for the coming of the Messiah. "The awaiting of the Messiah," says Lévinas, "is the duration of time itself – waiting for God – but here the waiting no longer attests to the absence of Godot, who will never come, but rather to a relationship with that which is not able to enter the present, since the present is too small to contain the Infinite."[14] The relationship is the key. So understood, time is the drawing nigh unto the Holy One that Lévinas describes when he says, "Time is the most profound relationship that man can have with God, precisely as a going towards God. ... 'Going towards God' is meaningless unless seen in terms of my primary going towards the other person. I can only go towards God by being ethically concerned by and for the other person."[15] In this going toward God by going toward the other person we ignite the messianic side of the soul.

Inasmuch as my responsibility for the other person is infinite, it is also a responsibility to and for the Infinite One, where time and eternity merge in a surpassing of my ontological horizon. Recall in this connection another insight from Lévinas: "To be *for* a time that would be without me, *for* a

[14] Emmanuel Lévinas, "Revelation in the Jewish Tradition," trans. Sarah Richmond, in Sean Hand, ed., *The Lévinas Reader* (Oxford: Basil Blackwell, 1989), 203.
[15] Emmanuel Lévinas, "Dialogue with Emmanuel Lévinas," in Richard A. Cohen, ed., *Face to Face with Lévinas* (Albany: SUNY Press, 1986), 23.

time after my time, over and beyond the celebrated 'being for death,' is not an ordinary thought which is extrapolating from my own duration; it is the passage to the time of the other. Should what makes such a passage possible be called *eternity?*"[16] His question, of course, is rhetorical. This "being for a time after my time" is precisely what it means to die for the sake of another; it is martyrdom and witness, a *Kiddush HaShem*. The "I am that I am not" of the messianic side of the soul lies in this being for a time that would be without me. It is the very project of redemption, where the redemption that I must bring about for humanity is also a redemption of the Holy One Himself. If "the salvation of God is identical with the salvation of Israel," as it is written in the Midrash (*Vayikra Rabbah* 9:3; see also *Midrash Tehillim* 1:13:4), it is because the messianic presence of the Holy One in this realm rests on Israel's accomplishing the task of redemption for which it is chosen. With the advent of the messianic era, says God, "The redemption will be Mine and yours; as if to say: 'I will be redeemed with you'" (*Shemot Rabbah* 15:12). The messianic responsibility does not lie with Israel alone, however, as we see in the talmudic teaching that each soul must accomplish the task for which it was created in order to open the way for the "the son of David" (*Yevamot* 63b; *Avodah Zarah* 5a; *Niddah* 13b). That assignation is what unnerves the anti-Semite: rejecting the Jew, the anti-Semite rejects the messianic project, the messianic accountability, that makes him or her a human being.

"The line of the horizon vanishes as one approaches it," in the words of André Neher, "but the Jew knows that even if the horizon vanishes, in its vanishing it turns toward a vertical position. The point of turning towards the vertical is the 'maybe' of the Messiah."[17] What Neher refers to as the "vertical" is the dimension of height and meaning that constitutes time itself, where the "maybe" of an undetermined future derives from the "certainty" of an immemorial past. And I am implicated by both. As Lévinas states it, the immemorial past so central to Jewish tradition "signifies starting from an irrecusable responsibility, which devolves on the ego and precisely is significant to it as a commandment."[18] A commandment to do what? Not to serve by waiting but to wait by serving. For the irrecusable responsibility not only *devolves* on the

---

[16] Emmanuel Lévinas, *Collected Philosophical Papers*, trans. Alphonso Lingis (Dordrecht: Martinus Nijhoff, 1987), 92.

[17] André Neher, *They Made Their Souls Anew*, trans. David Maisel (Albany: SUNY Press, 1990), 61–62.

[18] Emmanuel Lévinas, *Time and the Other*, trans. Richard A. Cohen (Pittsburgh, Pa.: Duquesne University Press, 1987), 113.

ego – it *dissolves* the ego to reveal the spark of the Messiah that abides in every soul. For the ego is the primary obstacle to the coming of the Messiah, both within us and beyond us.

To speak in such a way about the messianic side of the soul is all very well, but in the face of the anti-Semitism that culminated in the Holocaust it might be a bit presumptuous if not altogether offensive. After the Holocaust, however, the task of being there for the sake of another is more urgent than ever, and that is where the messianic cry of "Here I am" comes to bear. Indeed, when we encounter Jews who in the time of the Shoah remained devoted to God and to one another, we touch on an Ultimate, to borrow a phrase from Fackenheim. If the task of the messianic side of the soul is to effect a *tikkun,* or mending of creation, he writes, *"the* Tikkun *which for the post-Holocaust Jew is a moral necessity is a possibility because during the Holocaust itself a Jewish* Tikkun *was already actual.* This simple but enormous, nay, world-historical truth is the rock on which rests any authentic Jewish future, and any authentic future Jewish identity."[19] The move toward an authentic Jewish identity is a move to overcome the anti-Semite in my soul. Because faith is not a matter of belief, Eliezer Berkovits can assert, "In the presence of the holy faith of the crematoria, the ready faith of those who were not there is vulgarity. But the disbelief of the sophisticated intellectual in the midst of an affluent society – in the light of the holy disbelief of the crematoria – is obscenity."[20] Speaking from a Jewish perspective, disbelief can be holy when, insisting on the truth of what Jewish tradition places in our care, it insists on a certain fidelity on the part of the One who insists on our fidelity to one another. Here holy disbelief is not so much an absence of faith as it is the presence of outrage in the midst of faith. Indeed, it is not about belief at all.

After Auschwitz the wait for the Messiah is an impatient wait, an outraged wait, a wait made not only of doing but also of questioning. Questioning what? Not the truth of Torah but the devotion of God Himself to the Covenant of Torah. Remaining in the Covenant, we remain within the relation, and we have good reason for our outcry; abandoning the Covenant, we have no grounds for complaining. If we abandon the Torah and the loving relation that it commands, the outrage and the question amount to no more than the self-serving, arrogant

---

[19] Emil L. Fackenheim, *To Mend the World: Foundations of Post-Holocaust Jewish Thought* (New York: Schocken Books, 1989), 300; emphasis in the original.

[20] Eliezer Berkovits, *Faith after the Holocaust* (New York: Ktav, 1973), 5.

indignation of the anti-Semite. Only when we adhere to the Torah are we in a position to argue with God, as the Torah commands us to do, a commandment that is implicit in Abraham's assertion: "I take it upon myself to speak to my Lord" (Genesis 18:27). The Patriarch's first conversation with God after sealing the Covenant of Circumcision is an argument for the sake of the righteous of Sodom and Gomorrah. It is the one place in the Torah where we find God speaking to Himself: "Shall I hide from Abraham what I am about to do?" (Genesis 18:17). Determining whether Abraham understands the meaning of the Covenant, God *wants* Abraham to confront Him and put to Him the crucial question: "Will the Judge of the world be unjust?" (Genesis 18:25). And so we must ask and act, with God, for God, against God, for the sake and salvation of God.

The anti-Semite would put an end to this questioning of the Holy One; anyone who would be as God cannot tolerate any questioning of God. And yet precisely in a certain questioning of God the holy spark of the soul of the Messiah is manifest. Anti-Semitism is anti-Messianism, whether in the form of the creedal affirmation that salvation is settled, a smug intellectualism, or a totalitarian utopianism. Rooted in a longing for resolution, anti-Semitism is a longing to be relieved of the infinite responsibility that harangues the ego. Because who we are is rooted in this responsibility, Messianism has little to do with the pious recitation of a creed. Hence, unlike many anti-Semitic -isms, Judaism does not divide humanity into the damned and the saved on the basis of belief; according to Jewish teaching, the righteous dwell among the nations, even among those who reject Judaism. Waiting and working for the coming of the Messiah, the Jew longs for the world to take on a certain character, not to adopt a certain creed. The unsettling presence of the Jew forces the anti-Semite not into a "belief system" but into an "awakening," as Lévinas puts it, "a demand that no obedience equals."[21] For the presence of the Jew is a constant reminder that we are forever in debt and that redemption is always yet to be determined. There is no settling the accounts: no payment will do, because payment is always due. And so among the anti-Semites it is a truism that the Jews control the banks and ledgers of the world.

To determine the end is to settle the account. Therefore *the Messiah is precisely the one who has not yet appeared*, which means I am the one

---

[21] Lévinas, *Of God Who Comes to Mind*, 59.

who is eternally responsible. How long must we labor for the coming of the Messiah? According to the *Pesikta Rabbati*, 365,000 years (1:7). Which is to say: the wait is infinite, as our responsibility is infinite. Thus, said Rabbi Samuel ben Nachman, in the name of Rabbi Yonatan, "Cursed be the bones of those who calculate the end. For they would say, since the predetermined time has come, and yet the Messiah has not come, he will never come. Nevertheless, wait for him" (*Sanhedrin* 97b). In this *nevertheless* we have the needful response to anti-Semitism: do not calculate the "end" – hasten it. The time of the coming of the Messiah that is *now* is the time for which I am always too late, because it is always *already*: the Messiah abides in the nexus of the *not yet* and the *already*. To be sure, in the Talmud it is written that there will be no Messiah because those days have already passed, in the time of Hezekiah (*Sanhedrin* 99a); the point, however, is not to put an end to the task but to underscore its infinite duration. Even though – and precisely because – I am too late, I must hasten the coming of the Messiah.

If Democritus has something in common with Stokely Carmichael, it is because each of us has something in common with Adam. Because the adamic soul that harbors a trace of anti-Semitism also has its messianic side, however, we are as responsible for our Jew hatred as we are for our acts of loving kindness toward another. As anti-Semitism stems from despair, so is Messianism rooted in joy. Yitzchak Ginsburgh notes, in fact, that the Hebrew word for "Messiah," *Mashiach*, "can be understood as a permutation of the word *yismach*, meaning 'he will rejoice' or of the word *yesamach*, meaning 'he will make others rejoice.'"[22] For the divine presence, says the Talmud, abides neither "in levity nor in vain pursuits, but only in rejoicing" (*Pesachim* 117a). Why? Because only in rejoicing can we liberate ourselves from the self. And rejoicing is tied to thanksgiving. Recalling that the root of the word for "Jew," *Yehudi*, is *hodah*, which is to "give thanks," we realize that to be a Jew is to be grateful. If overcoming anti-Semitism entails assuming the Jewish condition, as Lawrence Newman did, it entails taking on a stance of gratitude before we see what there is to be grateful for. Indeed, no one is more ungrateful than an anti-Semite: filled with despair, in his or her soul there is no room for gratitude. Coming to the end of our investigation, we find that without gratitude, there is no room for the messianic side of the soul, the one antidote to anti-Semitism. When that side of the

---

[22] Yitzchak Ginsburgh, *Rectifying the State of Israel: A Political Platform Based on Kabbalah* (Jerusalem: Linda Pinsky Publications, 2003), 123.

soul ignites in the cry of "Here I am," it bursts into flames of joy and thanksgiving. Hence in the Midrash Rabbi Yochanan teaches in the name of Rabbi Menachem the Galilean that in the messianic age all prayers will cease except the prayers of joy and thanksgiving (*Midrash Tehillim* 2:56:4). Such prayers are a yea-saying to the mission for which every soul is chosen. That mission is to rid ourselves of the anti-Semite within us.

Bibliography

Aaron, David. *In Their Own Words: Voices of Jihad*. Santa Monica, Calif.: Rand Corporation, 2008.

Abrabanel, Don Isaac. *Abrabanel on Pirke Avot*. Trans. Abraham Chill. New York: Sepher-Hermon, 1991.

Abu-Amr, Ziad. *Islamic Fundamentalism in the West Bank and Gaza: Muslim Brotherhood and Islamic Jihad*. Bloomington: Indiana University Press, 1994.

Albo, Joseph. *Sefer HaIkkarim: Book of Principles*. 5 vols. Trans. Isaac Husik. Philadelphia: Jewish Publication Society, 1946.

Alexander, Edward. "Israelis against Themselves." In Edward Alexander and Paul Bogdanor, eds., *The Jewish Divide over Israel: Accusers and Defenders*. New Brunswick, N.J.: Transaction Publishers, 2008, pp. 33–46.

Alexander, Edward, and Paul Bogdanor, eds. *The Jewish Divide over Israel: Accusers and Defenders*. New Brunswick, N.J.: Transaction Publishers, 2008.

Alexander, Yonah. *Palestinian Religious Terrorism: Hamas and Islamic Jihad*. Ardsley, N.Y.: Transnational Publishers, 2002.

Alter, Yehudah Leib. *The Language of Truth: The Torah Commentary of the Sefat Emet*. Trans. Arthur Green. Philadelphia: Jewish Publication Society, 1998.

Améry, Jean. *At the Mind's Limits: Contemplations by a Survivor on Auschwitz and Its Realities*. Trans. Sidney Rosenfeld and Stella P. Rosenfeld. New York: Schocken Books, 1986.

Anti-Defamation League. *Holocaust Denial in the Middle East: The Latest Anti-Israel Propaganda Theme*. New York: Anti-Defamation League, 2001.

App, Austin J. *The Six Million Swindle: Blackmailing the German People for Hard Marks with Fabricated Corpses*. Tacoma Park, Md.: Boniface Press, 1973.

Applebaum, Shimon. *Jews and Greeks in Ancient Cyrene*. Leiden: Brill, 1979.

Aquinas, Thomas. *On Faith*. Trans. Mark D. Jordan. Notre Dame, Ind.: University of Notre Dame Press, 1990.

Summa Theologica: Volume III – Part II, Second Section. Dominican trans. New York: Cosimo, 2007.

Arendt, Hannah. *Antisemitism: Part One of the Origins of Totalitarianism.* New York: Harcourt Brace Jovanovich, 1968.

The Origins of Totalitarianism. New York: Harcourt Brace & Company, 1979.

Aron, Milton. *Ideas and Ideals of the Hassidim.* Secaucus, N.J.: Citadel, 1969.

Ateek, Naim Stifan. *Justice and Only Justice: A Palestinian Theology of Liberation.* Maryknoll, N.Y.: Orbis Books, 1989.

Atkins, Stephen E. *Holocaust Denial as an International Movement.* Westport, Conn.: Praeger, 2009.

Augustine. *The City of God.* Trans. Marcus Dods. New York: Random House, 2000.

Nicene and Post-Nicene Fathers: First Series Volume VI: Sermon on the Mount, Harmony of the Gospels, and Homilies on the Gospels. Ed. Philip Schaff. New York: Cosimo, 2007.

Azzam, Abdullah. *Defense of the Muslim Lands: First Obligation after Iman.* Trans. Brothers in Ribat. Available at http://www.ayyaz.com.pk/Books/Shaykh .Abdullah.Azzam/Defence.of.the.Muslim.Lands.-.the.First.Obligation.After .Iman.pdf.

Baal HaTurim. *Commentary on the Torah: Bereshis.* Trans. Avie Gold. Brooklyn: Mesorah, 1999.

Baeck, Leo. *The Essence of Judaism.* Revised ed. Trans. Victor Grubenwieser and Leonard Pearl. New York: Schocken Books, 1948.

Baerwald, Thomas J., and Celeste Fraser. *World Geography: Building a Global Perspective.* Upper Saddle River, N.J.: Prentice Hall, 2007.

The Bahir. Trans. Aryeh Kaplan. York Beach, Maine: Samuel Weiser, 1979.

Al-Banna, Hasan. *Five Tracts of Hasan al-Banna: A Selection from the Majmuat Rasail al-Imam al-Shahid Hasan al-Banna.* Trans. Charles Wendell. Berkeley: University of California Press, 1978.

Memoirs of Hasan al Banna Shaheed. Trans. M. N. Shaikh. Karachi: International Islamic Publishers, 1981.

Bardèche, Maurice. *Nuremberg ou la terre promise.* Paris: Le Sept Couleurs, 1948.

Barnes, Jonathan, ed. *Early Greek Philosophy.* Trans. Jonathan Barnes. New York: Penguin, 2002.

Bat Ye'or. *The Dhimmi: Jews and Christians under Islam.* Teaneck, N.J.: Fairleigh Dickinson University Press, 1985.

The Decline of Eastern Christianity under Islam: From Jihad to Dhimmitude. Madison, N.J.: Fairleigh Dickinson University Press, 1996.

Beck, Edward S. "Scholars for Peace in the Middle East (SPME): Fighting Anti-Israelism and Anti-Semitism on the University Campuses Worldwide." In Manfred Gerstenfeld, ed., *Academics against Israel and the Jews.* Jerusalem: Jerusalem Center for Public Affairs, 2007, pp. 134–146.

Beham, Markus P. "'Borrowed' Concepts: The Pitfalls of 'Atrocity Labeling' in Contemporary Historiography." In Marija Wakounig and Markus Peter Beham, eds., *Transgressing Boundaries: Humanities in Flux.* Berlin: Lit Verlag, 2013, pp. 73–92.

Beiser, Frederick C. "Kant's Intellectual Development: 1746–1781." In Paul Guyer, ed. *The Cambridge Companion to Kant*. Cambridge, U.K.: Cambridge University Press, 1992, pp. 2–61.

Berkovits, Eliezer. *Faith after the Holocaust*. New York: Ktav, 1973.

Bernstein, Perez. *Jew-Hate as a Sociological Problem*. Trans. David Saraph. New York: Philosophical Library, 1951.

Bigsby, C. W. E. *Arthur Miller: A Critical Study*. Cambridge, U.K.: Cambridge University Press, 2005.

Billington, James H. *Fire in the Minds of Men: Origins of the Revolutionary Faith*. New Brunswick, N.J.: Transaction Publishers, 1999.

Bin Laden, Osama. *Messages to the World: The Statements of Osama bin Laden*. Ed. Bruce Lawrence. Trans. James Howarth. London: Verso, 2005.

Bird, Michael F., and Joseph R. Dodson, eds. *Paul and the Second Century*. London: T&T Clark, 2011.

Bloch, Ernst. *The Spirit of Utopia*. Trans. Anthony Nassar. Stanford, Calif.: Stanford University Press, 2000.

Bogdanor, Paul. "Chomsky's Ayatollahs." In Edward Alexander and Paul Bogdanor, eds., *The Jewish Divide over Israel: Accusers and Defenders*. New Brunswick, N.J.: Transaction Publishers, 2008, pp. 115–134.

"The Devil State: Chomsky's War against Israel." In Edward Alexander and Paul Bogdanor, eds., *The Jewish Divide over Israel: Accusers and Defenders*. New Brunswick, N.J.: Transaction Publishers, 2008, pp. 77–114.

"Norman G. Finkelstein: Chomsky for Nazis." In Edward Alexander and Paul Bogdanor, eds., *The Jewish Divide over Israel: Accusers and Defenders*. New Brunswick, N.J.: Transaction Publishers, 2008, pp. 135–160.

Bonner, Michael. *Jihad in Islamic History: Doctrine and Practices*. Princeton, N.J.: Princeton University Press, 2006.

Bostom, Andrew G. "Jihad Conquests and the Imposition of *Dhimmitude* – A Survey." In Andrew G. Bostom, ed., *The Legacy of Jihad: Islamic Holy War and the Fate of Non-Muslims*. Amherst, N.Y.: Prometheus Books, 2005, pp. 24–124.

The Legacy of Jihad: Islamic Holy War and the Fate of Non-Muslims. Amherst, N.Y.: Prometheus Books, 2005.

Brunner, Constantin. *The Tyranny of Hate/The Roots of Antisemitism*. Trans. Graham Harrison. Ed. Aron M. Rappaport. Lewiston, Idaho: Edwin Mellen Press, 1992.

Buber, Martin. *On Judaism*. Trans. Eva Jospe. Ed. Nahum N. Glatzer. New York: Schocken Books, 1967.

Bukay, David, ed. *Muhammad's Monsters: A Comprehensive Guide to Radical Islam for Western Audiences*. Green Forest, Ark.: Balfour Books, 2004.

Burns, Robert A. *Christianity, Islam, and the West*. Lanham, Md.: University Press of America, 2011.

Butz, Arthur R. *The Hoax of the Twentieth Century: The Case against the Presumed Extermination of European Jewry*. Torrance, Calif.: Historical Review Press, 1976.

Cain, Andrew, and Josef Lössl, eds. *Jerome of Stridon: His Life, Writings and Legacy*. Surrey, U.K.: Ashgate Publishing, 2009.

Calvin, John. *Institutes of the Christian Religion.* Trans. Henry Beveridge. Peabody, Mass.: Hendrickson, 2003.

Camus, Albert. *The Myth of Sisyphus.* Trans. Justin O'Brien. New York: Random House, 1955.

Caputo, John D. "Heidegger's Scandal: Thinking and the Essence of the Victim." In Tom Rockmore and Joseph Margolis, eds., *The Heidegger Case: On Philosophy and Politics.* Philadelphia: Temple University Press, 1992, pp. 265–281.

Cargas, Harry James. *Reflections of a Post-Auschwitz Christian.* Detroit, Mich.: Wayne State University Press, 1989.

Carmichael, Joel. *The Satanizing of the Jews: Origin and Development of Mystical Anti- Semitism.* New York: Fromm International Publishing Corporation, 1992.

Chamberlain, Houston Stewart. *Richard Wagner.* Trans. G. Ainsle Hight. London: J. M. Dent, 1900.

The Foundations of the Nineteenth Century. Vol. 1. Trans. John Lees. London: John Lane, 1911.

Chayim ben Attar. *Or HaChayim.* 5 vols. Trans. Eliyahu Munk. Jerusalem: Munk, 1995.

Chehab, Zaki. *Inside Hamas: The Untold Story of the Militant Islamic Movement.* New York: Nation Books, 2007.

Cheyette, Bryan, and Laura Marcus, eds. *Modernity, Culture, and "the Jew."* Stanford, Calif.: Stanford University Press, 1998.

Chomsky, Noam. *Fateful Triangle: United States, Israel and the Palestinians.* London: Pluto Press, 1999.

Middle East Illusions. Lanham, Md.: Rowman & Littlefield, 2003.

Chrysostom, John. *Discourses against Judaizing Christians.* Washington, D.C.: Catholic University Press of America, 1979.

Clement of Alexandria. The Miscellanies or Stromata. Trans. William Wilson. In Alexander Roberts and James Donaldson, eds., *Clement of Alexandria: Ante Nicene Christian Library Translations of the Writings of the Fathers to AD 325, Part Four.* Whitefish, Mont.: Kessinger, 2007, pp. 349–470.

Cohen, Arthur A., ed. *Arguments and Doctrines: A Reader of Jewish Thinking in the Aftermath of the Holocaust.* New York: Harper & Row, 1970.

"Thinking the *Tremendum.*" In Michael L. Morgan, ed., *A Holocaust Reader: Responses to the Nazi Extermination.* New York: Oxford University Press, 2001, pp. 183–196.

Cohen, Hermann. *Reason and Hope: Selections from the Jewish Writings of Hermann Cohen.* Trans. Eva Jospe. Cincinnati, Ohio: Hebrew Union College Press, 1993.

Religion of Reason out of the Sources of Judaism. Trans. Simon Kaplan. Atlanta, Ga.: Scholars Press, 1995.

Cohen, Richard A., ed. *Face to Face with Levinas.* Albany: SUNY Press, 1986.

Cohen, Victor, ed. *The Soul of the Torah: Insights of the Chasidic Masters on the Weekly Torah Portions.* Northvale, N.J.: Jason Aronson, 2000.

Cohn-Sherbok, Dan. *Anti-Semitism.* Stroud, U.K.: The History Press, 2002.

Conrad, Joseph. *The Secret Sharer.* New York: St. Martin's Press, 1997.

Crétella, Henri. "Self-Destruction." In Alan Milchman and Alan Rosenberg, eds., *Martin Heidegger and the Holocaust*. Atlantic Highlands, N.J.: Humanities Press, 1996, pp. 150–166.

Culi, Yaakov. *The Torah Anthology: MeAm Lo'ez*. Vol. 1. Trans. Aryeh Kaplan. New York: Moznaim, 1977.

Cyprian. "Three Books of Testimonies against the Jews." In Alexander Roberts and James Donaldson, eds., *The Writings of Cyprian Bishop of Carthage II: Ante Nicene Christian Library Translations of the Fathers down to AD 325, Part Thirteen*. Whitefish, Mont.: Kessinger, 2004, pp. 78–98.

Dalin, David G., and John F. Rothman. *Icon of Evil: Hitler's Mufti and the Rise of Radical Islam*. New York: Random House, 2008.

Darré, Richard Walther. *Um Blut und Boden: Reden und Aufsätze*. Munich: Zentralverlag der NSDAP, 1940.

Democritus. Maxims. Trans. Jonathan Barnes. In Jonathan Barnes, ed. *Early Greek Philosophy*. Trans. Jonathan Barnes. New York, Penguin, 2002, pp. 203–253.

Derrida, Jacques. *De l'esprit*. Paris: Éditions Galilee, 1987.

Descartes, René. *Meditations on First Philosophy*. Trans. Donald A. Cress. 3rd ed. Indianapolis, Ind.: Hackett, 1993.

D'Hippolito, Joseph. "Patriarch of Terror." FrontPageMag.com, 4 January 2005. Available at http://archive.frontpagemag.com/readArticle.aspx ?ARTID=10031.

Dmowski, Roman. "The Jews and the War." Trans. Richard S. Levy. In Richard S. Levy, ed., *Antisemitism in the Modern World: An Anthology of Texts*. Lexington, Mass.: D. C. Heath and Company, 1991, pp. 182–192.

Dostoyevsky, F. M. The *Possessed*. Trans. Andrew R. MacAndrew. New York: New American Library, 1962.

Dribben, Judith. *And Some Shall Live*. Jerusalem: Keter Books, 1969.

Drumont, Édouard. *Les Juifs contre la France*. Paris: Librairie Antisémite, 1899.

Dunn, Geoffrey D. *Tertullian (The Early Church Fathers)*. London: Routledge, 2004.

Eaglestone, Robert. *Postmodernism and Holocaust Denial*. Duxford, U.K.: Icon Books, 2001.

Ellis, Elizabeth Gaynor, and Anthony Esler. *World History*. Upper Saddle River, N.J.: Prentice Hall, 2007.

Erwin, Edward ed. *The Freud Encyclopedia: Theory, Therapy, and Culture*. New York: Routledge, 2002.

Evans, Harold. *They Made America*. New York: Little, Brown, 2004.

Fackenheim, Emil L. *Quest for Past and Future: Essays in Jewish Theology*. Bloomington: Indiana University Press, 1968.

God's Presence in History: Jewish Affirmations and Philosophical Reflections. New York: Harper & Row, 1970.

"Jewish Existence and the Living God: The Religious Duty of Survival." In Arthur A. Cohen, ed., *Arguments and Doctrines: A Reader of Jewish Thinking in the Aftermath of the Holocaust*. New York: Harper & Row, 1970, pp. 252–269.

Jewish-Christian Relations after the Holocaust: Toward Post-Holocaust Theological Thought. Chicago: The Joseph Cardinal Bernardin Jerusalem Lecture, 1977.

The Jewish Return into History. New York: Schocken Books, 1978.

What Is Judaism? New York: Macmillan, 1987.

To Mend the World: Foundations of Post-Holocaust Jewish Thought. New York: Schocken Books, 1989.

Encounters between Judaism and Modern Philosophy. New York: Basic Books, 1993.

Jewish Philosophers and Jewish Philosophy. Ed. Michael L. Morgan. Bloomington: Indiana University Press, 1996.

"Jewish Faith and the Holocaust: A Fragment." In Michael L. Morgan, ed., *A Holocaust Reader: Responses to the Nazi Extermination.* New York: Oxford University Press, 2001, pp. 115–121.

Falk, Avner. *Anti-Semitism: A History and Psychoanalysis of Contemporary Hatred.* Westport, Conn.: Praeger, 2008.

Farías, Victor. *Heidegger and Nazism.* Trans. Paul Burrell. Philadelphia: Temple University Press, 1989.

Fasching, Darrell J. *Narrative Theology after Auschwitz: From Alienation to Ethics.* Minneapolis, Minn.: Fortress, 1992.

Faurisson, Robert. *The Problem of the Gas Chambers.* Newport Beach, Calif.: Institute for Historical Review, 1980.

Feldman, Louis H. *Jew and Gentile in the Ancient World.* Princeton, N.J.: Princeton University Press, 1993.

Feuerbach, Ludwig. *The Essence of Christianity.* Trans. George Eliot. New York: Harper & Row, 1957.

Fichte, Johann Gottlieb. *Addresses to the German Nation.* Ed. George Armstrong Kelly. New York: Harper & Row, 1968.

Finkel, Avraham Yaakov. *Kabbalah: Selections from Classic Kabbalistic Works from Raziel HaMalach to the Present Day.* Southfield, Mich.: Targum Press, 2002.

Finkelstein, Louis. *Akiba: Scholar, Saint and Martyr.* New York: Atheneum, 1981.

Firestone, Reuven. *Jihad: The Origin of Holy War in Islam.* Oxford, U.K.: Oxford University Press, 1999.

Flannery, Edward H. *The Anguish of the Jews: Twenty-three Centuries of Anti-Semitism.* New York: Macmillan, 1965.

Flaubert, Gustave. *Madame Bovary.* Trans. Geoffrey Wall. New York: Penguin Books, 2002.

Ford, Henry. *The International Jew: The World's Foremost Problem.* Eastford, Conn.: Martino Fine Books, 2010.

Frankel, Jonathan. *The Damascus Affair: "Ritual Murder," Politics, and the Jews in 1840.* Cambridge, Eng.: Cambridge University Press, 1997.

"Assimilation and the Jews in Nineteenth-Century Europe: Towards a New Historiography?" In Jonathan Frankel and Steven J. Zipperstein, eds., *Assimilation and Community: The Jews in Nineteenth-Century Europe.* Cambridge, U.K.: Cambridge University Press, 2004, pp. 1–37.

Frankel, Jonathan, and Steven J. Zipperstein, eds. *Assimilation and Community: The Jews in Nineteenth-Century Europe*. Cambridge, U.K.: Cambridge University Press, 2004.

Fraser, Ronnie. "The Academic Boycott of Israel: Why Britain?" In Manfred Gerstenfeld, ed., *Academics against Israel and the Jews*. Jerusalem: Jerusalem Center for Public Affairs, 2007, pp. 198–213.

Freud, Sigmund. *Moses and Monotheism*. Trans. Katherine Jones. New York: Vintage Books, 1955.

Gager, John G. *The Origins of Anti-Semitism: Attitudes toward Judaism in Pagan and Christian Antiquity*. Oxford, U.K.: Oxford University Press, 1983.

Garaudy, Roger. *The Founding Myths of Modern Israel*. Newport Beach, Calif.: Institute for Historical Review, 2000.

Geiger, Abraham. "Jewish Scholarship and Religious Reform." In Paul Mendes-Flohr and Jehuda Reinharz, eds., *The Jew in the Modern World: A Documentary History*. 2nd ed. Oxford, U.K.: Oxford University Press, 1995, p. 233.

Gerstenfeld, Manfred, ed. *Academics against Israel and the Jews*. Jerusalem: Jerusalem Center for Public Affairs, 2007.

"Academics against Israel and the Jews." In Manfred Gerstenfeld, ed., *Academics against Israel and the Jews*. Jerusalem: Jerusalem Center for Public Affairs, 2007, pp. 17–82.

Gilman, Sander L. *Jewish Self-Hatred: Anti-Semitism and the Hidden Language of the Jews*. Baltimore, Md.: Johns Hopkins University Press, 1986.

"Otto Weininger and Sigmund Freud: Race and Gender in the Shaping of Psychoanalysis." In Nancy Anne Harrowitz and Barbara Hyams, eds., *Jews and Gender: Responses to Otto Weininger*. Philadelphia: Temple University Press, 1995, pp. 103–120.

Ginsburgh, Yitzchak. *The Alef-Beit: Jewish Thought Revealed through the Hebrew Letters*. Northvale, N.J.: Jason Aronson, 1991.

Glass, James M. *Jewish Resistance during the Holocaust: Moral Uses of Violence and Will*. New York: Palgrave Macmillan, 2004.

Glazerson, Matityahu. *Building Blocks of the Soul: Studies on the Letters and Words of the Hebrew Language*. Northvale, N.J.: Jason Aronson, 1997.

Gobineau, Arthur de. *The Inequality of Human Races*. Trans. Adrain Collins. New York: G. P. Putnam's Sons, 1915.

Goebbels, Joseph. *Die Tagebücher von Joseph Goebbels: Sämtliche Fragmente*. Ed. Elke Fröhlich. Munich: K. G. Saur, 1998.

Goldschläger, Alain. "The Canadian Campus Scene." In Manfred Gerstenfeld, ed., *Academics against Israel and the Jews*. Jerusalem: Jerusalem Center for Public Affairs, 2007, pp. 154–162.

Goodwin, George M., and Ellen Smith, eds. *The Jews of Rhode Island*. Hanover, N.H.: Brandeis University Press and the University Press of New England, 2004.

Gottfried, Martin. *Arthur Miller: His Life and His Work*. Cambridge, Mass.: Da Capo Press, 2006.

Gouri, Haim. *Facing the Glass Booth: The Jerusalem Trial of Adolf Eichmann*. Trans. Michael Swirsky. Detroit, Mich.: Wayne State University Press, 2004.

Greenberg, Eric J. "Open Season on Jews." *The Jewish Week*, 11 May 2001.

Gregory of Nyssa. Against Eunomius. In Philip Schaff and Henry Wace, eds., *A Select Library of Nicene and Post-Nicene Fathers of the Christian Church: Select Writings and Letters of Gregory, Bishop of Nyssa.* Trans. William Moore and Henry Austin Wilson. New York: The Christian Literature Company, 1893, pp. 33–249.

Grosser, Paul E., and Edwin G. Halpern. *Anti-Semitism: The Cause and Effects of a Prejudice.* Secaucus, N.J.: Citadel Press, 1979.

Gunaratna, Rohan. *Inside Al Qaeda: Global Network of Terror.* New York: Columbia University Press, 2002.

Guyer, Paul, ed. *The Cambridge Companion to Kant.* Cambridge, U.K.: Cambridge University Press, 1992.

"Hamas Leader Rantisi: The False Holocaust." MEMRI, 27 August 2003. Available at http://www.memri.org/bin/articles.cgi?Page=subjects&Area=antisemitism&ID=SP5580.

Hand, Sean, ed. *The Levinas Reader.* Oxford, U.K.: Basil Blackwell, 1989.

Hanke, Lewis, and Jane M. Rausch, eds. *People and Issues in Latin American History: The Colonial Experience.* Princeton, N.J.: Markus Wiener Publishers, 2006.

Harris, Christina Phelps. *Nationalism and Revolution in Egypt: The Role of the Muslim Brotherhood.* The Hague: Mouton & Co., 1964.

Harrowitz, Nancy Anne, and Barbara Hyams, eds. *Jews and Gender: Responses to Otto Weininger.* Philadelphia: Temple University Press, 1995.

Hazony, Yoram. *The Jewish State: The Struggle for Israel's Soul.* New York: Basic Books, 2001.

HeChasid, Yehuda. *Sefer Chasidim.* Trans. Avraham Yaakov Finkel. Northvale, N.J.: Jason Aronson, 1997.

Hegel, G. W. F. *Early Theological Writings.* Trans. T. M. Knox. Chicago, Ill.: University of Chicago Press, 1948.

The Philosophy of Right. Trans. S. W. Dyde. New York: Cosimo, 2008.

Phenomenology of Spirit (The Phenomenology of Mind). Trans. J. B. Baillie. Digireads.com Publishing, 2009.

Heidegger, Martin. *Sein und Zeit.* 2nd ed. Tübingen: Max Niemeyer, 1929.

Kant and the Problem of Metaphysics. Trans. J. S. Churchill. Bloomington: Indiana University Press, 1962.

Vom Wesen des Grundes. 5th ed. Frankfurt am Main: Klostermann, 1965.

Poetry, Language, Thought. Trans. Albert Hofstadter. New York: Harper & Row, 1971.

Nietzsche. 2 vols. Trans. D. Krell. San Francisco: Harper & Row, 1979.

"Martin Heidegger: A Philosopher and Politics: A Conversation." In Guenther Neske and Emil Kettering, eds., *Martin Heidegger and National Socialism.* Trans. Lisa Harries. New York: Paragon, 1990, pp. 175–195.

"The Self-Assertion of the German University." In Guenther Neske and Emil Kettering, eds., *Martin Heidegger and National Socialism.* Trans. Lisa Harries. New York: Paragon, 1990, pp. 5–13.

Beiträge zur Philosophie. In *Gesamtausgabe*, vol. 65. Frankfurt: Vittorio Klostermann, 2003.

Heine, Heinrich. *Words of Prose*. Trans. E. B. Ashton. New York: L. B. Fischer, 1943.

The Complete Poems of Heinrich Heine: A Modern English Version. Trans. Hal Draper. Boston: Suhrkamp/Insel, 1982.

Herf, Jeffrey. *Nazi Propaganda for the Arab World*. New Haven, Conn.: Yale University Press, 2009.

Heschel, Abraham Joshua. *Man Is Not Alone*. New York: Farrar, Straus and Giroux, 1951.

God in Search of Man. New York: Farrar, Straus and Giroux, 1955.

The Prophets. 2 vols. New York: Harper & Row, 1962, 1975.

Israel: An Echo of Eternity. New York: Farrar, Straus and Giroux, 1969.

A Passion for Truth. New York: Farrar, Straus and Giroux, 1973.

Between God and Man: An Interpretation of Judaism. New York: Free Press, 1997.

Hilberg, Raul. *The Destruction of the European Jews*. Chicago, Ill.: Quadrangle Books, 1961.

Hitler, Adolf. *Mein Kampf*. Munich: Zentralverlag der NSADP, 1927.

Mein Kampf. Trans. Ralph Manheim. Boston: Houghton Mifflin, 1971.

Hoggan, David. *The Myth of the Six Million*. Los Angeles, Calif.: Noontide Press, 1969.

Holmes, Colin. "Alexander Ratcliffe: Militant Protestant and Antisemite." In Tony Kushner and Ken Lunn, eds., *Traditions of Intolerance: Historical Perspectives on Fascism and Race Discourse in Britain*. Manchester, U.K.: University of Manchester Press, 1989, pp. 196–217.

Holtz, Barry W. *Back to the Sources: Reading the Classic Jewish Texts*. New York: Simon & Schuster, 1984.

Honsik, Gerd. *Freispruch für Hitler?: 36 Ungehörte Zeugen wider die Gaskammer*. Vienna: Burgenländischer Kulturverband, 1988.

Horowitz, Isaiah. *The Generations of Adam*. Trans. and ed. Miles Krassen. New York: Paulist Press, 1996.

Huberband, Shimon. *Kiddush Hashem: Jewish Religious and Cultural Life in Poland during the Holocaust*. Trans. David E. Fishman. Ed. Jeffrey S. Gurock and Robert S. Hirt. Hoboken, N.J.: Ktav and Yeshiva University Press, 1987.

Hyams, Barbara, and Nancy Anne Harrowitz. "A Critical Introduction to the History of Weininger Reception." In Nancy Anne Harrowitz and Barbara Hyams, eds., *Jews and Gender: Responses to Otto Weininger*. Philadelphia: Temple University Press, 1995, pp. 3–20.

Ibn Khaldun. *The Muqudimmah: An Introduction to History*. Trans. Franz Rosenthal. New York: Pantheon, 1958.

Ibrahim, Raymond, ed. *The Al Qaeda Reader*. Trans. Raymond Ibrahim. New York: Doubleday, 2007.

Idel, Moshe. *Language, Torah, and Hermeneutics in Abraham Abulafia*. Albany: SUNY Press, 1989.

Ignatius of Antioch, "Letter to the Magnesians." In William A. Jurgens, ed., *The Faith of the Early Fathers*. Vol. 1. Collegeville, Minn.: The Order of St. Benedict, 1970, pp. 19–20.

"To the Philadelphians." In Andrew Louth, ed., *Early Christian Writings: The Apostolic Fathers*. Trans. Maxwell Staniforth. London: Penguin Books, 1987, pp. 91–98.

Irenaeus. *Against Heresies*. Ed. Paul Böer. Rome: Veritatis Splendor Publications, 2012.

Jacobs, Louis. *Hasidic Prayer*. New York: Schocken Books, 1972.

Jaeger, Werner. *Early Christianity and Greek Paideia*. Cambridge, Mass.: Harvard University Press, 1961.

Jerome. *Commentary on Galatians*. Trans. Andrew Cain. Washington, D.C.: Catholic University of America Press, 2010.

Jorisch, Avi. *Beacon of Hatred: Inside Hizballah's Al-Manar Television*. Washington, D.C.: Washington Institute for Near East Policy, 2004.

Judaken, Jonathan. *Jean-Paul Sartre and the Jewish Question: Antisemitism and the Politics of the French Intellectual*. Lincoln: University of Nebraska Press, 2006.

Juel, Donald. *Messianic Exegesis: Christological Interpretation of the Old Testament*. Minneapolis, Minn.: Fortress Press, 1992.

Jurgens, William A., ed. *The Faith of the Early Fathers*. Vol. 1. Collegeville, Minn.: The Order of St. Benedict, 1970.

Justin Martyr. *Dialogue with Trypho*. Trans. Thomas B. Falls. Washington, D.C.: Catholic University of America Press, 2003.

Juvenal. *The Sixteen Satires*. Trans. Peter Green. London: Penguin Books, 1998.

Kalmanovitch, Zelig. "A Diary of the Nazi Ghetto in Vilna." Trans. and ed. Koppel S. Pinson, *YIVO Annual of Jewish Social Studies* 8 (1953): 9–81.

Kamen, Henry. *The Spanish Inquisition: A Historical Revision*. New Haven, Conn.: Yale University Press, 1998.

Kant, Immanuel. *Religion within the Limits of Reason Alone*. Trans. Theodore M. Greene and Hoyt H. Hudson. New York: Harper & Brothers, 1960.
Anthropology from a Pragmatic Point of View. Trans. Victor Lyle Dowdell. Carbondale: Southern Illinois University Press, 1978.
The Conflict of the Faculties. Trans. Mary J. Gregor. New York: Abaris, 1979.
Grounding for the Metaphysics of Morals. Trans. James W. Ellington. Indianapolis, Ind.: Hackett, 1981.
The Critique of Practical Reason. Trans. Lewis White Beck. New York: Macmillan, 1985.
Critique of Pure Reason. Trans. and ed. Marcus Weigelt. New York: Penguin Classics, 2008.

Kaplan, Chaim A. *The Warsaw Diary of Chaim A. Kaplan*. Trans. and ed. Abraham I. Katsh. New York: Collier, 1973.

Kapustyan, Dimitry, and Matt Nelson. *The Soul of Terror: The Worldwide Conflict between Islamic Terrorism and the Modern World*. Washington, D.C.: International Affairs Press, 2007.

Karsh, Efraim. *Arafat's War: The Man and His Battle for Israeli Conquest*. New York: Grove Press, 2003.

Katz, Jacob. *From Prejudice to Destruction: Anti-Semitism, 1700–1933*. Cambridge, Mass.: Harvard University Press, 1980.

Katz, Steven T. *The Holocaust in Historical Context.* Vol. 1: *The Holocaust and Mass Death before the Modern Age.* New York: Oxford University Press, 1994.

Ka-tzetnik 135633. *Shivitti: A Vision.* Trans. Eliyah De-Nur and Lisa Herman. New York: Harper & Row, 1989.

Kaddish. Trans. Nina De-Nur. New York: Algemeiner Associates, 1998.

Katznelson, Yitzhak. *Vittel Diary.* Trans. Myer Cohn. 2nd ed. Tel-Aviv: Hakibbutz Hameuchad, 1972.

Kelly, J. N. D. *Early Christian Creeds.* 3rd ed. London: Continuum, 1972.

Keter Shem Tov. Brooklyn: Kehot, 1972.

Khadduri, Majid. "The Law of War: The Jihad." In Andrew G. Bostom, ed., *The Legacy of Jihad: Islamic Holy War and the Fate of Non-Muslims.* Amherst, N.Y.: Prometheus Books, 2005, pp. 305–319.

Khomeini, Ruhullah. *Islamic Government.* New York: Manor Books, 1979.

Islam and Revolution: Writings and Declarations of Imam Khomeini (1941–1980). Trans. Hamid Algar. Berkeley, Calif.: Mizan Press, 1981.

Kierkegaard, Søren. *Concluding Unscientific Postscript.* Trans. David Swenson and Walter Lowrie. Princeton, N.J.: Princeton University Press, 1941.

The Sickness Unto Death. Trans. Walter Lowrie. Princeton, N.J.: Princeton University Press, 1941.

Fear and Trembling. Trans. Alastair Hannay. New York: Penguin Books, 1985.

Kisiel, Theodore. "Heidegger's Apology: Biography and Philosophy and Ideology." In Tom Rockmore and Joseph Margolis, eds., *The Heidegger Case: On Philosophy and Politics.* Philadelphia: Temple University Press, 1992, pp. 11–54.

Kitov, Eliyahu. *The Book of Our Heritage.* 3 vols. Trans. Nathan Bluman. New York: Feldheim Publishers, 1973.

Kitzur Shulchan Arukh – Code of Jewish Law. 4 vols. Compiled by R. Solomon Ganzfried. Trans. Hyman E. Goldin. Rev. ed. New York: Hebrew Publishing Co., 1961.

Korn, Eugene B., and John Pawlikowski. *Two Faiths, One Covenant? Jewish and Christian Identity in the Presence of the Other.* Lanham, Md.: Rowman & Littlefield, 2005.

Kramer, Martin. "Columbia University: The Future of Middle Eastern Studies at Stake." In Manfred Gerstenfeld, ed., *Academics against Israel and the Jews.* Jerusalem: Jerusalem Center for Public Affairs, 2007, pp. 103–107.

Kressel, Neil J. *"The Sons of Pigs and Apes": Muslim Antisemitism and the Conspiracy of Silence.* Washington, D.C.: Potomac Books, 2012.

Kruk, Herman. *The Last Days of the Jerusalem of Lithuania: Chronicles from the Vilna Ghetto and the Camps, 1939–1944.* Ed. Benjamin Harshav. Trans. Barbara Harshav. New Haven, Conn.: Yale University Press, 2002.

Küntzel, Matthias. "National Socialism and Anti-Semitism in the Arab World," *Jewish Political Studies Review* (17, Spring 2005). Available at http://www.jcpa.org/phas/phas-kuntzel-s05.htm.

Jihad and Jew-Hatred: Islamism, Nazism and the Roots of 9/11. Trans. Colin Meade. New York: Telos Press, 2007.

Kushner, Tony, and Ken Lunn, eds. *Traditions of Intolerance: Historical Perspectives on Fascism and Race Discourse in Britain.* Manchester, U.K.: University of Manchester Press, 1989.

LaCapra, Dominick. *Writing History, Writing Trauma.* Baltimore, Md.: Johns Hopkins University Press, 2001.

Lamm, Norman. *The Religious Thought of Hasidism: Text and Commentary.* Hoboken, N.J.: Ktav, 1999.

Lang, Berel. *Act and Idea in the Nazi Genocide.* Syracuse, N.Y.: Syracuse University Press, 2003.

Langmuir, Gavin I. *History, Religion, and Antisemitism.* Berkeley: University of California Press, 1990.

Laqueur, Walter. *The Changing Face of Antisemitism: From Ancient Times to the Present Day.* Oxford, U.K.: Oxford University Press, 2006.

ed. *Voices of Terror.* New York: Reed Press, 2004.

Lazare, Bernard. *Antisemitism: Its History and Causes.* Lincoln: University of Nebraska Press, 1995.

Lehmann, Ernst. *Biologischer Wille: Wege und Ziele biologischer Arbeit im neuen Reich.* Munich: Zentralverlag der NSDAP, 1934.

Leuchter, Fred A., Robert Faurisson, and Germar Rudolf. *The Leuchter Reports: Critical Edition.* Chicago, Ill.: Theses and Dissertations Press, 2005.

Levi, Primo. *The Reawakening.* Trans. Stuart Wolf. Boston: Little, Brown, 1965.

The Drowned and the Saved. Trans. Raymond Rosenthal. New York: Vintage Books, 1989.

Survival in Auschwitz: The Nazi Assault on Humanity. Trans. Stuart Woolf. New York: Simon & Schuster, 1996.

Levin, Andrea. "Updated: Tony Kushner's Anti-Israel Falsehoods Thwart CUNY Award." *CAMERA*, 11 May 2011. Available at http://www.camera.org/index. asp?x_context=8&x_nameinnews=181&x_article=2033.

Lévinas, Emmanuel. *Totality and Infinity.* Trans. Alphonso Lingis. Pittsburgh, Pa.: Duquesne University Press, 1969.

Otherwise Than Being or Beyond Essence. Trans. Alphonso Lingis. The Hague: Nijhoff, 1981.

Ethics and Infinity. Trans. Richard A. Cohen. Pittsburgh, Pa.: Duquesne University Press, 1985.

"Dialogue with Emmanuel Lévinas." In Richard A. Cohen, ed., *Face to Face with Levinas.* Albany: SUNY Press, 1986, pp. 13–33.

Collected Philosophical Papers. Trans. Alphonso Lingis. Dordrecht: Martinus Nijhoff, 1987.

Time and the Other. Trans. Richard A. Cohen. Pittsburgh, Pa.: Duquesne University Press, 1987.

"Revelation in the Jewish Tradition." Trans. Sarah Richmond. In Sean Hand, ed., *The Levinas Reader.* Oxford, U.K.: Basil Blackwell, 1989, pp. 190–210.

"Zionisms." Trans. Roland Lack. In Sean Hand, ed., *The Levinas Reader.* Oxford, U.K.: Basil Blackwell, 1989, pp. 267–88.

Difficult Freedom: Essays on Judaism. Trans. Sean Hand. Baltimore, Md.: Johns Hopkins University Press, 1990.

Nine Talmudic Readings. Trans. Annette Aronowicz. Bloomington: Indiana University Press, 1990.

Outside the Subject. Trans. Michael B. Smith. Stanford, Calif.: Stanford University Press, 1994.

Basic Philosophical Writings. Ed. Adriaan T. Peperzak, Simon Critchley, and Robert Bernasconi. Bloomington: Indiana University Press, 1996.

Proper Names. Trans. Michael B. Smith. Stanford, Calif.: Stanford University Press, 1996.

Of God Who Comes to Mind. Trans. Bettina Bergo. Stanford, Calif.: Stanford University Press, 1998.

New Talmudic Readings. Trans. Richard A. Cohen. Pittsburgh, Pa.: Duquesne University Press, 1999.

God, Death, and Time. Trans. Bettina Bergo. Stanford, Calif.: Stanford University Press, 2000.

Is It Righteous to Be? Interviews with Emmanuel Levinas. Ed. Jill Robbins. Stanford, Calif.: Stanford University Press, 2001.

Levy, Richard S., ed. *Antisemitism in the Modern World: An Anthology of Texts.* Lexington, Mass.: D. C. Heath and Company, 1991.

Lewis, Bernard. *Semites and Anti-Semites: An Inquiry into Conflict and Prejudice.* New York: W. W. Norton & Co., 1986.

Lindemann, Albert S. *Esau's Tears: Modern Anti-Semitism and the Rise of the Jews.* Cambridge, U.K.: Cambridge University Press, 1997.

Lipstadt, Deborah E. *Denying the Holocaust: The Growing Assault on Truth and Memory.* New York: The Free Press, 1993.

Littell, Franklin H. *The Crucifixion of the Jews: The Failure of Christians to Understand the Jewish Experience.* Macon, Ga.: Mercer University Press, 1986.

Loeve, Yehuda. *Maharal of Prague: Pirke Avos.* Trans. and ed. R. Tuvia Basser. Brooklyn: Mesorah, 1997.

Lohse, Bernhard. *Martin Luther's Theology: Its Historical and Systematic Development.* Minneapolis, Minn.: Augsburg Fortress, 1999.

Losurlo, Domenico. "Heidegger and Hitler's War." In Tom Rockmore and Joseph Margolis, eds., *The Heidegger Case: On Philosophy and Politics.* Philadelphia: Temple University Press, 1992, pp. 141–164.

Louth, Andrew, ed. *Early Christian Writings: The Apostolic Fathers.* Trans. Maxwell Staniforth. London: Penguin Books, 1987.

Löwith, Karl. "Last Meeting with Heidegger." In Guenther Neske and Emil Kettering, eds., *Martin Heidegger and National Socialism.* Trans. Lisa Harries. New York: Paragon, 1990, pp. 157–159.

Lustig, Arnošt. *A Prayer for Katerina Horovitzova.* Trans. Jeanne Nemcova. New York: Harper & Row, 1973.

Luther, Martin. *On the Jews and Their Lies, 1543.* Trans. Martin H. Bertram. Available at http://www.jrbooksonline.com/PDF_Books/JewsAndTheirLies.pdf, 2001.

The Table Talk. Trans. and ed. Thomas S. Kepler. New York: Dover, 2005.

Lyotard, Jean-François. *The Differend: Phrases in Dispute.* Trans. Georges Van Den Abbeele. Minneapolis: University of Minnesota Press, 1988.

Heidegger and "the Jews." Trans. Andreas Michael and Mark S. Roberts. Minneapolis: University of Minnesota Press, 1990.

Mack, Michael. *German Idealism and the Jew: The Inner Anti-Semitism of Philosophy and German Jewish Responses*. Chicago, Ill.: University of Chicago Press, 2003.

Maier, Charles S. *The Unmasterable Past: History, Holocaust, and German National Identity*. Cambridge, Mass.: Harvard University Press, 1998.

Maimonides. *The Guide for the Perplexed*. Trans. M. Friedlaender. New York: Dover, 1956.

Maimonides' Commentary on the Mishnah: Tractate Sanhedrin. Trans. Fred Rosner. New York: Sepher-Hermon Press, 1981.

The Essential Maimonides. Trans. and ed. Avraham Yaakov Finkel. Northvale, N.J.: Jason Aronson, 1996.

Mamet, David. *The Wicked Son: Anti-Semitism, Self-Hatred, and the Jews*. New York: Schocken Books, 2006.

Manasheh ben Yisrael. *Nishmat Chayim*. Jerusalem: Yerid Haseferim, 1995.

Marcus, Itamar, and Barbara Crook. "Hamas Video: 'We will drink the blood of the Jews.'" *Palestine Media Watch*, 14 February 2006. Available at http://www.pmw.org.il/latest%20bulletins%20new.htm#b140206.

Maritain, Jacques. *Antisemitism*. London: Centenary Press, 1939.

Marx, Karl. "On Bruno Bauer's *The Jewish Question*." In Karl Marx. *Early Writings*. Trans. and ed. T. B. Bottomore. New York: McGraw-Hill, 1964, pp. 1–40.

Marx, Karl, and Friedrich Engels. *Manifesto of the Communist Party*. Authorized English translation. Radford, Va.: Wilder Publications, 2007.

Matas, David. *Aftershock: Anti-Zionism and Anti-Semitism*. Toronto: Dundurn, 2005.

Mattogno, Carlo. *The Myth of the Extermination of the Jews*. Chicago, Ill.: Theses and Dissertations Press, 2009.

Mattogno, Carlo, and Germar Rudolf. *Auschwitz-Lies: Legends, Lies, and Prejudices on the Holocaust*. Chicago, Ill.: Theses and Dissertations Press, 2005.

Maududi, Abul Al'a. *Selected Speeches and Writings*. Trans. S. Zakir Aijaz. 2 vols. Karachi: International Islamic Publishers, 1981.

Jihad in Islam. Lahore: Islamic Publications, 2001.

Meijer, Roel, ed. *Global Salafism: Islam's New Religious Movement*. New York: Columbia University Press, 2009.

Mekilta de-Rabbi Ishmael. 3 vols. Trans. Jacob Z. Lauterbach. Philadelphia: Jewish Publication Society, 1961.

Mendelssohn, Moses. *Jerusalem or On Religious Power and Judaism*. Trans. Allan Arkush. Introduction and commentary by Alexander Altmann. Hanover, N.H.: Brandeis University Press, 1983.

Mendes-Flohr, Paul, and Jehuda Reinharz, eds. *The Jew in the Modern World: A Documentary History*. 2nd ed. Oxford, U.K.: Oxford University Press, 1995.

Michael, Robert. *Holy Hatred: Christianity, Antisemitism, and the Holocaust*. New York: Palgrave Macmillan, 2006.

Midrash on Psalms (Midrash Tehillim). 2 vols. Trans. William G. Braude. New Haven, Conn.: Yale University Press, 1959.

Midrash Rabbah. 10 vols. Ed. and trans. H. Friedman et al. London: Soncino, 1961.

Midrash Tanchuma. 2 vols. Jerusalem: Eshkol, 1935.

Milchman, Alan, and Alan Rosenberg, eds. *Martin Heidegger and the Holocaust.* Atlantic Highlands, N.J.: Humanities Press, 1996.

Miller, Arthur. *The Death of a Salesman.* New York: Penguin Books, 1998.

Focus. New York: Penguin Books, 2001.

Millgram, Abraham Ezra. *Jerusalem Curiosities.* Skokie, Ill.: Varda Books, 2002.

Milton-Edwards, Beverley. *Islamic Politics in Palestine.* London: I. B. Tauris, 1999.

Minerbi, Sergio. "The Vatican and the Standoff at the Church of the Nativity." Jerusalem Center for Public Affairs, 15 March 2004. Available at http://jcpa.org/jl/vp515.htm.

Mishnah, The. Trans. Jacob Neusner. New Haven, Conn.: Yale University Press, 1988.

Moin, Baqer. *Khomeini: Life of the Ayatollah.* New York: St. Martin's Press, 1999.

Morgan, Michael L., ed. *A Holocaust Reader: Responses to the Nazi Extermination.* New York: Oxford University Press, 2001.

Morris, Benny. *Righteous Victims: A History of the Zionist-Arab Conflict, 1881–1998.* New York: Vintage Books, 2001.

Moss, Leonard. *Arthur Miller.* Boston: Twayne Publishers, 1980.

Mosse, George L. *Toward the Final Solution: A History of European Racism.* New York: Howard Fertig, 1978.

Moussalli, Ahmad S. *Radical Islamic Fundamentalism: The Ideological and Political Discourse of Sayyid Qutb.* Beirut: American University of Beirut, 1992.

Murawiec, Laurent. *The Mind of Jihad.* Cambridge, U.K.: Cambridge University Press, 2008.

Nachman of Breslov. *Restore My Soul (Meshivat Nefesh).* Trans. Avraham Greenbaum. Jerusalem: Chasidei Breslov, 1980.

Tikkun. Trans. Avraham Greenbaum. Jerusalem: Breslov Research Institute, 1984.

Nachmanides. *Commentary on the Torah.* 2 vols. Trans. Charles B. Chavel. New York: Shilo, 1971.

The Disputation at Barcelona. Trans Charles B. Chavel. New York: Shilo, 1983.

Nasrallah, Hassan. "Excerpts from Speech by Hizbullah Secretary-General Nasrallah." *Israel Ministry of Foreign Affairs,* 9 April 2000. Available at http://www.mfa.gov.il/MFA/MFAArchive/2000_2009/2000/4/Excerpts%20from%20Speech%20by%20Hizbullah%20Secretary-Genera.

"Hizbullah Leader Nasrallah: Great French Philosopher Garaudy Proved Holocaust a Myth." *MEMRI,* 7 February 2006. Available at http://www.memri.org/bin/articles.cgi?Page=archives&Area=sd&ID=SP108806.

Voice of Hezbollah: The Statements of Sayyed Hassan Nasrallah. Ed. Nicholas Noe. Trans. Ellen Khouri. London: Verso, 2007.

Nathan of Nemirov. *Rabbi Nachman's Wisdom: Shevachay HaRan and Sichos HaRan.* Trans. Aryeh Kaplan. Ed. Aryeh Rosenfeld. New York: A. Kaplan, 1973.

Nechunia ben Hakanah. *Sefer HaTemunah.* Jerusalem: Nezer Sharga, 1998.

Neher, André. *The Prophetic Existence*. Trans. William Wolf. New York: A. S. Barnes, 1969.

———. *They Made Their Souls Anew*. Trans. David Maisel. Albany: SUNY Press, 1990.

Neske, Guenther, and Emil Kettering, eds. *Martin Heidegger and National Socialism*. Trans. Lisa Harries. New York: Paragon, 1990.

Nettler, Ronald L. *Past Trials and Present Tribulations: A Muslim Fundamentalist's View of the Jews*. Oxford, U.K.: Pergamon, 1987.

Newman, Louis I., ed. *The Hasidic Anthology*. New York: Schocken Books, 1963.

Nicosia, Francis R. *Zionism and Anti-Semitism in Nazi Germany*. Cambridge, U.K.: Cambridge University Press, 2008.

Nietzsche, Friedrich. *Beyond Good and Evil*. Trans. Walter Kaufmann. New York: Vintage Books, 1966.

———. *Also sprach Zarathustra*. In *Werke*, vol. 1. Munich: Carl Hanser Verlag, 1967.

———. *The Will to Power*. Trans. Walter Kaufmann and R. J. Hollingdale. Ed. Walter Kaufmann. New York: Random House, 1968.

———. *The Gay Science*. Trans. Walter Kaufmann. New York: Vintage Books, 1974.

Nolte, Ernst. *Der europäische Bürgerkrieg, 1917–1945: Nationalsozialismus und Bolschewismus*. Berlin: Propyläen Verlag, 1987.

Nomberg-Przytyk, Sara. *Auschwitz: True Tales from a Grotesque Land*. Trans. Roslyn Hirsch. Chapel Hill: University of North Carolina Press, 1985.

Origen. *An Exhortation to Martyrdom, Prayer, and Selected Works*. Trans. Rowan A. Greer Mahwah, N.J.: Paulist Press, 1988.

von Oven, Wilfred. *Mit Goebbels bis zum Ende*. Tübingen: Rudolf Grabert-Verlag, 1974.

Ozick, Cynthia. "The Modern 'Hep! Hep! Hep!'" In Edward Alexander and Paul Bogdanor, eds., *The Jewish Divide over Israel: Accusers and Defenders*. New Brunswick, N.J.: Transaction Publishers, 2008, pp. 1–6.

Parkes, James William. *The Conflict of the Church and the Synagogue: A Study in the Origins of Antisemitism*. New York: ACLS Humanities E-Book, 2008.

Patai, Raphael. *The Messiah Texts*. New York: Avon, 1979.

Peli, Pinhas H. *The Jewish Sabbath: A Renewed Encounter*. New York: Schocken Books, 1988.

Pérez, Joseph. *The Spanish Inquisition: A History*. Trans. Janet Lloyd. New Haven, Conn.: Yale University Press, 2006.

Pesikta de-Rab Kahana. Trans. William G. Braude and Israel J. Kapstein. Philadelphia: Jewish Publication Society, 1975.

Pesikta Rabbati. 2 vols. Trans. William G. Braude. New Haven, Conn.: Yale University Press, 1968.

Peters, Rudolph. *Jihad in Classical and Modern Islam: A Reader*. Princeton, N.J.: Markus Wiener, 1995.

Philo. *Philo's Flaccus: The First Pogrom*. Trans. Pieter W. van der Horst. Leiden: Brill, 2003.

Pine, Lisa. *Nazi Family Policy, 1933–1945*. Oxford, U.K.: Berg Publishers, 1999.

Pirke Avos. Brooklyn, N.Y.: Mesorah, 1984.

Pirke de Rabbi Eliezer. Trans. Gerald Friedlander. New York: Hermon Press, 1970.

Plato. *Phaedo.* Trans. David Gallop. Oxford, U.K.: Oxford University Press, 2009.

Theaetetus. Trans. Benjamin Jowett. Rockville, Md.: Serenity Publishers, 2009.

Polen, Nehemia. *The Holy Fire: The Teachings of Rabbi Kalonymus Kalman Shapira.* Northvale, N.J.: Jason Aronson, 1999.

Prager, Dennis, and Joseph Telushkin. *Why the Jews? The Reason for Antisemitism.* New York: Simon & Schuster, 2003.

"Protocols of the Elders of Zion." In Richard S. Levy, ed. *Antisemitism in the Modern World: An Anthology of Texts.* Lexington, Mass.: D. C. Heath and Company, 1991, pp. 151–164.

Proudhon, Pierre-Joseph. *Carnets de P.-J. Proudhon.* Ed. Pierre Haubtmann. Paris: Marcel Rivière, 1961.

Al-Qaeda Manual. In Walter Laqueur, ed. *Voices of Terror.* New York: Reed Press, 2004, pp. 401–409.

Qassem, Naim. *Hizbollah: The Story from Within.* Trans. Dalia Khalil. London: SAQI, 2005.

Qutb, Sayyid. *Social Justice in Islam.* Trans. John B. Hardie. New York: Octagon Books, 1963.

"Our Struggle with the Jews." Trans. Ronald L. Nettler. In Ronald L. Nettler. *Past Trials and Present Tribulations: A Muslim Fundamentalist's View of the Jews.* Oxford, U.K.: Pergamon, 1987, pp. 72–89.

Ma'alim fi al-tariq [Milestones], 13th legal ed. Cairo: Dar al-Da'wa, 1989.

In the Shade of the Quran. Trans. M. A. Salahi and A. A. Shamis. Alexandria, Va.: Al Saadawi Publications, 1997.

Basic Principles of the Islamic Worldview. Trans. Rami David. Preface by Hamid Algar. North Haledon, N.J.: Islamic Publications International, 2006.

Rabinovich, Itamar, and Jehuda Reinharz, eds. *Israel in the Middle East: Documents and Readings on Society, Politics, and Foreign Relations, Pre-1948 to the Present.* 2nd ed. Lebanon, N.H.: University Press of New England, 2008.

Rahner, Karl. *Foundations of Christian Faith: An Introduction to the Idea of Christianity.* Trans. William V. Dych. New York: Crossroad, 1994.

Rashi, *Commentary on the Torah.* 2 vols. Trans. M. Rosenbaum and N. M. Silbermann. Jerusalem: The Silbermann Family, 1972.

Rassinier, Paul. *Le passage de la ligne.* Paris: Éditions Bressanes, 1948.

Le drame des Juifs européens. Paris: Le Sept Couleurs, 1964.

Reinhart, Tanya, and Jon Elmer. "A Slow, Steady Genocide," *Z Magazine/Z Net,* 11 September 2003. Available at http://cosmos.ucc.ie/cs1064/jabowen/IPSC/php/art.php?aid=4278.

Ringelblum, Emmanuel. *Notes from the Warsaw Ghetto.* Trans. and ed. Jacob Sloan. New York: Schocken Books, 1974.

Roberts, Alexander, and James Donaldson, eds. *The Writings of Cyprian Bishop of Carthage II: Ante Nicene Christian Library Translations of the Fathers down to AD 325, Part Thirteen.* Whitefish, Mont.: Kessinger, 2004.

Clement of Alexandria: Ante Nicene Christian Library Translations of the Writings of the Fathers to AD 325, Part Four. Whitefish, Mont.: Kessinger, 2007.

Robertson, Ritchie. "Historicizing Weininger: The Nineteenth-Century German Image of the Feminized Jew." In Bryan Cheyette and Laura Marcus, eds., *Modernity, Culture, and "the Jew."* Stanford, Calif.: Stanford University Press, 1998, pp. 23–39.

Robinson, Armin, ed. *The Ten Commandments.* New York: Simon & Schuster, 1944.

Rockmore, Tom. *On Heidegger's Nazism and Philosophy.* Berkeley: University of California Press, 1992.

Rockmore, Tom, and Joseph Margolis, eds. *The Heidegger Case: On Philosophy and Politics.* Philadelphia: Temple University Press, 1992.

Rohling, August. *Der Talmudjude.* 4th ed. Münster: Adolph Russell's Verlag, 1872.

Roques, Henri. *The Confessions of Kurt Gerstein.* Newport Beach, Calif.: Institute for Historical Review, 1989.

Rosenberg, Alfred. *Der staatsfeindliche Zionismus.* Hamburg: Deutsch Völkische Verlagsanstalt, 1922.

Der Mythus der 20. Jahrhunderts: Eine Wertung der seelisch-geistigen Gestaltenkämpfe unserer Zeit. Munich: Hoheneichen Verlag, 1934.

Race and Race History and Other Essays. Ed. Robert Pois. New York: Harper & Row, 1974.

Rosenfeld, Alvin. *The End of the Holocaust.* Bloomington: Indiana University Press, 2011.

Rosenzweig, Franz. *On Jewish Learning.* Ed. N. N. Glatzer. New York: Schocken Books, 1955.

The Star of Redemption. Trans. William W. Hallo. Boston: Beacon Press, 1972.

Franz Rosenzweig's "The New Thinking." Trans. and ed. Alan Udoff and Barbara Galli. Syracuse: Syracuse University Press, 1999.

Understanding the Sick and the Healthy: A View of World, God, and Man. Trans. Nahum Glatzer. Cambridge, Mass.: Harvard University Press, 1999.

Roukema, Riemer. *Jesus, Gnosis and Dogma.* London: Continuum, 2010.

Rubenstein, Richard L. *After Auschwitz: History, Theology, and Contemporary Judaism.* 2nd ed. Baltimore, Md.: Johns Hopkins University Press, 1992.

Rubin, Barry. *Revolution Until Victory?: The Politics and History of the PLO.* Cambridge, Mass.: Harvard University Press, 1994.

Rubin, Theodore Isaac. *Anti-Semitism: A Disease of the Mind.* New York: Continuum, 1990.

Rudolf, Germar. *The Rudolf Report: Expert Report on Chemical and Technical Aspects of the "Gas Chambers" of Auschwitz.* Chicago, Ill.: Theses and Dissertations Press, 2003.

Ruether, Rosemary Radford. *Faith and Fratricide: The Theological Roots of Anti-Semitism.* New York: Seabury Press, 1974.

Ruthven, Malise. *A Fury for God: The Islamist Attack on America.* London: Granta, 2004.

Saadia Gaon. *The Book of Belief and Opinions (Sefer Emunot Vedeot)*. Trans. Samuel Rosenblatt. New Haven, Conn.: Yale University Press, 1976.

Sacks, Jonathan. *Crisis and Covenant: Jewish Thought after the Holocaust*. Manchester, U.K.: Manchester University Press, 1992.
Future Tense: Jews, Judaism, and Israel in the Twenty-first Century. New York: Schocken Books, 2010.

Salton, George Lucius. *The 23rd Psalm: A Holocaust Memoir*. Madison: University of Wisconsin Press, 2002.

Sartre, Jean-Paul. *Anti-Semite and Jew: An Exploration of the Etiology of Hate*. Trans. George L. Becker. New York: Schocken Books, 1976.

Schaff, Philip, and Henry Wace, eds. *A Select Library of Nicene and Post-Nicene Fathers of the Christian Church: Select Writings and Letters of Gregory, Bishop of Nyssa*. Trans. William Moore and Henry Austin Wilson. New York: The Christian Literature Company, 1893.

Schechtman, Joseph B. *The Mufti and the Fuehrer: The Rise and Fall of Haj Amin el-Husseini*. New York: Thomas Yoseloff, 1965.

Schneerson, Menachem M. *Torah Studies*. Adapted by Jonathan Sacks. 2nd ed. London: Lubavitch Foundation, 1986.

Scholem, Gershom. *Kabbalah*. New York: New American Library, 1974.

Schopenhauer, Arthur. *Parerga and Paralipomena: Short Philosophical Essays*. 2 vols. Ed. E. F. J. Payne. Oxford: Clarendon Press, 1974 and 2000.

Sforno, Ovadiah. *Commentary on the Torah*. 2 vols. Trans. Raphael Pelcovitz. Brooklyn, N.Y.: Mesorah, 1987–1989.

Shahak, Israel. *Jewish History, Jewish Religion: The Weight of Three Thousand Years*. London: Pluto Press, 1997.

Shaikh, Nermeen. *The Present as History: Critical Perspectives on Global Power*. New York: Columbia University Press, 2007.

Shapira, Kalonymos Kalmish. *Esh Kodesh*. Jerusalem: Vaad Chasidei Pisetsenah, 1997.
Sacred Fire: Torah from the Years of Fury 1939–1942. Trans. J. Hershy Worch. Ed. Deborah Miller. Northvale, N.J.: Jason Aronson, 2000.

Shem Tov ibn Falaquera. *Sefer HaNefesh*. Jerusalem: Sefrit Mekorot, 1970.

Shermer, Michael, and Alex Grobman. *Denying History: Who Says the Holocaust Never Happened and Why Do They Say It?* Berkeley: University of California Press, 2000.

Sifre on Deuteronomy. New York: Jewish Theological Seminary, 1993.

Sluga, Hans. *Heidegger's Crisis: Philosophy and Politics in Nazi Germany*. Cambridge, Mass.: Harvard University Press, 1993.

Smallwood, E. Mary. *The Jews under Roman Rule: From Pompey to Diocletian: A Study in Political Relations*. Leiden: Brill, 1976.

Solomon ibn Gabirol. *Selected Religious Poems*. Ed. I. Davidson. Trans. Israel Zangwill. Philadelphia: Jewish Publication Society, 1952.

Soloveitchik, Joseph. *The Halakhic Mind: An Essay on Jewish Tradition and Modern Thought*. New York: Free Press, 1986.

Soulen, R. Kendall. *The God of Israel and Christian Theology*. Minneapolis, Minn.: Augsburg Fortress, 1996.

Spector, Stephen. *Evangelicals and Israel: The Story of American Christian Zionism.* New York: Oxford University Press, 2009.

Spencer, Robert. *The Myth of Islamic Tolerance: How Islamic Law Treats Non-Muslims.* Amherst, N.Y.: Prometheus Books, 2005.

The Truth about Muhammad: The Founder of the World's Most Intolerant Religion. Washington, D.C.: Regnery Publishing, 2006.

Spinoza, Baruch. *Theological-Political Treatise.* Trans. Samuel Shirley and Seymour Feldman. 2nd ed. Indianapolis, Ind.: Hackett, 2001.

Stäglich, Wilhelm. *Der Auschwitz-Mythos.* Torrance, Calif.: Historical Review Press, 1984.

Steinsaltz, Adin. *The Thirteen Petalled Rose: A Discourse on the Essence of Jewish Existence and Belief.* Trans. Yehuda Hanegbi. New York: Basic Books, 1980.

The Long Shorter Way: Discourses on Chasidic Thought. Trans. Yehuda Hanegbi. Northvale, N.J.: Jason Aronson, 1988.

On Being Free. Northvale, N.J.: Jason Aronson, 1995.

(with Josy Eisenberg). *The Seven Lights: On the Major Jewish Festivals.* Northvale, N.J.: Jason Aronson, 2000.

Steinsaltz, Adin, and Josy Eisenberg. *The Seven Lights: On the Major Jewish Festivals.* Northvale, N.J.: Jason Aronson, 2000.

Stern, Kenneth S. *Holocaust Denial.* New York: American Jewish Committee, 1993.

Still, Todd D. "Shadow and Light: Marcion's (Mis)Construal of the Apostle Paul." In Michael F. Bird and Joseph R. Dodson, eds., *Paul and the Second Century.* London: T&T Clark, 2011, pp. 91–107.

Strauss, Leo. *Studies in Platonic Political Philosophy.* Chicago, Ill.: University of Chicago Press, 1985.

The Rebirth of Classical Political Rationalism: An Introduction to the Thought of Leo Strauss. Selected by Thomas L. Pangle. Chicago, Ill.: University of Chicago Press, 1989.

Tacitus. The Histories. In *The Annals and the Histories.* Ed. Moses Hadas. Trans. Alfred Church and William Brodribb. New York: Modern Library, 2003, pp. 361–576.

Taheri, Amir. *Holy Terror: Inside the World of Islamic Terrorism.* Bethesda, Md.: Adler & Adler, 1987.

Tal, Uriel. *Christians and Jews in Germany: Religion, Politics and Ideology in the Second Reich, 1870–1914.* Ithaca, N.Y.: Cornell University Press, 1975.

Tanna debe Eliyahu. The Lore of the School of Elijah. Trans. William G. Braude and Israel J. Kapstein. Philadelphia: Jewish Publication Society, 1981.

Tertullian, "Against the Jews." In Geoffrey D. Dunn, ed. *Tertullian (The Early Church Fathers).* London: Routledge, 2004, pp. 43–73.

Thion, Serge. *Verite historique ou verite politique? Le dossier de l'affaire Faurisson: la question des chambers a gaz.* Paris: La Vieille Taupe, 1980.

Timmerman, Kenneth R. *Preachers of Hate: Islam and the War on America.* New York: Three Rivers Press, 2004.

Tolstoy, Leo. *Confession.* Trans. David Patterson. New York: W. W. Norton, 1983.

Anna Karenina. Trans. Constance Garnett. New York: Random House, 1994.

Tosefta. Jerusalem: Wahrmann, 1970.

Trachtenberg, Joshua. *The Devil and the Jews: The Medieval Conception of the Jew and Its Relation to Modern Antisemitism.* Philadelphia: Jewish Publication Society, 1983.

von Treitschke, Heinrich. "A Word about Our Jews." Trans. Richard S. Levy. In Richard S. Levy, ed., *Antisemitism in the Modern World: An Anthology of Texts.* Lexington, Mass.: D. C. Heath and Company, 1991, pp. 68–72.

Trifkovic, Serge. *The Sword of the Prophet: Islam: History, Theology, Impact on the World.* Boston: Regina Orthodox Press, 2002.

Van den Haag, Ernest. *The Jewish Mystique.* New York: Stein and Day, 1969.

Varner, William. *Ancient Jewish-Christian Dialogues: Athanasius and Zacchaeus, Simon and Theophilus, Timothy and Aquila.* Lewiston, N.Y.: Edwin Mellen, 2005.

Verrall, Richard. *Did Six Million Really Die? The Truth at Last.* 2nd rev. ed. Torrance, Calif.: Historical Review Press, 2011.

Vidal-Naquet, Pierre. *Assassins of Memory: Essays on the Denial of the Holocaust.* Trans. Jeffrey Mehlman. New York: Columbia University Press, 1992.

Vital, Chayim. *The Tree of Life (Ets Chayyim).* Trans. D. W. Menzi and Z. Padeh. Northvale, N.J.: Aronson, 1999.

Kedushah. Jerusalem: Eshkol, 2000.

Voltaire. *Philosophical Dictionary.* Trans. Theodore Besterman. New York: Penguin, 1984.

Wagner, Peter. *Wir werden frei sein: Leopold Zunz, 1794–1886.* Detmold: Gesellschaft für Christlich-Jüdische Zuzammenarbeit, 1994.

Wagner, Richard. *Art and Politics.* Trans. William Ashton Ellis. Lincoln: University of Nebraska Press, 1995.

Judaism in Music and Other Essays. Trans. W. Ashton Ellis. Lincoln: University of Nebraska Press, 1995.

Wakounig, Marija, and Markus Peter Beham, eds. *Transgressing Boundaries: Humanities in Flux.* Berlin: Lit Verlag, 2013.

Wallach, Luitpold. *Liberty and Letters: The Thought of Leopold Zunz.* London: East and West Library, 1959.

Wasser, Hersh. "Daily Entries of Hersh Wasser." Trans. Joseph Kermish, *Yad Vashem Studies*, 15 (1983): 201–82.

Weininger, Otto. *Sex and Character.* Authorized English translation from the German. 6th ed. New York: G. P. Putnam's Sons, 1907.

Weinreich, Max. *Hitler's Professors: The Part of Scholarship in Germany's Crimes against the Jewish People.* New Haven, Conn.: Yale University Press, 1999.

Weissman, Moshe, ed. *The Midrash Says.* 5 vols. Brooklyn, N.Y.: Bnay Yakov Publications, 1980.

Wiesel, Elie. *Legends of Our Time.* New York: Avon, 1968.

A Beggar in Jerusalem. Trans. Lily Edelman and Elie Wiesel. New York: Random House, 1970.

Ani Maamin: A Song Lost and Found Again. Trans. Marion Wiesel. New York: Random House, 1973.

The Oath. New York: Avon, 1973.

Souls on Fire: Portraits and Legends of Hasidic Masters. Trans. Marion Wiesel. New York: Vintage, 1973.

"The Holocaust as Literary Inspiration." In Elie Wiesel, et al. *Dimensions of the Holocaust.* Evanston, Ill.: Northwestern University Press, 1977, pp. 5–19.

A Jew Today. Trans. Marion Wiesel. New York: Random House, 1978.

The Testament. Trans. Marion Wiesel. New York: Summit Books, 1981.

Wiesel, Elie. *Against Silence: The Voice and Vision of Elie Wiesel.* 3 vols. Ed. Irving Abrahamson. New York: Holocaust Library, 1985.

Twilight. Trans. Marion Wiesel. New York: Summit, 1988.

Evil and Exile. Trans. Jon Rothschild. Notre Dame, Ind.: University of Notre Dame Press, 1990.

From the Kingdom of Memory: Reminiscences. New York: Summit Books, 1990.

Messengers of God: Biblical Portraits and Legends. Trans. Marion Wiesel. New York: Simon & Schuster, 2005.

Night. Trans. Marion Wiesel. New York: Hill and Wang, 2006.

et al. *Dimensions of the Holocaust.* Evanston, Ill.: Northwestern University Press, 1977.

Wiesenthal, Simon. *The Sunflower: On the Possibilities and Limits of Forgiveness.* Trans. H. A. Piehler. New York: Schocken Books, 1998.

Williams, Arthur Lukyn. *Adversus Judaeos: A Bird's-Eye View of Christian Apologiae Until the Renaissance.* Cambridge, U.K.: Cambridge University Press, 1935.

Wilson, Marvin R. *Our Father Abraham.* Grand Rapids, Mich.: Wm. B. Eerdmans, 1989.

Wistrich, Robert S. *Antisemitism: The Longest Hatred.* New York: Schocken Books, 1994.

"Islamic Judeophobia: An Existential Threat." In David Bukay, ed., *Muhammad's Monsters: A Comprehensive Guide to Radical Islam for Western Audiences.* Green Forest, Ark.: Balfour Books, 2004, pp. 195–219.

A Lethal Obsession: Anti-Semitism from Antiquity to the Global Jihad. New York: Random House, 2010.

Wood, Allen W. "Rational Theology, Moral Faith, and Religion." In Paul Guyer, ed., *The Cambridge Companion to Kant.* Cambridge, U.K.: Cambridge University Press, 1992, pp. 394–416.

Wright, Lawrence. *The Looming Tower: Al-Qaeda and the Road to 9/11.* New York: Alfred A. Knopf, 2006.

Wundt, Max. *Deutsche Weltanschauung.* Munich: J. F. Lehmans, 1928.

Wyschogrod, Edith. *Spirit in Ashes: Hegel, Heidegger, and Man-Made Death.* New Haven, Conn.: Yale University Press, 1985.

Yaakov Yosef. *Toledot Yaakov Yosef al HaTorah.* 2 vols. Jerusalem: Agudat Beit Vialipoli, 1944.

Yakira, Elhanan. *Post-Zionism, Post-Holocaust: Three Essays on Denial, Forgetting, and the Delegitimation of Israel.* Trans. Michael Swirsky. Cambridge, U.K.: Cambridge University Press, 2010.

Yalkut Shimoni. 5 vols. Jerusalem: Chotzet Sefarim, 1993.

Yamauchi, Edwin M. *Gnostic Ethics and Mandaean Origins*. Piscataway, N.J.: Gorgias Press, 2004.

Yaqoub, Muhammad Hussein. "We Will Fight, Defeat, and Annihilate Them." *Al-Rahma TV*, 17 January 2009. Available at http://memri.org/bin/latestnews .cgi?ID=SD227809.

Yockey, Francis Parker. *Imperium: The Philosophy of History and Politics*. 4th ed. Los Angeles, Calif.: Noontide Press, 2008.

al-Zawahiri, Ayman. *His Own Words: Translation and Analysis of the Writings of Dr. Ayman al-Zawahiri*. Trans. and analysis by Laura Mansfield. Lulu.com, 2006.

The Zohar. 5 vols. Trans. Harry Sperling and Maurice Simon. London: Soncino, 1984.

Index

Abbas, Mahmoud, 97, 184–85
Abel, 23
Abrabanel, Don Isaac, 273
Abraham, 2, 19, 31, 65, 81, 181, 239, 285
Abu-Amr, Ziad, 95
Abulafia, Abraham, 9
Adam, 8, 12–15, 62, 74, 137, 145, 205, 252, 254, 275, 278, 286; question put to, 20, 22, 73, 225
Agasy, Yosef, 246
Aggadah, 169, 251
Ahmadinejad, Mahmoud, 178
Akiva, Rabbi, 8, 253
Albo, Joseph, 7, 204
Alexander, Edward, 235–36, 242–43, 245
Allah, 4, 19, 81, 89, 94; and Adolf Hitler, 184; and jihad, 82, 84–86, 91–92, 101, 103–5, 196, 220; Party of, 89–90, 99
Ali, Burhanuddin, 83
Alloush, Ibrahim, 182
Alter, Yehudah Leib, 14
Amalek, 27, 89, 134
Améry, Jean, 22, 26–27, 28
al-Amin, Ibrahim, 99
ibn Anas, Malik, 83
Angel of Death, 16, 160, 164
Anidjar, Gil, 212–13
Aoude, Ibrahim, 212–13
Apostles' Creed, 59
App, Austin J., 175, 178
Aquinas, Thomas, 65, 66–67, 68, 75, 280
Arabisches Freiheitskorps, 96
Arafat, Yasser, 96–97

Arendt, Hannah, x, 36–37, 174, 251
Aryans, 43, 129–30, 135, 137–38, 147, 246
Ascher, Saul, 116
al-Assad, Bashar, 210
Athanasian Creed, 59
Athanasius of Constantinople, 70
Athens, 108–9
Atkins, Stephen, 131, 182
Augustine, 58, 61, 65, 68, 75
Auschwitz, 3, 5, 145, 193, 194, 199, 221; as anti-creation, 158–59; and Athens, 109; Commanding Voice of, 180–81; and the Covenant, 171; and Jerusalem, 205–6; and the Messiah, 284; Rosh Hashanah in, 154; uniqueness of, 161–62, 167
Avrahami, Yossi, 89
Azzam, Abdullah, 103, 104, 105

Baal Shem Tov, 6, 62, 77, 157, 169
Baeck, Leo, 170, 202
Baker, Mona, 214
Baladhuri, 86
al-Banna, Hasan, 83n, 85, 91–93, 95, 97, 101, 106, 217
Banu Qurayzah, 94, 98
Bar Kochba Revolt, 33
Bardèche, Maurice, 174, 178, 179
Bauch, Bruno, 138
Bauer, Bruno, 235
Bäumler, Alfred, 138
Begun, Vladimir, 211
Beinin, Joel, 241
Bellow, Saul, 258